Love Letters from Golok

LOVE LETTERS
FROM GOLOK

A Tantric Couple in Modern Tibet

HOLLY GAYLEY

COLUMBIA UNIVERSITY PRESS *NEW YORK*

Columbia University Press
Publishers Since 1893
New York   Chichester, West Sussex
cup.columbia.edu
Copyright © 2017 Columbia University Press
Paperback edition, 2018
All rights reserved

Library of Congress Cataloging-in-Publication Data
Names: Gayley, Holly, author.
Title: Love letters from Golok : a tantric couple in modern Tibet /
Holly Gayley.
Description: New York : Columbia University Press, 2016. |
Includes bibliographical references and index.
Identifiers: LCCN 2016009736 (print) | LCCN 2016040859 (ebook) |
ISBN 9780231180528 (cloth : alk. paper) | ISBN 9780231180535 (pbk. : alk. paper) |
ISBN 9780231542753 (electronic)
Subjects: LCSH: Tā-re Bde-chen-lha-mo, Mkha'-'gro
Rin-po-che—Correspondence. | O-rgyan-'jigs-med-nam-mkha'-gling-pa,
Rin-po-che, 1944–2011—Correspondence. | Buddhists—China—Golog Zangzu
Zizhizhou—Correspondence. | Rnying-ma-pa (Sect)—China—
Golog Zangzu Zizhizhou.
Classification: LCC BQ7662.9.A2 G38 2016 (print) | LCC BQ7662.9.A2 (ebook) |
DDC 294.3/9230922 [B]—dc23
LC record available at https://lccn.loc.gov/2016009736

Columbia University Press books are printed on permanent
and durable acid-free paper.

Printed in the United States of America

Cover design: Rebecca Lown

གནས་སྐྱོངས་ཕན་བདེའི་ལེགས་ཚོགས་དཔལ་ཡོན་རྒྱས། །
མུན་སྐྱིང་བསྟན་པའི་སྒྲོན་མེ་ཕྱོགས་བཅུར་སྦར། །
ས་གསུམ་བཀྲ་ཤིས་དགེ་བཅུའི་སྣང་བས་ཁྱབ། །
ཕྱོགས་ལས་རྣམ་པར་རྒྱལ་བའི་རྟེན་འབྲེལ་འགྲིགས། །

May prosperity and glory proliferate, benefitting the Land of Snows.
May the lamp of Buddhist teachings blaze in dark lands in ten directions.
May auspiciousness and the ten virtues pervade the three worlds.
May coincidence click into place, completely victorious in all directions.

— Khandro Tāre Lhamo, 1978

Contents

CONTENTS

Illustrations

All photos by the author, unless otherwise indicated.

Acknowledgments

THIS BOOK WOULD not have been possible without the blessings of Namtrul Jigme Phuntsok, known locally as Namtrul Rinpoche, who lent his support from the very inception of this project during my first visit to Golok in 2004. Year after year, he graciously hosted me at Nyenlung Monastery, allowed me to observe and participate in ritual activities there, shared with me crucial source material, and tirelessly answered my inquiries about his teaching career and collaboration with Khandro Tāre Lhamo. In addition, I benefited from the learned contributions of Ringu Tulku and Lama Chönam in translating difficult passages in the source material for this book; the counsel of Tulku Thondup at key points during research; stories shared by Khenpo Rigdzin Dargye, which he gathered for a new account of Tāre Lhamo's life, as yet unpublished; and input from Tulku Laksam Namdak and Gelek Nyima, who helped bring the epilogue up to date during a final visit to Serta in 2014 prior to finishing this book.

A number of scholars contributed their invaluable insights and support along the way. First and foremost, Janet Gyatso provided sustained guidance and careful readings throughout the process of crafting this project. As advisor and mentor, she has been a treasured conversation partner, challenging me to think theoretically and comparatively across sources and disciplines. I cannot thank her enough for all her help during graduate school and beyond. My appreciation also extends to Leonard van der Kuijp, Diana Eck, Anne Blackburn, Anne Monius, Parimal Patil, Lauran Hartley, Gray Tuttle, and Kurtis Schaeffer, who offered input at various stages in the conception, research, composition, and revision of this project into a book. Anonymous reviewers also provided valuable suggestions in the final stages prior to publication.

I would like to express my appreciation to all who shared their time and expertise while I was in the field, especially scholars affiliated with Qinghai Minorities University and its Gesar Research Institute, teachers and students at the ETP program at Qinghai Normal University, and singers, poets, and writers in the county seat at Serta and in Tawu, the capital of Golok Prefecture. I could not have fathomed the variegated forms of versification in the correspondence between Namtrul Rinpoche and Tāre Lhamo without their guidance. In addition, I am grateful to Tibetan friends who joined me on trips to Golok and neighboring areas as traveling companions, research assistants, and ad-hoc interpreters. They enabled my research in so many ways—by hosting me in their homes, helping me to make contacts, and accompanying me on visits to lamas, monasteries, and sacred sites in their homeland. My appreciation also goes to the many disciples of Tāre Lhamo and Namtrul Rinpoche who allowed me to interview them and whose stories are recounted, often anonymously, in this book. During field research, I traveled on many a bumpy road with various colleagues and friends, whom I thank for their good company and cheer.

I would like to acknowledge the support of a Fulbright-Hays award, which enabled the initial year of research on this project in 2005-6, based in Xining and traveling into Golok and neighboring areas for several weeks at a time. Harvard University provided a writing grant upon my return from the field, and colleagues in the doctoral program there served as beneficial conversation partners during the early stages of writing. Since then, the Kayden Research Grant at the University of Colorado Boulder and the American Academy of Religion funded subsequent trips to Golok and Serta in which I continued my research alongside other projects. Additionally, the resources provided by the Tibetan Buddhist Resource Center have been instrumental. My thanks to the late Gene Smith for his time and advice over the years, as well as to the TBRC staff and volunteers, who continue to sustain his vision and make available vital resources for Tibetan studies.

The University of Colorado Boulder has been an ideal place to complete this project. I am appreciative to my Tibetan and Himalayan Studies colleagues, Emily Yeh, Carole McGranahan, and Ariana Maki, for their support and collaboration, particularly in launching the Tibet Himalaya Initiative; to the Center for Asian Studies for providing forums for faculty to showcase their work and promoting Asia-related events on campus; to the Center for Humanities and the Arts for supporting two research leaves that facilitated the completion of this book and significant work on a second project; and to my colleagues within the Department of Religious Studies, who have offered encouragement and mentorship. I am grateful for departmental support in pursuing research opportunities and for a Kayden Research Grant to cover a subvention for the index. Colleagues from nearby institutions, Naropa University and the Tsadra Research Center in Boulder, have provided further inspiration and collaborative opportunities. In bringing this book to fruition, I am particularly indebted to Wendy Lochner, Christine Dunbar, Leslie Kriesel, and other staff at Columbia University Press.

Finally, I could not have persevered without the kindness of friends and family. My appreciation goes especially to Brigitta Karelis and Jonna Fleming for serving as sounding boards throughout the writing process; to Rick Merrill, who helped inspire the extensive revision from dissertation to book; and to my furry companions, Buster and Poky, who must have imagined that I had a really good bone to chew on all these years. Last but not least, I would like to thank my parents, Joan and Oliver Gayley, for all the support and encouragement they have given me throughout my education and early career as a scholar.

It has been an honor to work on this project, and I thank all who have assisted me along the way. May the lives and letters of Tāre Lhamo and Namtrul Rinpoche be an inspiration to others as they have been to me. Lha gyal lo!

Note on Transliteration and Translation

TIBETAN TERMS ARE rendered phonetically throughout the main body of this book in order to make it accessible to the general public with an interest in Buddhism and contemporary Tibet, as well as to scholars in Asian studies and religious studies who may not be specialists in Tibetan language and literature. The first occurrence of Tibetan terms is accompanied by the Wylie transliteration in parentheses. Sanskrit (Skt.) and Chinese (Ch.) are included where relevant.

For proper names, the glossary provides an equivalence between my phonetic renderings of people and place names and their Wylie transliteration. While phonetic renderings are used in the main body of the book, Wylie is used when citing sources and interviews in the notes and bibliography. Exceptions are made in the case of Tibetan teachers, scholars, and authors who have published English-language works and are therefore known primarily by the phonetic renderings of their names. In these cases, and when citing authors of Tibetan works translated into English, I follow the transliteration of names as rendered in their publications.

All the translations contained in this book are my own, except in the few instances where indicated. In citing primary sources by and about Tāre Lhamo and Namtrul Rinpoche, I provide abbreviations for sources, as listed before the notes section, followed by the page and line number so that scholars and translators may reference the original.

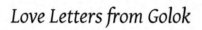

Love Letters from Golok

Introduction

Journey to Golok

LET ME BEGIN with a tale of healing from the nomadic region of Golok,[1] situated on the eastern reaches of the Tibetan plateau. It involves seven strands of hair, sent by a female tantric master to her ailing beloved. Reporting visions day and night of her "companion who has never been separate even for an instant," she sent strands of her own hair alongside a tantric liturgy and protection circle—which she revealed through visionary means— as relics and a ritual to heal him.[2] In the accompanying letter, she assured him that these items would dispel any obstacles to the two of them joining together as a couple, including the distance that separated them and his recurring bouts of illness.

Healing is a persistent theme in the correspondence between the eminent tantric couple Khandro Tāre Lhamo (1938–2002) and Namtrul Jigme Phuntsok (1944–2011), known locally as Namtrul Rinpoche (and not to be confused with Khenpo Jigme Phuntsok, the monastic founder of Larung Buddhist Academy in Serta).[3] Through the fifty-six letters they exchanged between 1978 and 1980, while separated by province borders, the future couple asserted their inseparability across lifetimes and exchanged visionary recollections of their myriad past lives together in India and Tibet. On a personal level, they expressed their blossoming affection in folksy terms using the local song styles of ordinary nomads. And in a prophetic voice, they articulated their shared destiny to heal and restore Buddhist teachings, practices, and institutions in the aftermath of the Cultural Revolution (1966–76).

Int.1 Rolling hills surrounding Drongri, a sacred mountain in the vicinity of Golok.

The healing power of union between tantric partners is a recurrent motif in Tibetan literature,[4] but takes on new meaning in the context of modern Tibet under Chinese rule.[5] Ordinarily, it is a youthful female who extends the longevity of an elder master, but in this case, Tāre Lhamo was already forty years old when she initiated a courtship and correspondence with Namtrul Rinpoche, a reincarnate lama six years her junior.[6] Beyond that, her visionary talents and ritual prowess were harnessed in service of the larger mission of revitalizing Buddhism in the region of Golok—whether bestowing a long-life empowerment on the foremost Buddhist teachers who survived the Maoist period or revealing esoteric teachings and rituals with Namtrul Rinpoche during the 1980s and '90s. In one letter, Namtrul Rinpoche compares Tāre Lhamo to the moon exerting its influence on the tides, thereby causing the ocean of the Nyingma teachings of Tibetan Buddhism to swell.[7]

What do moments like these in the lives and letters of a contemporary tantric couple convey about gender and agency within a Buddhist framework?

How did Tāre Lhamo and Namtrul Rinpoche interweave the personal and prophetic dimensions of their courtship and correspondence? How did they understand their partnership to effect a healing process at a critical historical juncture in modern Tibetan history?

A Buddhist Tantric Couple

Steeped in esoteric Buddhism from their youth, Tāre Lhamo and Namtrul Rinpoche formed part of a nexus of Nyingma leaders in Golok who survived the Maoist period and spearheaded the revitalization of Buddhism in the region from the 1980s forward. As economic and cultural liberalization got under way in China, the two forged a bond through an epistolary courtship that lasted more than a year and crisscrossed borders between her homeland of Padma County (Qinghai Province) and his in neighboring Serta (Sichuan Province).[8] Their correspondence led to a lasting partnership, teaching and traveling together as a couple for more than twenty years in Golok and neighboring regions. Video footage from the late 1990s shows a rare sight: a Buddhist tantric couple seated side by side on ceremonial thrones, conducting rituals for large assemblies of Buddhist monastics and Tibetan laity. As the first study of the lives and letters of Tāre Lhamo and Namtrul Rinpoche, this book provides an intimate portrait of Tibetan lifeworlds and revitalization efforts by Buddhist leaders who remained in their homeland through the vagaries of Chinese Communist rule.

In many ways, Tāre Lhamo's life story is emblematic of her times. Born as the daughter of Apang Terchen (1895–1945),[9] a prominent figure in the Nyingma tradition of Tibetan Buddhism in Golok, she received instruction from many of the region's great masters of the twentieth century. Following the socialist transformation of Tibetan areas in the late 1950s, she suffered tremendous personal losses and spent her twenties and thirties consigned to manual labor. In the late 1950s, she lost her first husband, a scion of the prominent Dudjom line,[10] and her three brothers, all reincarnate lamas who died in prison.[11] Most likely, gender played a role in her averting imprisonment and surviving the period unscathed. Later, she lost her only son, who passed away before reaching the age of ten.[12] During the years leading up to and including the Cultural Revolution, when the physical vestiges of Buddhism were dismantled and religious practice forbidden, Tāre Lhamo served as a local heroine to her community through tales of her miracles, providing a beacon of hope amid the devastation. From this tragedy, at once personal and collective in scale, she emerged at the age of forty remarkably poised for action.

At the end of the Maoist period, Tāre Lhamo initiated a courtship and correspondence with Namtrul Rinpoche, who would become her second husband.[13] Namtrul Rinpoche was only a teenager in the late 1950s and thereby escaped the fate of her first husband and other prominent lamas. Enthroned in his youth as the Namkhai Nyingpo incarnation at Zhuchen Monastery in Serta,[14] Namtrul Rinpoche received a traditional monastic education and trained closely under the lamas and cleric-scholars at Zhuchen, including his main teacher, Zhuchen Kunzang Nyima. Based on his education, after the socialist transformations of Tibetan areas, he served as a secretary for his work unit and managed to sequester himself on retreat for periods of time. With monasteries forcibly closed and monastics defrocked, Namtrul Rinpoche also married and had a son, Laksam Namdak, who was recognized as the reincarnation of his own teacher and today serves as the lineage holder for the teachings that Namtrul Rinpoche and Tāre Lhamo revealed together.

Via secret messenger between 1978 and 1980, the couple exchanged an extended series of "love letters"—the first collection of its kind to come to light in Tibetan literature—combining personal expressions of affection with prophetic statements about their shared destiny. The letters contain avowals of their growing fondness and longing to be together, visionary recollections of their past lives as a couple, prophecies about their future revelatory activities, and references to sexuality in the context of tantric practice and the distinctively Tibetan process of treasure revelation.[15] With a rich array of folk and poetic styles, the letters offer insight into the gendered exchanges of this Buddhist tantric couple as they negotiated the terms of their union and envisioned the historic role they would play in Golok and beyond. Based on the bond they forged in their correspondence, in 1980 Tāre Lhamo left her homeland, against the wishes of her relatives and in contravention of state restrictions on travel, to join Namtrul Rinpoche in Serta.

Given its historical context, this correspondence provides a rare window into the religious imagination out of which the revitalization of Buddhism in Tibetan areas of China was inaugurated during the 1980s. In prophetic terms, Tāre Lhamo and Namtrul Rinpoche conceived of their shared destiny as "healing the damage of degeneration times" (*snyigs dus kyi rgud pa gso*).[16] The language of "healing" suggests the restorative work needed in the wake of collective trauma, given the "damage" or rupture in Tibetan social life, religious observances, cultural expression, and systems of meaning during the previous two decades—from the socialist transformation in the late 1950s through the death of Mao Zedong in 1976. With this language, Tāre Lhamo and Namtrul Rinpoche drew on well-established lore in the Nyingma tradition whereby periods of decline and strife call forth the revelation of esoteric teachings and ancient relics, referred to as "treasures" (*gter ma*),[17] meant to restore Buddhism and, as a corollary, the welfare of Tibetans. The revelatory content of treasure texts is generally traced to teachings by Padmasambhava, the eighth-century Indian tantric master credited with a pivotal role in establishing Buddhism in Tibet during the imperial period (seventh to ninth century) when the Tibetan empire dominated vast tracts of central Asia.[18] Sharing visionary recollections of their past lives, including as direct disciples of Padmasambhava—for her, Yeshe Tsogyal, and for him, Namkhai Nyingpo—Tāre Lhamo and Namtrul Rinpoche laid claim to a sense of continuity in their very personhood and in their prophetic revelations. Moreover, their persistent usage of the language of healing signals the heroic role that they envisioned for themselves in their religious vocation as tertöns or "treasure revealers" (*gter ston*).

This heroic conception of their historic role is important to my overall concern in this book with Buddhist conceptions of agency and healing cultural trauma among Tibetans as a minority in China. The life stories and letters of Tāre Lhamo and Namtrul Rinpoche provide a rich body of literature within which to explore ideas of agency in Buddhist terms, because they afford the rare occasion to compare the third-person voice of their idealized hagiographic portraits with the more humanizing first-person voice of their letters to each other. These sources shed much light on gendered representations of agency in Tibetan literature as well as the visionary processes through which contemporary Buddhist masters retrieved sources of authority from the distant past in order to confront their historical moment. I analyze these sources as minority voices in China that provide an alternative history of recent decades, seeking to establish cultural continuity and thereby to heal the trauma from the turbulent decades of the Maoist period.

Int.2 Image of Namtrul Rinpoche and Tāre Lhamo as found on a disciple's shrine.

As the culmination of their correspondence, Tāre Lhamo and Namtrul Rinpoche joined together into a lasting partnership and religious career, teaching and traveling during the 1980s and '90s while collaborating in the visionary process of revealing treasures. Following the inauguration of economic and cultural liberalization across China by Deng Xiaoping,[19] which allowed for public religious expression after an almost twenty-year hiatus, Tāre Lhamo and Namtrul Rinpoche began their religious career as a couple. Along with a handful of surviving Nyingma masters in Golok and northern Kham, they formed part of what David Germano has called a "vibrant, multipronged Ter [treasure] movement that has emerged as one of the most powerful and vital strategies for the renewal of traditional Tibetan culture among Nyingma traditions in Tibet."[20] From the 1980s forward, based at Nyenlung Monastery, which they rebuilt in Serta,[21] the couple traveled widely to discover and disseminate their treasures, while sponsoring construction projects and establishing ritual programs at numerous monasteries in and around Golok.

Gendered Lens

The distinctive representation of Tāre Lhamo and Namtrul Rinpoche as a tantric couple in Tibetan literary and audio-visual sources has motivated my focus on gender as a central rubric within my broader concern to recover the minority voices of Tibetans in post-Mao China. The couple's lives and writings are inextricably linked in the available Tibetan literary sources: their interwoven and jointly published life stories,[22] their twelve-volume corpus of collaborative revelations,[23] and their correspondence in fifty-six letters as collected and published in a single volume.[24] In terms of audio-visual sources, Nyenlung Monastery has produced numerous photographs and posters of the couple, cassette tapes featuring devotional songs by and about them, and VCDs (video compact discs) featuring short biographies and archival footage of the couple from the 1990s.[25] Most recently, a towering memorial structure featuring their photographs behind glass has been constructed at Nyenlung Monastery, above the outdoor pavilion where they used to teach together at their annual dharma gathering (*chos tshogs*).

I foreground Tāre Lhamo in analyzing sources by and about this couple in order to call attention to gender in representing agency and to recover female contributions to revitalizing Buddhism in the post-Mao era. This is particularly important due to the tendency in Tibetan sources and Western scholarship to elide the contributions of Buddhist women to Tibetan history, with the exception of specific recovery projects, of which there are a small but growing number.[26] Although Tibetan women have been active and vibrant in Nyingma communities as the consorts of prominent lamas and teachers in their own right, their names and religious roles are often mentioned only in passing in Tibetan sources.[27] While Tāre Lhamo and Namtrul Rinpoche were partners in the revelatory process, as acknowledged in their published life stories and joint corpus of revelations, it would nonetheless be easy for her to fade from view under the assumption that she played a secondary and supportive role to his.[28] This is particularly the case given that Namtrul Rinpoche outlived her by almost a decade and gained increased visibility through the sizeable number of Han Chinese followers with a keen interest in Tibetan Buddhism who made their way to Nyenlung Monastery.

As a female tantric master in her own right, Tāre Lhamo was prominent in Golok in her youth and a heroine to her local community during much of the Maoist period. Early on, she was recognized as an emanation of Yeshe Tsogyal and two prominent figures from the previous generation in Golok, one female and one male, namely Sera Khandro (1892–1940) and Tra Gelong Tsultrim Dargye (1866–1937). Later in life, she proved to be unusual among contemporary female religious figures in the extent to which she traveled and taught widely throughout Golok and beyond, side by side with Namtrul Rinpoche. While there are a handful of well-known female tantric masters, called *khandroma* (*mkha' 'gro ma*),[29] in Tibetan regions of China today, few others have had such a wide-ranging public presence or literary legacy. Tāre Lhamo is one of the few to enter the literary record with a life story and significant corpus of writings and one of only three contemporary female tertöns known to Western audiences through scholarly sources on the treasure tradition available in English.[30] Notably, in the early 1990s, Tāre Lhamo garnered international attention for recognizing one of the reincarnations of Dudjom Rinpoche Jigdral Yeshe Dorje, the former head of the Nyingma lineage in exile.[31] In 2003, her life story appeared in a Tibetan journal issue dedicated to tantric women (*sngags ma*) published by the Ngakmang Research Institute, where Tāre Lhamo stands alongside the likes of Yeshe Tsogyal, Mingyur Paldrön, and Sera Khandro as one of the remarkable Nyingma women in Tibetan history.[32] More recently, in 2013, Larung Buddhist Academy produced a sixteen-volume anthology of the lives of Buddhist women from India and Tibet, which contains the biographies of only a few contemporary Tibetan women serving as Buddhist teachers, including Tāre Lhamo.[33]

My foregrounding of Tāre Lhamo in this study can also be justified on the grounds of her greater renown in the early phase of her teaching career with Namtrul Rinpoche, in large part because of her status as the daughter of the regionally celebrated tertön Apang Terchen.[34] Indeed, the first large-scale teachings and rituals they conducted in the mid-1980s involved transmitting her father's revelations at Tsimda Gompa, the monastery he founded, to a gathering of lamas and monks from more than fifty newly reestablished monasteries in the region. This gave the couple immediate stature based on her birthright as her father's lineage heir.[35] In a further indication of her regional prominence, Namtrul Rinpoche appropriated aspects of Tāre Lhamo's identity and integrated them into his own: his identification as the activity emanation of her father in publications from 2000 and 2001 and as a reincarnation of Drime Özer, the consort and teacher of Sera Khandro, in a VCD produced by Nyenlung Monastery circa 2003.[36] Neither of these attributions appears in the couple's correspondence or is highlighted in the earliest version of their life stories; instead, they emerged publicly in close proximity to Tāre Lhamo's passing in 2002, suggesting a concern with lineage continuity.

There are three different versions of Tāre Lhamo's life, two of which interweave her story with that of Namtrul Rinpoche and one in which she is a stand-alone protagonist. The focus of this book, alongside their correspondence, is the earliest and authorized versions of the couple's life stories, *Spiraling Vine of Faith: The Liberation of the Supreme Khandro Tāre Lhamo* and *Jewel Garland: The Liberation of Namtrul Jigme Phuntsok*, composed by Pema Ösal Thaye and published together in 1997 in a single paperback book, *Cloud Offerings to Delight the Vidyādharas and Ḍākinīs*.[37] I consider these "authorized" versions since they were commissioned by the couple, written with their input, and published with state sanction through the County Office of the Bureau for Cultural Research in Serta.[38] Pema Ösal Thaye masterfully constructs their lives into a story of heroism with gendered idiosyncrasies, such as the way that Tāre Lhamo's youth is interwoven with the stories of her female antecedents, Yeshe Tsogyal and Sera Khandro, in *Spiraling Vine of Faith* and the distinctive narration of the post-Mao era with a tantric couple as the protagonist in *Jewel Garland*.

Using this as a basis, Abu Karlo produced an abbreviated and largely derivative work synthesizing their stories, *Jewel Lantern of Blessings: An Abridged Biography of the Tertön Couple, the Lord of Siddhas Zhuchen Namtrul and Khandro Tāre Dechen Lhamo*, published in 2001.[39] It adds little new information but makes a decisive intervention by characterizing Tāre Lhamo as the "wisdom consort" (*shes rab kyi grogs*) to the "great tertön" (*gter chen*) Namtrul Rinpoche even as it describes the distinctive process of their collaboration in revealing treasures.[40] This may be the result of a difference in the structure of this version of their intertwined lives, since here Abu Karlo integrates their activities together as a couple into her life story, and his characterization functions as a transition into that period. Whatever its function or rationale, Abu Karlo's intervention gives Namtrul Rinpoche primacy in their partnership and has been influential through its translation into Chinese and wide circulation among their Han Chinese disciples in multiple formats, including a glossy magazine-size book incorporating photographs.[41]

As a counterbalance, in the newest version of her life story, still in progress and as yet unpublished,[42] Tāre Lhamo is the central figure. Khenpo Rigdzin Dargye, a cleric-scholar from her homeland of Padma County,[43] casts Tāre Lhamo as an emanation of the female bodhisattva Tārā and emphasizes her visionary and wonder-working abilities in youth. This version of her life, which Rigdzin Dargye generously shared with me in 2014 in draft form, highlights Tāre Lhamo's revelation of treasures with multiple collaborators, her ritual prowess at extending the lives of others, and her miraculous ability to heal the sick and aid the recently deceased. While my study focuses on the former, due to its distinctive and masterful way of narrating recent Tibetan history, I will make comparative references to the other two versions of Tāre Lhamo's life story along the way.

Entering the Namthar

I first encountered Tāre Lhamo through her *namthar*, or story of "complete liberation" (*rnam thar*), in a Tibetan literature class at Harvard University with Janet Gyatso.[44] This genre of Tibetan literature recounts the life story of an accomplished tantric master, one understood to be liberated either at the outset, as in the case of a reincarnate lama, or by the end of the story as its culmination. Our class read through the first portion of the text together, which turned out not to be about her at all. Instead, the first part of *Spiraling Vine of Faith*,[45] recounts in abbreviated form the life stories of Yeshe Tsogyal and Sera Khandro,[46] among the illustrious series of her past lives. Later, on my own, I continued with the story of Tāre Lhamo's youth up to the age of forty, when she met Namtrul Rinpoche. Thereafter, the account of their travels and teachings together in the 1980s and '90s is found in his namthar, *Jewel Garland*, in which the couple are joint protagonists. Published together in the paperback book *Cloud Offerings to Delight the Vidyādharas and Ḍākinīs*, which totals 161 pages, their namthars are substantial but not exhaustive. The narrative style is episodic, structured as a series of short chronological vignettes, with no long passages describing people or places, nor a sense of the activities of everyday life. The condensed nature of each episode relies on culturally assumed knowledge of local figures, regional lore, and sacred sites.

I realized early on that only by spending time in Golok and visiting the places where Tāre Lhamo and Namtrul Rinpoche traveled, revealed treasures, and conducted large-scale rituals could I become an informed reader of these texts.

This initial encounter drew me to the grasslands of Golok on numerous research trips over a ten-year period between 2004 and 2014. On the eastern edge of the Tibetan plateau, Golok is a nomadic region characterized by rolling grasslands, often treeless, unlike the arid high plateaus of central Tibet to the west or the forested ravines of Kham to the south. The terrain is punctuated by several major rivers—the Ser, Do, Mar, and Ma (which becomes the Yellow River)—and bookended by the sacred mountain ranges Amnye Machen to the northwest and Nyenpo Yutse to the southeast. Ecologically, it is considered to be "high pasturage" suitable for a life of nomadic pastoralism.[47] Herding yaks and other livestock has been a mainstay occupation alongside trade and, more recently, the harvesting of medicinal herbs. Tāre Lhamo's homeland of Padma County is distinctive to the extent that it occupies the lush valley of the Mar River and is one of the main areas in Golok amenable to agriculture. For that reason, Padma County has a high population density and the greatest concentration of Buddhist monasteries in the region. These are primarily affiliated with the Nyingma tradition of Tibetan Buddhism, as are the monasteries in neighboring Serta County to the south. Because of the Nyingma predominance, Golok and neighboring areas of northern Kham have historically served as a hub for treasure revelation.

My impetus to travel to Golok and neighboring Serta was to fill in the missing gaps of Tāre Lhamo's life story. I also hoped to acquire a complete copy of the treasure corpus (*gter chos*) containing her joint revelations with Namtrul Rinpoche.[48] With these tasks in mind and joined by a colleague,[49] in 2004 I ventured for the first time to Nyenlung, the monastery in Serta County that Tāre Lhamo and Namtrul Rinpoche rebuilt and where they resided together from 1980 until her death in 2002. Much to my surprise and delight, in that meeting, Namtrul Rinpoche generously gave me their entire treasure corpus in twelve volumes as well as the treasure corpus of her father, the locally renowned Apang Terchen, in sixteen volumes.[50] He also described the circumstances surrounding their correspondence and offered me a facsimile edition of the collected letters, which he and Tāre Lhamo exchanged during their courtship, in their entirety.

Of the twenty-nine volumes that I carried back to Chengdu that sum-mer, I sensed immediately that the letters were special. Given prohibitions on travel and the province border separating the couple at that time, their correspondence provided the principal medium of their courtship. As Nam-trul Rinpoche later told me, prior to 1980, when Tāre Lhamo joined him at Nyenlung, they had only met once for an extended visit he made to her homeland the previous year. Over the next several years, I worked through the variegated content and genres in the fifty-six letters and addenda, total-ing 188 pages and almost entirely in verse. As I consulted with Tibetan lamas, scholars, poets, and singers, I realized the versatility and virtuosity in their use of folk and poetic styles as they crafted a shared destiny and conveyed a range of sentiments, erotic and amorous. As exchanges conveyed secretly across province borders, their letters provide a more intimate portrait of the couple than available in the idealized accounts found in their namthars, a perfect basis for comparison.

In that first meeting, Namtrul Rinpoche also invited my colleague and me to join him on pilgrimage. The following day, he planned to travel to Padma County and visit the monastery Tashi Gomang to lead a feast offer-ing (tshogs mchod), a ritual performed in order to purify tantric commit-ments and accumulate merit, and a public empowerment (khrom dbang), a tantric initiation ceremony meant as a blessing for the general public. It was his first time traveling on a pilgrimage-cum-teaching tour since the death of Tāre Lhamo in 2002. Together with our driver, we joined the cara-van of cars and trucks filled with disciples (both Tibetan and Chinese) mak-ing the journey from Serta County northward along a winding dirt road. We became part of the entourage, and Namtrul Rinpoche occasionally stopped the caravan to point out sacred sites to us along the way.

During this first visit and each of my subsequent trips to Golok, in some sense, I entered the namthar—witnessing the people, places, and events of Tāre Lhamo and Namtrul Rinpoche's life story firsthand. In Golok, I inhabited the domain of prophecy and auspicious signs, blessings and meaningful con-nections, pilgrimage and aspiration prayers. Research questions to Namtrul Rinpoche sometimes generated the spontaneous composition of advice or rituals,[51] and my own translation and research efforts were seen as a way to propagate their lineage abroad. In journeying to Golok and environs, I had entered not just a place but an entire worldview, where the actions of and environment around a Buddhist master are imbued with special meaning.

[12]

Int.3 Procession to welcome Namtrul Rinpoche to Tashi Gomang.

Even on the sidelines, while observing rituals such as the feast offering and public empowerment at Tashi Gomang, I became a participant in the sphere of activity centered around the teacher, constituted among the faithful in the ongoing life story of Tāre Lhamo and Namtrul Rinpoche.

Ritual at Tashi Gomang

Outside of Tashi Gomang,[52] a line of Tibetan monks formed in the open meadow. Dressed in ceremonial garb, they wore yellow cloaks draped over their maroon monastic robes and donned cone-shaped hats fringed with tassels. The yellow and maroon vividly contrasted with the lush hue of grasses covering the meadow and hillsides after the summer rains. The procession began, and the line of approximately fifty monks moved forward, curving snakelike along the dirt road leading to the monastery. The low drone of Tibetan horns filled the air, punctuated by the clang of cymbals and the whine of an oboe-like instrument (*rgya gling*). Escorted by this procession was Namtrul Rinpoche, seated in a land cruiser covered in white ceremonial silk scarves. It is traditional for the monks and laity to welcome visiting teachers by traveling partway along the route to greet them and escorting them into the monastery. The monks walked in order of ordination rank, with the youngest trailing behind. A throng of nomads and residents from the nearby county seat lined the road, some bowing in reverence, others with necks stretched out in order to catch a glimpse of him.

Having joined Namtrul Rinpoche on pilgrimage, my colleague and I stood at the sidelines, documenting the procession in photographs and on video. Some monks also had cameras and video equipment out, making us feel less intrusive. We found a spot by the side of the road, a bit ahead of the jostling crowd, to shoot as the procession passed. It was a typical scene in some regards—foreign researchers capturing an exotic moment in a distant land—a scene laden with a long legacy of power relations in which representation is not a neutral act of documentation, but instead presumes privileged access and affords interpretive control.[53] At Tashi Gomang, I marveled at being able to witness a ritual that in the namthar would have been described in a single line. As foreigners, my colleague and I were invited to join the monks inside the assembly hall during the main ritual, while the bulk of the laity—more than a thousand locals—crowded into the courtyard outside. A speaker had been hooked up to the roof of the monastery so that they could listen to the prayers being recited. That day, it was as if I had lifted my eyes from the page back in Cambridge to find that suddenly the namthar had become a living world all around me.

That hypothetical single line in the namthar was suddenly a long afternoon spent chanting in a crowded assembly hall. Now I could see how the event was structured: who attended public rituals, where they sat, how they processed in and out, what happened during the ritual, the liturgies used for chanting, and the teachings given. I could witness how, although the laity was consigned to outside the monastery during the main ceremony, the food that had been offered and blessed during the feast was later distributed to them. Afterward, Namtrul Rinpoche's throne was set up on the steps to the assembly hall facing the courtyard for the public empowerment. The monks sat up front in a crescent with the laity behind them, spread out in the courtyard as before. At the end, the crowd swelled around his throne in order to receive blessings.

Since then, I have viewed comparable scenes recorded when Tāre Lhamo was still alive. A set of VCDs produced by Nyenlung introduces the monastery and provides a brief overview of their life stories, followed by devotional songs and footage of their teachings and travels going back to the late 1990s.[54] The viewer joins the tantric couple on virtual pilgrimage, visiting some of the same sites that Namtrul Rinpoche did in 2004, as the couple gives empowerments to the young Dudjom reincarnation in the inner chamber of their residence, leads a procession to consecrate the large stūpa at the administrative seat of Padma County, conducts rituals in a tent at the base of the Nyenpo Yutse mountain range, and teaches in the assembly hall at Nyenlung, overflowing with Tibetan and Chinese disciples. In footage of their travels and teachings, the viewer witnesses the rare phenomenon of a tantric couple conferring empowerments together, side by side on ceremonial thrones, both reading the liturgy, performing the gestures, and blessing the assembly with ritual implements. At Tashi Gomang, there is even a glimpse of Tāre Lhamo standing alone in the field outside the monastery, receiving white ceremonial scarves (*kha btags*) from a long line of disciples from her homeland, while Namtrul Rinpoche stands back to allow them to greet her.

Unbeknown to us that day, my colleague and I were also captured on video. When I returned to Padma County in 2006, a set of VCDs had been released chronicling Namtrul Rinpoche's 2004 pilgrimage.[55] Featuring both Tāre Lhamo and Namtrul Rinpoche on the cover, the VCDs follow his pilgrimage with footage of each stop along the way, including his visit to Tashi Gomang. The video is accompanied by devotional songs, some written by Tāre Lhamo, emphasizing her continuing presence for their religious community and authorizing Namtrul Rinpoche as the steward of their teachings. One short clip features the foreign researchers, video recorder rolling and camera clicking away. In an ironic twist, it shows the monks capturing us in the process of capturing them. Rather than standing outside the frame as *observers*, "neutrally" recording the scene, in that VCD, we are located within the scene as *participants*, subsumed into the flow of activity centered around Namtrul Rinpoche. This ethnographic vignette raises the issue of representation, central to this book, and shows that one's interlocutors in research are by no means passive "objects of study" but have their own agendas and frames in which to place the researcher.[56] By appearing in this video clip, my colleague and I were incorporated within a framework of meaning that positions Buddhist masters at the center of public activity and the apex of social values. We were constituted as part of the crowd of disciples and admirers, confirming Namtrul Rinpoche's stature and prestige and by extension Tāre Lhamo's own.

Minority Voices

The ritual occasion at Tashi Gomang exemplifies the large-scale Buddhist gatherings that I encountered in the mid-2000s, including construction projects, consecration ceremonies, and other conspicuous signs of the revitalization of Tibetan culture. If unfamiliar with modern Tibetan history, a first-time visitor might not realize that most monasteries standing in Tibetan areas of China today have been rebuilt from the rubble left after the Maoist period. Nor would one necessarily realize that ordinary public religious observances that permeate Tibetan life—pilgrims circumambulating monasteries, the elderly spinning prayer wheels, monks gathered in large assembly halls reciting prayers, and large-scale rituals and festivals—were forbidden for almost two decades. Tibetans know this history all too well, and one lama chided me when I marveled at the many new buildings on his monastery's grounds, indicating that the scale of Buddhist institutions has yet to approach what once existed.

Apart from researchers and travelers who have ventured to the Tibetan plateau, many in the West have not heard much, if anything, about cultural revitalization efforts by Tibetans within China. In general, the Tibetan people are disparately represented in the media as either the victims of "cultural genocide" or the benefactors of "peaceful liberation" at the hands of the Communist state.[57] In their discussion of these diametrically opposed viewpoints, Ashild Kolas and Monika Thowsen highlight that the realities on the ground are not so black and white. The Chinese Communist state's claim to protect and promote Tibetan culture effectively erases its culpability in the destruction of most visible signs of Tibetan culture during the Maoist period, culminating in the Cultural Revolution. However, the exile Tibetan counterclaim that Tibetan areas in China have been turned into a "cultural wasteland" makes the Cultural Revolution stand for more than sixty years of Communist rule, discounting the significant changes brought about by economic and cultural liberalization.[58] Both versions homogenize the role of the state in recent Tibetan history, despite major shifts in state policy toward minorities as well as the gap between policy and implementation that has led to local variations in how policy affects minority groups.[59] More importantly, such representations narrowly focus on state policy, rendering invisible the substantial achievements by Tibetans within China in revitalizing their own culture since the 1980s.[60]

Despite China's attempt to celebrate cultural revitalization as evidence that Tibetans are thriving under Communist rule, we need to ask how Tibetans themselves construe their own recent history. Where do we look for Tibetan voices and self-representations? For minorities in China, who do not have direct access to political discourse and for whom major media venues like television and newspapers are state-controlled, literature and the arts have become important sites for intellectual discourse and debate.[61] In the last decade, scholars have begun to examine the revival of Tibetan arts and literature in order to retrieve minority voices, highlighting the complexity of self-representation, coded mechanisms for dissent, and debates about the very nature of Tibetan modernity.[62] Although secular literature composed by Tibetan writers received attention in the anthology *Modern Tibetan Literature*,[63] there has been no comparable study of religious literature to investigate how Buddhist masters are adapting Tibetan literary genres to address contemporary concerns.[64]

This study seeks to recover minority voices within Buddhist literature recently published in China, and to highlight their representations of Tibetan agency. Here I follow Laura Ahearn's definition of "agency" as the "socioculturally mediated capacity to act,"[65] highlighting the ways human actors are situated in social and cultural systems that both constrain and provide resources for their endeavors.[66] Representations in art and literature are culturally situated within specific notions of personhood and causation as well as conventions for ascribing agency according to literary genre and artistic style. In a Buddhist context, notions of karma and past lives feature prominently in conceptions of personhood, creating a relational and composite identity that complicates how we might ordinarily associate agency with autonomy.[67] Meanwhile, certain genres of literature allow for the assertion of forms of agency beyond the boundaries of secular and state discourse, creating an alternative vantage point from which to narrate recent history. Overall, cultural conventions play a significant role in how Tibetans today invoke symbols, ideals, and authoritative paradigms in order to explain events, to conceive of possibilities, and to articulate and authorize a course of action. One of the tasks of this book, then, is to discern how specific examples of religious literature function to restore a sense of Tibetan agency in Buddhist terms.

In my focus on the lives and letters of an eminent tantric couple, I share a microhistorical approach with the contributors to the seminal volume *Buddhism in Contemporary Tibet: Religious Revival and Cultural Identity*.[68] Each focused on the role of a single monastery, ritual, or individual as exemplary of the constituent features of the Buddhist revival more broadly. Similarly, I re-create for the reader the rich tapestry in which the lives of this contemporary Buddhist tantric couple unfolded and show how the literary imagination—the shared vision and prophetic mission that Tāre Lhamo and Namtrul Rinpoche created in their correspondence— became actualized in the form of their prodigious religious activities and represented in the hagiographic portrait of their career together in the 1980s and '90s.[69] Informed by field research during numerous visits to the region between 2004 and 2014, I focus on literary representations of their lives—their hagiographic portraits and their own voices in epistolary exchanges at a moment of tremendous historical uncertainty—as windows into how Tibetans have understood and represented the rupture and revival of Buddhism on the Tibetan plateau in the second half of the twentieth century.

In its capacity to reassert systems of meaning, hagiographic and epistolary literature can be considered an alternative source for memory work and reconstructing the past, not as a means of establishing facts, but as Tibetan self-representations that offer an alternative to the official account by the state. Perhaps these are best described as "subaltern pasts," in Dipesh Chakrabarty's use of the term, pasts articulated by subordinated minority groups in terms outside the epistemological limits of the discipline of history.[70] For Chakrabarty, "minority" refers to a marginal social position and relegation to inferior status vis-à-vis the dominant group, as well as the subordination of "life-worlds" that harbor "irrational" elements marginalized in the mainstream discourse of the secular state, such as religious premises.[71] In China, religious discourse is potentially subversive because it offers the possibility not only to assert an alternative version of events but also to construct a narrative rooted in an alternative episteme, or worldview, with its corresponding set of beliefs, values, and authority.

Although their purpose is not to narrate history per se, in the process of recounting the lives of contemporary Buddhist masters—who are subaltern vis-à-vis the state but elite in their local contexts—hagiographic accounts present the events of recent Tibetan history within a Buddhist framework. A striking example is the use of "collective karma" (*spyi mthun las*) to frame the turbulent decades of the Maoist period in *Spiraling Vine of Faith*.[72] While it may seem odd for a Buddhist author to attribute the events of history to the collective deeds of the Tibetan people in an indeterminate past, this choice can be regarded as part of a literary strategy to reclaim agency on behalf of Tibetans. More importantly, as I argue in chapter 2, karma serves as a vital interpretive schema through which local historians and monastics like Pema Ösal Thaye make sense of collective trauma and encompass the devastating events of the Maoist period within Buddhist systems of meaning. In this way, karma serves as a narrative device, retrospectively asserting interpretive command over events otherwise outside of Tibetan control.

Broadly speaking, narrating trauma is an exercise in constructing meaning out of the shattered ruins of the past. According to trauma theorists, the ability to create a narrative is central to the healing process as a means to repair and adapt systems of meaning and encompass the memory of trauma within them.[73] Unlike the dialogic format of psychoanalysis, in the case of collective trauma, this active process must be performed by a select group—cultural carriers such as artists, elders, intellectuals, or religious figures—on behalf of the society as a whole. In a colonial context or under other forms of interethnic domination,[74] the restoration of meaning involves ascribing cultural significance to devastating historical events and thereby encompassing the damage caused as a result within a local episteme. What is crucial is a useable history that can serve as an alternative to the official state history and a rallying point for collective action. As the anthropologist Michael Jackson emphasizes, making meaning through storytelling generates not just an "intellectual grasp of events" but a "symbolic restructuring" of them. This becomes an important way to gain mastery over the events of history, whether personal or collective. For this reason, Jackson refers to storytelling as "a vital human strategy for sustaining a sense of agency in the face of disempowering circumstances."[75] In other words, narrating trauma provides a way to restore systems of meaning after an abrupt and overwhelming event or period of devastation.

As such, it could be regarded as part and parcel of constructing subaltern pasts—in this case, by reasserting the centrality of Tibetans as actors in their own history.

This symbolic restructuring of events, a prominent feature in their hagiographic corpus, begins in their own voice in the letters that Tāre Lhamo and Namtrul Rinpoche exchanged at the cusp of the post-Mao era between 1978 and 1980. Therein they tacitly subsume the turbulent decades of the Maoist period within a Buddhist framework as "degenerate times" and announce their own revelatory activities as the means to "heal the damage" to Buddhist practice, teachings, and institutions in Tibetan areas. This serves as a potent narrative device allowing the couple to maintain an orientation toward the future, specifically toward their own visionary means to restore Buddhism through treasure revelation, recovering esoteric teachings and ancient relics from Tibet's imperial past. The optimistic and heroic tenor of their letters, replete with images of regeneration, the language of healing, and declarations of victory over dark forces, is stunning given the historical devastation out of which they had just emerged. Their namthars, *Spiraling Vine of Faith* and *Jewel Garland*, follow suit in focusing on moments of heroism during the Maoist period and their revitalization efforts in the 1980s and '90s, rather than detailing the extent or nature of the actual damage. Such epistolary and hagiographic works thereby create a vibrant alternative to "scar literature," a literary trend among modern Chinese and Tibetan writers that emerged in the 1980s to recount the trauma associated with the Cultural Revolution in fictional and allegorical terms.

In exploring literary works by and about Tāre Lhamo and Namtrul Rinpoche, I provide poignant examples of how Tibetans represent their own recent history. These illustrate an alternative approach to narrating history and agency within a Buddhist framework, rooted in premodern notions of causation and personhood. The works offer not just a different story, but a story with *different premises* that positions Tibetans themselves, particularly Buddhist masters, as the principal agents in history. I highlight how Tāre Lhamo and Namtrul Rinpoche, as well as their hagiographer, Pema Ösal Thaye, draw on long-standing symbols, discourses, and practices within the tradition of treasure revelation in order to imagine, inspire, effect, and narrate the revitalization of Buddhism as part of a synergistic group of Nyingma masters in the region of Golok. Their voices and those of their followers provide a striking account of Tibetan agency.

Recentering Tibetan Lives

Notably, in *Spiraling Vine of Faith* and *Jewel Garland*, the Chinese Communist state is rarely mentioned, apart from scant references to policies during the Maoist period and the colophon, which acknowledges a local government agency that enabled its publication. This is no doubt as much due to the religious nature of the genre as it is a product of self-censorship on the part of Pema Ösal Thaye, seeking to avoid politically sensitive content. Instead, the principal actors are Tāre Lhamo and Namtrul Rinpoche, who are portrayed with heightened agency as visionaries and ritual virtuosos engaged in recovering lineages of teachings through treasure revelation and reconstituting Tibetan community in ritual terms. In this way, hagiographic literature effectively decenters Beijing and recenters Buddhist masters as the principal agents in Tibetan society and history.

Charlene Makley has described the revitalization of Tibetan culture from the 1980s forward as a "mandalization process" in which recounting stories about the lives of Buddhist masters is a constituent feature. According to her definition, the mandalization process repositions the reincarnate lama, and by extension Buddhist institutions, at the apex of social value and the center of public life.[76] (Note that a *maṇḍala* can be a two- or three-dimensional representation of the domain of a tantric deity; often the deity in union with a consort resides at the center, which is also the apex.) The work of namthar as a genre in the contemporary context, according to Makley, is to reposition the Tibetan people as the faithful beneficiaries of the moral authority and ritual prowess of Buddhist masters.[77] Drawing out the implications of this assertion, one could suggest that hagiographic literature, with its leitmotif of engendering faith (*dad pa*), has played and continues to play a pivotal role in reconstituting Tibetan social worlds around Buddhist leaders, values, and institutions in the post-Mao period.

In promoting a mandalization process, hagiographic literature can thus be seen as a constitutive feature of cultural revitalization by Tibetans in China. As a literary genre, namthar is flourishing alongside audio-visual materials focused on Buddhist masters, such as poster images, devotional songs, and even music videos on monastery-produced VCDs showcasing their activities that proliferate in public spaces throughout Tibetan areas.[78] Moreover, the publication of namthars is part of a broader movement to

Int.4 Pema Ösal Thaye, a local historian and disciple of Tāre Lhamo and Namtrul Rinpoche.

recover local history in Golok by Tibetans themselves since liberalization in the 1980s. Pema Ösal Thaye is an important contributor as a Buddhist monastic and government worker who is the publisher, author, and editor of numerous namthars, histories, and edited volumes dedicated to preserving Tibetan culture.[79] On the county level in Serta in Sichuan Province, his effort is a smaller-scale version of the work of the poet Ju Kalzang at the prefecture level in Tawu, the capital of Golok Prefecture in Qinghai Province.[80] Both endeavors share the common purpose of recovering local history and publishing works by religious figures from the region of Golok, which in its broadest sense includes neighboring Serta. As a compiler of local histories and the namthars of Buddhist masters, Pema Ösal Thaye has made a significant contribution to the mandalization process described by Makley.

While Makley emphasizes the role of mandalization in the reassertion of Tibetan masculinities, both lay and monastic, since the 1980s, the case of Tāre Lhamo and Namtrul Rinpoche is a prominent exception to the rule. In Tāre Lhamo's namthar, *Spiraling Vine of Faith*, it is the khandroma at the center of the action, and Pema Ösal Thaye crafts a type of agency explicitly identified with the *ḍākinī*, a category of female tantric deities. Moreover, in the telling of her life with Namtrul Rinpoche, as recounted in *Jewel Garland*, the reader finds not a solitary lama at the center of the maṇḍala but the iconographically more traditional *yab-yum*. Literally meaning "father" and "mother," *yab-yum* refers to the tantric couple representing the union of "method and wisdom" (*thabs shes*) in Buddhist tantric symbolism. Although the yab-yum is prevalent in Buddhist tantric iconography, the consort of a male lama typically receives little mention in hagiographic literature.[81] However, due to Tāre Lhamo's stature as the daughter of Apang Terchen and as a khandroma in her own right, she and Namtrul Rinpoche traveled and taught together, revealing a significant corpus of ritual manuals and esoteric instructions, and this is reflected in their hagiographic representation as joint protagonists and acknowledged collaboration in their jointly attributed treasure revelations. In *Jewel Garland*, they are depicted as the charismatic centerpiece of large-scale public rituals in which they forge connections with the hundreds and thousands in attendance. These narrative accounts showcase the tantric prowess of the couple, transforming the natural and social world through acts of consecration and initiation.

What I am proposing is that we examine how agency is construed within a Buddhist framework in a way that recenters Tibetans, and specifically

Buddhist masters, female and male, as agents of their own history. The assertion of Tibetan agency in Buddhist terms in the sources for this study can be read as a response to the specific challenges posed by a competing episteme embodied in state policy, Communist discourse, secular values, and market forces, all of which have tended to marginalize Tibetans within the larger Han-dominated Chinese nation. This response inscribes new meaning into the events of recent history and serves to heal the cultural trauma that Tibetans have undergone as a result of social upheaval and disruption of cultural and religious practices, particularly during the Maoist period.[82] Examining these literary representations as sites for reasserting Buddhist interpretive schemas and systems of meaning, I link the processes of writing literature, making meaning, and taking action in the revitalization of Buddhism as effected by Tāre Lhamo and Namtrul Rinpoche, and through which recent Tibetan history has been narrated.

Sources for This Book

The literary accounts central to this book narrate recent Tibetan history from several different temporal orientations, authorial voices, and literary genres. I start with an analysis of *Spiraling Vine of Faith: The Liberation of the Supreme Khandro Tāre Lhamo*, which is the namthar of Tāre Lhamo as narrated in the third-person voice of Pema Ösal Thaye. A retrospective account of her early life up through the turbulent decades of the Maoist period, *Spiraling Vine of Faith* creates an idealized hagiographic portrait of Tāre Lhamo in Buddhist terms as a local heroine. In chapter 1, I perform a gendered analysis of this work, asking how a cultural space is created for female religious authority in the otherwise male-dominated religious milieu in Golok. Specifically, I look at the use of authoritative female antecedents in the long prelude to her life story and place this within the social context in Golok, where her status as the daughter of Apang Terchen ensured her inclusion in esoteric Nyingma circles. In chapter 2, I show how historical events and hagiographic interventions are interwoven in miracle tales that provide a means of restoring a sense of Tibetan agency after a period of collective trauma. Scholars of trauma such as Judith Herman have argued for the importance of crafting a narrative in the healing process in order for individuals to regain a sense of mastery over overwhelming and devastating events, originally outside their own control. I build on her work and recent studies on collective trauma to theorize about the role of hagiography in healing cultural trauma.

I then introduce and translate selections from the correspondence between Tāre Lhamo and Namtrul Rinpoche, an invaluable counterpart to this idealized portrait, which provide a more humanizing and multi-faceted representation in which their own voices come to the fore. Their amorous and prophetic exchanges are composed almost entirely in verse and draw on a range of styles from ornate Indic-inspired poetry to Tibetan folk songs, and their choice of literary style in each letter influences the content and tone of the correspondence. For example, ornate poetry marks the for-mality of their initial exchanges, while bardic verse drawing on the Gesar epic (a pan-Tibetan epic of Arthurian proportions) is reserved for bold declara-tions of their certain victory over the dark and demonic forces of their times. In turn, prophetic passages allowed Tāre Lhamo and Namtrul Rinpoche to construct their identity as a couple, based on myriad past lives together, and to chart the locations of treasures awaiting revelation in the landscape of Golok and neighboring regions. Yet right alongside that, local song styles offer more folksy imagery, equating their destined union to the inseparabil-ity of a snow lion and its mountain perch, a juniper branch and its berries, and thunderclouds hovering over the grasslands. In her preference for oral folk genres, Tāre Lhamo gradually induces Namtrul Rinpoche to eschew the erudite poetics of his monastic training for the exuberance of folk songs. Because of this, much of their correspondence has a fresh, colloquial tone, akin to the love poems of the Sixth Dalai Lama but with a distinctively east-ern Tibetan flavor.

As part and parcel of their religious vocation, they engaged in the "sport of attraction" in preparation for the tantric rite of sexual union that con-stitutes an integral part of treasure revelation. In chapter 3, I explore the dynamic interplay of love and destiny, arguing that the affection shared between Tāre Lhamo and Namtrul Rinpoche in their epistolary exchanges activated their visionary propensities in preparation for their collaborative revelatory activities and ultimately galvanized them into action. I pay spe-cial attention to gender in tracing how they negotiated the terms of their union and created a shared narrative as a tantric couple across lifetimes. In chapter 4, I turn to the historical contingencies and challenges that Tāre Lhamo and Namtrul Rinpoche faced and how they navigated those within a clearly articulated Buddhist rubric of causation, drawing on forces in the distant past to imagine realizing their vision for the future. I examine the language and metaphors they employed to foresee restoring Buddhist teachings and the welfare of Tibetans in the post-Mao period, including: "healing" (*gso ba*) the damage of degenerate times, in a prophetic key derived from the treasure tradition; "rescuing" (*skyob pa*) beings, assuming a heroic stance as bodhisattvas or buddhas-to-be; and achieving "victory" (*rgyal kha*) over demonic and barbaric forces in the performative language of bardic verse. In this way, the couple engaged in a creative dialogue, harnessing the terminology and imagery from various genres of Tibetan verse to conceive of the possibility of revitalizing Buddhism and script their own roles within it. As an extended and initially private exchange, their correspondence provides a distinctive perspective on the agency of Tibetans on the cusp of the post-Mao era.

Coming full circle, chapter 5 returns to the writing of namthar, showcasing the couple's endeavors from the 1980s forward, after Tāre Lhamo left her homeland to join Namtrul Rinpoche in Serta. Specifically, I analyze *Jewel Garland: The Liberation of Namtrul Jigme Phuntsok*, in which the second half recounts their joint activities from 1980 to 1995. This last source is both retrospective, recounting their religious efforts up to its publication, and concurrent, as the writing of namthars is a project constitutive of cultural revitalization itself. Returning to the genre of namthar after an excursus into their letters shows how the shared vision and prophetic mission constructed in the correspondence were actualized in their prodigious religious activities and translated into an idealized hagiographic representation. In contrast to the intimate words exchanged in their letters, *Jewel Garland* portrays the public personae and heightened agency of a tantric couple whose visionary talents and ritual prowess form the basis of their many accomplishments promoting the revitalization of Buddhism in Golok. I highlight the recurring paradigm of forging "connections" (*'brel ba*), which draws attention to the ways that Buddhist masters are understood to reconstitute people and places as Tibetan through their teachings and ritual activities. This account of the 1980s and '90s illustrates, in microhistorical terms, how the revitalization of Buddhism in the post-Mao period unfolded within a single region with its corresponding network of Buddhist teachers, monasteries, and ritual systems. The epilogue closes the book with a discussion of the couple's activities after 1995, when *Jewel Garland* was completed; their ongoing community after Tāre Lhamo passed away in 2002; and their legacy as a tantric couple since Namtrul Rinpoche's passing in 2011.

Through a close examination of these three main literary sources—in conjunction with other historical and biographical sources as well as interviews conducted between 2004 and 2014—I explore an eminent example of the religious imagination out of which the restoration of Buddhist institutions and practices was conceived and represented by Tibetans within China. While it is important to describe the achievements of Tibetans in reconstructing monasteries and other visible cultural forms,[83] it has not been enough only to build buildings. What has also had to be restored are systems of meaning that came under attack during the Maoist period and have been undermined in intermittent reeducation campaigns in recent decades, intensifying in the wake of the March 2008 protests, despite claims by the state regarding freedom of religion.[84] Nonetheless, it is also possible for subordinated groups to resist dominant systems of meaning. In the Tibetan case, one form that this resistance has taken is the assertion of a Buddhist worldview in the face of epistemological challenges posed by CCP rhetoric and state policy. In other words, Tibetan leaders have not only been rebuilding Buddhist institutions, they have also been reasserting a Buddhist episteme as a total worldview.

A New Namthar?

Though my purpose here is not to compose a new namthar, this book does provide a chronological account while analyzing literary sources by and about Tāre Lhamo and Namtrul Rinpoche. In its chronology, it follows the arc of Tāre Lhamo's life, analyzing the principal textual sources associated with each phase in successive sections, and I integrate Namtrul Rinpoche into the narrative at the point at which they began to correspond. Because I arrived at Nyenlung in 2004, two years after Tāre Lhamo passed away, I traveled the length and breadth of Golok in order to gather stories about her—from her homeland in Padma County to monasteries throughout the region where she and Namtrul Rinpoche conducted large-scale rituals and provided financial aid for reconstruction. I was able to interview the people who knew her best: her husband, Namtrul Rinpoche; their hagiographer, Pema Ösal Thaye; her close disciple, Rigdzin Dargye, who is currently finishing a new

Int.5 Elderly female relative of Tāre Lhamo at Tsimda Monastery in Padma
County.

namthar about her; and female relatives and friends in youth, like Adrön and Achung, who lived through the Maoist period with her. In addition, at Nyenlung Monastery and elsewhere, I had the opportunity to participate in the activities of the couple's ongoing religious community.

This field research has allowed me to triangulate the first-person perspective of their correspondence and the third-person account in their hagiographies with the social context of lived religion in Golok, oral tales of Tāre Lhamo's life, and firsthand accounts that Namtrul Rinpoche shared with me. This ability to bridge text and context provides an invaluable touchstone throughout the book. It allows me not only to fill in gaps in information in the life stories of Tāre Lhamo and Namtrul Rinpoche as found in published accounts, particularly for the turbulent decades of the Maoist period, but also to share insights into the selection process of crafting a literary representation of a tantric couple. The process of selectivity is all the more pronounced today due to self-censorship in publications resulting from the sensitive nature of the "Tibet question" in China. While in the field, my sense was that the more I understood about the world outside the text, the more I could learn about representational strategies within the namthars and correspondence.

That said, there are important ways that I intervene in the representation of Tāre Lhamo's life as intertwined with Namtrul Rinpoche's in these literary sources. First and foremost, I give more weight to the letters they exchanged at the cusp of the post-Mao era than does *Jewel Garland*. There, prophetic selections from the letters appear alongside prophecies by local religious figures in order to confirm their union and to introduce Tāre Lhamo into the narrative. By contrast, in this book, I examine both the prophetic and the personal dimensions of their correspondence in order to get a more rounded picture of this tantric couple, juxtaposing their own self-representation with the hagiographic portrait of their lives by Pema Ösal Thaye. My purpose is to explore the human side of their relationship and the creative negotiation of their received heritage: how their partnership developed, how they handled the contingencies of the historical moment, and how they appropriated and transformed the resources available to them from treasure lore, folk and literary genres, and tantric practices.

As an additional intervention, I invert the order of their life stories by following the chronology of Tāre Lhamo's life. In publication, *Cloud Offerings to Delight the Vidyādharas and Ḍākinīs* begins with Namtrul Rinpoche's namthar, *Jewel Garland*. After an account of his youth, it presents excerpts from their correspondence as a way to introduce Tāre Lhamo into the narrative and then focuses on the couple's activities together. Her own namthar, *Spiraling Vine of Faith*, follows. In a parallel but inverted structure, this study begins with Tāre Lhamo's life story, introduces Namtrul Rinpoche through an analysis of their correspondence, and finally examines their joint role in the revitalization of Buddhism. The crucial difference is that I am putting Tāre Lhamo first, as the primary object of this study. Namtrul Rinpoche and others whom I interviewed were fully aware that my primary interest lay in Tāre Lhamo's life story, and the importance of such a project was never questioned by anyone in their religious community. Ironically, the only person who questioned my motives was another khandroma, who objected to the idea that women should be privileged as a category of inquiry.[85]

The ordering of their namthars—his first, hers second—reflects a gendered hierarchy within their religious community at Nyenlung, which sponsored the publication of *Cloud Offerings*. There Namtrul Rinpoche is considered the principal; he walked first in ceremonial processions, and though they conducted tantric initiations seated side by side, his throne in the main shrine hall remained just a few inches higher than hers. My own interest in Tāre Lhamo and positioning of her as the centerpiece of this study is grounded in a feminist impulse—and growing academic trend—to retrieve Tibetan women from the literary and historical record.[86] This impulse launched the project in 2004 and remained at its core during field research, even as I gradually came to realize that a study of Tāre Lhamo's life and writings could not feasibly be separated from her long-standing collaboration and hagiographic fusion with Namtrul Rinpoche. This ordering also reflects a trajectory in their own careers, whereby Tāre Lhamo's renown in Golok as the daughter of Apang Terchen gave their teachings early visibility and a large following among Tibetans, while later Namtrul Rinpoche came to the fore with the growth of Nyenlung Monastery and a burgeoning community of Chinese disciples.

Rather than endeavoring to present a more complete account of their lives, my interest lies in understanding strategies of representation, specifically the difference between the idealized account of their hagiographic construction and the more complex and decidedly human terms of their correspondence in their own voices. In line with recent trends in the study of hagiography, I leave aside epistemological questions: separating fact from fiction, history from myth, and the natural from the supernatural.[87] Instead, this book explores the production of meaning in texts by and about Tāre Lhamo and Namtrul Rinpoche. In other words, rather than ask questions about truth, I take up issues of meaning. How might the idealized account of Tāre Lhamo's miracles during the years leading up to and including the Cultural Revolution, as contained in *Spiraling Vine of Faith*, function as alternative history and serve to heal cultural trauma? How do Tāre Lhamo and Namtrul Rinpoche construct the distant past and envision future possibilities through their courtship and correspondence? How does the narration of their joint activities in *Jewel Garland* portray and participate in the revitalization of Buddhism in Golok?

That said, in presenting a study of the lives and letters of Tāre Lhamo and Namtrul Rinpoche, I do not seek to foreclose the possibility of its interpretation within a hagiographic frame. Early in my research, Namtrul Rinpoche cited a prophecy that the treasure teachings of this eminent couple will one day reach America. That my research offered a potential vehicle to help fulfill that prophecy no doubt helped motivate him to spend many patient hours answering my questions in interviews over the years. Certainly, this analysis of their lives and letters will introduce English-speaking audiences to Tāre Lhamo and Namtrul Rinpoche. The circulation and use of this book will ultimately decide how it is read. Likely one day it will journey back to Golok and serve as testimony to their significant legacy as a tantric couple, kept alive by his son, Tulku Laksam Namdak, and their ongoing religious community.

ONE

Daughter of Golok

Tāre Lhamo's Life and Context

THE DAUGHTER OF Apang Terchen, a prominent treasure revealer in Golok, Tāre Lhamo was identified as an extraordinary child in prophecies surrounding her birth. Prior to pregnancy, her mother, Damtsik Drolma, received pronouncements from two local Buddhist figures that they planned to reincarnate in her home.[1] When Tāre Lhamo was just an infant, her family went on pilgrimage to Lhasa, where the eminent Dudjom Rinpoche Jigdral Yeshe Dorje (1904–87) recognized her as an emanation of Yeshe Tsogyal, a figure central to treasure lore as the Tibetan consort of the eighth-century Indian tantric master Padmasambhava, and Sera Khandro (1892–1940), a female tertön from the previous generation in Golok.[2] The former identification was pivotal to the role that Tāre Lhamo later claimed through her treasure revelations, which are understood to be teachings received directly from Padmasambhava or a comparable figure in a previous life, and the latter gave her an immediate female antecedent of regional prominence, even through Sera Khandro would have still been alive when Tāre Lhamo was born (1938). The combination of her birth into the religious elite of Golok and early recognition of her emanation status allowed Tāre Lhamo access to esoteric teachings in the male-dominated religious milieu of Golok and paved the way for her to become a Buddhist teacher of considerable renown, alongside Namtrul Rinpoche later in life.

Despite her exalted status from birth, one peculiarity of Tāre Lhamo's life story is that it rarely stands alone in published accounts.[3] In her namthar,

1.1 Khandro Tāre Lhamo in the late 1970s. Original photographer unknown.

Spiraling Vine of Faith: The Liberation of the Supreme Khandro Tāre Lhamo, her life is refracted through a host of female figures—divine, mythic, and human. In the opening verses of praise, she is identified with the enlightened female deities Samantabhadrī, Vajravārāhī, and Sarasvatī, and her namesake, the female bodhisattva of compassion Tārā, is also invoked. Beyond that, the first half of the text consists of extended excepts from the life stories of two female predecessors, Yeshe Tsogyal and Sera Khandro,[4] one of the figures who reportedly approached Damtsik Drolma to announce her reincarnation plans. Only after that, halfway through, is there finally an account of Tāre Lhamo's own life. It begins with her religious training in youth, briefly mentions her first marriage to a scion of the Dudjom line, and then presents a series of miracle tales used to narrate her twenties and thirties, during the socialist transformation of Tibetan regions in the Maoist period. Then her namthar abruptly ends. The latter part of her life, in which she traveled and taught extensively with Namtrul Rinpoche, is subsumed into his namthar, *Jewel Garland*, in which Tāre Lhamo serves as a joint protagonist.[5]

What can learn about Tāre Lhamo herself, when the hagiographic construction of her identity is so deeply relational? Rather than producing an "imaginary singularity" of the autonomous individual,[6] Tibetan life writing frequently constructs the identity of a Buddhist master as composite, an amalgam across many lifetimes. Janet Gyatso has highlighted the importance of such "connections" with respect to the lives of treasure revealers, who draw on past life associations to legitimate their revelations, while Sarah Jacoby has drawn attention to the importance of the "relational self" in autobiographical writings by Tibetan women.[7] *Spiraling Vine of Faith* represents somewhat of an extreme case, given the extent to which it emphasizes Tāre Lhamo's identification with female antecedents in the extended preamble to her birth, taking up half of her namthar and threatening to overwhelm her own story. In line with this, the correspondence between Tāre Lhamo and Namtrul Rinpoche also features a relational conception of identity, constructing their public personae as a couple through a series of past life connections across time and space. This raises a conundrum: where is the locus of agency within the proliferation of past lives? To what extent does such a relational identity enhance or delimit agency, specifically for Tibetan women who have managed to make it into the literary record with a significant legacy of writings by or about them?

Just as Tāre Lhamo begins to come into focus as a remarkable woman in *Spiraling Vine of Faith*, the namthar ends, and her religious career is subsumed into *Jewel Garland*, where her identity becomes fused with that of Namtrul Rinpoche. Here the "eminent couple" (*skyabs rje yab yum*) is the protagonist, acting in concert and sometimes even speaking in one voice. A comparable interweaving occurs in their abbreviated namthar, *Jewel Lantern of Blessings*, though in that case their activities as a couple are embedded in her story. Likewise, in their correspondence, her voice intermingles with that of Namtrul Rinpoche as they negotiate the terms of their union and construct their identity as a couple based on visionary recollections of their past lives together and prophecies about their future revelations. What we find in these published literary sources, epistolary and hagiographic, is neither the autonomous individual of Western humanism nor the fragmentary self (and decentered agency) of poststructuralism.[8] Rather, her identity is composite, densely layered, and accretive in nature, embedded in a web of connectivity.

In *Spiraling Vine of Faith*, this connectivity entails her simultaneous identification with and reliance on female deities, producing a paradox in the representation of female agency. Typical of Tibetan hagiographic literature more broadly, *Spiraling Vine of Faith* portrays female agency as the domain of ḍākinīs, a class of female deities who are central to Buddhist tantric iconography, ritual, and visionary experience and who can also be embodied by actual women like Tāre Lhamo.[9] In her namthar, she is aided by the ḍākinīs, said to be continually by her side, and is herself cast as a living *khandroma*, the Tibetan term that translates the Sanskrit ḍākinī. Thus, on the one hand, *Spiraling Vine of Faith* features a panoply of female deities who appear in visions to Tāre Lhamo and her predecessors to offer inspiration, advice, and prophecies. And on the other hand, Tāre Lhamo is presented as a ḍākinī-in-action, performing miraculous feats on behalf of her local community during the turbulent decades of the Maoist period, when Tibetans faced severe repression under Chinese Communist rule. This slippage between the representation of exceptional historical women and the deflection of agency to a divine source, I argue, both authorizes and delimits the scope of female agency.

This chapter explores issues of gender and agency in the life of Tāre Lhamo as written and lived in the social context of the tight-knit treasure scene in Golok. After providing a brief summary of her life, I shift between literary text and social context to examine how a cultural space is created for female religious authority in a male-dominated milieu. I ask whether Tāre Lhamo's religious authority derives primarily from links with men in Golok's treasure scene, especially her prominent father, or from her associations with female antecedents in the symbolic system of Tibetan Buddhism. Addressing this question takes us into the complex politics of reincarnation and overlapping networks of clan, lineage, and monastic affiliation in Golok. It also takes us into the literary world of namthar through a less commonly explored gate. While Tibetan autobiography has been the subject of several recent studies,[10] this chapter explores the genre of namthar in a hagiographic key, as an idealized account of the life of a Buddhist master narrated by a devoted disciple.[11] I am particularly interested in the impact of third-person narration on the construction of female agency, which I will later contrast with Tāre Lhamo's own voice and self-representation in her epistolary exchanges with Namtrul Rinpoche. *Spiraling Vine of Faith* itself has several discernible vantage points due to the composite nature of the text, which offer a fertile basis for comparison and create a synthesis within the work to construct Tāre Lhamo unequivocally as a Buddhist tantric heroine.

By delving into issues of gender and agency, this chapter provides the necessary background to understand how Tāre Lhamo served as a heroine for her local community during the socialist transformation of Tibetan areas and went on to become an important Buddhist leader in Golok during the post-Mao era. While her relational and composite identity might seem at first to diffuse her agency, her association with the figure of the ḍākinī became important to narrating a devastating chapter of Tibetan history in a redemptive key. Relational and composite identity is likewise central to the ways that Tāre Lhamo and Namtrul Rinpoche conceived of their shared destiny in their correspondence and imagined the possibility of revitalizing Buddhist teachings, practices, and institutions in the wake of the Cultural Revolution. Furthermore, re-creating a web of connectivity is central to the hagiographic portrait of the couple in *Jewel Garland*, which highlights their connections to people and places as the very means by which they reconstituted Tibetan communities and Buddhist networks during their extensive teachings and travels in the 1980s and '90s.[12] To recover subaltern pasts, we first need to gain a footing in the literary world of namthar and the social context of Golok, beginning with the ways that religious identities are formed and how gender and agency operate in those settings.

Life of Tāre Lhamo

This brief overview of Tāre Lhamo's life in historical terms is a summary of what I have garnered from multiple sources: the namthars and letters introduced in this book, interviews with people close to Tāre Lhamo throughout Golok,[13] audio-visual materials produced by Nyenlung Monastery, and other written accounts, such as the biographies of related figures and local monastic histories. I present the facts as best as I have been able to discern them rather than analyze stories (literary or oral) about her as representations—my tack for the bulk of the book.

Tāre Lhamo was born in 1938, the daughter of Apang Terchen Orgyan Trinle Lingpa (1895–1945), alias Pawo Chöying Dorje,[14] a prominent tertön in Golok from the Apang family with an illustrious past life pedigree, and Damtsik Drolma, the daughter of a local chieftain who was also regarded as an emanation of Yeshe Tsogyal. Apang Terchen's homeland was Dartsang, but like most religious figures in nomadic Golok, he was highly mobile, shifting his residence regularly between what are today Padma County in Qinghai Province and Serta County in Sichuan Province. At the time of Tāre Lhamo's conception, Apang Terchen and Damtsik Drolma were staying at the sacred mountain Drongri, the abode of a local protector in the region. However, her birthplace was closer to Tsimda Gompa, the monastery in Padma County that Apang Terchen founded, in a valley between gently rolling hills called Bökyi Yumo Lung. Tāre Lhamo was the fourth of five children and the only girl among them.[15]

Because of her elite status, Tāre Lhamo had considerable access to esoteric teachings in her youth. She began her religious training under her father and received the transmission for the entirety of his treasure revelations at a young age. In 1945, he passed away when she was only nine years old (by Tibetan reckoning), but remarkably, not before they had revealed a treasure together.[16] During the rest of her youth, she traveled extensively on pilgrimage throughout the region of Golok, accompanied by her mother, and received teachings from many of the eminent religious figures of her day, including Rigdzin Jalu Dorje (1927–61), the fourth in a line of Dodrupchen incarnations,[17] and Dzongter Kunzang Nyima (1904–58), the grandson of Dudjom Lingpa. As the daughter of a tertön, Tāre Lhamo was able to join the encampments of Nyingma masters, where she participated in religious

1.2 Statue of Apang Terchen in the Vajrasattva temple at Tsimda Monastery.

gatherings, receiving initiations and instructions in various tantric ritual cycles, such as the *Nyingtik Yabshi (Snying thig ya bzhi)*. Tāre Lhamo became a close disciple of Dzongter Kunzang Nyima,[18] who served as her principal teacher, giving her the empowerment, authorization, and instructions for his treasures and formally investing her as the trustee (*chos bdag*) for his *sādhana* cycle of Yeshe Tsogyal.

In 1957, at the age of twenty, Tāre Lhamo joined the encampment of Dzongter Kunzang Nyima and married his son Mingyur Dorje (1934–59), who was nicknamed Tulku Milo.[19] The encampment, which served as Dzongter Kunzang Nyima's main residence for more than two decades, was located at Lunghop (also known as Rizab), at the base of a mountain outside of Dartsang. In the previous generation, it was common for a Buddhist master in Golok to attract students to a hermitage at a far remove from other habitations. As disciples gathered around a charismatic teacher, an encampment (*sgar*) would form with no permanent structures, only the black yak-hair tents used by nomads as homes. According to his son, Pema Thegchok Gyaltsen, several thousand disciples gathered around Dzongter Kunzang Nyima in this encampment as a fluid and vibrant community.[20] As family members, the young couple formed part of an inner circle to whom Dzongter Kunzang Nyima bestowed esoteric Dzogchen teachings from his own treasure corpus (*gter chos*) and that of his grandfather Dudjom Lingpa, of whom he was recognized as the speech emanation (*gsung sprul*).[21]

Tāre Lhamo and Tulku Milo lived at Rizab, and apart from the general atmosphere of the encampment, it is difficult to know what their short time together entailed except that she gave birth to a son. *Spiraling Vine of Faith* dedicates a paragraph to Tāre Lhamo's first marriage but never mentions her son.[22] I heard only one story about her marriage with Tulku Milo from one of her close friends. It seems too frivolous to be worthy of inclusion in a namthar but gives some sense of the humor and affection between the young couple. One time when Tulku Milo and Tāre Lhamo were approaching their summer residence at dusk, Tulku Milo claimed that he saw a wild animal and said to her, "You go ahead and I'll defend you." At first, Tāre Lhamo felt afraid, but then as she passed by, she saw that it was only a tower of yak dung (which nomads gather to use as fuel). Tulku Milo was only teasing. The story is short and sweet. In it, we glimpse Tāre Lhamo as a young woman, taking solace in the protection of her husband (four years her senior) only to learn that she had fallen for a lighthearted prank.

One can imagine the laughter that may have accompanied the telling of such a story, which is so recognizably human—despite their incarnation status and roles as religious figures of local import—and at the same time distinctive to Golok.

Within a year or two, all this had changed. As the Chinese Communist state consolidated its control over Tibetan regions in the late 1950s, socialist reforms swept through Golok. There were massive arrests of Tibetan elite—religious figures, wealthy traders, and clan leaders—as part of a shift in state policy toward minorities. One lama living in exile described the situation at Dodrupchen Monastery in Padma County in stark terms, stating that any monk of rank who held a title, even the *chöpon* (shrine master, *mchod dpon*) and *umdze* (chant master, *dbu mdzas*), was imprisoned and very few survived. During the late 1950s, Tāre Lhamo lost her teachers, Dzongter Kunzang Nyima and Rigdzin Jalu Dorje; her first husband, Tulku Milo; and her three brothers, Gyurme Dorje, Wangchen Nyima, and Thubten Chökyi Nyima. I learned during field research that Dzongter Kunzang Nyima passed away due to natural causes, but the rest died in prison.

In all likelihood, gender and age played into why Tāre Lhamo and the younger reincarnate lamas who were only teenagers during the late 1950s, like Namtrul Rinpoche and Pema Thegchok Gyaltsen, were not perceived as a threat and were spared imprisonment at that time.[23] According to one close friend, Tāre Lhamo once came close to being arrested. When the authorities arrived, her son asked her to come home soon, and Tāre Lhamo promised that she would. According to this statement—considered to be prophetic given that it was uttered by a khandroma—though she was taken away to jail at the county seat, she returned unscathed soon afterward. No one learned why she was released, though others corroborated that she had been taken away and then allowed to return home.

Several people I interviewed insisted that Tāre Lhamo had never been subjected to harsh treatment during this period, and there is no indication in *Spiraling Vine of Faith* that she endured physical abuse, which was routine during struggle sessions. Yet others avowed that, like so many elites, she underwent struggle sessions at the county seat, and a childhood friend confided that Tāre Lhamo had been beaten seriously. On one harrowing occasion, officials placed her bare chest on a hot wood-burning stove. As narrated to me, Tāre Lhamo reflected on the far greater sufferings of beings in the hell realms, and as a result she had no burn marks afterward. This is a miracle tale that cannot be found in *Spiraling Vine of Faith*, no doubt because it touches on a politically sensitive topic. There are other comparable tales that Rigdzin Dargye has gathered for a new namthar of Tāre Lhamo focused on her youth in Padma County,[24] some of which are included in chapter 2.

The 1960s began with widespread famine that accompanied the failed policy of the Great Leap Forward. One lama characterized this famine as a time when Tibetans were like hungry ghosts on earth, surviving on thin soup of *tsampa* or roasted barley (*rtsam pa*) and vegetables; resorting to roots, herbs, and even bark for nourishment; and growing ill and dying when too weak to digest these things. During these years, by all accounts, both literary and oral, Tāre Lhamo was a source of solace to those around her through miracles addressing the needs of her local community. Some miracle tales that I heard while in Golok can also be found in *Spiraling Vine of Faith*, but others cannot. For example, one elderly woman who shared a household with Tāre Lhamo during the 1960s told me that some evenings her body would lie cold as if dead, while Tāre Lhamo sojourned to celestial realms, bringing back sacred substances to distribute to and nourish those around her.

With the onset of the Cultural Revolution in 1966, monasteries in Golok, as elsewhere, were looted and physically damaged. The main Vajrasattva temple at Tsimda Gompa was destroyed, and only the main Vajrasattva image survived.[25] Around this time, Tāre Lhamo had a liaison with Sera Khandro's grandson, Doli Nyima (b. 1946), and the two revealed several treasures together.[26] Apparently, Doli Nyima had been imprisoned at some point in the mid-1960s, but in a miracle tale omitted from *Spiraling Vine of Faith*, Tāre Lhamo secured his release by secretly sending a message to him in prison along with several objects, including her ring and belt.[27] Sometime after his release, he disappeared and was never seen again. I was told that Tāre Lhamo often dreamed of him and continued to search for him throughout the 1960s.[28]

Tāre Lhamo lost her only son to illness in 1966, and later on her mother died of old age. When her son fell sick and died at the age of nine, she reportedly pulled at her hair until much of it fell out. By the early 1970s, one friend said that Tāre Lhamo appeared ragged and thin, like a vulture dressed in a worn-out Chinese coat. Accounts like this, not in *Spiraling Vine of Faith*, show Tāre Lhamo's distress and vulnerability during these long and arduous years in a way that her hagiographic idealization does not permit.

During the 1960s and '70s, she was consigned to manual labor in her homeland of Markhok in Padma County. For the most part, Tāre Lhamo tended livestock, including the menial tasks of herding, milking, making butter, and gathering dung. Periodically, she also engaged in more grueling tasks, such as digging irrigation ditches, loading wood onto yaks, or hauling stones to build pens for livestock. During this period, along with her attendant, Thopa, she stayed with two different families, the Tharwa from 1962 to 1971 and the Chabdrol from 1972 to 1977. She remained under close supervision in a small cluster of black tents that functioned as a work unit. In the Tharwa family, there were twelve members in the work unit, divided into three family groups: one to milk yaks, one to herd livestock, and one to tend to household chores.[29] The work unit was responsible for fifty government-owned yaks, and each member received food in return for their labor.

During field research, I had the opportunity to meet one of the families with whom Tāre Lhamo stayed. When I asked if she could practice Buddhism in those years, they laughed. Didn't I know religious observance was illegal during that period? But once the laughter died down, they began to tell me how people would surreptitiously come to Tāre Lhamo's tent late at night to request a prognostication, lungtan (lung bstan) or phowa ('pho ba), the transference of consciousness, for a deceased family member. It became apparent that Tāre Lhamo had continued her religious practice in secret. In addition, she dictated treasures and other compositions to Thopa, which amounted to five volumes.[30] These were later incorporated into the twelve-volume treasure corpus shared jointly with her second husband, Namtrul Rinpoche.

Tāre Lhamo emerged from this period as one among a small cohort of surviving religious figures from her generation in Golok who had not fled into exile or died in prison. They could be considered second-tier religious figures, whether by age, gender, or rank. Namtrul Rinpoche and Pema Thegchog Gyaltsen, though incarnate lamas, were teenagers in the late 1950s. Important figures in the revitalization of Buddhism in the post-Mao period like Khenpo Jigme Phuntsok and Khenpo Munsel were cleric-scholars, who under different circumstances might have assumed a lesser rank than incarnate lamas. Likewise, khandromas such as Tāre Lhamo and Kachö Wangmo may have held more prominent and active teaching roles because of the dearth of surviving lamas.[31] After so much had been destroyed, the key tasks included not only rebuilding visible signs of Tibetan culture but also reviving ritual forms, esoteric knowledge, and the transmissions for lineages. The older generation was key because they had received formal training, particularly the transmissions for esoteric rituals and teachings, before religious observances were forbidden in Golok for nearly twenty years—from 1958 to 1978, with a brief reprieve from 1962 to 1965.[32] When the political climate began to shift in the late 1970s after the death of Mao, this group of surviving religious figures became the natural leaders to spearhead a revival.

In 1978, Tāre Lhamo initiated a correspondence with Namtrul Rinpoche, a lama six years her junior who lived across the border in Serta County, Sichuan Province. Her initial letter contained a prophecy predicting a treasure awaiting the pair at the sacred mountain range Nyenpo Yutse in eastern Golok, accompanied by one of her own revelations, a Yeshe Tsogyal sādhana. Thus began an extended correspondence conducted secretly by private messenger across province borders along the rugged two-day route separating them. Their courtship took place mainly through letters; the future couple only met for one extended visit in 1979, when Namtrul Rinpoche undertook the journey to Markhok to visit her, accompanied by a single attendant.[33] In early 1980, Tāre Lhamo risked state censure that tightly controlled movement in Tibetan areas and traveled with a small party to join Namtrul Rinpoche in Nyenlung, which served as their base for the next two decades of teaching and traveling together.

From 1980 forward, Tāre Lhamo and Namtrul Rinpoche contributed to the revitalization of Buddhism in Golok as part of a nexus of Nyingma masters. The eminent couple led the effort to rebuild Nyenlung, the monastery where they resided in Namtrul Rinpoche's homeland in Serta County, and Tsimda, the monastery that Tāre Lhamo's father founded in Padma County. They also contributed to the reconstruction of at least ten other monasteries, donating funds, establishing ritual programs, and visiting regularly to teach.[34] Additionally, they sponsored the construction of stūpas, temples, images, and other sacra to sanctify the land after its desecration during the Maoist period, including a Gesar temple that stands at the base of the Amnye Machen mountain range.

During this time, Tāre Lhamo and Namtrul Rinpoche traveled widely to discover and disseminate their treasures, considered to be esoteric teachings from Tibet's imperial past hidden in the landscape for posterity.

They revealed treasures at sacred sites throughout Golok and beyond, including Nyenpo Yutse in Jigdril County, Amnye Machen in Machen County, Drongri in Serta County, and Drakar Tredzong to the north of Golok. On pilgrimage, they journeyed and revealed treasures as far west as central Tibet and as far east as Wutai Shan in central China, where they joined a key figure in the post-Mao period, Khenpo Jigme Phuntsok of Larung Buddhist Academy, on pilgrimage in 1987 with approximately 10,000 others from the region.[35] Annually, they toured monasteries in Serta and Padma counties as well as other counties in Golok, and also taught regularly in a Nyingma enclave in Rebkong in northern Amdo. During these tours, they gave teachings to monastics and laity alike, disseminating their own treasures as well as those of Tāre Lhamo's father, Apang Terchen.

Tāre Lhamo and Namtrul Rinpoche were also important in reestablishing the regional lore of King Gesar of Ling. They built a temple to Gesar at the base of Amnye Machen outside of Tawu, the prefecture capital of Golok, registered as one of six official cultural sites dedicated to Gesar that are recognized by the government.[36] They also revealed a rendition of one section of the Gesar epic, included as the twelfth volume of their treasure collection. The volume became the basis for a sacred dance and dance troupe, established in Serta, which toured monasteries in the region. Indicating their prominence in this regard in 2000, Tāre Lhamo and Namtrul Rinpoche served as the guests of honor presiding over a conference on research into Gesar at the county seat of Serta.[37] This was to be one of Tāre Lhamo's last public appearances.

Later in 2000, Tāre Lhamo fell ill and visited the hospital in Barkham with what may have been esophageal cancer.[38] Various ritual remedies were attempted to extend her life. Tāre Lhamo herself sponsored the ransoming (srog bslu) of 10,000 yaks and sheep, saving them from slaughter in order to accumulate merit. In addition, long-life rituals were performed on her behalf by lamas in Golok and India, to no avail. Namtrul Rinpoche performed a long-life ritual for her in the hospital, knowing that it would be impossible to save her.[39] At some point, she moved to a hospital in Chengdu, the capital of Sichuan Province, but in the warm weather her condition deteriorated. Tāre Lhamo passed away on March 26, 2002. Hundreds of lamas from the surrounding area attended her cremation at Nyenlung Monastery. Today, a gilded and jewel-laden reliquary (sku gdung), containing her relics, stands in a shrine room within the family complex at Nyenlung.

Tight-Knit Treasure Community

Tāre Lhamo's achievements are considerable, given the personal misfortunes she endured and the tumultuous historical period in which she came of age. What factors laid the ground for her to play a significant role in revitalizing Buddhism in Golok? How did she, as a Tibetan woman, gain the stature to become a leader in its male-dominated religious milieu and in addition, a khandroma worthy of a namthar? To address these questions, let us consider how Tāre Lhamo was constituted as part of the treasure community in Golok in her youth, and how this enabled her to draw on resources from her Nyingma roots to reconstruct a sense of cultural continuity at the end of the Maoist period. A brief introduction to Golok and its treasure scene—and a discussion of Tāre Lhamo's structural and symbolical embeddedness within it—will allow us to appreciate more fully her rise to prominence and the rhetorical strategies in representing her agency in *Spiraling Vine of Faith.*

Religious life in Golok and its thriving treasure scene up through the middle of the twentieth century synthesized local and regional networks of affiliation. Although Golok shares in many of the institutions, practices, and mythos of Tibetan Buddhism in its broadest sense, it is linguistically and culturally distinct,[40] and until the 1950s, was "famed for the ferocity and independence of its people."[41] Fostering a distinctive identity, the mythic origins of its clans (*tsho ba*) link the people of Golok genealogically as a group, one of the main networks of affiliation in the region.[42] Clan divisions formed the basis of Golok's political system from approximately the fifteenth century forward, and as a loose confederation of clans, the region remained for the most part independent from outside political control until forcible incorporation into the PRC in 1952.[43] In the religious arena, by contrast, Golok has been thoroughly integrated into broad regional networks of sectarian affiliation with a strong influence from Kham to the south. Of the Buddhist monasteries in Golok Prefecture today, most belong to the Nyingma sect and are considered branch monasteries (*dgon lag*) of major monasteries in Kham, such as Katok, Payul, and Dzogchen.[44] Historically the Nyingma sect was the first to arrive in Golok in 1493, with the founding of Drakar Gompa as a branch of Katok, and it has remained the predominant force.[45]

This Nyingma predominance has made Golok fertile ground for a vibrant and tight-knit community engaged in treasure revelation. Much of this constellated around two major figures: Jigme Trinle Özer (1745–1821), the First Dodrupchen, who was a principal disciple of Jigme Lingpa and spread the *Longchen Nyingtik* (*Klong chen snying thig*) in the regions of Dege and Golok; and Dudjom Lingpa (1835–1903), a tertön from Dartshang whose legacy has loomed large in the Nyingma milieu of Golok, with each generation of his scions boasting eminent reincarnate lamas and tertöns.[46] Tāre Lhamo was tied to both these figures through her two main teachers, Rigdzin Jalu Dorje (known locally as Tulku Riglo), the fourth in the Dodrupchen incarnation line, and Dzongter Kunzang Nyima, the grandson and speech incarnation of Dudjom Lingpa as well as a tertön in his own right. Tāre Lhamo married into the Dudjom family; her first husband, Tulku Milo, was the great-grandson of Dudjom Lingpa and son of Dzongter Kunzang Nyima. The proliferation of treasure lineages meant that the region became more than an outgrowth of Buddhist monasteries beyond

1.3 Tsimda Gompa, the monastery that Apang Terchen founded in 1925.

its borders: it was a major site for the production of significant Nyingma cycles of esoteric teachings.

Treasure revelation has operated within overlapping networks of affiliation, while retaining a distinctive character. Charismatic tertöns, like Tāre Lhamo's father, Apang Terchen, founded new monasteries and ritual systems that became gradually integrated into existing monastic networks while retaining a distinctive lineage of transmission. In 1925, he founded the monastery Tsimda Gompa on the presumption contained in a prophecy he revealed that Samye Temple in central Tibet and Payul Tarthang Monastery in Golok would be threatened by fire if a water spirit (Tib.: *klu*, Skt.: *nāga*) at the Mar River was not tamed through the construction of a monastery.[47] Given the import of these institutions to the Nyingma, the prophecy provided ample incentive for general agreement to his plan. Once constructed, Tsimda Gompa was connected into existing monastic networks as a branch of Katok Monastery.

Despite this affiliation, stewardship of the monastery has remained in his clan, the Pongyu. After Apang Terchen's death, leadership initially passed to his son, Wangchen Nyima. When the monastery reopened in the early 1980s, responsibility would have fallen to Tāre Lhamo as Apang Terchen's only surviving child, but she moved to Nyenlung, across the province border in Sichuan, to reside with Namtrul Rinpoche. The couple remained the spiritual heads of Tsimda, while administrative leadership fell to the acting head of the monastery, Jamyang Nyima.[48] He is from the Pongyu clan, as are most of the monks who populate Tsimda Gompa. This follows a broader pattern in Golok in which monasteries are affiliated with one or more clans that support them and provide their monks, cleric-scholars, and lamas. This could be characterized as clan-based monasticism rather than a feudal system of elite dominating the serfdom, as it is so often described in Chinese Communist Party propaganda.

Indicating the preeminence of family in the transmission of terma lineages, the ritual cycles that Apang Terchen introduced were passed to Tāre Lhamo and her brothers as principal lineage holders. Regardless of the broad regional networks of monastic affiliation, lineages for treasure cycles are often transmitted through the family even as their ritual programs are established at specific monasteries. Incarnation lines also play an important role in linage transmission, yet the treasure tradition co-opts that institution in distinctive ways by creating its own incarnation lines and also identifying incarnations within the family of a tertön. Dudjom Lingpa spawned a line of three incarnations; the most well known internationally was Dudjom Rinpoche Jigdral Yeshe Dorje, but notably, the other two were his grandsons, Dzongter Kunzang Nyima and Sönam Detsun. Apang Terchen also spawned four emanations, including his own nephew, Jigme Wangdrak Dorje (known locally as Tulku Tsebo, abbreviating his alias Apang Tulku Orgyan Tsewang Drakpa), and more unusually, the current Sakya Trizin or "throne holder" of the Sakya tradition of Tibetan Buddhism. As mentioned, Namtrul Rinpoche served as his activity emanation—a late identification that occurred well after he and Tāre Lhamo had joined together as a couple.[49]

Within the treasure scene in Golok, the practice of recognizing incarnations has functioned as a way to confirm the children of prominent tertöns and lamas as notable religious figures and future lineage holders. This follows the broader trend among the Nyingma of transmitting lineages for specific ritual cycles and esoteric teachings through the family. All of Apang Terchen's children were identified as reincarnations of local religious figures, even his first child (a male) who died at birth, suggesting that the identification may have happened in utero.[50] Tāre Lhamo's eldest brother, Gyurme Dorje, was born in 1928 and recognized as a reincarnation of Adzom Drukpa, a prominent holder of the *Longchen Nyingtik* lineage in Kham.[51] Her next brother, Wangchen Nyima, was born in 1931 as the reincarnation of Sönam Gyurme, a chief and lama of the Washul clan.[52] A tertön in his own right, Wangchen Nyima took over the responsibilities of his father after his death, becoming the head of Tsimda Gompa and helping to arrange Tāre Lhamo's first marriage. Her younger brother, Thubten Chökyi Nyima, was locally regarded (but not widely accepted) as the reincarnation of Do Rinpoche, Khamsum Zilnön Gyepa Dorje, the grandson of Do Khyentse Yeshe Dorje, who passed away in 1939.[53]

Due to the elite practice of recognizing incarnations within the families of prominent lamas, Tāre Lhamo's recognition as a manifestation of Yeshe Tsogyal is arguably derivative of her family ties. Indeed, her recognition was principally in the hands of already established religious figures, including her father. As previously mentioned, Dudjom Rinpoche Jigdral Yeshe Dorje, the former head of the Nyingma lineage in exile, delivered the following prophecy in front of the Jowo Śākyamuni at the Jokhang Temple during Tāre Lhamo's infancy, when her family visited Lhasa:

Joint emanation of Vārāhī, mother of victorious ones, and Tsogyal,
Bearing the name of the Do Kham ḍākinī, Sukha,
The reincarnation of that one is the mantra-born, Tāre.
Her deeds and activities will spread in regions of India, Tibet, and China.
Whoever encounters her, she will guide to celestial realms.[54]

In this prophecy and others, included in *Spiraling Vine of Faith*, Tāre Lhamo
is identified with a series of female figures: the tantric deity Varjavārāhī;
the preeminent lady of treasure lore, Yeshe Tsogyal; and a female tertön of
the previous generation, Sera Khandro (Sukha is the Sanskrit for the one
rendering of her name, Bde ba'i rdo rje). While the appropriation of such
illustrious female antecedents clearly serves as a means to authorize Tāre
Lhamo, importantly, this was done on her behalf at birth by tertöns already
ensconced with religious authority. I would aver that such appropriation
allows Nyingma masters to make room for women who enter their circle of
close relations as wife, consort, or daughter in order to constitute them as
authorized participants in an otherwise male-dominated milieu.[55]

While her status as the daughter of Apang Terchen was arguably the key
factor enabling her active participation in Nyingma circles, her identification with Yeshe Tsogyal provided her with an eminent past life pedigree
and further distinction as exceptional and worthy of a place of prominence
among Nyingma leaders.[56] It was also pivotal to her status as a tertön later
in life, since those who reveal treasures necessarily trace their past lives
to the imperial period as a direct disciple of Padmasambhava or a comparable master. More generally, such past life identifications situate religious
figures in a ranking of incarnate lamas that becomes visible in the public
domain on ritual or ceremonial occasions through the seating order and
height of thrones.

Although her female antecedents are emphasized in prophecies and also
in her hagiographic representation, in fact Tāre Lhamo was recognized in
her youth as a joint emanation (*zung 'jug gi sprul ba*) of two local figures of
the preceding generations, one male and one female. Thus, in addition to
being a manifestation of Yeshe Tsogyal, she was an emanation of a leading
monk, Tra Gelong Tsultrim Dargye (1866–1937), who approached her mother
before his death to say, "My reincarnation will take birth in your home," and
the female tertön Sera Khandro, also known as Uza Khandro Dewe Dorje,
who reportedly gave Tāre Lhamo's mother a red knotted protection cord

and said: "Preserve this well and one day when the knot disappears, I will arrive in your house."[57]

Her identification with these two figures has an anomaly beyond the intriguing and unusual gender-bending involved.[58] As mentioned, most likely Sera Khandro was still alive when Tāre Lhamo was born in 1938, since available sources give the date of her passing as 1940.[59] By contrast, the foreword to a recently published collection of Tra Gelong's writings gives the date of his passing as 1937,[60] and it would be entirely plausible that his followers would want to procure the child of a prominent religious figure as his reincarnation, particularly one predicted by the master himself. But would they have selected a girl knowingly? It is entirely possible that Tāre Lhamo was identified in utero as the reincarnation of Tra Gelong (as occurred with the first child of Apang Terchen and Damtsik Drolma) and then later identified with Sera Khandro in order to provide her with a proximate female antecedent. When I questioned her hagiographer, Pema Ösal Thaye, on this discrepancy of dates between Tāre Lhamo's birth and Sera Khandro's passing, he smiled enigmatically.[61]

Notably, there is no record of Tāre Lhamo receiving or holding the transmission for teachings by either Tra Gelong or Sera Khandro. At a young age, she was entrusted with ritual implements belonging to Tra Gelong but refused the option to return to his former residence to train as a nun.[62] Even though her father was a disciple of Sera Khandro and established Tsimda Gompa at one of her hermitages, there is no record that he transmitted any of Sera Khandro's treasure cycles to Tāre Lhamo. Moreover, Tāre Lhamo was never formally enthroned as her reincarnation. Indeed, she was just one of several Buddhist figures in her generation identified with either of her proximate antecedents.[63] Rather than receiving the transmission of teachings by either of them, *The Concise History of Tsimda Gompa* and *Spiraling Vine of Faith* concur that Apang Terchen transmitted the entirety of his own treasure revelations to his daughter. This indicates the primacy of family ties within the Nyingma over and above incarnation or emanation status.

Given her father's importance and the practice of recognizing children within the family of Nyingma masters, I would suggest that Tāre Lhamo's status as the daughter of Apang Terchen should be considered primary and her emanation status secondary. Yet even as an elite daughter of Golok, she required an anchor in the symbolic system of Tibetan Buddhism to achieve prominence. This anchor was provided at birth through those prophecies

delivered by established Nyingma masters and became central to her hagiographic representation in *Spiraling Vine of Faith*. Let us now turn to examine
the gendered pedigree marshaled in the construction of Tāre Lhamo's identity in her namthar through a close reading of *Spiraling Vine of Faith*.

Hagiographic Idealization

As a third-person account by a disciple, *Spiraling Vine of Faith* represents the
devotional side of namthar as a genre, providing an idealized portrait of
Tāre Lhamo as an object of veneration. To compose a namthar is to stake
a claim to realization on behalf of the protagonist, as the genre denotes
a story of "complete liberation" (Skt.: *vimokṣa*; Tib.: *rnam thar*),[64] the pinnacle of the Buddhist path.[65] Within the wide-ranging variety of this genre,
Janet Gyatso makes a crucial distinction between the "studied diffidence"
of Tibetan lives narrated autobiographically and the "studied reverence"
of third-person accounts. In the studied diffidence of Tibetan autobiography, authors grapple with the tension between self-promotion, inherent in
autobiographical writing, and cultural dictates of humility, strongly present
in Tibetan culture when speaking about oneself in the first person. By contrast, namthars narrated in the third person are not so encumbered and, as
Gyatso states, "Tibetan biographers often present the life of their master in
glorified, idealized terms."[66]

The tendency toward idealization in the third-person voice of namthar
is reminiscent of Patrick Geary's characterization of the "glorification of
a saint" in much of medieval Christian hagiography: "the virtues of the
saint appear even before birth, and difficulties, temptations, and conflicts
serve not to perfect but only to manifest a perfection already present."[67]
Geary makes this statement as a corrective to the general presumption that
hagiographic literature necessarily presents a saint as an exemplar to be
emulated. Often, the opposite is the case, whether in Christian or Buddhist
literary contexts, when the saint is cast as an object of veneration and credited with salvific powers.[68] That said, saints may function differently for different constituencies, such that one and the same person can serve as both
an exemplar and an object of veneration. As Kurtis Schaeffer points out,
the widely circulated namthar of Milarepa by Tsangnyön Heruka "inspires
yogins to practice, kings to offer patronage, commoners to have faith, and

heretics to convert."[69] Nonetheless, narrative voice plays an important role in either humanizing or elevating its subject. As Andrew Quintman argues, Milarepa becomes the most humanized and individual in his namthar by Tsangnyön in part through the literary conceit of its narration in Milarepa's first-person voice, blurring the line between autobiography and biography.[70]

Although narrated in the third person, *Spiraling Vine of Faith* can be situated in a gray zone between autobiography and biography. Tāre Lhamo and Namtrul Rinpoche not only commissioned *Spiraling Vine of Faith*—as well as his namthar, *Jewel Garland*—but also provided much of the narration, which they dictated to Pema Ösal Thaye. Thus, although their namthars were compiled by a disciple, the creative process directly involved the input and oversight of the protagonists, whose voices come through in quotes and the inclusion of excerpted letters from their correspondence in *Jewel Garland*. Of course, there were other contributors. Included in *Spiraling Vine of Faith* are episodes recounted by local elders in and around Serta, prophecies by Buddhist masters of her day, and excerpts from the life stories of her female antecedents.[71] Her hagiographic construction was in the hands of many, at least in part a product of social memory rather than the exclusive handiwork of her hagiographer. This exemplifies what William Lafleur calls a process of "reciprocal generation," denoting how the stories of saints take shape over time and with community participation.[72]

That said, its third-person voice allows for a hagiographic idealization that would not have been possible if Pema Ösal Thaye had merely recorded their stories as scribe and presented them in the first person. Though he insists in his statement of authorial intent that he arranged the narrative according to the stories of others exactly as they were recounted to him,[73] he nevertheless plays a major role in setting the tone, structure, and framework. First and foremost, he marshals authoritative female paradigms in which to frame Tāre Lhamo's activities, including referring to her by the epithet the "supreme ḍākinī" (*mkha' 'gro mchog*) throughout her adulthood and also describing her as a bodhisattva (*byang chub sems dpa'*) and female *siddha* (*grub thob mo*) in relation to her miracle tales during the years leading up to and including the Cultural Revolution. Beyond this, Pema Ösal Thaye selected and arranged stories that emphasize her early heroism, eliding the personal side of her life, particularly the hardships and misfortunes of the Maoist period.

In describing this as hagiographic idealization, I am not suggesting that in *Spiraling Vine of Faith*, Tāre Lhamo merely instantiates a preexisting ideal—as John Stratton Hawley suggested in the heyday of studies on comparative sainthood in the late 1980s—or repeats a perennial paradigm, as Mircea Eliade would have it.[74] I question the assumption that paradigms offer themselves up for imitation as if cultural (re)production was an automatic process devoid of human agency. Instead, the construction of sainthood should be understood as an emergent process in relation to, on the one hand, received tradition in the form of symbols, ideals, and idioms, and on the other hand, a given historical moment within a context of competing discourses and interests. Hagiography understood as a process accounts for situated actors (saint, hagiographer, community) who appropriate and recast authoritative paradigms in response to the exigencies of their specific historical conjuncture. Moreover, unlike the flattened individuality that can result when an authoritative paradigm overruns its subject, the idiosyncrasies of Tāre Lhamo's story come through clearly, and *Spiraling Vine of Faith* retains a distinctly local flavor that reflects and responds to the particularity of its historical circumstances.

Divinization of Female Agency

To return to Gyatso's distinction, I suggest that the narrative strategies of "studied diffidence" and "studied reverence" become intensified in life writings by and about accomplished Tibetan women. In the first person, the intensification of diffidence takes shape in gender-specific gestures of humility, such as when a female author disparages her "inferior body" (*lus dman*) and prays for rebirth as a male in the next life, as discussed by Sarah Jacoby in relation to the autobiographical writings of Sera Khandro.[75] By contrast, in third-person accounts such as *Spiraling Vine of Faith*, the intensification of reverence involves the elevation of the female protagonist beyond ordinary women through her identification as a ḍākinī, who manifests in this world already fully enlightened.

In Tibetan life writings, it is not unusual for female saints to be identified with the ḍākinī, a class of enlightened female deities in Buddhist tantra. Indeed, Tāre Lhamo's own association with various ḍākinīs stems from her primary identification as an emanation of Yeshe Tsogyal, whose widely known namthar, revealed by the seventeenth-century tertön Taksham Nuden Dorje, identifies her with the female deities Samantabhadrī,

Vajravārāhī, and Sarasvatī.[76] In another eminent case, the Tibetan princess, nun, and yoginī Chökyi Drönma (1422–55) was identified so strongly with Vajravārāhī (*Rdo rje phag mo*) that her incarnation line—the Dorje Phagmo line, which still survives today—is named after this female tantric deity.[77] Even Orgyan Chökyi (1675–1729), the self-effacing shepherdess-turned-hermitess whose autobiography is filled with gender-specific challenges to her spiritual pursuits, including being relegated to her teacher's kitchen after becoming a nun, is referred to as a ḍākinī in the posthumous preamble and colophon by the editor of her namthar.[78] Of equally humble origins, the illiterate nomad Sönam Paldren, who probably lived in the fourteenth century, is cast in her namthar as a "wisdom ḍākinī" (*ye shes mkha' 'gro*) and the emanation of Vajravārāhī.[79] Therefore, it should come as no surprise that the life story of the royally born Chökyi Drönma begins "Homage to Vajravārāhī!" and proceeds to describe how "Vajravārāhī, the female buddha, took a human body and enjoyed the magic dance of Mahāmudrā in this world."[80] Given such examples, one must wonder if there a cultural discomfort in representing an exceptional Tibetan woman qua woman and therefore a tendency to identify her as a ḍākinī.

This gendered form of hagiographic idealization takes shape in what I term "the divinization of female agency." In *Spiraling Vine of Faith*, the process involves two facets: elevating and distancing. Her hagiographer elevates Tāre Lhamo by identifying her as an emanation of female deities and simultaneously distances her from ordinary women and the "faults" (*skyon*) attributed to them. Pema Ösal Thaye simply states, "Free from all the faults of women, from a young age, this venerable protector of beings had uncontrived compassion and spontaneous mastery of mind."[81] While we do not learn what these faults might be, the traits of ordinary women are rhetorically excluded from the criteria for religious authority. Also, her compassion and mastery of mind appear "spontaneously," in an "uncontrived" manner, not due to her own accomplishment. In this way, Tāre Lhamo is marked as extraordinary from birth, by virtue of her status as an emanation of female tantric deities rather than through her own efforts and achievements, and thereby set apart from ordinary women and the possibility of emulation.

Tāre Lhamo is fashioned as an enlightened being from the very outset of *Spiraling Vine of Faith*. Her namthar begins in a reverential tone with an homage in verse form, which identifies her with a series of illustrious female figures drawn from the symbolic imaginary of Tibetan Buddhism:

the primordial buddha Samantabhadrī, the female tantric deity Vajravārāhī, the Indian goddess Sarasvatī, and the highly mythologized Tibetan yoginī Yeshe Tsogyal.[82] Her namesake, the bodhisattva and savioress Tārā, is also invoked, though not explicitly identified with her.[83] These figures serve as authoritative female antecedents, creating a cultural space for Tāre Lhamo's public representation as a religious figure of standing.

That said, her identification as a ḍākinī is not restricted to the open-ing verses of *Spiraling Vine of Faith*. Throughout most of the namthar, she is referred to as the "supreme ḍākinī," though I use the Tibetan equiva-lent, the "supreme khandro," in my translations in this book to convey a local flavor.[84] It is the symbol of the ḍākinī as much as any particular female deity that provides a cultural space for exceptional women.[85] This is evident in the very term for the category of female religious specialists in Tibet to which Tāre Lhamo belonged prior to assuming the mantle of a tertön. The Tibetan term *khandroma (mkha' 'gro ma)*, which translates the Sanskrit *ḍākinī*, refers to female religious specialists who are neither monastics nor ordinary laywomen. Instead, they tend to live as tantric adepts or *ngakmas (sngags ma)*, dedicating their time primarily to esoteric tantric practices. Whereas *ngakma* refers to a religious vocation to which any Tibetan woman may aspire, *khandroma* is reserved as an epithet for woman credited with a high degree of realization. Bearing the title Khandro as part of their name, khandroma typically live either as recluses or as the consorts of male lamas, particularly in the Nyingma sect, and Tāre Lhamo played both of these roles at different times in her life.

Significantly, the term *khandroma* suggests the ontological derivation of female religious authority, based on the correlation with the tantric arche-type of the ḍākinī as identified by others. By contrast, the male correlate *drupthob (Skt.: siddha, Tib.: grub thob)*, meaning "accomplished one," ety-mologically emphasizes individual achievement and attendant powers that derive from spiritual realization. I call this a correlate because *drupthob* is an epithet used commonly in Golok to refer to men who fill a similar role to khandroma outside of monastic settings by performing healings, delivering prophecies, transferring the consciousness of the dead, and giving esoteric teachings.[86] Although Tibetans use *drupthob* and *khandroma* for people due to their personal realization and perceived powers, the female designation masks personal achievement while the male designation highlights it. The very use of *khandroma*, then, is a way that realized women are divinized and separated ontologically from other women. This may serve to accord female religious figures a high status without threatening to disrupt the structure of male dominance in the religious arena.

After the opening verses, Pema Ösal Thaye explicitly locates Tāre Lhamo's enlightenment long ago in a previous eon. Witness the opening prose lines of the text, which refer to her by her full name:

> The speech emanation of the mother of the victorious ones, Vajravārāhī, the supreme Khandro Rinpoche Tāre Dechen Gyalmo, amassed an ocean of the two accumulations long ago in innumerable eons past. Having purified the two obscurations together with karmic residues, she reached buddhahood as the essence of blissful Samantabhadrī.[87]

These opening lines refer to Tāre Lhamo as the speech emanation of the female tantric deity Vajravārāhī and displace her enlightenment to a mythic time in eons past.[88] Pema Ösal Thaye thereby deflects agency for her spiritual realization, relegating her pursuit of the Buddhist path—amassing the two accumulations and purifying the two obscurations—to a time so long ago that is beyond the human capacity to fathom.[89] Nevertheless, this attainment warrants her identification with Samantabhadrī, the primordial buddha in female form. Thus, like Geary's "virtues of the saint" that "appear even before birth," Tāre Lhamo's enlightenment is said to have occurred well before her journey even begins.

However, this alone would not distinguish her hagiographic representation from that of male counterparts. After all, *Jewel Garland* also begins by stating that Namtrul Rinpoche "reached original enlightenment immeasurable eons ago." In addition, Pema Ösal Thaye identifies Namtrul Rinpoche with the "original protector" (*gdod ma'i mgon po*), an epithet for Samantabhadra, and the buddha Vajradhara before detailing his past lives, also associationg him with the "three secrets" (body, speech, and mind) of Padmasambhava. Yet a gendered difference is that Namtrul Rinpoche's past life genealogy takes up one page and the life of his previous incarnation another page,[90] compared to the twenty-five pages taken up with Tāre Lhamo's past lives in *Spiraling Vine of Faith*.

Moreover, in discussing Namtrul Rinpoche's religious training in youth, *Jewel Garland* highlights his achievements in tantric practice in a way that *Spiraling Vine of Faith* never does for Tāre Lhamo. He studied treatises on the sūtras and tantras with cleric-scholars such as Khen Rinpoche Jigme Senge, who transmitted the preliminaries (*sngon 'gro*) for tantric practice to him. Enthroned as the Fourth Namkhai Nyingpo incarnation of Zhuchen Monastery, Namtrul Rinpoche received the complete treasure collections of Rigdzin Dudul Dorje and Rigdzin Longsal Nyingpo from Zhuchen Kunzang Nyima. During his studies at Zhuchen, he took monastic ordination at the age of thirteen and received teachings from Zhuchen Pande Chökyi Nyima. Later, in the mid-1960s, he received further empowerments and esoteric instructions from Lama Rigdzin Nyima, despite the prohibition on religious practice at the time. Thereafter, *Jewel Garland* portrays Namtrul Rinpoche practicing in various sacred sites and hermitages in the region. Although his monastic education involved a systematic study of the traditional ten fields of knowledge (*rig gnas*) that Tāre Lhamo did not receive, having never ordained as a nun, there are certain similarities with the portrayal of her religious training in youth, particularly the focus on receiving various cycles of esoteric teachings from great masters and practicing at sacred sites in the region.

In marked contrast to the hagiographic portrait of Tāre Lhamo is the depiction of Namtrul Rinpoche's achievement of realization (*rtogs pa*), for which there is no parallel in *Spiraling Vine of Faith*. Witness the emphasis on practice and attainment in the following:

From that point onward until now, he principally practiced at major sites and hermitages such as Sholung Gomkhang and Lhalung Drakar. He recited approximately thirteen hundred million propitiations to the three roots and continuously offered *gaṇacakra* feasts. Internally, he struck the vital point of his tantric commitments in stabilizing creation and completion, thereby attaining realization along the paths and *bhūmis*. In particular, he put into practice the dharma cycles of esoteric precepts on luminosity according to the Great Perfection. Purifying the patterns of intellectual fabrication and dualistic grasping, he attained spontaneous realization transcending conceptuality. Great mind treasures burst forth. As he had loosened the knots in the channels at the head and throat, the transmission for teaching and propagating the sūtras and tantras of the old and new [schools]—as well as the orally transmitted and revealed [teachings], the support for maturation and liberation—expanded forth, as did all the activities of the three spheres [of dharma]. Maintaining the continuity of the precious Buddhist teachings without faltering, he became a great holy man, holder of the teachings of all systems of dharma in an unbiased way, with followers like the constellations in the sky.[91]

This passage represents Namtrul Rinpoche's attainment of realization based on various tantric practices including "creation and completion," which entails the visualization of tantric deities and other esoteric techniques related to the subtle body.[92] The teachings of Dzogchen or the Great Perfection (*rdzogs pa chen po*), the specialty of the Nyingma tradition, are highlighted as the basis for his attainment of "spontaneous realization transcending conceptuality" (*blo 'das rang byung gi rtogs pa*) and his subsequent access to "mind treasures" (*dgongs gter*), one of the main categories of revelations alongside "earth treasures" retrieved from the Tibetan landscape.[93] Here Pema Ösal Thaye clearly depicts Namtrul Rinpoche's realization as the result of his own efforts, engaging in tantric practice in this life.[94]

By contrast, Tāre Lhamo's path to enlightenment—if one can be discerned in *Spiraling Vine of Faith*—takes place across her past lives, portrayed through a series of female antecedents. In the brief space of a few sentences, her lives across the eons are delineated by evoking just two female figures from *Prajñāpāramitā* literature: a certain daughter of a merchant who assists the noble Sadāprarudita in making offerings to the bodhisattva Dharmodgata, and Gaṅgādevī, a female disciple of the Buddha who appears before him to proclaim her resolute intention to attain buddhahood.[95] Due to their merit and resolve, both figures are prophesized to attain buddhahood, although ironically only after they undergo a sex change and become male.[96] Given that these figures also appear in Taksham Nuden Dorje's life of Yeshe Tsogyal, it seems that Tibetan authors may have self-consciously contravened their Indian heritage on this point by omitting any reference to sex change and deliberately maintaining the female gender of such literary figures for the very purpose of creating authoritative antecedents for Tibetan women. Even though her past life genealogy contains a mix of male and female figures,[97] Pema Ösal Thaye sustains a focus on her female antecedents. The names listed that are most easily recognizable are Yeshe Tsogyal, the Tibetan consort and female disciple of Padmasambhava in treasure lore; Ne'u Chung, one of the prominent ladies of Ling in the Gesar epic; the female siddha Lakṣmīṅkarā from medieval India, whose story appears in Abhayadatta's *Lives of Eighty-Four Siddhas* (*Caturaśīti-siddha-pravṛtti*); and a celebrated female tertön of the preceding generation in Golok, Sera Khandro.

Tellingly, this emphasis on female antecedents in the hagiographic portraits of Tibetan women can also be found in other sources. An apt point of comparison is the namthar of Mingyur Paldrön (1699–1769), the daughter of the renowned tertön Terdak Lingpa (1646–1714), who established the Mindrolling tradition in central Tibet alongside his brother Lochen Dharmaśrī. Mingyur Paldrön shares with Tāre Lhamo an elite birth as the daughter of a tertön and identification as an emanation of Yeshe Tsogyal, though she was raised in the cosmopolitan milieu of eighteenth-century central Tibet and trained at Mindrolling Monastery. Yet despite receiving extensive training in religious matters in preparation to be a lineage holder, Mingyur Paldrön was denied training in secular subjects that her male counterparts studied.[98] More to the point, her namthar composed by a devoted male disciple, Gyurme Ösal, emphasizes her female antecedents in recounting her past life genealogy. In an ironic and self-reflexive moment recorded in her namthar, which Alison Melnick has highlighted, Mingyur Paldrön insists to Gyurme Ösal that he include her male past lives as well as her female ones, which he then does in cursory fashion.[99] As another point of comparison, in the extensive prose autobiography of her immediate antecedent, Sera Khandro—a work in more than 400 folios, distinct from the short autobiography excerpted in *Spiraling Vine of Faith*—there is a substantial prelude invoking female antecedents, parallel to the opening frame of Yeshe Tsogyal's namthar revealed by Taksham Nuden Dorje. Sarah Jacoby proposes that this prelude serves as an extra measure of legitimation, necessary due to gender and also Sera Khandro's lack of familial roots in Golok, having fled her elite Lhasa upbringing to follow her destined consort, Drime Özer.[100]

Two female figures are given priority in Tāre Lhamo's hagiographic construction and heighten the portrayal of her enlightenment prior to birth. *Spiraling Vine of Faith* excerpts significant passages from the namthars of Yeshe Tsogyal and Sera Khandro, quoting them wholesale from other sources. These excerpts take up most of the first half of the namthar— an undeniable sign of the importance of gender-specific antecedents to authorize Tāre Lhamo as a female religious figure. The first is a condensed summary of Yeshe Tsogyal's life, taken directly from the sixth chapter of Taksham Nuden Dorje's well-known version of her namthar. This is a summary of her accomplishments in verse that is framed as Yeshe Tsogyal's own voice.[101] The second is a short autobiography of Sera Khandro, also in verse, which *Spiraling Vine of Faith* copies verbatim. This text is twenty-six pages in the original as found in Sera Khandro's four-volume treasure corpus,[102] and it is reproduced almost in its entirety in *Spiraling Vine of Faith*. If read as part of Tāre Lhamo's journey to enlightenment, enacted across lifetimes, these sources suggest radically different portrayals of female agency and complement her own story in distinctive ways.

Equal to All the Buddhas

The inclusion of a condensed summary of Yeshe Tsogyal's life contributes to the displacement of Tāre Lhamo's enlightenment to the distant past and her portrait as an object of veneration. The verse passage highlights Yeshe Tsogyal's many accomplishments in summary fashion.[103] While touching on some of the events in her life story—her retreat at Tidro, her ransom of Atsara Sale, and her practice of Vajrakīla—this excerpt focuses on her meditative attainments. These include obtaining the inner heat of *cāṇḍālī* (*gtum mo*); raising a corpse from the dead in order to ransom Atsara Sale to be her consort; extracting medicine from herbs; taming demons; experiencing visions of Amitāyus; attaining mastery over the inner yogic channels, vital drops, and winds; and obtaining the immortal status of a *vidyādhara*. Notably, such meditative attainments are altogether absent in Tāre Lhamo's own story, and their displacement to Yeshe Tsogyal's serves to consign such achievements to her previous lives and also shore up her stature as a realized being.

It would be difficult to imagine a stronger claim, or one more significant as a representation of female agency. In no uncertain terms, Yeshe Tsogyal is depicted achieving a high degree of accomplishment, described as the invincibility and immortality of a vidyādhara,[104] an elevated rank in Buddhist tantra that denotes a "knowledge holder" who has attained mastery over the elements of the phenomenal world and the energies of the subtle body. Indeed, her accomplishment is represented in no uncertain terms as "equal to all the buddhas" (*sangs rgyas kun dang mnyam*).[105] This claim is intensified by an addition from Pema Ösal Thaye, the only instance in which *Spiraling Vine of Faith* strikes a seemingly feminist note. As a closing frame for the excerpt, Pema Ösal Thaye pronounces that Yeshe Tsogyal is the equal of Padmasambhava—who is regarded by Tibetans as a second Buddha—in body, speech, mind, quality, and action.[106] Thus *Spiraling Vine of Faith* offers a portrait of a Tibetan woman attaining realization on par with buddhas and tantric heroes, even Padmasambhava himself, as an authoritative antecedent for Tāre Lhamo.

Perhaps most striking is the declarative tone of the verses, which seem to defy the dictum of "studied diffidence" for autobiographic speech. In Yeshe Tsogyal's namthar, Taksham Nuden Dorje frames the verses as "the words of the lady [herself]" (jo mo'i bka'), and it is possible that the excerpt represents a preexisting oral tradition. The style closely resembles a "song of experience" (nyams mgur), one of the few genres of Tibetan literature in which declarative statements about one's own meditative attainments are readily found.[107] In line with the force of these statements, Taksham's extensive third-person account, in which the verses are embedded, depicts Yeshe Tsogyal with a high degree of agency, escaping her would-be suitors who pursued her with their armies, enduring harsh austerities in long periods of retreat, withstanding the attacks of bandits and hunters, and even transforming rape into a tantric empowerment that she bestowed upon her attackers. Yet tellingly, in line with the divinization of female agency, Taksham Nuden Dorje depicts Yeshe Tsogyal in the preamble of her story as an emanation of Sarasvatī, who is specifically summoned by Padmasambhava in order to help him establish Buddhism in Tibet.

In this vein, Yeshe Tsogyal is an especially important antecedent for the few female tertöns known to us, because of her key role in treasure lore as the consort of Padmasambhava and scribe for his teachings hidden as treasures. In this role, she is said to have encoded Padmasambhava's teachings in the elusive symbolic script of the ḍākinīs and concealed them for posterity in Tibetan and Himalayan regions. Janet Gyatso describes her as the "the foremost female figure of the Rnying ma tradition" and "preeminent female exemplar with whom Tibetan Buddhist women have been identified."[108] Yeshe Tsogyal has served as an authoritative antecedent for exceptional Tibetan women, like Tāre Lhamo and her mother, who became incorporated into the religious elite as well as for other female tertöns, such as Jomo Menmo, Kunga Bumpa, Sera Khandro, and Khandro Chöchan.[109] Although we know little about Yeshe Tsogyal as a historical figure, her presence in Tibetan lives continues to be central in the visionary experience of tertöns who seek her help in decoding their treasures, in the ritual life of Nyingma practitioners who supplicate her for blessings through liturgies dedicated to her, and in the religious activities of those women deemed to be her emanations.

Showcasing Yeshe Tsogyal's achievements and identifying her with Tāre Lhamo prepares the reader to encounter a remarkable woman whose miraculous abilities have a very definite genealogy. Perhaps the most significant lines for invoking Yeshe Tsogyal—and by extension Tāre Lhamo—as an object of veneration come toward the end of the excerpted verses. Yeshe Tsogyal's beneficent power and concern for Tibetans is emphasized in an poignant first-person statement, found in the sixth chapter of Taksham Nuden Dorje's version of her namthar and also excerpted in *Spiraling Vine of Faith*. These lines express her beneficent concern for future generations of Tibetans and portray her blessings as coextensive with the Tibetan landscape as follows:

> Throughout the whole land of Tibet[110]
> there are countless places where I practiced.
> There is not any handful or bit of earth
> that has not been blessed by me.
> Truly, in the future, the signs of truth successively
> will burst forth, extracted one by one as treasures.
> Thus, in an inconceivable number of little places,
> filled with my hand- and footprints in rock,
> mantras, seed syllables, and statues are arranged,
> left behind as the basis of faith for the future
> with aspirations to benefit those connected [with me].[111]

This passage draws on the premise that the places visited by a Buddhist master become sanctified by their very presence, and especially by their ritual and meditative practice. In this evocative passage, the whole of Tibet is said to be blessed by Yeshe Tsogyal's practice, marked by her presence, and packed with treasures. These tokens left for future generations, in emic terms, localize the presence of Yeshe Tsogyal, remaining latent until activated by the tertön.

By excerpting these verses, *Spiraling Vine of Faith* rouses the reverence that Tibetans already have for Yeshe Tsogyal and transfers that sentiment to Tāre Lhamo as her emanation. This passage also models the compassionate activity of an enlightened being and thereby foreshadows the idealization of Tāre Lhamo as a ḍākinī-in-action during the years leading up to and including the Cultural Revolution. Throughout *Spiraling Vine of Faith*, Tāre

Lhamo is portrayed in a homologous role to Yeshe Tsogyal as a beneficent presence for those around her. In the homage, she is likened to the sun that shines across the snowy land of Tibet; in the account of her youth, she practices in all the major and minor places of pilgrimage in Golok, further sanctifying them with her presence; and in the miracle tales of early adulthood, she serves as a local heroine in troubled times.

A Woman's Lot

The excerpted autobiography of Sera Khandro presents a more humanizing account than the declarative verses of Yeshe Tsogyal that precede it in *Spiraling Vine of Faith*. This is the short autobiography of Sera Khandro in twenty-six pages, *The Excellent Path of Devotion: An Abridged Story of a Mendicant's Experience in Response to Questions from Vajra Kin*, which has been translated separately by Christina Monson and Sarah Jacoby.[112] In versified format, through dialogues with visionary apparitions and terse summaries of the main periods of her life, it depicts the challenges that Sera Khandro faced by leaving behind her elite Lhasa upbringing and journeying to Golok as a teenager in pursuit of her religious aims. This short work leaves out the details of her life circumstances, such as her fraught entanglements with other consorts, which Jacoby chronicles and analyzes with respect to Sera Khandro's extensive autobiography. In the following, I will only be concerned with her short autobiography's function within Tāre Lhamo's namthar, not with the facts of Sera Khandro's life as a historical figure or her representation in other sources.[113]

As it appears in *Spiraling Vine of Faith*, her story provides a foil for Tāre Lhamo's own by expressing, in her self-effacing autobiographical voice, the enormous challenges of a Tibetan woman traversing the Buddhist path. As a proximate antecedent, Sera Khandro's story of struggles and hard-won accomplishments helps to explain, at least in the logic of its inclusion, why Tāre Lhamo's story unfolds with an emphasis on her early talents and miracles, despite the historical tragedy that beset Golok—and Tibetan areas more widely—in her youth. In that way, its inclusion in her namthar serves to further displace Tāre Lhamo's accomplishments to her past lives. Yet also importantly, Sera Khandro's poignant struggles as a woman seeking to establish herself in the Nyingma milieu in Golok provide the only site in

Spiraling Vine of Faith where the gender-specific challenges of a female practitioner are explicitly addressed.

Given that Sera Khandro had a comparable but not identical pedigree of female antecedents as Tāre Lhamo,[114] we might ask why her story is filled with such challenges whereas Tāre Lhamo is portrayed as a dauntless heroine, enlightened from birth. What accounts for the difference? On the one hand, in terms of life circumstances, Sera Khandro lacked the family roots in Golok to facilitate her entry into religious life there and faced considerable challenges that Tāre Lhamo, having been born into the region's religious elite, never did. On the other hand, in terms of literary representations, we might look to narrative voice for another perspective on this question. The juxtaposition of their stories in *Spiraling Vine of Faith* reveals telling parallels and divergences in the representation of female agency in autobiographical and biographical modes for recounting the lives of exceptional Buddhist women in Tibetan literature. As found therein, the life story of Sera Khandro is narrated with the studied diffidence of a first-person account in which she continually deflects agency to the prophetic voice of those who appear to her in visions. By contrast, Tāre Lhamo's life is narrated in the studied reverence of a third-person account, through which Pema Ösal Thaye deflects her agency in certain ways—like locating her enlightenment in past lives—in order to heighten her agency in other ways, most strikingly in the tales of her numerous miracles.

Although the representations of female agency in the lives of Tāre Lhamo and her predecessors differ, they share one feature in common: the centrality of the ḍākinī. Even the declarative statements attributed to Yeshe Tsogyal preface her practice of austerities and many achievements with a statement that these were "encouraged by signs from the ḍākinīs" (*mkha' 'gro'i brdas bskul*).[115] And by the end of the verses, she is identified as "inseparable from Vārāhī herself." Pointedly, in her excerpted short autobiography, Sera Khandro supplicates the ḍākinīs and other visionary apparitions to ask for guidance at major turning points in her life. While Tāre Lhamo is referred to as the "supreme ḍākinī" throughout her adult years, at one point, her miracles are nonetheless summarily ascribed to the handiwork of the ḍākinīs, whose "lingering breath" (*kha rlangs ma yal ba*) is said to have never left her side.[116] In each case, the ḍākinī is credited with the capacity to incite action rather than an ordinary woman.

In *Spiraling Vine of Faith*, a key difference in the representation of agency in the stories of Tāre Lhamo and Sera Khandro is the degree to which the protagonist herself is divinized. Tāre Lhamo is repeatedly identified with enlightened female deities, not only in the opening homage but also in prophecies included in the account of her birth. The prophecy by Dudjom Rinpoche attributes salvific powers to Tāre Lhamo, in particular her ability to guide others to a celestial realm (*mkha' spyod zhing*) associated with the *khecarī*, another class of female deity. This suggests that anyone who establishes a connection (*'brel ba*) by encountering her in person, through her relics, and perhaps even via her namthar may benefit from her grace. The protracted account of her past lives further reinforces her exceptional stature.

By contrast, in her short autobiography as excerpted in *Spiraling Vine of Faith,* Sera Khandro spends a mere four lines on her past life genealogy and otherwise portrays herself in explicitly human terms as the beneficiary of guidance and encouragement from ḍākinīs.[117] One striking episode provides the basis for comparison with a parallel tale in Tāre Lhamo's life, to be discussed in the next chapter. It takes place in the early part of Sera Khandro's story, depicting her reliance on prophetic signs in order to resist parental dictates to marry and cope with public scorn after running away to Golok to pursue a religious life.[118] In such cases, the deflection of agency to the ḍākinīs and other visionary apparitions in effect authorized her decisions. With reference to her autobiographical writings more generally, Sarah Jacoby has theorized Sera Khandro's "ḍākinī dialogues" as a kind of "autobiographical ventriloquy," a strategy to validate her decisions and actions in an authoritative voice other than her own.[119] The hermitess Orgyan Chökyi likewise invoked the ḍākinīs to authorize her composition of an autobiography after her master said, "There is no reason to write a liberation tale for you—a woman."[120] In similar terms, by externalizing her aspirations in the language of guidance and prophecies by the ḍākinīs, Sera Khandro is able to present her actions as sanctioned by a higher authority.

In this episode, Sera Khandro disparages her gender after being confronted with social barriers to her religious aspirations. Unlike Tāre Lhamo's birth into the tight-knit treasure scene in Golok, when Sera Khandro arrives from Lhasa as a runaway teenager, she reports being treated poorly and becoming destitute. She attributes this to gender in repeated references to her body as inferior, stating, "Due to my lowly body and being destitute of wealth, / I received an array of contempt and scorn from everyone."[121]

In such excerpted passages, the question of agency is explicitly tied to gender in *Spiraling Vine of Faith*. Note how she questions her ability to pursue her religious aspirations in a female body in the following lament:

> Due to various ill-natured criticisms,
> [Others] see me as lacking in good qualities.
> As the object of contempt and wrong views,
> Leave aside [bringing any] benefit to beings,
> I am the cause of ruin to myself and others.
> Because of that, casting away this worthless body of mine,
> I pray for a male body, endowed with the dharma.[122]

Here Sera Khandro appears ready to cast away her female body as an insurmountable barrier to pursuing a religious vocation. While statements like this indicate that Tibetan women have internalized negative gender stereotypes to a certain extent, in a fascinating twist, these very moments in Tibetan literature also provide the opportunity for the determinacy of gender to be questioned.[123]

Indeed, this moment of crisis functions as a turning point in the narrative and provides an opportunity for divine intervention. In response, the Great Mother of Space (Dbyings kyi yum chen) appears and categorically rejects the determinacy of gender. She then utters a long prophecy that organizes Sera Khandro's life into a wider framework of meaning through recourse to destiny. We should not, however, mistake such prophecies as illustrative of a conception of predetermination. The Great Mother delineates two scenarios depending on Sera Khandro's own choice whether or not to follow the guidance of the ḍākinīs. If she does, her aspiration to benefit beings will be fulfilled; if she does not, her treasures will remain hidden. The Great Mother also gives her the following advice: "As a messenger appointed by the mother ḍākinīs, rely on the principle of coincidence. [Meanwhile,] it's vital to take care and be resourceful."[124] This double message aptly expresses a complementary but seemingly contradictory relationship between prophetic destiny and human agency in the treasure tradition, to be taken up in chapter 4. Fulfilling her destiny to discover treasures requires favorable circumstances, but her own resourcefulness (*thabs mkhas pa*) is also key. Destiny is not a given; rather, it is a possibility to be seized, which requires determination, resourcefulness, and action.

Dauntless in Youth

While Sera Khandro's religious aspirations were at odds with her social milieu in early life, the opposite was true for Tāre Lhamo. Turning to the story of Tāre Lhamo's youth, *Spiraling Vine of Faith* depicts her embeddedness in the tight-knit treasure community of Golok, starting with her birth into her religious vocation as the daughter of a tertön. Here her father's stature is highlighted by the inclusion of his robust past life genealogy.[125] As other indicators of her special status, wondrous signs are recorded accompanying her birth—resounding music, shimmering rainbows, and billowing perfume—following a standard trope in Tibetan hagiographic literature to indicate the exceptional nature of the protagonist. Together the verses of praise identifying her with tantric deities, excerpted accounts of her female antecedents, her father's stature as a tertön, prophecies delivered early in her life, and the wondrous signs at birth create a sense of anticipation and expectation for her exceptional life story.

From an early age, Tāre Lhamo is depicted as forthright and dauntless, a girl who acts decisively without hesitation. In her youth, she is entrusted with the property of Tra Gelong and also given the option to return to his former residence to train as a nun. As recounted in *Spiraling Vine of Faith*, the attendant of Tra Gelong named Alogowa came to retrieve Tāre Lhamo soon after she was born, saying simply, "This is my lama." At that point, Tāre Lhamo's father diplomatically suggested that Alogowa come back and ask Tāre Lhamo herself about "returning" to Tra Gelong's former residence when she was a bit older. Alogowa duly visited again some years later. At that point, the narrative reads: "Her father, the great tertön, said to his esteemed daughter, 'You may become a venerable nun or remain a householder.' She replied, 'I am determined to be both venerable and a householder.'"[126] In this episode, Tāre Lhamo is portrayed as capable of determining the direction of her own life, even as a young girl. In her choice to be neither a renunciant nor a layperson, she resists social categories and envisions her own future. The coupling of "venerable" (*jo btsun*) and "householder" (*khyim 'dzin*) here anticipates her vocation as a tantric adept who marries yet remains dedicated to full-time religious pursuits, as is common in the Nyingma tradition. Thus Tāre Lhamo rejects the offer from Alogowa in favor of a religious education at home with her father, who gives her ritual initiations into the

Nyingtik Yabzhi cycle in addition to the transmission of the entirety of his own treasure corpus.

Later, *Spiraling Vine of Faith* portrays an early treasure revelation as accidental when responding bravely to an attack by a pack of dogs. This is a fascinating representation of agency in which Tāre Lhamo's forthright character and lack of hesitation allow her to defend herself and also unintentionally reveal a treasure. Since she is only fourteen by Tibetan reckoning, she is referred to as the "supreme maiden" (*srad mo mchog*) rather than the "supreme khandro."

> At the age of fourteen, while staying at Shukchung Sangngak Ling in the Do Valley, once she went to circumambulate Dodrupchen Monastery. In a place called the "great open plain," a pack of dogs attacked her. As they were chasing after her, the Supreme Maiden without hesitation gathered up lots of rocks and threw them [at the dogs]. In particular, on top of a large boulder, there was one dark stone. Fearlessly, she grabbed it to cast it at the dogs. That evening, when she returned home, she still had the dark stone in her pocket. When she showed it to her mother, [it turned out to be] a treasure casket with a red syllable Vaṃ protruding on top. How amazing! Her mother said, "Last night I had a sign in a dream that a marvel would occur. This is good for the most part." Saying that, she affixed [the dark stone] around [Tāre Lhamo's] neck, out of sight. From that point forward, having awakened the karmic propensity for profound treasures, she revealed various material treasures, including statues, caskets, and yellow scrolls.[127]

Tāre Lhamo's first revelation is recounted as a seeming accident in a scene typical of Golok, where packs of dogs roam freely and frequently menace people. Tibetans routinely fend them off by throwing rocks, and it is in the process of gathering rocks and seeking high ground that Tāre Lhamo stumbles upon this treasure, confirmed by her mother. Later Tāre Lhamo surrendered the rock to one of her exalted teachers, Rigdzin Jalu Dorje, after he queried her about whether she had one of his "treasure allotments" (*gter skal*); he responded with delight when she presented it to him.[128] This haphazard revelation is cast as the direct result of her personal character, rather than divine or prophetic intervention of any sort, and it becomes the occasion for Pema Ösal Thaye to pronounce that her propensity for treasure revelation had been awakened and that henceforth she began to reveal treasures.

In a common hagiographic trope, Tāre Lhamo is also portrayed as devout in youth and endowed with early visionary propensities. The following passage highlights this and also provides the context for her rhetorical separation from "all the faults of ordinary women":

> Regarding this eminent protector of beings, from a young age, she was free from all the faults of ordinary women and had uncontrived compassion and spontaneous mastery of mind. She had faith in deities and lamas and [experienced] extensive visions [of them]. In particular, just by uttering the name of the Great Orgyan, the hairs of her body would stand on end and tears would well in her eyes. Again and again, she experienced visions and prophecies of the king of victors, Padmākara, and oceans of the infinite three roots [lamas, yidams, and ḍākinīs].[129]

This statement confirms Tāre Lhamo's visionary capacities and close connection to Padmasambhava, alias the Great Orgyan and Padmākara, but the content of these visions is not divulged, and in general the reader gets less of a sense for Tāre Lhamo's subjective experience than in the excerpts about her predecessors included in Spiraling Vine of Faith.

Instead, Pema Ösal Thaye cites a passage about the characteristics of "emissaries of Padma who extract treasures" (gter 'byin pad ma'i pho nya), which curiously consists of a generic set of Buddhist qualities such as faith, generosity, renunciation, and compassion.[130] This is a device that allows him to indirectly affirm her status as a tertön and elaborate her qualities in general terms. It is her intense faith, "uncontrived compassion," and "spontaneous mastery of mind," the very qualities that set her apart from "ordinary women," that make her receptive to visionary experience. Yet once again these are portrayed as innate rather than developed through her own efforts, traceable to her association with authoritative female antecedents.

Meanwhile, throughout her youth, Tāre Lhamo is shown devoted to religious practice, touring major and minor sacred sites of the region accompanied by her mother. Teachings and prophecies from Golok masters continue to punctuate her story. For example, once while attending a sacred dance (presumably of the Gesar epic) at Dodrupchen Monastery, "The great lord of siddhas, Rigdzin Jalu Dorje, showed her a mask of Ne'u Chung from among the images of female deities and said, 'You are an emanation of her.'"[131] Another time, Lingtrul Rinpoche introduced her to the mountain deity Nyenpo Yutse by pouring tsampa (roasted barley) on a piece of crystal and thereby producing a magical illusion of the mountain range in order to indicate the location of various treasure sites. His statement, "One day, the time will come when this is useful," presaged her numerous revelations at the sacred site later in life.[132] Later, when visiting Nyenpo Yutse, her principal teacher Dzongter Kunzang Nyima announced to Tāre Lhamo and his daughter Lhacam Chökyi Drolma (both considered to be emanations of Yeshe Tsogyal and Sera Khandro): "You two resided in Takmo Yangdzong at this place together with the great Guru [Padmasambhava] and his disciples."[133] This references their identification with Yeshe Tsogyal and, as a test of their visionary capacity, Dzongter Kunzang Nyima requested them to locate the treasure gate (gter sgo) for the Distillation of the Ḍākinīs' Realization (Mkha' 'gro dgongs 'dus) and to place a long-life arrow at the spot. The conclusion of the episode is somewhat ambiguous. Despite her early visionary talents, Tāre Lhamo did not know the whereabouts of the site and was able to complete the test only because of the previous "tour" of treasure sites at Nyenpo Yutse she had received from Lingtrul Rinpoche by magical means. Nevertheless, such interactions with local tertöns and their prophetic content further confirm her exceptional status and identity with illustrious female antecedents.

The account of her youth showcases Tāre Lhamo's embeddedness in the local treasure scene of Golok, interacting with prominent teachers and receiving prophecies and teachings. In addition to esoteric teachings received from her father, Tāre Lhamo received oral instructions for the Nyingthik Yabshi from Rigdzin Jalu Dorje and Thubten Trinle Palzangpo and later joined the encampment of Dzongter Kunzang Nyima, where she participated fully in religious gatherings. Spiraling Vine of Faith notes that Dzongter Kunzang Nyima gave her the empowerment, authorization, and instructions for the entirety of his own treasure corpus. Moreover, he formally invested her as the trustee (chos bdag) for his sādhana cycle of Yeshe Tsogyal. Together with her elder brother, Dzongter Kunzang Nyima presided over the arrangement of her first marriage to his own son, Tulku Milo (alias Mingyur Dorje or Pema Ösal Nyingpo); however, the account of her marriage is restricted to a single paragraph, and we never learn his fate in the namthar. Instead, Tāre Lhamo is depicted continuing to devote her time to religious practice, particularly the sādhana of her namesake Tārā.

While portraying Tāre Lhamo as steeped in the esoteric milieu of Nyingma circles in Golok and devoted to religious practice, Pema Ösal

Thaye does not directly correlate her training and practice to any attainment of realization, as he does for Namtrul Rinpoche in *Jewel Garland*.[134] The reader only gets a glimpse of what might be Tāre Lhamo's liberation toward the end of *Spiraling Vine of Faith*, in a series of recorded visions. In early 1989, during a feast offering to the ḍākinīs, Tāre Lhamo had a vision in which she toured various ḍākinī lands, including Dhumathala, where she encountered Varjavārāhī in person.[135] In the vision as recorded, Varjavārāhī acknowledges their inseparability and invites her to partake of sanctified substances from a gaṇacakra feast being held by the ḍākinīs. Upon tasting it, Tāre Lhamo experiences "the wisdom of nondual bliss and emptiness" (*bde stong gnyis med kyi ye shes*). If this is indeed where Tāre Lhamo's liberation is to be found in her namthar, then even here we do not see her achieving enlightenment; rather, her gnosis is granted to her by the ḍākinīs—albeit in a double of herself as Varjavārāhī.

Reflecting on representations of female agency in *Spiraling Vine of Faith*, we must be especially careful to distinguish between hagiographic portraits and the actual agency of historical women. Whereas Sera Khandro downplays her extraordinary life and accomplishments due the constraints of autobiographical writings, Pema Ösal Thaye goes to great lengths to highlight the exceptional and miraculous aspects of Tāre Lhamo's story during the period when Tibetan agency was most constricted. From the onset of socialist transformations in Golok in the late 1950s, when she was consigned to manual labor, Tāre Lhamo is portrayed as an altruistic miracle worker. This gives us a clue that there is more at stake than gender. In the next chapter, I trace the representation of her agency through the miracles used to narrate this devastating chapter of Tibetan history and argue that her miraculous activities are central to narrating those decades in a redemptive key.

At this point, we are in a position to reflect on the conundrum of agency, raised at the outset of this chapter: How can one speak of individual agency for Buddhist masters whose identities are explicitly and publicly understood to be composite and relational? Given the elaborate preamble to her life story, taking up nearly half of *Spiraling Vine of Faith*, how does her amalgamated identity influence the representation of Tāre Lhamo's agency?

I propose that it is precisely through this amalgam of social relations with prominent lamas in Golok and symbolic identification with authoritative female antecedents that agency is conferred on Tāre Lhamo in her hagiographic representation. While her own meditative attainments are not described in any detail, the reader can infer them through the list of accomplishments attributed to Yeshe Tsogyal. Even the struggles that Sera Khandro undergoes in order to be socially recognized in the Nyingma milieu in Golok could be read as another iteration of Tāre Lhamo's traversing of the Buddhist path in past lives. Indeed, her dauntless youth and heroism during the Maoist period could be explained within the logic of the namthar by the hard work of her proximate antecedent. The overall effect is that Tāre Lhamo emerges as an enlightened tantric heroine by birthright who nonetheless must confront the challenges of her historical circumstances.

Overall, Tāre Lhamo's portrayal in *Spiraling Vine of Faith* captures well the tension between heightened agency and its deflection in Tibetan life writings about exceptional women. Pema Ösal Thaye deflects agency for Tāre Lhamo's spiritual qualities and miracles by relegating her enlightenment to past lives and identifying her with female antecedents. On that basis, from the outset of her story, it is clear that Tāre Lhamo is no ordinary woman; rather, she is the manifestation of female deities and tantric heroines of yore. While this seems to preclude her ability to function as an exemplar, it does serve to authorize her own agency once *Spiraling Vine of Faith* finally arrives at the point of telling her story. In her youth, she is depicted traveling widely to monasteries and sacred sites throughout Golok and joining the encampments of Nyingma masters to receive tantric initiations and esoteric instructions. And during the devastation following the socialist transformation of Tibetan areas, she emerges as a powerful and benevolent figure. Precisely because of her exceptional nature, Tāre Lhamo can be portrayed with heightened agency during this period of collective trauma.

As we will see in the next chapter, Tāre Lhamo's representation as a ḍākinī-in-action allows for a distinctive style of narrating recent Tibetan history in *Spiraling Vine of Faith*. Just as the ḍākinī spontaneously appears in response to the petitions of the faithful, in episodes used to narrate these turbulent decades, Tāre Lhamo suddenly arrives on the scene of many a crisis to resolve it through miraculous means. In ḍākinī fashion, she also appears in visions to male lamas incarcerated in prison in order to console them and to predict their release. Based on her identification with female deities and authoritative antecedents in the symbolic system of Tibetan Buddhism, Tāre Lhamo is able to embody a particularly Buddhist form of Tibetan agency during the narration of the Maoist period. In line with the broader aims of this book to recover minority voices and subaltern forms of agency, the next chapter demonstrates how Tibetan authors within the PRC, like Pema Ösal Thaye, have employed hagiography to recenter Tibetans as actors in their own recent history and to reclaim interpretive control over traumatic events by placing them within an explicitly Buddhist framework.

TWO

Local Heroine

The Hagiography of Cultural Trauma

THE APOGEE OF *Spiraling Vine of Faith* recounts a devastating period of recent Tibetan history. Although the Chinese occupation of Tibetan areas began with a gradualist policy of assimilation, this was abandoned in the late 1950s in favor of socialist transformation. At that point, many religious figures were imprisoned or subjected to reform through labor for the duration of the Maoist period. However, *Spiraling Vine of Faith* contains no overt discussion of state policy and provides no details about Tāre Lhamo's living conditions; her circumstances can only be glimpsed in the background. Instead, her hagiographer, Pema Ösal Thaye, narrates the years leading up to and including the Cultural Revolution through a series of miracle tales that portray Tāre Lhamo as a tantric heroine and ḍākinī-in-action during troubled times.

The devastation of the Maoist period serves as the background and stage for *Spiraling Vine of Faith* to showcase the compassionate intervention of Tāre Lhamo. The specter of famine, prison, hard labor, death, and natural disasters is present, yet the narrative stays focused on the redeeming moments amid the chaos. In the course of her miracles, we do catch "an unflinching side glance at the chasm"[1]—an image of a corpse-strewn landscape, the physical exhaustion of hard labor, the panic of people fleeing a rockslide, and the isolation of reincarnate lamas in prison. Yet, in keeping with her identification with illustrious female antecedents, Tāre Lhamo is represented with heightened agency, exhibited in miracles that mitigate the impact of the devastation on her local community. While her activities are grassroots in scale, they nevertheless presume salvific powers, as when she is depicted multiplying the supply of rice during famine or rescuing a deceased person from the ravages of hell.[2] By casting a Buddhist heroine in the foreground of the devastation of the Maoist period, miracle tales allow for a symbolic restructuring of events, the process by which, according to anthropologist Michael Jackson, storytelling serves as a powerful vehicle for healing collective trauma.[3]

In this way, *Spiraling Vine of Faith* provides a distinctive mode of narrating recent Tibetan history, whereby the traumatic events of the Maoist period serve as the backdrop to the miraculous deeds of a tantric heroine. As a contemporary namthar composed according to classical genre conventions, it is an important example of how this genre is being configured anew as a means not merely to engender faith (as namthars traditionally do) but to heal or restore faith (*dad pa'i gso*).[4] What is being promoted is not just faith in individual Buddhist masters or the continuity of their lineage but faith in Buddhism itself. By constructing Tāre Lhamo as an emanation of enlightened beings, *Spiraling Vine of Faith* implicitly suggests that buddhas and bodhisattvas did not abandon the Tibetan people during this period; rather, they lived among them and intervened in the immediate crises within their community.

In their capacity to restore faith in a Buddhist worldview, contemporary namthars may play a significant role in healing cultural trauma. Trauma—whether personal or collective—poses a threat to systems of meaning, including cultural values and religious beliefs, due to the incomprehensibility of cataclysmic events within received frames of reference.[5] A trauma shared by a collective may be termed "social trauma" when it involves a rupture to systems of social organization due to war, disease, famine, economic collapse, or political upheaval, or "cultural trauma" when colonial domination or state intervention poses a fundamental threat to a social group by disrupting cultural practices and imposing an alien worldview.[6] Although the Tibetan experience during the Maoist period fits into both categories of collective trauma, I will primarily discuss cultural trauma, since my concern is with making meaning in the narration of this period in *Spiraling Vine of Faith*.

Cultural trauma is insidious because it destabilizes systems of meaning, the very resource that can protect against anomy when individuals or groups are faced with misfortune. In a recent study on the Cultural Revolution as trauma, Ban Wang discusses how "trauma shatters a culture's repertoire of representational and expressive means" as well as "the shared, collective matrix of meaning that keeps alive cultural continuity and personal identity."[7] The nexus of meanings and practices of a given society ordinarily serves as a buffer to trauma by providing frameworks through which to interpret events as well as ritualized methods of healing, such as occasions for collective mourning. When cultural systems are disrupted during periods of social upheaval, the impact of collective trauma is intensified.[8] In addition to coping with the effects of catastrophe, there is the added burden of how to interpret and represent traumatic events. Because of this, it may take a number of years, even decades, after a cataclysmic event for cohesive narratives and other forms of representation that make sense of it to emerge.[9] As Arthur Kleinman and Veena Das have emphasized, the process of narrating trauma facilitates the "retrieval of voice in the face of recalcitrance of tragedy" and enables those who survived to reclaim the power to make sense of the world around them.[10]

This chapter explores the representation of the years leading up to and including the Cultural Revolution in *Spiraling Vine of Faith* as an alternative history and hitherto unexamined way to narrate cultural trauma. I demonstrate how the conventions of namthar as a genre provide a way for Pema Ösal Thaye to narrate trauma in a redemptive key, symbolically restructuring events. This contrasts significantly with the two dominant modes of representing this period in Tibetan literature, scar literature and exile testimonials, which both (in quite different ways) seek to expose the atrocities of the Maoist period. Redemption in this case is not the final victory of good over evil, nor justice meted out by international courts, nor even necessarily the end of the trauma. Rather, redemption comes about through the compassionate intervention of an enlightened heroine and the restoration of systems of meaning that this makes possible. *Spiraling Vine of Faith* restores faith by showcasing Tāre Lhamo's many miracles that testify to the continued efficacy of Buddhist practices and teachings, even under the most tragic circumstances. The proliferation of namthars about historical and contemporary Buddhist masters published since the 1980s indicate their importance to reconstructing Tibetan identity in Buddhist terms.[11] Here I suggest that contemporary namthars may be significant sites for an alternative narration of recent history, by participating in the process of making meaning, and hence healing, in the wake of collective trauma.

What's Left Out?

While typical in its idealized portrait of the life of a Buddhist master, *Spiraling Vine of Faith* allows for a particular way of narrating history. By emphasizing the exceptional aspects of Tāre Lhamo's public persona constructed through past lives, prophecies, and miracles, Pema Ösal Thaye highlights her heightened agency against the backdrop of historical devastation. Even though he states that she was able to "embrace misfortune,"[12] the specifics of her personal losses are never mentioned: the deaths of her three brothers and first husband during the socialist transformation of Tibetan areas and her only son during the Cultural Revolution. *Spiraling Vine of Faith* glosses over these, simply stating that "because of the extreme turbulence of the times, she experienced a mix of myriad joys and sorrows."[13] In this statement, it is not difficult to sense a certain caution on the part of her hagiographer. Overall, *Spiraling Vine of Faith* omits the nitty-gritty details of daily life and instead presents the exceptional aspects of Tāre Lhamo's identity and activities in constructing her as an object of veneration.

In all likelihood, such details were omitted as too controversial, due to the ongoing sensitivity of the "Tibet question" in China. After all, her namthar was published in 1997 under the jurisdiction of Serta County officials and in cooperation with the County Office of the Bureau for Cultural Research. For this reason, Pema Ösal Thaye had to be especially careful to avoid any politically sensitive topics. But beyond pragmatic reasons, I would also suggest that such details do not serve the purpose of namthar. In its classical form, namthar is not meant to be a testimonial of an ordinary person who survived tragedy.[14] Instead, the genre emphasizes the enlightened activities of a Buddhist master, particularly when narrated by a devoted disciple.

For this reason, I suggest that the genre of namthar is remarkably well positioned to narrate the years leading up to and including the Cultural Revolution in a redemptive key. There is a fortuitous collusion between restrictions on what is permissible to say, given the political sensitivity of the topic, and the dictates of genre conventions that favor an idealized account when narrated by a third party. These concerns dovetail so as to

2.1 Stūpas dedicated to Tāre Lhamo's mother and son at Tsimda Monastery.

omit any potentially controversial details. The narrative style of namthar is often episodic, moving between chronologically arranged episodes introduced by the age of the protagonist or the date when the event occurred. In this way, it is reminiscent of other Tibetan writing practices, such as historical chronicles and diary keeping.[15] This style means that long descriptive passages of the quotidian, whether social setting or daily routine, are not expected by the reader as they would be in a Western biography, novel, or travelogue.

These quotidian details, if included, would expose Tāre Lhamo's misfortunes and hardships that resulted from state policy and, as a result, epitomize the very things that are politically sensitive and would be risky to describe. Recall that she spent the 1960s and '70s consigned to manual labor as a herder, sometimes forming part of a work crew to dig irrigation ditches and carry stones to build pens for livestock. There is also oral testimony that Tāre Lhamo was subjected to harsh treatment during struggle sessions, though she never went to prison. In the collusion of self-censorship and studied reverence, Pema Ösal Thaye invents a particular way of telling her story that emphasizes her miracles and never overtly describes social conditions or her treatment as a "black hat," a term used to label reactionaries during this period.[16] The result is a narration of cultural trauma focused on Tāre Lhamo's heroism.

In *Spiraling Vine of Faith*, only on rare occasions is state policy made explicit as a force in her life. The narration of this period opens by describing widespread famine, but Pema Ösal Thaye does not reference the state policies that precipitated it. By 1960, Golok had suffered from an alarming 50 percent reduction in livestock and unprecedented famine induced by collectivization, among other factors.[17] Previously, in the early 1950s, the Chinese Communist Party (CCP) had dictated a gradualist policy throughout Tibetan areas, in accordance with the view that the pace of socialist reform should be tailored to local conditions in areas dominated by minority populations. Pastoralist production remained under Tibetan control and proceeded according to traditional practices. However, in the late 1950s, in the face of armed resistance in Tibetan areas, socialist transformation was inaugurated unilaterally. In 1959, collectivization was imposed throughout Golok, although the process was not completed until the mid-1960s or later.[18] The result was a swift decline from relative prosperity to unprecedented poverty.[19] In the early 1960s, when the Panchen Lama made a tour of Tibetan areas in Qinghai, Gansu, and Sichuan provinces, he was "appalled by the deterioration in living standards and of the economy caused by ill-conceived communisation programmes and ruthless suppression by the PLA."[20] Not only famine but also a decline in the population, with the young men altogether missing in some areas, was readily evident.[21]

Indeed, famine spread across China between 1959 and 1961 as a result of the failed policies of the Great Leap Forward. It cost millions of lives, estimated between 16.5 and 30 million across the country.[22] The Great Leap Forward diverted significant resources from the agricultural sector to the industrial sector, including labor and grain procurements, in an attempt to swiftly industrialize.[23] Concurrently, collectivization had shifted incentive structures in agricultural production, resulting in a lower grain output than anticipated, and exacerbating this, agricultural labor was often diverted locally to nonagricultural tasks, such as smelting iron in backyard steel mills.[24] Thus, collectivization had unanticipated consequences across China, and widespread famine meant that the state could not easily redress a crisis in one area with resources from another.

Though never explicitly mentioned, collectivization and its effects are evident in the background of Tāre Lhamo's miracle tales. *Spiraling Vine of Faith*'s coverage of the period opens by describing the famine and a massive death toll with "human and horse corpses strewn across all the mountains and valleys."[25] In subsequent tales, Tāre Lhamo participates in work crews loading timber onto wild yaks and constructing stone pens for them, and I was told that she also took part in digging irrigation canals to expand the arable land and increase the production of wheat, favored among Han cadres over the Tibetan staple crop of barley. However, Pema Ösal Thaye only mentions Tāre Lhamo's participation in manual labor as the setting for her miracles.[26] It is possible that any discussion of collectivization was omitted, since this would be assumed knowledge among informed readers, literate Tibetans from the Golok region and environs. But this also suggests the collusion between avoiding any politically sensitive content and constructing Tāre Lhamo as an object of veneration, by focusing on her miracles and omitting explicit reference to her personal hardships.

The Cultural Revolution is the only state policy mentioned by name (Ch.: *wenhua dageming*; Tib.: *rig gnas gsar brje*), rather strangely in the context of a policy that required Tibetans in Golok to round up and kill stray dogs and rodents. Although I have been unable to trace the historicity of this policy, it is not all that unusual within the context of campaigns during the Maoist period. Take, for example, the infamous Anti-Sparrow Campaign inaugurated during the Great Leap Forward. Residents of both cities and the countryside were required to engage in pest control by killing sparrows, rats, flies, and mosquitoes. One exile Tibetan reports that in Lhasa, the corpses of pests had to be turned in each day to one's group leader.[27] Given the problem of stray dogs in Tibetan areas and plateau pikas that damage the grasslands in Golok, it would not be surprising if local Party officials inaugurated a similar campaign to eliminate them. Indeed, a comparable drive to eliminate stray dogs was part of a twenty-point plan formulated by Red Guards in Lhasa at the outbreak of the Cultural Revolution.[28] These kinds of campaigns were especially offensive to Tibetans, as they ran directly counter to the Buddhist ethical dictate against killing any living creature. In *Spiraling Vine of Faith*, Tāre Lhamo's own response was to consider taking her own life rather than that of a dog.[29] In her reaction, there may be an implicit critique of the anti-Buddhist nature of state policy.

The Cultural Revolution was the final and most intense attack on Buddhist practices and institutions in Tibetan areas during the Maoist period. Religion had already been under siege for almost a decade. In Lhasa, the estates of large monasteries had been redistributed during land reforms that followed the 1959 Lhasa Uprising, and monks who had participated in the uprising had been imprisoned. Deprived of their economic base, the monastic population dwindled. Moreover, a number of monasteries in Kham had been bombed as the Chinese Communist state quelled armed resistance among Tibetans.[30] In the late 1950s and early '60s, Tibetans were subjected to ideological training to raise class consciousness and induce revolutionary fervor. Ordinary Tibetans were encouraged to recount the evils of the "old society" and disavow the "three feudal lords"—the aristocracy, religious leaders, and former officials. During the Cultural Revolution, this was taken to new heights in the campaign to smash the "four olds" (old ideas, old culture, old customs, and old habits). Thus at the onset of the Cultural Revolution in 1966, wholesale destruction of monasteries, temples, and other religious structures was actively undertaken.

Spiraling Vine of Faith does not reference details about the damage to Buddhist institutions, and we know less about what happened during the Cultural Revolution in Golok than about Lhasa, where it is well documented that the Red Guards took to the streets, banging cymbals and drums, searching houses to confiscate religious objects, parading religious figures through the streets in dunce caps, and ravaging temples.[31] Monasteries in Golok had already closed in 1958, though eight were allowed to reopen briefly in 1962 and then closed again in 1966 with the onset of the Cultural Revolution.[32] The *Annals of Golok History* records the destruction of "cultural artifacts of great value" (*rig dngos 'gangs che ba*) and mentions that monasteries were "struck with severe loss and damage" (*gyong gud tshab phog*) during this period, listing the destruction of existing assembly halls, monks' quarters, and stūpas containing ancient objects (*gna' rdzas*).[33] Since many Golok monasteries had been encampments with few permanent structures, it is difficult to assess the degree of material damages.

Narrating Cultural Trauma

Although *Spiraling Vine of Faith* makes little mention of the destruction that occurred during the Cultural Revolution, other well-known genres of literature do, and these make for salient points of contrast to the hagiographic deployment of miracle tales to narrate cultural trauma. Within the PRC, the predominantly Chinese genre of scar literature (*shanghen wenxue*) emerged in the 1980s to publicly expose wounds from the Cultural Revolution in fiction and memoirs that tacitly criticized the excesses of the Maoist era. Scar literature was made possible by the new freedom of expression inaugurated by Deng Xiaoping that encouraged criticism of the "decade of chaos" as a means to distance the new regime from the excesses of the Cultural Revolution, which was summarily blamed on the Gang of Four.[34] Nevertheless, this literature presented an alternative to the master narrative of the state and its teleological notion of a history culminating in a Communist utopia.[35] Tibetans also produced scar literature, referred to as "tales of wounds to the Tibetan psyche" (*bod kyi sems rma'i sgrung gtam*),[36] although these works tended to be more allegorical and did not appear until the mid-1980s due to an initial caution on the part of Tibetan writers.

Among the Tibetan community in exile, there has been an entirely different approach to narrating trauma, embodied in the outpouring of testimonials documenting human rights violations experienced under Chinese Communist rule. I refer to these as "exile testimonials," by which I mean autobiographical accounts by Tibetans who escaped to India and provided a personal account of hardships, such as imprisonment or torture. Auto-biographies of this type are for the most part composed in English for an international audience.[37] Since the authors are native Tibetan speakers, stories are often elicited through an interview process and then translated and assembled into a cohesive narrative by a native English speaker who serves as either coauthor or ghostwriter. Less frequently, exile testimonials are first composed in Tibetan as a literary work and then translated into English.[38] While the autobiographies of lamas and aristocrats share with other Tibetan life writings a focus on the activities of prominent figures, what I am calling exile testimonials depart from these norms by recounting eyewitness and personal accounts of state violence against ordinary Tibet-ans in China. The emphasis is on realistic portrayal of everyday life, both inside and outside prison, presenting a factual account of general condi-tions as well as the subjective experience of the narrator.[39]

While scar literature and exile testimonials both aim to expose the atroc-ities of the Maoist period, there are significant differences between these genres. First and foremost, scar literature restricts its critique to the Cul-tural Revolution as a leftist aberration in the otherwise infallible leadership of the Communist Party, whereas exile testimonials recount the violence of the Maoist period as a synecdoche for the whole Chinese occupation of Tibet. While realism is important to both, scar literature frequently takes the form of historical fiction. By contrast, in exile testimonials, the authenticity of the narrator as witness to events is crucial for providing firsthand evidence to document human rights abuses. Moreover, while the state accepts nar-ratives that criticize the Cultural Revolution and therefore permitted scar literature to flourish in China, it rejects claims of torture,[40] which can only be made publicly outside China by those who have escaped into exile. In this regard, exile testimonials take part in the broader international discourse on human rights and thereby introduce humanistic concerns into Tibetan life writing.

The narration of the Maoist period in *Spiraling Vine of Faith* is significantly different from both scar literature and exile testimonials. Here the focus is not on the hardships endured by Tibetans; instead, the narrative concen-trates on the heroism of Tāre Lhamo amid the mayhem. Since its account of the Maoist period consists of miracle tales, an obvious difference between Tāre Lhamo's namthar and these other genres is the lack of concern with literary realism. Indeed, *Spiraling Vine of Faith* departs from both genres by narrating recent Tibetan history within a Buddhist framework. It represents a minority voice, in Chakrabarty's sense, which narrates historical events outside of the epistemological limits of secular history.

A Buddhist Framework

The Buddhist framework can be seen clearly in the way that Pema Ösal Thaye frames the years between 1959 and 1978 in *Spiraling Vine of Faith*. This period is bracketed by statements about karma, ascribing the widespread famine to the collective karma (here previous negative deeds) of Tibetans. The namthar describes this as a time of extreme anguish due to famine throughout the land "by the force of collective karma."[41] Famine is neither described as a "natural" occurrence nor attributed to state policies emanating from Beijing, such as the Great Leap Forward. Rather, the cause is attributed to karma (*las*), which is "collective" or "common to the public" (*spyi mthun*). *Jewel Garland* features a comparable statement: "In the year of the iron rat [1960], by the force of collective karma, the region in general and all its specific [domains] were afflicted by famine."[42] Causality in these framing statements is articulated by combining the word for power, force, or influence (*dbang*) with the agentive or instrumental particle (*byed sgra*), here to indicate the cause of the famine. More typically, the agentive particle is used to indicate the subject of a sentence, the agent or doer (*byed pa po*) of the action, and thereby serves as a key marker for ascriptions of agency in Tibetan literature.

At the close of this period, the advent of liberalization is similarly attributed to collective karma. *Spiraling Vine of Faith* proclaims, "In the meritorious sky of the Land of Snow, the youthful sun of the [Buddhist] teachings dawned in a renewed propagation."[43] This is a poetic turn of phrase that heralds a dramatic change, the rising of the sun anew over the "Land of Snow" (*gangs ljongs*), a standard epithet for Tibet. The sun is correlated to the renewed propagation of Buddhism, which by implication clears away the darkness of the previous decades. This is euphemistically attributed to the merit (*bsod nams*) of Tibetans, referencing the accumulation of virtuous deeds that ripens as positive circumstances. Once again, collective karma is invoked, this time for a favorable change in historical circumstances.[44] No mention is made of state policy—neither the Great Leap Forward nor the policy of "reform and opening" (*gaige kaifang*) inaugurated by the Third Plenum of the Eleventh National Congress in 1978 is referenced.[45] Instead, the karma of Tibetans supersedes the policies of the Chinese Communist state as the causal explanation for historical events within this hagiographic context.

The use of karma to frame this period is provocative for a number of reasons. First and foremost, doctrinally karma refers to a retributive system propelled by the volitional actions of the individual. As such, it provides a model of causation that underscores Buddhist cosmology as a whole, particularly how individuals are understood to take rebirth within it.[46] By contrast, in *Spiraling Vine of Faith*, karma is marshaled as an explanation for the fortune of a collective, indeed, the fate of an entire people. Examples of karma shared by a group can be found in early Buddhist sources, but no systematic notion of collective karma can be discerned from them.[47] That said, the use of "collective karma" can also be found in the writings of Buddhist modernists in Southeast Asia, particularly the notion of "national karma" in relation to social justice movements.[48]

The use of karma in *Spiraling Vine of Faith* is also provocative because it appears to "blame the victim." Why appeal to karma to explain historical events pragmatically driven by policy decisions in Beijing? Why claim responsibility, albeit obliquely by recourse to indeterminate previous actions, on behalf of Tibetans as a people for events by and large beyond their control? Perhaps this is simply a way to avoid the question of state culpability in a context where publication requires self-censorship. While this is entirely plausible, karma may also have a significant function in the articulation of subaltern pasts. I would suggest that the hagiographic appropriation of collective karma provides an important mechanism in *Spiraling Vine of Faith* to decenter Beijing and recenter Tibetans as the principal actors in their own history.

Instead of treating ascriptions of agency as assertions to be judged by the epistemic parameters of secular history, it may be more profitable to view them as representational strategies that intersect with culturally specific conventions related to literary genres or oral frames of reference. Without a culturally nuanced approach, one might blandly read the evocation of karma in *Spiraling Vine of Faith* as a passive acceptance of historical events as "fate." Indeed, karma has been widely misunderstood in the West to be synonymous with fatalism since Buddhism's early encounter with British colonialism.[49] Contra such a mistaken association, I argue that the use of karma to frame historical events can be read as an assertion of agency, because it asserts *interpretive control*. It makes meaning in the face of anomy and reestablishes a sense of mastery in the wake of traumatic events.[50] In other words, the ability to explain misfortune, even when one cannot directly act to change it, prevents the collapse of systems of meaning.

Based on research in Buddhist communities in Southeast Asia, Charles Keyes has found that karma frequently serves as an explanation of last recourse, when all remedial action fails and nothing more can be done to rectify the situation.[51] In this usage, karma shores up meaning in the face of human misfortune beyond one's immediate control by affirming the moral order of the cosmos. It offers an answer to the "why me" or "why us" question provoked by seemingly random tragedies and needless suffering. Because of this, sociologists like Max Weber and Peter Berger have heralded karma as the most comprehensive and rational theodicy, or solution to the problems of evil and suffering in a morally constituted universe.[52] In this light, karma can be seen as part of an active process of meaning making invoked to prevent a collapse into anomy, by addressing the haunting question of "why" that accompanies unjust and undeserved suffering within a Buddhist interpretive schema.[53] Karma thus provides a way to make meaning in the face of tragedy, when remedial action fails,[54] and thereby assert interpretive control over circumstances.

Additionally, karma serves as a potent framing device, because it asserts a Buddhist view of history against the master narrative of the state. In other words, karma provides a means to narrate an alternative and specifically Buddhist version of recent Tibetan history. It elides Chinese Communist state policy as the engine driving the fate of Tibetans and instead asserts Tibetans' own control over their destiny, albeit through actions in the distant and indeterminate past. By marshaling the explanatory power of karma, Tibetans like Pema Ösal Thaye restore cultural meanings in the face of a devastating chapter of history and reassert Tibetan agency in Buddhist terms. This is quite different than exposing the wounds caused by the Cultural Revolution in scar literature or documenting human rights abuses in exile testimonials. Instead, *Spiraling Vine of Faith* symbolically restructures events by creating a Buddhist framework for Tāre Lhamo's activities in this period.

Heroine in Troubled Times

In *Spiraling Vine of Faith*, the Maoist period is narrated through a dozen or so miracle tales. The years from 1959 to 1978, spanning Tāre Lhamo's twenties and thirties, are bracketed off as "extremely turbulent" (*yo lang drag po*). This characterization implicitly contests state-sanctioned historiography by extending the so-called "decade of chaos" (referring to the Cultural Revolution) to two decades, starting with the socialist transformation in Tibetan areas. Throughout this period, Tāre Lhamo is portrayed as a dauntless heroine, addressing the immediate crises in her local community. The representation of her agency in these miracle tales relies on the cumulative perspective that the reader has gained in *Spiraling Vine of Faith* by encountering Tāre Lhamo first as an emanation of enlightened beings, next in her previous lives as Yeshe Tsogyal and Sera Khandro through biographical excepts in their own first-person voices, and finally in her youth through the account of her religious training with prominent Nyingma masters. The various facets of Tāre Lhamo's identity assure the reader of her extraordinary status and undergird the depiction of her heightened agency during the nadir in collective agency for Tibetans as a whole.

On top of her identity as a ḍākinī, constructed through her identification with illustrious female antecedents, Pema Ösal Thaye adds two other authoritative Buddhist paradigms to the framing of this period, which are not necessarily gendered. Her identity as the "supreme khandro" remains, but added to that are the Mahāyāna ideal of the bodhisattva (awakened being) and the tantric ideal of the *siddha* (accomplished one). These two paradigms are used to call attention, respectively, to her beneficent activities and her power over the phenomenal world in the miracle tales to follow. The first of these is mentioned in the opening lines describing the period:

> From the ages of twenty-two to forty-one,[55] because of the extreme turbulence of the times, [Tāre Lhamo] experienced a mix of myriad joys and sorrows. Nevertheless, she was able to embrace misfortune. Whatever her activities, inwardly she approached [them] with the discipline of a bodhisattva. Her mindstream was brimming with *bodhicitta*, and she took up with singular earnest the benefit of others, directly and indirectly.[56]

Here Pema Ösal Thaye orients the reader to view Tāre Lhamo in heroic terms, embracing her own misfortunes and facing the ensuing calamity with others at the forefront of her mind. Whatever her outer activities (herding, carrying stones, gathering wood), the reader should not be fooled. Although the khandroma performed the tasks of an ordinary nomad, *Spiraling Vine of Faith* insists that her mind was nevertheless filled with altruistic intent, encapsulated in the term *bodhicitta*, meaning "awakened mind or heart." With this statement, Pema Ösal Thaye proposes that inwardly Tāre Lhamo remained true to Buddhist principles, approaching all activities with the discipline of a bodhisattva, one who dedicates his or her existence to the benefit of others. Thus Pema Ösal Thaye sets up the expectation that Tāre Lhamo will not succumb as a victim to circumstances but will heroically work for the benefit of those around her. The reader is thus prepared for a certain type of narration of this period, akin to the salvific activities of bodhisattvas like Tārā or Guanyin.

2.2 Black tent made of yak wool, typical of nomads in Golok.

Nevertheless, a tension can be detected in *Spiraling Vine of Faith*'s representation of Tāre Lhamo's agency during this period. She appears to be simultaneously confined by her circumstances and able to transcend them. In these episodes, the reader can detect that she had been consigned to manual labor, yet Pema Ösal Thaye highlights her tantric prowess, heralding Tāre Lhamo as a "female siddha who commands the inexhaustible treasure of the sky."[57] This phrase represents her with infinite resources at her command to meet the challenges of the times and echoes the divinization of her agency in *Spiraling Vine of Faith* as a whole.[58] Notably, the explicit claim to her possession of supramundane powers occurs in a story dated to 1959, near the outset of the time when historically Tibetans were losing control over their lives in the midst of socialist transformation.

Given the claim to mastery on her behalf, it may seem puzzling that her miracles are so modest in scale. *Spiraling Vine of Faith* shows Tāre Lhamo performing grassroots miracles to solve local dilemmas, even when the calamity was widespread. Her first miracle of the period is a good example, referencing the famine that struck Golok in 1960, when she was only twenty-three by Tibetan reckoning (twenty-two by the international standard).

> At the age of twenty-three, by the force of collective karma, the whole land was devastated by famine. Because the Supreme Khandro was a female siddha who commanded the inexhaustible treasury of the sky, each measure of rice that she cooked multiplied to be more than enough to feed eighteen people. Everyone was in a state of amazement.[59]

In this passage, Tāre Lhamo is depicted performing a "loaves and fishes" type of miracle, directed at the immediate needs of the people around her. Each time she cooked a measure of rice, she fed eighteen people, a recurring number in these episodes that may reflect the members of her work unit at some point. As mentioned, the historical processes at work are attributed to the irrevocable force of collective karma. Yet the crisis at the local level is subject to Tāre Lhamo's miraculous intervention.

The incongruence between the scope of her agency and the scale of her miracle, as depicted in this episode, may illustrate a more general challenge in representing the Maoist period in the genre of namthar. Within a Buddhist episteme that generally credits tantric masters with salvific powers, why were such masters powerless to prevent the collective trauma of Tibetans as a people, let alone in many cases their own confinement to prison or hard labor? Instead of leading the reader into a state of anomy through invoking such questions or emphasizing the tragic nature of the period, Pema Ösal Thaye highlights a grassroots form of agency that remained during the chaos, as conceived in religious terms.

Raw images of death and mayhem form the backdrop of her miracles, evoking the collective memory of trauma that would be part of the personal experience or received cultural knowledge for Tibetans from Golok or its environs. Another miracle tale provides a particularly devastating view of the carnage. It involves a sky burial, traditionally a Tibetan way of disposing of the dead by chopping up the corpse and feeding it to vultures, necessary due to high-altitude conditions in which permafrost prevents burial and scarcity of wood mitigates against cremation (except in the case of high lamas).

> One time, a horseman named Norbu died. In general, during these times, because of the human and horse corpses strewn across all the mountains and valleys, there were no vultures. Before the Supreme Khandro arrived, there was nothing to be done. [When she arrived] she commanded two corpse cutters named Zangkyong and Tenzang, "Place the corpse on top of a boulder." They did as she said, and five vultures appeared—who were the emanations of a set of five ḍākinīs—and partook of [the corpse] without leaving any residual.[60]

When Tāre Lhamo arrived, the scene contained a pressing problem and sense of despair: "there was nothing to be done." There was a corpse but no vultures to perform the traditional sky burial. The image of horror—"corpses strewn across all the mountains and valleys"—is not concealed as much as relegated to the background. In the foreground of the action is Tāre Lhamo as heroine, transforming the situation. In miracles such as this, *Spiraling Vine of Faith* depicts Tāre Lhamo offering immediate relief to pragmatic dilemmas and intervening to rescue others when no other recourse seemed possible.

By foregrounding her miracles, the narrative remains focused on redeeming moments amid the chaos. As a result, social calamities particular to this historical period are transformed within a hagiographic framework as sites for her compassionate intervention. In the passage above, Tāre Lhamo arrived on the scene and took charge. She ordered the traditional chopping to take place, and lo and behold, five vultures appeared. Because there were five and because Tāre Lhamo was a khandroma, the scene became imbued with special meaning for the observers. The vultures were *understood* to be the emanation of five ḍākinīs arriving at her command.[61] And there is no reason to think that this event did not happen just as described. The miracle is not in the event but in how it was perceived by those present and later constructed as a tale showcasing her marvelous deeds. Pema Ösal Thaye also employs the context of her miracle to provide a devastating image of the chaos of this period, suggesting that so many people and livestock died that even the quintessentially Tibetan vultures could not keep up with the carnage.

In *Spiraling Vine of Faith*, Tāre Lhamo is credited with the powers of a tantric adept in a construction of agency in which the capacity for heroic action is claimed for the spiritually realized. In another miracle, she prevented a rockslide that threatened to injure a group of people with a simple gesture of her hand, alluding to the tantric use of *mudrās* to influence the phenomenal world. While the context for this event is not given, the gathering of people and animals along a road with unstable rocks above suggests the extensive road construction in Tibetan areas during that period. Note the juxtaposition in the passage between the effortless miracle by Tāre Lhamo and the distress and helplessness of others.

> Another time, a rockslide was under way [that included] a large boulder. On the road, animals were injured. When she arrived, the people there were ready to flee. By merely pointing her finger [at the rockslide], the Supreme Khandro rendered the large boulder unable to move. All were amazed.[62]

This passage begins with a description of chaos before Tāre Lhamo arrives and saves the day, merely by pointing her finger. In terms of ascribing agency, the passage uses two agentive particles, one after "Supreme Khandro," indicating her as the principal actor or subject, and one after her finger pointing, indicating the instrument by which she accomplished the action of preventing the rockslide. As before, the tale traces the transformation of the scene from panic to relief, from chaos to order, from dilemma to resolution. In the process, feelings of despair and helplessness among the victims and onlookers are converted into amazement at Tāre Lhamo's miracle.

A shift also takes place for readers as they follow the transformed emotions in the beneficiaries of Tāre Lhamo's miracles. One might analyze this as a shift in aesthetic response by turning to classical Indian aesthetic theory, in which her hagiographer Pema Ösal Thaye as learned monk would be well versed. According to that, each emotional state (Skt.: *bhāva*; Tib.: *'gyur*) portrayed in literature (or the performing arts) arouses a corresponding aesthetic experience (Skt.: *rasa*; Tib.: *nyams*) in the audience. In the episode above, the emotion of fear (locals fleeing a rockslide) would seem to initially evoke the corresponding aesthetic experience of apprehension in the audience.[63] However, this state would be transformed through the miracle (Tāre Lhamo making a gesture with her hand to stop the rockslide). The transformation is signaled by a stock refrain following her miracles, "all were amazed" (*thams cad ngo mtshar*). As those in the tale are struck with amazement, Indian literary theory suggests that the corresponding experience roused in the audience would be wonder.[64] Thus, the aesthetic response of the reader shifts from a state of apprehension to a state of wonder, which not surprisingly in Buddhist sources is regarded to be conducive of faith.[65]

Using contemporary reader-response theory instead, it might be possible to identify another kind of shift in aesthetic response. Wolfgang Iser discusses how the repertoire of any literary work is drawn from the world beyond the text, including social norms, literary antecedents, and historical context.[66] These form the familiar background against which elements are selected and combined in the foreground in order to facilitate the action and provoke new meanings during the reading process. As Iser suggests, "new meanings come to the fore but at the same time, it drags its original context in its wake."[67] In other words, the juxtaposition of context in the background and action in the foreground facilitates a transformation in the reader's outlook and a new synthesis, a revision of the view of the background in light of the foreground. In terms of narrating trauma, this synthesis involves a shift in orientation toward events of recent history, revised in light of Tāre Lhamo's compassionate intervention. Memories of collective trauma are thereby reinscribed, or symbolically restructured in anthropologist Michael Jackson's terms, from sites of despair and helplessness by associating them with the compassionate activities of Buddhist masters and the vindication of Tibetan agency.

The key to this shift in orientation is the Buddhist framework in which *Spiraling Vine of Faith* portrays events of the Maoist period. The episodes evoke memories of catastrophe—famine, rampant death, hard labor, natural disasters, and mass imprisonment—and insert Tāre Lhamo, rescuing victims and amazing onlookers. This representation of her heightened agency and miraculous powers is made possible through the genre of namthar, which permits a wholly Buddhist narration of the period and hence the inclusion of miracles otherwise outside the bounds of secular history. Moreover, only through miracle tales is a Tibetan (and explicitly Buddhist) triumphalism possible, given the historical circumstances of the wholesale attack on traditional culture during the years leading up to and including the Cultural Revolution. Within a hagiographic frame, Tāre Lhamo is depicted surmounting the tragic circumstances of the day, suggesting that the devastation of socialist transformation was never total.

Beneficiary of the Ḍākinīs

As a point of comparison, let me briefly discuss how Namtrul Rinpoche is portrayed during the 1960s and '70s, noting differences due to their respective ages and genders. Given that he was a teenager in 1960, *Jewel Garland* allows for the anguish that he felt with the advent of famine, whereas Tāre Lhamo is presented stoically as embracing misfortune with others at the forefront of her mind. Pema Ösal Thaye reports a vision that Namtrul Rinpoche had that year of Yeshe Tsogyal, who promised to benevolently protect him, stating: "Although you will experience some situations of suffering, you will never be separated from me even for an instant."[68] In maternal fashion, she suckles him at her breast with an elixir to protect him from thirst, hunger, and cold. After that, his physical strength and radiance are said to have increased, and the namthar pronounces that his anguish about these conditions was purified. Here we witness Namtrul Rinpoche as a vulnerable youth, requiring protection in a way that Tāre Lhamo does not in her portrayal as a dauntless heroine.

On several occasions, as he grows into adulthood, *Jewel Garland* presents Namtrul Rinpoche as a beneficiary of the ḍākinīs, who provide him with protection throughout this period. In early 1970, now in his mid-twenties, he has a vision of a ḍākinī from the sphere of wisdom, who warns him of impending imprisonment but also assures him that the protectors will be close at hand and that the duration will not be long. After only two months, "he was released from prison, like the sun freed from the clouds."[69] Within the Buddhist framework of namthar, the cause of his imprisonment is attributed to karma or past deeds (*sngon las*) in conjunction with immediate circumstances (*'phral rkyen*). While in prison, he heroically refuses to kill a female *dzo* (*mdzo,* a hybrid of yak and cow) in an episode parallel to Tāre Lhamo's refusal to kill a dog when it is demanded by state policy (discussed later in this chapter). Later, during his thirties, a ḍākinī is credited with healing him from grave illness while he is practicing in solitary retreat.[70]

Otherwise, the focus of this period in *Jewel Garland* is on Namtrul Rinpoche's dedication to religious practice in secret and his emerging visionary talents. The namthar mentions him receiving teachings (presumably in secret) from Rigdzin Nyima, who bestows his entire treasure corpus in 1966 and appoints him the dharma trustee (*chos bdag*) for them.[71] Rigdzin Nyima likewise authenticates an early treasure revelation by Namtrul Rinpoche containing a section of the sādhana of the eight command deities (*bka' brgyad*).[72] In the late 1960s, Namtrul Rinpoche had a vision of the fourteenth-century tertön, Rigdzin Gödem,[73] predicting that he would become a holder of Apang Terchen's corpus of revelations. Then a few days later he reportedly found two sheets of paper blowing in the wind, containing a short wealth sādhana by Apang Terchen. After he practiced this sādhana earnestly, Pema Ösal Thaye relays that the cattle and harvest in the local area for that year were healthy as a result.[74] *Jewel Garland* mentions several of the practices that Namtrul Rinpoche engaged in during this period and the signs of accomplishment, for which there is no parallel in *Spriraling Vine of Faith,* given its emphasis on Tāre Lhamo as enlightened from birth.

There are also several miracle tales attributed to Namtrul Rinpoche in *Jewel Garland,* which all take place in the mid-1970s, toward the end of the Maoist period, after he reaches the age of thirty.[75] These offer noticeable parallels to tales in *Spiraling Vine of Faith,* though they are far fewer (a third in number) and less central to his hagiographic portrait for the period. Just as Tāre Lhamo is credited at the outset of famine in 1960 with multiplying each portion of rice she cooked to feed her entire work unit, Namtrul Rinpoche is depicted in the mid-1970s in his role as secretary for his work unit as being able to increase the allotments of butter he dispersed by conferring a "sky-treasury mantra blessing."[76] There is also an episode involving vultures identified with the five ḍākinīs, though it is not depicted as a miracle per se.[77] In a clear parallel, both are also credited with saving a girl's life by predicting that she would not die.[78]

Why such close parallels? It could be simply that Tāre Lhamo and Namtrul Rinpoche shared a repertoire of ritual practices and prophetic utterances, perceived as efficacious by those around them. Another possibility is that it appealed to Pema Ösal Thaye, in his selection process of the stories shared with him, to show certain convergences between the two prior to their union. Notwithstanding, overall their hagiographic portraits for this period diverge in significant ways. While Namtrul Rinpoche is represented as vulnerable to anguish as a teenager, he progressively garners a more heroic stance as the narrative continues and he practices for extended periods in retreat. By contrast, in *Spiraling Vine of Faith*, miracle tales constitute the entirety of its narration for two "extremely turbulent" decades from 1959 to 1978, and it makes no mention of her practicing in secret, even through local oral sources suggest as much. Either Pema Ösal Thaye did not have access to those sources, being from Serta rather than her homeland of Markhok in Padma County, or he chose to differentiate their hagiographic portraits in this way. In their respective namthars, Pema Ösal Thaye highlights different facets of their experience coming of age in the Maoist period, showing Namtrul Rinpoche surviving under the protective care of ḍākinīs and maturing into a realized master through diligent practice, and focusing on miracle tales in which Tāre Lhamo repeatedly comes to the rescue of her community in moments of crisis.

Alternative Frames

Compared with other Tibetan sources, Pema Ösal Thaye's framing of the period as the result of collective karma is by no means standard; nor is the way he presents Tāre Lhamo in heroic terms working wonders for the benefit of her local community. Namthars for other prominent tertöns from the region—such as Khenpo Jigme Phuntsok (1933–2004) of Larung Buddhist Academy in Serta and Kusum Lingpa (1934–2009), whose monastery, Pal Lhundrup Thubten Chökor Ling, lies in Gabde County of Golok—each have a distinct way to frame the period and narrative approach to the protagonist during those decades. In the namthar of Khenpo Jigme Phuntsok, his disciple and successor Khenpo Tsultrim Lodrö marks the period discreetly as one of "great change" ('pho 'gyur chen po) starting in 1959, when the great Khenpo was twenty-six years old.[79] Thereafter

Tsultrim Lodrö recounts how he evaded capture and remained hidden in the mountains with a small group of disciples, continuing to teach and practice throughout the period. The most well-known miracle tale, recounted in detail, relates how the authorities arrived to escort Khenpo Jigme Phuntsok to a struggle session but were frightened off by his appearance, since his head had miraculously swollen, and it appeared to them as if he had a terrible disease. On another occasion, he was taken to prison but immediately released for reasons no one could discern. While such miracles were directed at the great Khenpo's own safety, the title of his namthar, *Medicine to Heal Faith* (*Dad pa'i gsos sman*), calls attention to the role of contemporary namthar in restoring faith by demonstrating the continuity of the Buddhist teachings in the lives of those eminent masters who survived the Maoist period.

In the namthar of Kusum Lingpa, known locally as Pema Tumpo, the situation is different, since he spent many years in prison.[80] The hagiographer, Abu Karlo, introduces the period allegorically as a terrible storm with fierce winds amassing clouds that blackened the radiant sky. He recounts how the blameless were falsely accused of crimes and how Kusum Lingpa (then in his mid-twenties) was condemned to many years in prison and hard labor. If there is a miracle to be found, it is in Kusum Lingpa's demeanor, which his namthar insists continued to exude joy and lucidity despite his circumstances. Abu Karlo emphasizes that Kusum Lingpa never broke his bodhisattva vow and managed to continue to teach and practice in secret, even revealing a significant body of treasure texts. His healing powers and generosity to the sick and destitute are mentioned, though the details of specific occasions are not recounted. In these comparative examples, drawn from third-person accounts of male tertöns from Tāre Lhamo's region and generation (though both were several years older than her), we hear a different type of story, one that emphasizes their means of survival and the vibrancy of their practice during this period in similar terms to the account of Namtrul Rinpoche discussed above.

For comparative purposes, it is instructive to consider the namthar of another female master from this generation, Do Dasal Wangmo (b. 1928),[81] who, like Tāre Lhamo, came from a family steeped in treasure revelation. Do Dasal Wangmo is the great-granddaughter of the tertön Do Khyentse Yeshe Dorje (1800–66) and the only surviving member of his family lineage (*gdung rgyud*). Since the 1980s, she has served as a medical doctor and teacher in Dartsedo, a main entry point onto the Tibetan plateau from Chengdu, as well as in other locations in Kandze Prefecture. Do Dasal Wangmo grew up in Minyak, where she studied religious and secular subjects at Palri Monastery, including astrology and medicine. Although her mother tried to persuade her to marry and continue the family lineage, she became a nun at the age of twenty-two and subsequently trained at Dzogchen Monastery outside of Dege. The teachings and empowerments she received there and elsewhere in her youth are given in detail in her namthar, titled simply *The Liberation of Do Dasal Wangmo*. During the 1960s, like Tāre Lhamo, she was consigned to manual labor, such as caring for livestock and clearing roads. Her hagiographer, Thubten Chödar, makes explicit mention of the hardships that Do Dasal Wangmo underwent while characterizing her as unharmed by them: "Remaining as a holy person, since she was someone who realized the equality of saṃsāra and nirvāṇa, how could she be harmed by baseless, illusory things?"[82] Otherwise, he says little about this period.

Miracles do not play a significant role in Do Dasal Wangmo's namthar, apart from auspicious signs that accompanied her birth and her early visionary propensities. Mention is made of her serving as a spirit medium in her youth, but only one instance is recounted. Overall, Thubten Chödar downplays any supernatural features of her life and includes a curious tangent about whether dragons exist scientifically after stating that she saw a dragon emerge from a well at a Gesar shrine in Dege. Instead, he foregrounds Do Dasal Wangmo's exertion in treating patients during her adult career as well as her religious teachings at select monasteries and efforts to publish the works of great masters from her family's tantric lineage. In this way, her namthar more closely resembles third-person accounts of the lives of earlier elite Tibetan women, like Chökyi Drönma and Mingyur Paldrön, which focus on their worldly accomplishments and activities, including their teaching careers, institution building, and publication efforts.

As another point of comparison, in Pema Ösal Thaye's own writings outside of publications under government auspices, he frames the period of 1959–78 in a different way. For example, in a locally produced pamphlet about a sacred site in Gyalrong, which contains a brief biography (in a dozen pages) of a khandroma known simply as Khandro Rinpoche (b. 1954), Pema Ösal Thaye marks the onset of the socialist transformation of Tibetan areas in more overt terms:

A foreign army came to the fore and instituted democratic reforms. Much agitation proliferated, such as the Cultural Revolution and so forth, leading to religious figures' imprisonment. On account of the various disturbances of the times such as the need for manual labor, those who practised the holy dharma became as rare as stars in the daytime.[83]

This more overt statement does not feature the collusion between the genre of namthar and self-censorship apparent in *Spiraling Vine of Faith*, nor the euphemistic framing of this time in the lives of Khenpo Jigme Phuntsok and Kusum Lingpa.[84] In contrast to his hagiographic portrait of Tāre Lhamo and perhaps due to her younger age, Pema Ösal Thaye depicts Khandro Rinpoche during the Cultural Revolution as a teenager remaining faithful to her religious conviction by reciting the mantra *Oṃ maṇi padme hūṃ* while doing nomadic chores such as threshing barley, milking cattle, and collecting dung for fuel. According to his brief account, Khandro Rinpoche only received religious training after the onset of economic and cultural liberalization, studying with Khenpo Munsel during the 1980s while married and raising a family, and only later in life became a teacher in her own right, establishing a retreat center at the Vairocana Cave in Gyalrong in 2003. For these reasons, the narration of a contemporaneous khandroma, even by the same author, reads quite differently.

As a final point of comparison, there are numerous other miracle tales associated with Tāre Lhamo as recorded by Rigdzin Dargye in his new, unpublished version of her life.[85] His manuscript remains close to oral accounts by elders in her homeland and references the names of specific families and individuals who would only be known to a local audience. In one such account, when three local families were gathered in black tents in a valley near Tsimda Monastery to collect medicinal herbs, dark clouds gathered in preparation for a hailstorm. As Rigdzin Dargye narrates the scene:

In a wrathful manner, the Supreme Khandro menacingly addressed the gods, demons, and humans of the whole of China, Tibet, and Mongolia: "What do you need as proof? None of you can rival me." Fierce hail fell all around the surrounding area, but at the place where the households and livestock were gathered, not even one hailstone fell even though the sky remained black. Those present were amazed and gained confident faith.[86]

Like the miracles included in *Spiraling Vine of Faith*, this tale showcases Tāre Lhamo's heightened agency in addressing a local dilemma. However, given that the threat of hail is a perennial concern among Tibetan nomads and not specific to the Maoist period, it could not effectively serve to narrate cultural trauma. In oral accounts, miracles tend to be personal in nature and also reflect perennial concerns, as when a childhood friend told stories of losing her yak herd and later her son, requesting Tāre Lhamo to intercede both times on her behalf. The first time, Tāre Lhamo performed some protection rituals and burned incense, and two days later, the entire herd came home of their own accord. The second time, when her childhood friend lost both her son and the herd, she panicked and prayed to Tāre Lhamo, calling out to her by a nickname, "Aze, please help me—I cannot find my son!" When she finally returned home, her son and the herd of yaks were waiting there.

Local Tibetans that I interviewed spoke in personal terms of gifts they received from Tāre Lhamo, advice or prophecies that she had delivered at their request, and small-scale rituals she had performed on their behalf. One woman from Jigdral County told me that she walked twenty kilometers to a public empowerment in order to seek out Tāre Lhamo to perform prayers and the transference ('pho ba) of consciousness for her father, who had just passed away. Though personally significant, perhaps such accounts lack a public character or a grand enough scale for inclusion in the authorized version of her namthar. Instead, Pema Ösal Thaye chose to focus on salvific miracles, broadly legible in Buddhist terms as signs of compassion and tantric prowess and specifically situated in the two decades from 1959 to 1978. Through such tales, he crafted a masterful narrative of tantric heroism within this period of collective trauma. Given notable differences among the hagiographic representations of other Buddhist masters, both male and female, in roughly the same generation and region, we can conclude that the representation of Tāre Lhamo as a tantric heroine in *Spiraling Vine of Faith* is not simply the result of the available material and not reducible to prevalent norms for representing the period. While sharing a concern with other namthars in demonstrating the continuity of Buddhism through the lives of surviving masters, *Spiraling Vine of Faith* is distinctive in its emphasis on miracle tales in order to craft a redemptive narrative of the Maoist period.

Making Sense of Miracles

In his use of miracles, Pema Ösal Thaye emphasizes the endurance of a shared interpretive schema among Tibetans rooted in Buddhist faith. As portrayed in *Spiraling Vine of Faith*, Tāre Lhamo remained the "supreme khandro" despite being consigned to manual labor, and in the eyes of witnesses to her many miracles, she had an ongoing ability to transcend circumstances at will. This is vividly illustrated in an episode that takes place while Tāre Lhamo is gathering wood, loading it onto wild yaks, and constructing a pen for them.

> [On] yet another [occasion], having gathered eighteen measures of wood earlier in the day, she was able to load them onto yaks who never before had been burdened with a load. At the time, she appeared fatigued by effort. [However,] while constructing a pen for livestock, [Tāre Lhamo lifted] a boulder that could not be carried by eighteen and added it to the [stone] wall, leaving her handprint on it. [This was] perceived in common by all.[87]

This is the only episode in her namthar recounting the type of activities that must have filled those long and arduous years for Tāre Lhamo. No more is said. We only learn that she performed a minor miracle in the midst of backbreaking work. Even so, the tale suggests that something more extraordinary is afoot: though appearing to be fatigued, she surmounts the predicament with supramundane powers.

Placing a handprint in rock is a stock miracle in Tibetan hagiographic literature but takes on new meaning here. The Tibetan and Himalayan landscape is scattered with impressions in rock, identified as the handprints and footprints of great tantric masters over the centuries. What gives Tāre Lhamo's act new significance? First and foremost, the tale suggests an opposition between how she appeared during the activities of everyday life and her capacity for action as a living ḍākinī in the eyes of Tibetans. Although she may have displayed the fatigue of an ordinary person performing manual labor, *Spiraling Vine of Faith* champions the underlying potential of her supramundane powers when she lifts a boulder by herself that a group of eighteen could not lift together, then leaves her handprint in rock. The triumphalism of this scene lies in its unequivocal assertion of the enduring agency of Buddhist masters and hence the validity of a Buddhist episteme under attack in the Maoist period.

This story is almost certainly one that circulated at the time, and I heard a different version of it orally in which the narrator emphasized that the imprint of all ten of her fingers could be clearly seen in the rock.[88] The assumption so often in the study of hagiography is that miracles represent late additions to the life of a saint accrued over time as legends pile up and pilgrimage sites proliferate. But there is another way to understand miracles if we acknowledge that these stories sometimes circulate in close proximity to events, which I believe to be the case here. Miracles could be understood as a *shared interpretation of events* that imbues a saint's activities with special meaning.

In the episode above and others, *Spiraling Vine of Faith* presents this very stance in claiming the veracity of the miracle. Pema Ösal Thaye uses the phrase "perceived in common by all," which more literally could be translated: "it was established as a common perception in all" (*kun la mthun snang du grub*). This phrase is repeated at the end of several episodes, through which the text itself suggests that miracles are established by a consensus on what was witnessed. Although expressions of amazement (*ngo mtshar*) are common in the genre of namthar, the specific phrase used by Pema Ösal Thaye—emphasizing their shared perception or interpretation—may reflect a modernist impulse. Instead of making a truth claim, just as Thubten Chödar pauses to ponder the empirical existence of a dragon, Pema Ösal Thaye stakes the miracles' validity on the testimony of witnesses. There is also another way to think about the deployment of this phrase. To regard something as a miracle is to see it within a shared interpretive schema, whereby the actions of a Buddhist master carry an aura of sanctity, authority, and efficacy. In the context of attempts by the Chinese Communist Party to awaken class consciousness and force Tibetans to confess the evils of the "old society," miracle tales highlight their persistence in interpreting events through a Buddhist episteme.

Indeed, *Spiraling Vine of Faith* insists that Tāre Lhamo's identity as a khandroma and emanation of Yeshe Tsogyal was never effaced, and the same claim is made for other religious figures. In another episode, she encounters the tertön Do-ngag Tenpe Nyima engaged in manual labor in the vicinity of Banak Gompa, no doubt as part of a work team forced to do agricultural labor. The namthar cleverly avoids this association and states that he appears to be plowing. What he is *actually* doing is revealing an earth treasure, which he offers to Tāre Lhamo, saying: "In a former life in Tibet, you were Yeshe Tsogyal, who satisfied the king as his consort. . . . From the coincidence of having tamed the ground and negative emotions, you will meet with supreme knowledge and treasures. How wondrous!"[89] In this statement, Tāre Lhamo is prophesized to be a tertön, based on her previous lifetime as Yeshe Tsogyal, and given a treasure as token of her future vocation. In this tale and others, a Buddhist explanation of events is asserted in direct opposition to the attempts by state policy to undermine the status of religious figures through struggle sessions and reform through labor. *Spiraling Vine of Faith* contrasts the outer appearance of Do-ngag Tenpe Nyima plowing the field with the "real" purport of his activities, which is to reveal a treasure, a teaching or relic connected to Tibet's imperial past. Once again, the memory of this period is reinscribed by asserting interpretive control over the events of recent history.

As a corollary, these miracle tales draw attention to how Tāre Lhamo has functioned for others, illustrating how Tibetans perceived her during this period, rather than necessarily what she herself felt and did. One of the clearest cases is an occasion recounted in *Spiraling Vine of Faith*, when Tāre Lhamo appeared in the sky to a reincarnate lama in order to predict his impending release from prison.

> One time, when the incarnate lama, Rigdzin Sang-ngak Lingpa, was in prison in Serta, Khandro Rinpoche came before him in the sky by means of a magical emanation . . . and prophesied, "Not long from now, you will be free from jail and we will meet." Later, in accordance with that prophecy, he was released from prison like the sun freed from clouds.[90]

In this passage, Tāre Lhamo is depicted iconically as a ḍākinī in a visionary apparition in the sky before Rigdzin Sang-ngak Lingpa (alias Sera Yangtrul). Her form and function in this episode are similar to female deities that appear elsewhere in *The Spiraling Vine of Faith* as consoling figures, uttering prophecies to assuage difficult circumstances. Here Tāre Lhamo, refracted through Rigdzin Sang-ngak Lingpa's vision, is shown predicting events and thereby also effecting his release. The episode suggests that she served as a beacon of hope, heralding a good outcome in what appeared to be a hopeless situation.[91]

In its portrayal of Tāre Lhamo as a source of solace to others during these turbulent decades, *Spiraling Vine of Faith* contests Communist propaganda of the Maoist period that denounced religious elites of the "old society" as feudal exploiters. Without any explicit comment or criticism, the genre of namthar is able to position her in such a way as to resist the Communist worldview being coercively imposed on Tibetans during the period represented. The miracle tales consistently represent Tāre Lhamo in Buddhist terms as imbued with compassion and endowed with the power to intervene on behalf of others to mitigate their suffering. Instead of bearing witness to the hardships that she and others endured, as a testimonial would, *Spiraling Vine of Faith* affirms the heightened agency of a Buddhist master in the eyes of Tibetans by insisting that her miracles were perceived in common by all present.The circulation of miracle tales at the time would have been acts of resistance to Communist propaganda, reeducation campaigns, and struggle sessions, which sought to force Tibetans to repudiate their allegiance to traditional authorities, particularly religious ones. Gathered, selected, and compiled into a namthar decades later, miracle tales evince and bolster a shared Buddhist episteme in relation to a period of collective trauma in which Tibetan culture was vociferously under attack.

I have argued thus far that *Spiraling Vine of Faith* forges a redemptive narrative through miracle tales that symbolically restructure the memory of trauma by inserting the compassionate intervention of a tantric heroine. But there are still other ways *Spiraling Vine of Faith* creates a redemptive narrative, which have to do with a continuity embodied by Tāre Lhamo herself and other Buddhist masters who survived these turbulent decades.

Amid the Ruins

Remarkably, *Spiraling Vine of Faith* depicts Tāre Lhamo emerging from the Maoist period unscathed. This presents a striking contrast to scar literature, which brought to light the physical and psychological wounds associated with the social upheaval and violence of the Cultural Revolution. As a namthar, *Spiraling Vine of Faith* is not particularly concerned with exposing the excesses of the period, except to the extent that they are redressed by Tāre Lhamo's miracles. Instead, Pema Ösal Thaye announces summarily in several episodes that her integrity remained intact. In similar terms to how Abu Karlo represents Kusum Lingpa, she is shown to have an unwavering commitment to Buddhist values. There is much at stake in this representation. The revitalization of Buddhism in Tibetan areas of the PRC relied on the survival of lineage holders with uncorrupted vows, who could transmit anew tantric rituals and esoteric teachings after their public practice had been forbidden for almost twenty years. A reflection of this concern, establishing the continuity of Buddhist vows and teachings has been an important aspect of contemporary namthars like those of Khenpo Jigme Phuntsok and Do Dasal Wangmo, surveyed earlier. Despite their diverse narrative frames and strategies for representing this period, these sources emphasize the continuity of the vows, practice, faith, and realization of their eminent Buddhist protagonists.

One striking episode showcases Tāre Lhamo's commitment to Buddhist principles, even at the cost of her own life. This is the only occasion recorded in *Spiraling Vine of Faith* when she herself needed rescuing. As previously discussed, during the Cultural Revolution, a local policy apparently required each citizen to kill a pest, either a dog or pika, and deliver its corpse to the authorities.[92] This policy must have been particularly offensive to those who had previously dedicated their lives to Buddhist practice, since to kill (even a rodent) would mean breaking one of the foundational precepts of Buddhist ethics. Here is Tāre Lhamo's reaction and the resolution to her dilemma:

According to a policy during the Cultural Revolution, [the people] were ordered to kill dogs and pikas. There was no way out of it. When [Tāre Lhamo heard] the order to kill, fierce compassion arose toward all sentient beings without bias, based on the abundant strength of benevolence in her mind. The Supreme Khandro thought, "I would rather die myself than kill those [animals]." Following from that thought, during an agitated [night of] sleep, the tantric protectress Dorje Rachigma appeared [to her] and said: "Don't be sad. Before morning, I will provide a dog corpse for you to present. It is not yet time [for you] to die! Since you must accomplish great benefit for the dharma and beings, you are not allowed to die." [The protectress] stamped her foot, and the ground quaked, reverberating throughout the area and rousing everyone from sleep. In that way, according to prophecy, the next morning there was a dog corpse, and she was freed from the horror of that policy.[93]

In this tale, Tāre Lhamo retains a heroic quality; she is ready to die rather than violate the Buddhist precept against killing. There is no trace of desperation and no cry for help, as in the comparable episode, discussed in the previous chapter, from the excerpted autobiography of Sera Khandro.[94] Recall that Sera Khandro contemplated casting away her female body as a runaway teenager, ill-treated upon her arrival in Golok. Whereas she articulated a failure of confidence in her ability to be of benefit, Tāre Lhamo is shown filled with compassion and concern for the lives of others. The horror of the event, as depicted, is not the suffering that she would endure but the idea that she would be compelled to cause others harm.

Though she never cries out for help, in a dream that night, the female protective deity Dorje Rachigma appears to Tāre Lhamo and promises to produce a resolution in the form of a dog's corpse (presumably fake). Moreover, in an affirmation of Tāre Lhamo's value to her local community, Dorje Rachigma forbids her to die. The rationale anticipates her activities in the 1980s and '90s to "accomplish great benefit for the dharma and beings." To punctuate this point, Dorje Rachigma stamps her foot, thereby producing an earthquake that radiates throughout the region and results in a dog corpse. In the end, Tāre Lhamo is released from breaking an ethical precept in order to fulfill the dreaded policy. Though she is on the receiving end of a miracle for a change, this episode portrays her unwavering commitment to Buddhist principles under duress, even at the cost of her own life.

The inclusion of this episode in *Spiraling Vine of Faith* serves to highlight her untarnished integrity, never compromised by the policies of the Maoist period. The same point is made more explicitly in a statement toward the end of the period: "Unsullied by the grime of broken *samaya* and with the swift potency of blessings, [her] many miracles persisted, said to be the lingering breath of the mother ḍākinīs."[95] This is a retrospective deflection of agency to the ḍākinīs. But it affirms once again that Tāre Lhamo never reneged on her Buddhist vows despite reeducation campaigns and struggle sessions in those two decades of turmoil.

The significance of this passage must be read within a reconfiguration of the tantric vow of *samaya* (*dam tshig*) in the post-Mao era. The vow consists of, among other things, a pledge of loyalty to one's teacher and lineage,[96] and its purity is a prerequisite to receiving (and of course bestowing) tantric initiations. In the 1980s, two of the foremost Buddhist masters still remaining on the Tibetan plateau, the Paṇchen Lama and Khenpo Jigme Phuntsok,

advocated not bestowing tantric initiations and esoteric teachings on anyone who had engaged in serious anti-Buddhist activities during the Cultural Revolution and thereby had broken their samaya vow.[97] As depicted,
Tāre Lhamo's pure samaya was instrumental to accessing the blessings of
ḍākinīs, which in turn empowered her many miracles. Thus her miraculous feats are linked not only to the agency of ḍākinīs but also to her own
steadfastness in upholding Buddhist principles. Tacitly, this statement also
provides a retrospective affirmation of Tāre Lhamo's legitimacy in transmitting tantric rituals and esoteric teachings that she received prior to the
prohibition on religious practice in Golok.

A provocative episode in *Spiraling Vine of Faith* toward the end of this
period implies that Tāre Lhamo emerged unharmed in other ways as well.
The episode involves a house set on fire by lightning. It suggests a sudden, unexpected event in which she emerged unscathed amid the ruins, and
I will read it allegorically as a representation of trauma:

> One time, when the Khandro herself was in bed, suddenly there was a fierce
> hailstorm. A bolt of lightning struck. The whole house collapsed into a heap of
> ashes, including [her] bed and mat. Dousing her clothing in water, [Tāre Lha-
> mo's] indestructible body remained without any harm whatsoever. All were
> amazed.[98]

If read allegorically, the storm could represent the Cultural Revolution as a
sudden jolt that razed everything to ashes. A storm had already been used
as an allegory for the Cultural Revolution in a work of Tibetan scar literature titled "Forest After the Rainstorm" (*Char shul gyi nags tshal*).[99] In this
case, Tāre Lhamo is depicted as impervious to harm even though trapped
in a burning house with everyone else. The implication is that although
she underwent the same hardships as others during the Maoist period, she
survived *without a scar*. Just as "the scar" in scar literature represents both
physical and psychological trauma, it would be fair to surmise that the reference to her "indestructible body" suggests a comparable unyielding state
of mind.[100] This is not too much of an interpretive leap, since *Spiraling Vine
of Faith* has already shown Tāre Lhamo to be unwavering in her commitment
to Buddhist vows and ethical principles.

In the context of narrating cultural trauma, Tāre Lhamo's ability to survive a disaster without harm has significant implications. What remained

after the Cultural Revolution was the untarnished integrity of Buddhist masters who survived unscathed and maintained their Buddhist principles and practice. After visible cultural symbols were destroyed, these religious figures—though labeled as "black hats" and subjected to struggle sessions— nonetheless remained living symbols of Buddhist ideals. As in the tale of the burning house, out of the ashes, something remains. And it is embodied in *Spiraling Vine of Faith* through Tāre Lhamo herself, who stands for the resilience of Buddhism as an dauntless heroine in troubled times and an untarnished vessel for esoteric transmissions.

Stories that have circulated outside *Spiraling Vine of Faith* also construct Tāre Lhamo as unscarred, even when subjected to physical abuse. According to an elder in Padma County, once during a struggle session Tāre Lhamo was stripped naked and left outside in the snow overnight with hands and feet bound. Rather than succumbing to hypothermia or frostbite, she engaged in the tantric practice of *tummo* or "inner heat" (Skt.: *caṇḍālī*, Tib.: *gtum mo*) and emerged unharmed.[101] Recall another oral account of a struggle session, mentioned in the previous chapter, in which her bare chest was placed on a hot wood-burning stove, yet she was able to rouse compassion for the greater suffering of others within Buddhist cosmology, specifically those reborn in hell.[102] These are significant stories for narrating trauma, suggesting that she retained mastery and resisted victimhood with its associated states of panic, helplessness, and dissociation. In the second account, as narrated, she had no burn marks. The implication of stories like these, both in and outside of *Spiraling Vine of Faith*, is that Tāre Lhamo retained no scar or wound, physical or mental, as the result of the hardships of those turbulent decades.

I would suggest that Tāre Lhamo's lack of scars is crucial to how *Spiraling Vine of Faith* constructs a redemptive narrative out of the chaos and trauma of the Maoist period. Within the devastation that forms the backdrop of her miracles, her namthar focuses on what remained intact and unharmed, namely Tāre Lhamo herself. By virtue of the divinization of her agency, Tāre Lhamo is depicted in a state of mastery throughout this period, able to transcend forces of nature and maintain a compassionate intent in service of others. In each episode, she rescues the day when those around her are in a state of despair or panic. Tāre Lhamo is always the heroine and never the victim. This acknowledges the historical conditions of the Maoist period yet asserts a Buddhist triumphalism in the midst of it.

Not Yet Time to Die

Tāre Lhamo not only survived unscathed but also is depicted as capable of dispelling obstacles and extending the lives of other Buddhist masters who remained. In 1978, she revealed a treasure called "The Indestructible Knot: A Long-Life Sādhana" (*Tshe sgrub rdo rje'i rgya mdud*), a ritual she bestowed on local religious figures in order to extend their lives.[103] This represents the first record of her treasures that she publicly bestowed upon others, and it is significant that the group consists of Nyingma masters who became leaders in the Buddhist revival in Golok, including Khenpo Jigme Phuntsok, Dodrupchen Thubten Trinle Palzangpo, Lama Rigdzin Nyima, Khenpo Munsel, Khenpo Chöthun, Payul Karma Chagme, Tsopu Dorlo, Shukjung Lama Tsedzi, Getse Khenpo Wangchen, Gartrul Rinpoche, Rigdzin Sang-ngak Lingpa, and Akong Khenpo Lozang Dorje. This is a virtual who's who of Golok reincarnate lamas and cleric-scholars who survived the Maoist period, and *Spiraling Vine of Faith* refers to them collectively as "defenders of the teachings and beings" (*bstan 'gro'i dpung gnyen*).[104] This unusual designation appears to highlight the historical context of Tibetan culture under siege. By conducting long-life ceremonies on their behalf, Tāre Lhamo proved to be a resource for other Buddhist leaders, and she is shown to have a special talent for extending life. Moreover, she is showcased in a ritual role that places her on par with these figures.

Spiraling Vine of Faith also credits Tāre Lhamo with the ability to revive what seems to be on the verge of death. In another episode, a local girl lay on her deathbed from severe illness, and her family brought a horse to Tāre Lhamo in order to request funeral rites to be done on her behalf. However, she refused the horse, pronouncing that the girl would not die:

> Around the same time, a girl named Soza Dröpo fell severely ill and seemed certain to meet with death. A stallion was brought to the Supreme Khandro [in order to request the transference of consciousness]. [She stated:] "It is not yet the time for her to die" and returned the horse [to the family]. People say because of this, the girl survived.[105]

Implied in this account is not just that Tāre Lhamo had the ability to prophesize the future but also that her declaration, "It is not yet the time for her to die," made it so. This interpretation is expressed in the conclusion of the tale—"people say because of this the girl survived"—which indicates that locals attributed the outcome to her prophecy.

The implication of this tale, from one vantage point, is that Tāre Lhamo could effect the survival of a dying person, a power reminiscent of Yeshe Tsogyal's well-known talent for raising the dead. In the treasure tradition, prophecy serves as performative speech with illocutionary force.[106] In other words, prophecies do not so much predict the future; *they make it so.* This represents a significant form of agency. From another vantage point, if read allegorically, the tale implies that Tāre Lhamo had the power to revive whatever seemed to be on the verge of death or destruction. This is a possible allegory for revitalization, not merely of the girl Soza Drӧpo but of Buddhism in Golok at the end of the Maoist period.

The placement of this tale is telling. It comes immediately after the declaration of the onset of the *yangdar,* a neologism that means "renewed propagation" (*yang dar*), echoing a standard and long-standing Buddhist structuring of Tibetan history into different periods of the propagation of Buddhism. The "early propagation" (*snga dar*) refers to the imperial period (seventh to ninth centuries), when the Tibetan empire controlled vast tracts of Central Asia and religious kings, retrospectively identified with celestial bodhisattvas, sponsored the translation of Buddhist canonical texts from Indic languages (primarily Sanskrit) into Tibetan. Tibetan histories generally characterize the subsequent collapse of the empire in the ninth century and the consequent political fragmentation as a dark era of decline precipitated by the persecution of Buddhism.[107] Beginning in the late tenth century, a "later propagation" (*phyi dar*) ensued as Tibetans once again traversed the Himalayan mountain range in search of Buddhist texts and masters in India. Some Amdo and Golok authors refer to this as an "intermediate propagation" (*bar dar*) and assign the "later propagation" to the fifteenth century forward, in connection with the later flowering of Buddhism in those regions.[108]

In this schema, the term *yangdar* signals a third (or fourth) major diffusion of Buddhism on the Tibetan plateau. Echoing the standard periodization of Tibetan history it draws an implicit parallel between the dark age after the persecution of Buddhism in the ninth century and the devastation to Buddhist institutions during the Maoist period.[109] The *Cultural History of Golok,* for example, uses a "renewed propagation of the teachings" (*bstan pa yang dar*) in this way. This source describes "a great decline in the Buddha's teachings" starting in the earth dog year (1958–59) that lasts more than two decades. In turn, it dates the yangdar to the iron monkey year (1980–81), beginning a new period "to rekindle once again the ember of [Buddhist] teachings in this land."[110] By encompassing recent historical events in a Buddhist framework, contemporary Tibetan authors can implicitly critique the Maoist period and also champion the reassertion of Tibetan culture and identity in Buddhist terms.

As previously mentioned, *Spiraling Vine of Faith* closes these two turbulent decades with a statement heralding the revitalization of Buddhism, proclaiming: "In the meritorious sky of the Land of Snow, the youthful sun of the [Buddhist] teachings dawned in a renewed propagation."[111] The tale of Tāre Lhamo restoring Soza Drönpo to life comes immediately thereafter. When it begins, stating "around the same time," the reference is to the inauguration of the yangdar. Pema Ösal Thaye links these two passages with the conjunction *dang* (meaning "and"), omitted from my translation since I present the passages separately. The gist of this combination would be something like: The sun of Buddhism rose in Tibet to be propagated once again, and Tāre Lhamo prevented a severely ill girl from dying by stating that it was not yet time for her to die. To further interpret this, applying the allegorical reading suggested above, the gist would be more like: The possibility to revitalize Buddhism emerged in Tibet, and Tāre Lhamo was able to revive what was on the verge of dying by declaring it so.

The illocutionary force of Tāre Lhamo's prophetic voice gives one of the final passages of *Spiraling Vine of Faith* its redemptive flourish. A series of her visions are included at the end of her namthar, after the main action concludes and Pema Ösal Thaye refers the reader to Namtrul Rinpoche's namthar, *Jewel Garland*, for an account of their activities together from 1980 forward. In one of these visions, dated to 1985, Tāre Lhamo and Namtrul Rinpoche are decked out in crowns and robes, prepared to bestow a tantric initiation. They arrive at a mountain with a turquoise lake at its base and a fruit-laden tree at its center, an image of fertility and regeneration. There together they proclaim that the time is ripe to revitalize Buddhist teachings and practices as follows:

Ah ho!
A sign to propagate the undamaged Buddhist teachings,
A sign to open the gates of profound treasures as speech,

A sign to sustain the practice of great secret mantra . . .
A sign to awaken karma, aspiration, and the entrustment,
A sign to reverse the chaos of degenerate times,
A sign to establish the welfare of all mother beings,
A sign to pacify conditions of plague and strife. . . .[112]

This declaration of signs has a prophetic cast, indicating the reversal of degenerate times. Within the treasure tradition, the revelation of treasures is attributed the power to intervene in order to restore the Buddhist teachings and the welfare of beings.[113] The awakening of aspiration and entrustment specifically refers to activating the latent propensity for treasure revelation in Tāre Lhamo and Namtrul Rinpoche as a couple.

This passage adds a redemptive flourish to the namthar, because it heralds the revitalization of Buddhism in no uncertain terms. It suggests that despite the nearly two-decade hiatus in Buddhist practice, the desecration of Buddhist sacra, and the closure of and damage to monasteries, the Buddhist teachings themselves were never destroyed. From the "undamaged Buddhist teachings" (rgyal bstan nyams med), the rest could be reconstituted. This likely refers to treasures, mentioned thereafter in this passage and generally said to lie buried in the Tibetan landscape or in the minds of the tertöns, impervious to the vagaries of history until they are needed to help restore Buddhism. Along these lines, in the preface to Cloud Offerings to Delight the Vidyādharas and Ḍākinīs, which contains their namthars, Pema Ösal Thaye credits their treasure revelations with the capacity to "heal the damage of degenerate times" (snyigs dus kyi rgud pa gsos), reiterating the language in the couple's own correspondence.[114] These triumphant lines mark the conclusion of Spiraling Vine of Faith, since the activities of Tāre Lhamo and Namtrul Rinpoche are recounted in his namthar, Jewel Garland. To declare the revitalization of Buddhism in such terms is to speak it into existence.

Spiraling Vine of Faith offers a distinctive way to narrate cultural trauma. Unlike exile testimonials and scar literature, which expose the wounds of the Maoist period, Pema Ösal Thaye's work purposefully constructs Tāre Lhamo as a tantric heroine who survived two decades of chaos without physical scars or damage to the integrity of her Buddhist commitments. Throughout this period, the namthar depicts her unambiguously in a state of mastery through omitting the very details that are the mainstay of testimonial literature: personal misfortunes, the hardships of forced labor, brutality during struggle sessions, and general conditions in Tibetan areas. While the namthars of her contemporaries emphasize their untarnished vows and continued practice, *Spiraling Vine of Faith* takes this one step further using the hagiographic trope of miracle tales in order to interject Tāre Lhamo as a heroine into the memory of traumatic events. This makes it possible to incorporate the devastation of those decades into a Buddhist master narrative that places Tibetans under the enduring compassionate protection of buddhas, bodhisattvas, and tantric masters.

Spiraling Vine of Faith thereby reinscribes the ideal of enlightened Buddhist masters as a central, active, and compassionate force in the lives of Tibetans, an ideal that was challenged by socialist condemnation of the "old society" in propagandist literature and through state policies that consigned former elites to prison or hard labor. This reinscription occurs in the very structure of the text. In each frame, Tāre Lhamo occupies center stage in an active role, creating the resolution to successive dilemmas. By contrast, victims and onlookers (for the most part unnamed) passively react, first with fear or despair to the crisis at hand and later with amazement to her miracle.

In episode after episode, the reader is positioned on the sidelines as witness to Tāre Lhamo's miracles. *Spiraling Vine of Faith* never encourages identification with Tāre Lhamo herself; after all, she has been presented as an emanation of female deities and Yeshe Tsogyal in person. She is thereby placed out of reach of ordinary folk as an exemplar and instead serves as an object of veneration by virtue of her illustrious antecedents and her salvific powers. The only footing left for the reader to assume is that of a bystander and witness, constituted within a mandalic framework as a potential beneficiary of her grace and at the periphery of the action.

Given its contemporary context, the hagiographic idealization of *Spiraling Vine of Faith* participates in the mandalization process described by Charlene Makley by positioning the reader among the faithful as witness to the wondrous deeds of Tāre Lhamo. Recall Makley's observation that stories about Buddhist masters have played and continue to play a key role in

cultural revitalization in Tibetan areas of the PRC since the 1980s by consti-
tuting Tibetan identity as "grounded in faith."[115] Indeed, faith (dad pa) can
be considered a leitmotif of namthar as a genre, and it is no coincidence
that the term appears in the title of Tāre Lhamo's hagiography, The Spiraling Vine of Faith.[116] The image of a "spiraling vine" ('khri shing), I was told by
one learned lama from Golok, is a standard metaphor for reliance. In the
context of a namthar, this metaphor implies the reliance of the faithful on
the compassion and blessings of a Buddhist master.[117]

In the opening verses of praise in Jewel Garland, Pema Ösal Thaye compares namthar to a seed planted in the field of faith: "In the field of faith
of fortunate beings without bias, I offer [this] namthar, unadorned by
hyperbole, as a seed that yields many fruits."[118] In this metaphor, faith
already exists, though it lies fallow, and the namthar plants a seed in
order for that faith to bear fruit. This is a powerful metaphor for reawakening faith in the post-Mao era through hagiographic accounts that show
how Buddhist teachings and lineages persisted through almost twenty
years of persecution in the very being of those surviving masters. Faith
serves more than one purpose; it is both faith in a Buddhist master and,
more broadly, allegiance to Buddhism and by extension, to Tibetan identity and culture.

In the process of crafting a potent and culturally specific form of narrating trauma, Spiraling Vine of Faith presents an idealized portrait of Tāre
Lhamo. I have argued that the omission of any discussion of her personal
hardships and misfortunes is crucial to how Pema Ösal Thaye narrates cultural trauma in a redemptive key. But this style of narration gives little sense
of the complexities of human agency within a Buddhist framework, not to
mention Tāre Lhamo herself as a Tibetan woman facing personal hardship
and the ravages of history. By crafting a hagiographic representation of her,
Spiraling Vine of Faith provides little information about the woman behind
the miracles.

Only through Tāre Lhamo's own voice in dialogue with Namtrul Rinpoche
do we get a much more complex picture of human agency at this critical juncture of recent Tibetan history. In their correspondence, exchanged between
1978 and 1980 at the cusp of economic and cultural liberalization, there is a
vision of agency that admits uncertainty and contingency while also claiming leverage over the unfolding of events in Buddhist terms—through ritual,
past life recollections, prophecy, and treasure revelation. These complexities

cannot be found in the third-person account of *Spiraling Vine of Faith*, which presents Tāre Lhamo unambiguously as a heroine with unfaltering mastery. For a more well-rounded picture, we turn to her correspondence with Namtrul Rinpoche in the next chapter, to their own voices and concerns as the future couple imagine their role together at this critical historical juncture. This will take us into the next phase of Tāre Lhamo's life, when *Spiraling Vine of Faith* leaves off, and integrate Namtrul Rinpoche more fully into our discussion.

THREE

Inseparable Companions
A Buddhist Courtship and Correspondence

DESPITE THE HARDSHIPS she had endured, by 1978, in her early forties, Tāre Lhamo felt optimistic enough to initiate a courtship and correspondence with Namtrul Rinpoche. In her opening letter, she proposed a shared future engaged in the revelation of treasures, esoteric teachings traced to Tibet's imperial past and understood to await them in the landscape of Golok and beyond. In somewhat cryptic language, the letter contains a prophecy delineating rituals and aspirations to be performed together at Nyenpo Yutse, one of the two main sacred mountain ranges of Golok, and predicts the site of a future revelation at Drakar Tredzong, a major pilgrimage site in Amdo with caves associated with the Nyingma progenitors Padmasambhava and Yeshe Tsogyal.[1] Accompanying the letter, she sent one of her own treasures, a sādhana or liturgical text dedicated to Yeshe Tsogyal.[2] This marked the beginning of an epistolary courtship cast in prophetic terms.

Over more than a year, Tāre Lhamo exchanged a total of fifty-six letters with Namtrul Rinpoche,[3] sent by secret messenger in batches along the arduous route separating them.[4] During this time, they only met during one extended visit, when Namtrul Rinpoche surreptitiously traveled to Markhok in 1979 to meet Tāre Lhamo and some of her close relatives.[5] Apart from what can be discerned in the letters themselves, we know little about what happened during this visit except that their efforts to forge a union intensified thereafter.[6] Movement across province borders was highly restricted, and the letters allude to Tāre Lhamo's difficulty gaining permission from the government and the consent of her relatives to leave her homeland. Risking possible censure, in early 1980,[7] she traveled with a small party across the border between Qinghai and Sichuan provinces to join Namtrul Rinpoche at Nyenlung, which served as their base for the next two decades traveling and teaching together.

Although the pretext for their courtship was the revelations of treasures, their correspondence also discloses the blossoming affection of a tantric couple. Alongside prophetic statements about their future revelations, the letters contain a plethora of amorous passages, as when Namtrul Rinpoche refers to Tāre Lhamo as dearer to him than his own eyes and heart or when she confesses to missing him one hundred (and even a thousand) times a day. The bond they developed had to do not only with awakening their visionary capacities as a couple but also with love, expressed as mutual affection, compatibility, and commitment. Throughout their correspondence, Tāre Lhamo and Namtrul Rinpoche convey in no uncertain terms their longing to be together and "converge in one household" (khang pa gcig tu 'dzoms).[8] For this reason, the collection could be deemed "love letters," the first of its nature to come to light in Tibetan literature.

As love letters, their exchanges abound in images of fertility and regeneration: thunder crackling, rain clouds bursting, sprouts shooting forth, lotus buds blooming, and bees circling to extract the nectar. In his reply to Tāre Lhamo's first letter, Namtrul Rinpoche depicts himself as a peacock dancing with delight at the "thunder" of her news, referring metaphorically to the prophecy contained therein.[9] This is, of course, an Indian image for fertility, heralding the monsoon and the season of love in which the peacocks dance to attract a mate. As he continues, Namtrul Rinpoche links fertility to the timeliness of treasure revelation: "Just as vegetation bursts forth when spurred by the seasons, / So too with the karmic inheritance of Padma's profound treasures."[10] In this couplet, the revelation of treasures is compared to lush vegetation bursting forth in the appropriate season. Given the historical context, the implication is that just as the fertility of spring follows the barrenness of winter, the revitalization of Buddhism follows its persecution due to a karmic inheritance or residue (las 'phro) from the distant past. This refers to the treasure teachings that Padmasambhava (here abbreviated Padma) and Yeshe Tsogyal are understood to have buried throughout the Tibetan and Himalayan landscape, to be revealed in times of degeneration and strife.

The exuberant tone of the letters is remarkable given the devastating chapter of history that they had just survived. Tāre Lhamo and Namtrul Rinpoche must have felt some reprieve as the Cultural Revolution came to a close with the death of Mao in 1976, since in the imagery of their correspondence, the season is spring—a time of new possibilities. In 1978, as Tāre Lhamo composed her first letter, the policy of "reform and opening" (*gaige kaifang*) was being inaugurated by Deng Xiaoping, though its effects would take several years to spread across China into Tibetan areas. This marked the end of Maoist revolutionary fervor and the beginning of liberalization in economic and cultural terms, which allowed public religious expression for the first time in almost twenty years.[11] In evoking springtime's renewal, Tāre Lhamo and Namtrul Rinpoche acknowledged the potential of this critical historical juncture and also gestured to the fecundity of courtship. A sense of exuberance circulates back and forth in the letters, which no doubt fueled their inspiration and awakened their visionary talents. For this reason, their correspondence provides a rare window into the prophetic terms in which Nyingma masters imagined the possibility of reviving Buddhism at the end of the Maoist period and also a unique vantage point through which to view the role of love, and affect more generally, in the process of revealing Tibetan treasures.[12]

In turning now to their correspondence, we proceed from a retrospective account of the Maoist period as narrated by a devoted disciple in *Spiraling Vine of Faith* to a prospective account in their own voices as the couple imagined their future activities in the post-Mao era. In her namthar, hagiographic idealization facilitates the symbolic restructuring of the events of recent history by focusing on the activities of a Buddhist heroine, while relegating the devastation of the Maoist period to the backdrop of her miraculous interventions. Their correspondence, by contrast, reveals the challenges the couple faced in an uncertain future, offering a more humanizing and multifaceted self-portrait in their own first-person voices. Yet because of this, we can discern their own ingenuity and creative response to changes in state policy by preparing through their epistolary courtship to play an active role in revitalizing Buddhism in Golok and beyond.

In exploring their more humanizing self-portraits, I am not proposing to read the letters as "transparent expressions of the private self."[13] Scholars of epistolary literature warn against such a reading, which takes letters to be unmediated expressions of a singular, cohesive self. Not only does Buddhist doctrine not accept such a view, but in their correspondence Tāre Lhamo and Namtrul Rinpoche construct a multiplicity of shared identities across lifetimes through their visionary recollections. Moreover, they invoke different registers and related authorial stances in negotiating the terms of their union. We can see this, for example, in modes of address: from formal gestures of praise and deference, related to their exalted incarnation status, to nicknames and terms of endearment though which they nurture a personal bond. To highlight the situated and fluid nature of their self-representation, I use the term "epistolary persona" to indicate the complex and relational identity that they construct in dialogue as they shift between registers and disclose various facets of themselves to each other.[14]

I am particularly interested in the role that gender and voice play in how Tāre Lhamo and Namtrul Rinpoche forged their partnership and sense of agency as a couple. Gender influences the subject positions they offer to each other, and their choice of different styles of versification shapes their self-representation. In what follows, I discuss the range of authorial voices and styles of versification that Tāre Lhamo and Namtrul Rinpoche marshal as they reconstruct a useable past through which to imagine an imminent future. I also situate their letters within Tibetan epistolary practices, cultural constraints on first-person expression, tantric practices involving sexuality, and folk conventions for articulating love. In this way, I illuminate how their correspondence provided the vehicle through which they created a lasting personal bond and launched their prophetic career together as tertöns or treasure revealers.

Gender and Epistolary Style

The multifaceted dimensions of this epistolary courtship are expressed in a rich array of styles that span the gamut of versification in Tibetan literature. Almost entirely in verse, the letters exchanged between Tāre Lhamo and Namtrul Rinpoche contain elements of ornate Indic-inspired poetry (*snyan ngag*), various styles of Tibetan folk songs (*dmangs glu*), and bardic verse (*sgrung glu*) evocative of the Gesar epic. As the styles shift, so do the authorial stances, rhetorical strategies in their self-representation, and content of their letters. In terms of content, the central themes include: prophecies about the location of treasures awaiting revelation, visionary recollections of their past lives as a couple, love songs expressing affection and their yearning to be together, pairings in the natural landscape indicating mutual compatibility, erotic imagery and references to the tantric rite of sexual union, and proclamations regarding the revitalization of Buddhism. In what I am calling the *interplay of love and destiny*, Tāre Lhamo and Namtrul Rinpoche shift between and synthesize the personal and prophetic aspects of their courtship.

There are at least four different modes in which these aspects interact and evolve in the correspondence. The first is an oscillation between the two, whereby a letter or section of a letter is primarily related to either their prophetic vocation as tertöns or the expression of personal sentiment. Here epistolary conventions and literary style play a key role in the way Tāre Lhamo and Namtrul Rinpoche construct their personae as a couple by alternating between various authorial stances. The second mode involves the development of a synergy whereby visionary recollections of their past lives elicit affective responses that strengthen their bond in this life. In turn, the affection shared between them encourages their visionary propensities and stimulates further past-life recollections and prophecies about the location of their treasures, thereby inaugurating the revelation process within the correspondence itself. The effect is to blur the boundary between love and destiny. In a third mode, they use folksy pairings of animals and their habitats, like a snow lion and its mountain abode, to depict their shared destiny in worldly terms and portray their personal bond as one of mutual compatibility and reliance. The fourth mode offers a final synthesis of the prophetic and personal in references to the tantric rite of sexual union and its role in treasure revelation.[15] This points beyond the correspondence itself to the consummation of their courtship and life together, sharing a single monastic seat, revealing treasures, and teaching side by side.

In the first mode, according to Tibetan epistolary conventions, the higher the stature of the addressee, the more ornate and honorific the praise and tone of the letter.[16] In his reply to Tāre Lhamo's first letter, Namtrul Rinpoche follows these conventions with such artfulness that he simultaneously expresses his high regard for her and shows off his own erudition and mastery of poetic forms. His letter is filled with praises of Tāre Lhamo delivered in elaborate metaphors and an ornate style. Following the Tibetan epistolary convention of opening a formal letter with praise and a deferential statement,[17] he begins with a verse of homage that invokes her identification with Yeshe Tsogyal and the female deities Samantabhadrī, Tārā, and Sarasvatī.

In the space of alpha-pure *dharmakāya*, Samantabhadrī,
In the realm of natural *saṃbhogakāya*, the mother Tāre,
Compassionate *nirmāṇakāya*, supreme goddess, the Lady of Speech,
Bear witness that the purport of aspirations by Yeshe Tsogyal—
[These] three aspects inseparable—be accomplished.

Before the *utpala* [lotus] at the ear of the celestial maiden,
Who arises as glorious among beings throughout space
From the sacred site, supreme Orgyan Khandro Ling,[18]
Like the ornament of sun and moon adorning unadorned space,

I bow down laden with the fruit of [my] news,
Like the supple stem of the verdant utpala flower,
In a radiant lake of liquid emerald jewels;
Or an unforgettable fruit tree, blooming undamaged
In a lake of karma, aspiration, and coincidence.[19]

Namtrul Rinpoche adds Tārā (as her namesake) to Tāre Lhamo's associations with female deities found in prophecies at her birth and later recounted in *Spiraling Vine of Faith,* and this allows him to create an elaborate gesture of deference. Invoking the standard iconography of Tārā, who holds a lotus stem in her left hand with the flower reaching to her ear, he imagines himself to be the lotus that bows to convey his news into her ear. His artful employment of epistolary conventions positions her in an elevated status from the outset of their relationship.

Namtrul Rinpoche's praise of her continues through the rest of the letter. After wishing for her good health, he praises the sādhana dedicated to Yeshe Tsogyal that Tāre Lhamo sent along with her initial letter and makes a formal request for her to teach widely. This corresponds to further conventions in a formal Tibetan letter, including an obligatory inquiry about the addressee's health and a petition or formal request.[20] To add another flourish, Namtrul Rinpoche creates an extended metaphor when wishing for her good health, comparing it to a full moon free from eclipse, then extending that metaphor into a praise of Tāre Lhamo as the moon with special enhancing powers as follows:

> Utterly perfect maṇḍala of aspiration and entrustment,
> The moon that increases the profound nectar,
> You, special friend, swell the ocean of early translations
> And grace the eastern ridge with good fortune and merit.[21]

In this verse, Tāre Lhamo is compared to the moon, which "increases the profound nectar" and causes "the ocean of the early translations" to swell.[22] "Early translations" (*snga 'gyur*) is a standard reference to the great translation projects of Tibet's imperial period, to which the Nyingma tradition traces their roots. Thus, as a corollary to the moon's influence on the tide, Tāre Lhamo is credited with the power to cause the ocean of the Nyingma teachings to swell. Beyond that, she is styled as a source of good fortune and merit in an image of moonlight on a (snowy) mountain range.

The stanza above is a good example of Namtrul Rinpoche's use of ornate poetry with its elaborate metaphors, stylized kennings, and trochaic meter. In an extended metaphor, it features four lines of nine syllables each and involves two standard kennings, "marked by a deer" for the moon and "water treasure" for the ocean.[23] Stylistically, it reflects Indian poetic conventions as found in the influential *Kāvyādarśa* by Daṇḍin. After its translation into Tibetan in the thirteenth century,[24] this text became the standard in Tibetan poetics and remained a prevailing poetic model until free verse gained traction in the late 1980s.[25] Namtrul Rinpoche uses ornate poetry in his early letters to convey formality, and this style provides the ideal medium for his elaborate praises of Tāre Lhamo. In a final literary flourish, again following Tibetan epistolary conventions,[26] he closes the letter with a request for her to continue corresponding in "a stream of letters like the Ganges" and an aspiration that likewise acknowledges her religious stature, wishing for her long life in a stock phrase reserved for Buddhist masters: "may your lotus feet remain on a vajra throne."[27]

By contrast, Tāre Lhamo's letters are less elaborate, eschewing the ornamental flourishes characteristics of either ornate poetry or formal epistolary conventions. Her first letter, inaugurating the correspondence, begins unceremoniously, "To the emanation of Namkhai Nyingpo," acknowledging his incarnation status, and ends equally briefly, "Offered to Pema Drime Ösal Lodrö Thaye / By the Devī: Secret seal." The closing uses his name in religion in youth and gives the Sanskrit for "lhamo" (*lha mo*), the second part of her name, meaning "goddess."[28] There are no extended praises or gestures of deference, which may reflect her higher status at the outset of their correspondence or simply the gap in their level of erudition. In his youth Namtrul Rinpoche was trained as a reincarnate lama at Zhuchen Monastery, where he would have studied the traditional ten fields of knowledge (*rig gnas*), including poetics and composition. Despite her status as the daughter of Apang Terchen, without monastic training or the education of aristocrats in central Tibet, Tāre Lhamo could read but not write the Tibetan script, and her attendant, Thopa, served as a scribe for the letters. Perhaps for this reason, linked as much to her gender as to her nonmonastic status, Tāre Lhamo turned to oral genres of bardic verse and folk song styles for most of her letters. Nonetheless, her first letter is formal to the extent that it includes verses demonstrating her command of esoteric Nyingma teachings, as below, and a prophecy about a future treasure revelation, translated in the next chapter:

> On the seventh day of the rabbit month, in the earth horse year of the 16th
>> Tibetan era:
> To the tulku of Namkhai Nyingpo,
> Free from extremes, removed from worldly concerns.
> In the dream of dependently arisen phenomena,
> There is nothing for the mind to reckon.
> In alpha-pure naked awareness-emptiness,
> No distortions by thoughts, good or bad, remain.
> Though unobstructed experience, the cognizing aspect,
> Flashed forth as the five lights manifesting wisdom,
> Free from extremes of permanence or absence,
> The sun of awareness, the definitive meaning, arises.
> Recognizing the nature of awareness as clear light,
> Just that is nonconceptual wisdom.

This opening could be read as esoteric instructions or alternatively a praise to Namtrul Rinpoche, given an ambiguity in Tibetan whereby extended passages of this type do not require pronouns. Moreover, in

3.1 Jokhang Temple in Lhasa, circumambulated by pilgrims.

her second letter, she returns the compliment by requesting Namtrul Rinpoche to teach in her own folksy metaphors, encouraging him to unfurl his turquoise mane as a snow lion and to spread his sturdy wings as a youthful garuḍa.[29] (A translation of this letter is included in the next chapter.) Tāre Lhamo's more direct style carried the day, and Namtrul Rinpoche eventually eschewed his initial formality for the expressiveness of folk songs.

In contrast to ornate poetry influenced by Indian literary models, Tibetan folk songs exhibit more direct language, frequent colloquialisms, and an affinity for distinctively Tibetan imagery. By her fourth letter, Tāre Lhamo shifts to the personal and shares her fondness for Namtrul Rinpoche in a "song of marvels" (kha mtshar glu), a folk style performed at the opening of celebratory gatherings to convey marvelous tidings (ngo mtshar ba'i gtam).[30] In a style from the region of Amdo, the selection below favors three lines per stanza and a meter of eight syllables per line.[31]

When traveling among dharma assemblies in Lhasa,
Meeting, meeting the golden face of the Jowo,
I cannot forget the potency of the Lord's blessing.

When wandering among thickets of juniper bush,
Warbling, warbling, the call of the cuckoo bird,[32]
I cannot forget the tune of its melodious song.

When meandering in the sublime six districts [of Ling],
Sustained, sustained by the affection of a youthful friend,
I can never forget your unwavering mind.[33]

In this song of marvels, Tāre Lhamo uses distinctively Tibetan images to call to mind her "youthful friend" (*grogs gzhon nu*), where "friend" can also stand for companion or lover.[34] Over successive verses, she refers to the sacred epicenter of Lhasa, where she recalls the face of the Jowo Śākyamuni, the revered image of the Buddha housed in the Jokhang Temple; to the alpine environment where juniper thrives, where she recalls the cry of the cuckoo bird—a harbinger of spring; and to divisions of Gesar's legendary kingdom of Ling, which local Tibetans place in Golok and northern Kham, where she recalls the affection of her youthful friend. In this passage, Tāre Lhamo uses a style of parallelism particular to Tibetan folk songs,[35] in which the first stanzas offer a series of analogies (*dpe*) and the last stanza provides the referent (*don*).[36] Each is given as an unforgettable marvel, but the last, which refers to Namtrul Rinpoche, is the main point of the song.

This shift from ornate poetry to folk song styles makes possible a growing intimacy between Tāre Lhamo and Namtrul Rinpoche in the midst of the mutual recognition of their exalted status as emanations of previous Buddhist masters.[37] This can be poignantly observed in different modes of address. Their correspondence is replete with terms of endearment such as "sweetheart" (*snying sdug*), "beloved" (*brtse gdung*, alt: *brtse grogs*), "darling" (*snying grogs*), "radiance of the heart" (*snying gi dwangs ma*), "dearest friend" (*grogs snying gces*), and "incomparable companion" (*grogs 'gran bral*).[38] In addition, they use nicknames for each other, Tarpo and Tsebo, following the local style of adding *lo, po,* or *bo* to the end of the first syllable of a Buddhist master's name: Tarpo from Tāre Lhamo and Tsebo from Namtrul Rinpoche's childhood name, Tsedzin.[39] Meanwhile, they continue to refer to each other by the names of their past lives. For Namtrul Rinpoche, this is primarily Namkhai Nyingpo, and for Tāre Lhamo, this is Yeshe Tsogyal and Sera Khandro as well as the female deities with whom she is associated.

Authorial Voice in Tibetan Letters

As the styles of versification shift, so do the authorial stances and rhetorical strategies in their self-representation signaled in a number of ways: a change in imagery and meter, the insertion of exclamatory phrases like "E ma!" or "Ha ha!," and the addition of a special orthographic mark, particular to treasure revelation, that sets it apart from ordinary speech.[40] These shifts are integral to the complex modulation of voices through which Tāre Lhamo and Namtrul Rinpoche negotiate their union as they flatter and cajole each other, predict and stipulate the terms of their relationship, and reconstruct the distant past in order to imagine a future together. Since stylistic shifts usually signal a change of content and tone, they maintain a certain degree of flexibility in their self-representation as they find ways to reassure each other of the constancy of their affection and confirm the joint nature of their destiny.

Within these shifts, one can detect a delicate balance between the self-effacing constraints of first-person expression in Tibetan and certain modes of assertion allowed in genres like prophecy or bardic verse. Midway through the correspondence, Tāre Lhamo alternates between the performative certainty of a prophetic voice and self-effacing statements that follow a Tibetan cultural imperative toward humility in the first-person. In her fifteenth letter, Tāre Lhamo refers to herself as "a gullible lady with thick latent tendencies" whose "transgressions and violations of samaya are great."[41] Yet later in the same letter, she boldly asserts that her aspiration to be with Namtrul Rinpoche is guided by the "prophetic vision of glorious Padma" (Padmasambhava) and "oath of the mother ḍākinīs."[42] Likewise, in her seventeenth letter, after confidently uttering a prophecy indicating the location of one of their treasures, she takes a self-deprecating tone and expresses sadness regarding her lack of accomplishments to date:

En route to the great benefit of beings and the teachings,
First, I did not fulfill the promise of samaya to the lord.

Second, I did not delight nor appease the mother ḍākinīs.

Third, I did not perform activities to protect the teachings.

Fourth, I did not accomplish the wishes of my father guru.

Although praised as a person benefiting mother beings,

I did not accomplish the benefit of a single creature.

In terms of supports, I did not build even one stūpa.

In terms of speech, I did not write even a single book.

In terms of mind, not even one student of mine attained liberation.

I don't want to stay; I feel sad and ashamed.[43]

In this passage, Tāre Lhamo uses a distinctively Tibetan style of enumerating a list in verse,[44] here detailing the things she has yet to accomplish, lending weight to her self-effacing statement. Her mention of broken samaya and lack of accomplishments to date directly contradicts her later hagiographic representation in *Spiraling Vine of Faith* as someone who emerged from the Maoist period with unstained samaya, having accomplished miraculous feats. This contradiction indicates the large extent to which authorial voice shapes representational strategies in Tibetan literature, as well as speech.[45]

Adopting a humble stance, typical of the first-person voice in Tibetan, Tāre Lhamo rejects the praise of others and focuses instead on her lack of outer activities: no building projects, no book publications, and no accomplished disciples. Notably, she does not mention the state policy forbidding the public expression of religion to account for her supposed shortcomings. Instead, she berates herself for not doing more to protect the teachings and benefit others. Implicit in her statement is the suggestion that this could be reversed through her union with Namtrul Rinpoche who, at this point in the correspondence, had arrived in Markhok to meet her relatives. The suggestion is that allied with him, she could fulfill her samaya or commitment to her "lord" (*rje*), probably referring to Padmasambhava, and accomplish the wishes of her father and guru, Apang Terchen. The context of this is key. Namtrul Rinpoche's namthar, *Jewel Garland*, represents an excerpt of this letter as her direct speech during his visit,[46] and the letter may have been a prepared statement delivered aloud in the presence of relatives. If that was the case, it would have operated as a strong form of persuasion. Rather than taking such statements literally, as transparent expressions of the self, we should view them as a cultural performance of humility that may have garnered support for her intended aims and attempted to compensate for her assertive prophetic statements earlier in the same letter.

As they negotiate the terms of their union, Tāre Lhamo and Namtrul Rinpoche make certain gendered subject positions available to each other. This is most pronounced in passages in which they appropriate each other's voices. On one occasion, Namtrul Rinpoche recounts a vision in which Tāre Lhamo appears to him in the form of Sera Khandro, one of her past lives, to console and advise him about his ongoing struggle with illness. By recounting this vision, he casts Tāre Lhamo as a ḍākinī, qualified to instruct him on how to overcome obstacles on the Buddhist path, and also as a female consort who facilitates the restoration of health in male lamas.[47] Namtrul Rinpoche thereby situates her in a gendered position that is both exalted and potentially subsidiary to his own. In turn, Tāre Lhamo displays her visionary talents in ways that at times defer to male authority. On one striking occasion from midway through the correspondence, she contends that her visions are hazy (rab rib) and then places a long visionary passage into Namtrul Rinpoche's voice, framed as his recollection of their past lives together.[48] Intensifying the modesty of her stance, Tāre Lhamo avows to have only "pretended to know" (shes mdog) in her previous visionary recollections and refers to herself as an imposter, "posing as the girl who recalls her past life as the Princess of Kharchen."[49] The Princess of Karchen refers to Yeshe Tsogyal, the all-important antecedent linking her to the source of her revelations and central to her public identity in prophecies by Buddhist masters during her youth.

Several hierarchies may be at work in their mutual gestures of praise and deference, including religious status, gender, and age. Tāre Lhamo was the daughter of Apang Terchen and a khandroma with close connections to the prestigious Dudjom line through her prior teacher-disciple and consort relationships, and Namtrul Rinpoche was an incarnate lama in Zhuchen Monastery in Serta, a branch of the Katok tradition. While it would be difficult to know how these differences were regarded at the time, he was also six years junior to her in age, signaled by her use of "youthful" (gzhon nu) in describing him at several points in the correspondence. Both these factors may account for the formality, elaborate praises, and deferential stance of his early letters. Gender also plays a key role in the ways they fashion their epistolary personae in relation to each other. I have already suggested how their choice of versification styles can be correlated to their respective levels of erudition, traceable to the gender norms of their social milieu, and how Namtrul Rinpoche evokes the gendered trope of the consort. Let me make a further point in relation to their statements of praise and deference.

In chapter 1, I suggested that gender intensifies the overarching postures of reverence and diffidence in relationship to narrative voice in Tibetan literature and namthar in particular. There is a parallel within epistolary literature. In Namtrul Rinpoche's writings, Tāre Lhamo is an amalgamation of the female deities Samantabhadrī, Tārā, and Sarasvatī in similar terms to prophecies delivered at her birth and in her later hagiographic portrait in *Spiraling Vine of Faith.* Beyond that, he credits her with the power that the moon exerts over the tides as one who can cause the ocean of the Nyingma teachings to swell, thereby invoking her visionary talents and capacity to reveal treasures. By contrast, in her own voice, Tāre Lhamo presents herself as "sad and ashamed" (*skyo ba ngo re tsha*) at her lack of accomplishments and as merely "posing" (*brdzu*) as a visionary who can recall her past life as Yeshe Tsogyal. In such statements, she seemingly disavows her visionary talents and ability to reveal treasures, which are traced to teachings received from Padmasambhava as a direct disciple. This is an especially ironic claim since, in treasure lore, Yeshe Tsogyal is credited with the "dhāraṇī of total recall" (*mi brjed pa'i gzungs*) as the scribe for Padmasambhava's teachings. However, such self-effacing statements are not meant to be taken at face value as statements of truth or "transparent expressions" of her own self-doubts. Rather, they are culturally situated statements of humility expected in the first-person voice according to Tibetan norms, which I suggest are intensified by gender.

We hardly find comparable statements in Namtrul Rinpoche's letters. While he salutes Tāre Lhamo with considerable literary flourish and offers a bow to her in the form of the goddess Tārā, he never expresses shame in that way or undermines his own authority, and she does not make a point to exalt him as a male deity. One self-effacing comment on his part stands out, when he refers to his own writings as the scribbles of a madman. In his sixth letter, he states: "These are scribbles, whatever arose in mind, / by the slightly impetuous madman priest, Tse."[50] Statements of this kind are a common way to speak about a spontaneous mode of writing in Tibetan. "Whatever arose in mind" (*yid shar cha*) gestures to an outburst of affection in this letter, while the term "madman" (*smyon pa*) can refer to a tantric master engaged in unconventional or transgressive behavior in the pursuit of soteriological aims.[51] To put this statement in context, Namtrul Rinpoche's letters maintain a focus on the prophetic aspect of their religious calling until his sixth letter, a short ditty combining tantric images and affective sentiments. Yet not until his ninth letter does he compose a lyrical song of recalling the beloved, free of tantric references and anchored wholly in the Tibetan landscape, to be discussed below. For this reason, I read his statement about the scribbles of a madman as a self-conscious first foray into intimacy that he feels necessary to explain away as impetuousness (*gdol spyod*). Otherwise, by her fourth letter and his ninth, folk song styles predominate, giving the correspondence a more colloquial and intimate tone overall. That said, they never leave their religious identities behind and shift back into prophecies and past-life recollections at regular intervals.

Despite her self-effacing gestures, Tāre Lhamo has a strong and variegated voice in her sustained dialogue with Namtrul Rinpoche. In humanizing terms, she presents herself as someone just as capable of declaring a prophecy as she is prone to daydreaming about her beloved or fretting over local gossip. It is notable that Tāre Lhamo is the one who initiated and set the tone for their correspondence, actively courting Namtrul Rinpoche. At one point, she depicts her pursuit of him in a striking metaphor: "circling, circling, the mind of the tigress circles the monkey."[52] While suggestive of courtship as a sport, or even a hunt, the metaphor coyly references their respective birth years—hers, 1938, the earth tiger year; his, 1944, the wood monkey year—within the twelve-year calendar and its five associated elements that make up the Tibetan sexagenary cycle.[53] Moreover, her visionary contributions to imagining and articulating their shared future as a couple are comparable to, if not more substantial than his.[54] Overall, she is the more prolific, composing 105 pages to his 72.[55] In all of this, Tāre Lhamo is neither a passive recipient of his advances nor merely a vehicle to enable the fulfillment of his visionary pursuits. As signaled in the correspondence, their union promised to be a true partnership.

Heightening what is at stake in the construction of their epistolary personae, the letters of Buddhist masters in Tibet have often been collected for posterity and published.[56] Given their affective content, the correspondence between Tāre Lhamo and Namtrul Rinpoche is certainly more private in nature than official or didactic letters of other Buddhist masters that have so far come to light.[57] Yet the very fact of their publication suggests a public dimension beyond expressing personal sentiments, though they surely do that in abundance. Notwithstanding its initial secrecy, the correspondence between Tāre Lhamo and Namtrul Rinpoche has now been published in several formats. A dozen or so letters were selected for inclusion in *Jewel Garland*, the namthar of Namtrul Rinpoche in which the couple serves as joint protagonists, published together with *Spiraling Vine of Faith* in 1997.[58] These excerpts emphasize the prophetic dimension of their union over and above their personal expressions of affection, indicating at least some initial discomfort with sharing the correspondence as a whole. Their correspondence in its entirety was later published in facsimile edition as an addendum to their treasure corpus, between 2003 and 2004, when Namtrul Rinpoche generously gave me a copy.[59] Since then, in 2013, it was published in paperback form, integrated into their treasure corpus along with writings by Namtrul Rinpoche composed following Tāre Lhamo's passing in 2002.[60] In addition, selections from several letters have recently been performed by well-known singers on a DVD produced by Nyenlung Monastery, rendering them into devotional songs for a popular audience.[61]

Past Lives as a Couple

As their letters progress, a synergy develops between the prophetic and personal dimensions of their courtship and correspondence. Their visionary recollections of past lives together, which Tāre Lhamo and Namtrul Rinpoche share back and forth, fuel their growing affection in this life. In turn, their expressions of affection likewise encourage their visionary propensities. This second mode of interplay between love and destiny can be seen vividly in passages where Tāre Lhamo and Namtrul Rinpoche recollect their connection across time and space through memories of past lives and reminiscences related to this life, bridging the temporal and spatial distances between them through the medium of memory.

Over the course of their correspondence, Tāre Lhamo and Namtrul Rinpoche stir each other's memory of events long ago, which took place in their myriad past lives together as a couple. For example, at one point Namtrul Rinpoche writes, "Here in the cool domain of Tibet, the land of snow mountains, / We came together across seven lifetimes. / ... Do you recall, joyous heart friend?"[62] In many more extensive passages, Tāre Lhamo and Namtrul Rinpoche create a series of linkages in common to seminal times and places in the history and mythos of Buddhism and its propagation in Tibet. Through their past-life recollections, they forge a sense of legitimacy as a couple, establishing connectivity in their very persons to the authoritative precedents of the tantric siddhas in India, the imperial court of central Tibet, and central figures in the legend of King Gesar anchored in Golok and northern Kham.

The longest series of past-life recollections occurs in her fifteenth letter, in which Tāre Lhamo pretends not to be able to remember much of the distant past and then places her memories in Namtrul Rinpoche's voice.[63] It provides a striking example of the deflection of agency in their correspondence, inflected by gender, and covers a large swath of time and space. The tantric scene in India is captured in a reference to Namtrul Rinpoche as a student of Hūṃchenkara, considered one of the eight *vidyādharas* of India and a source of Nyingma teachings; Tāre Lhamo indicates that she was his consort, a Kashmiri princess.[64] The time of the legendary King Gesar is evoked in her reference to Metok Lhadze, the princess of a kingdom to the south of Ling who figures in the epic,[65] and Munchen Thökar, a less easily identifiable male figure that may be an alternate name for the Prince of Jang, Yulha Thogyur, with whom Namtrul Rinpoche is mainly identified.[66] Then come their all-important lives in central Tibet at the temple at Samye, when Padmasambhava bestowed teachings to be revealed in the future as treasures; in this passage the couple are identified as Namkhai Nyingpo and Shelkar Dorje Tso, notably distinct from Tāre Lhamo's usual identification with Yeshe Tsogyal. Through such past-life identifications, they not only draw on the historical and mythic past to create a shared genealogy of lifetimes together but also anticipate the joint nature of their revelatory activities by occasionally naming the sites where treasures await them in the landscape.

The list of past lives found in their letters does not mesh perfectly with the identifications given to them in youth as recorded in their namthars. In their correspondence, Tāre Lhamo and Namtrul Rinpoche invent new identities in dialogue together, and their recollections produce overlapping identifications for certain periods. Despite her primary identification as an emanation of Yeshe Tsogyal, given to her in prophecies at birth, Tāre Lhamo assumes a past-life identification as Shelkar Dorje Tso, an accomplished female disciple of Padmasambhava within treasure lore.[67] And Namtrul Rinpoche, despite his incarnation status as the fourth Namkhai Nyingpo emanation of Zhuchen Monastery, is also identified by Tāre Lhamo as an emanation of Atsara Sale, the Nepalese consort of Yeshe Tsogyal whom she is said to have ransomed from slavery.[68] For the time of Gesar of Ling, both also have multiple identities. Identified in her youth as Ne'u Chung, a maiden of Ling,

3.2 Statue of Ne'u Chung at the Gesar Palace in Darlag County of Golok.

by Rigdzin Jalu Dorje, Tāre Lhamo takes on the identity of Metok Lhadze in several passages in their correspondence.[69] With the exception of Munchen Thökar mentioned above, Namtrul Rinpoche's identity remains fairly stable as Yulha Thogyur, the Prince of Jang who became a "converted hero" (dpa' thul) loyal to Gesar after his kingdom was conquered.[70] That multiple identities for the same period sometimes overlap does not seem to be a problem. In fact, there is no attempt in their letters to produce a linear sequence of past lives. Instead, what is important is to establish connectivity to seminal times and places in the history of Buddhism and Tibet and, more pointedly, to each other across time and space.

In constructing the legitimating source for their treasures, their main interest is the imperial period in central Tibet and Gesar's legendary rule in eastern Tibet, so their overlapping identities are concentrated at those times. Their past lives together form a key aspect of their public identity, through which they forge vital links to the source of their future revelations. For the imperial period when Buddhism first entered Tibet, they trace the prophetic entrustment of teachings by Padmasambhava to their previous lives as Yeshe Tsogyal and Namkhai Nyingpo and, in ancillary fashion, to the respective consorts of these figures, Atsara Sale and Shelkar Dorje Tso. Given that their revelations include a section of the Gesar epic, the final volume of their treasure corpus in its original twelve-volume format, their past lives traced to central figures in that epic are likewise crucial. One of the distinctive features of treasure revelation in Golok and northern Kham is the tendency for contemporary tertöns to trace their lives back both to the time of Padmasambhava and to the time of legendary King Gesar.[71]

It is important to emphasize the flexibility and accretive nature of past-life identifications within their correspondence, since these are not necessarily consistent with later writings about the couple or earlier writings by and about their antecedents. For example, although Tāre Lhamo was publicly identified as an emanation of Sera Khandro in her youth and Namtrul Rinpoche refers to her as such on several occasions in their correspondence, her past lives do not neatly match those of Sera Khandro as given in her own autobiographical writings. There are overlaps, such as Shelkar Dorje Tso and Kālasiddhi, but there are just as many discrepancies.[72] One reason for this may be that previous literary sources would not have been readily available for consultation in the wake of the Cultural Revolution. Sarah Jacoby remarks on the rarity of manuscripts of Sera Khandro's writings in the region before they were published in 2009.[73] Another reason is that, unlike incarnation lines associated with monastic seats and involving the formal enthronement of a single successor, emanations in the Nyingma tradition of Golok do not necessarily entail a one-to-one correlation. This was certainly the case for Tāre Lhamo, who was identified in her youth as the emanation of both Sera Khandro and Tra Gelong from the previous generation. Later in life, she accrued a third association as an emanation of Lushul Khenpo Könchok Drönme.[74]

In their exchange of letters, Tāre Lhamo and Namtrul Rinpoche continued to add past-life recollections and associations. Though the longest list is concentrated in Tāre Lhamo's fifteenth letter, past life recollections can be found in at least four of her other letters and seven letters by Namtrul Rinpoche.[75] Despite their repeated mention of seven lifetimes together in Tibet, with rare exception, these are not fleshed out beyond the imperial period and Gesar's legendary reign. An exception comes in his eighth letter,[76] in which Namtrul Rinpoche references the tertön Dudul Dorje (1615–72),[77] who played a role in rebuilding Katok Monastery in eastern Tibet, in connection with a Mingyur Paldrön—but not the famous daughter of Terdak Lingpa.[78] Curiously, neither of them suggests a correlation between Namtrul Rinpoche and Drime Özer, the teacher and destined consort of Sera Khandro, although Namtrul Rinpoche staked a claim to this association later in life.[79] Nor is his later association as one of four emanations of Apang Terchen mentioned.[80] The fact that Tāre Lhamo and Namtrul Rinpoche did not detail all of their seven lifetimes in Tibet together left open a certain flexibility for future associations beyond the correspondence itself. This flexibility reflects long-standing practices within the Nyingma tradition of Golok, in which multiple claims to be the emanation of a esteemed master coexist without fanfare and any single Nyingma master may be regarded as the emanation of several past figures who lived concurrently.

Recollection and Affect

In recalling their past lives, Tāre Lhamo and Namtrul Rinpoche follow a Buddhist literary practice established long ago in the *jātakas* and *avadānas*, Indian tales that recount the past lives of the Buddha and his disciples.[81] However, in contrast to the findings of Donald Lopez regarding Indic

Buddhist sources, their past-life recollections are vivid and accompanied by affect and emotional charge.[82] According to Lopez, recollections of this nature in early Buddhist sources are typically skeletal in nature, consisting of bare details such as place, name, clan, and caste, which he describes as "topographically flat, without affect."[83] By contrast, due to the implications of such memories for their imminent future, Tāre Lhamo and Namtrul Rinpoche share expressions of joy and longing upon exchanging such memories.

In their epistolary exchanges, the couple's connection across lifetimes fuels their longing in this life. Witness Tāre Lhamo's confession: "One hundred times a day, pining away, the spiritual support, / My congenial friend comes to mind. / The sketch of past lives becomes clearer; / The mind yearning, [my] loving affection increases."[84] Here she suggests that as they recall more about their past lives, her mind fills with yearning ('dun ma) and loving affection (brtse gdung) for Namtrul Rinpoche. He echoes this sentiment in emblematic statements such as: "Our connection from previous lives dawns in mind. / Happy and sad, tears fall like rain" and "The pattern of past lives becomes clearer, / Beloved, delighting the mind, I recall again and again!"[85] As these examples indicate, their past-life recollections are accompanied by affective responses that indicate the significance of the past for inspiring their own union and religious vocation in the future.

Notably, their past-life recollections emerge in an exuberant atmosphere of affection that facilitates the initial stages of the revelation process in ways yet to be noted in scholarship on the treasure tradition or, for that matter, in Tibetan treatises on the topic. As Tāre Lhamo and Namtrul Rinpoche exchange memories of past lives, these elicit joyful responses that further encourage the unfolding of the visionary process. What results is a feedback loop between memory and affect. As a result, Tāre Lhamo and Namtrul Rinpoche create a sense of shared destiny in dialogue as they fondly urge each other to recall more about their past lives and predict future revelations.

For example, early in the correspondence, in her fifth letter, composed on the tenth day of Sagadawa in the earth sheep year (1979),[86] when "the new moon brandishes a smile," Tāre Lhamo conveys how she found Namtrul Rinpoche's message "agreeable and pleasing to mind."[87] Expressing her delight at his "sweet, sweet words," she declares that "the fog of mind is cleared by [your] loving affection."[88] The term I am translating as "loving affection" (brtse gdung) appears frequently in the correspondence; it is a key term that indicates love in Tibetan and serves as a standard epithet for "beloved." In the next letter, referring to Namtrul Rinpoche as one who makes "the mind bubble with inspiration," she offers a song from the depths of her heart.[89] But instead of a love song, Tāre Lhamo delivers a prophecy about a golden treasure casket awaiting them within a white cliff at a place called Trachugmo Pass, where a seed syllable marks the top of a ravine.[90] This she characterizes as their shared allotment hidden as treasure, "the inheritance of Padma" and "the means to reverse the strife of degeneration."[91] By indicating the location of a treasure, albeit in cryptic terms, her prophecy is functionally equivalent to a "treasure certificate" (gter byang), the all-important document that initiates the revelatory process by providing clues about where the treasure has been hidden in the landscape.[92] Prophecies of this kind permeate their correspondence and, in this case, indicate that affective states, such as love or affection, can facilitate visionary recollection by clearing away mental obscurations (the "fog of mind") and allowing deep-seated memories to percolate into the mind. In delivering this prophecy, Tāre Lhamo claims to "remember vividly as if carved in stone,"[93] suggesting a type of memory immutably stored and contradicting her self-effacing claims to be an imposter who merely pretends to know.

From this and other passages, we can see the way love and destiny are intertwined in a mode whereby the affective dimension of their courtship serves to ignite the visionary process. In turn, the uncovering of their destiny through past-life recollections draws them closer, increasing their longing to be together in this life. The interplay between love and destiny in their correspondence suggests that the process of courtship may be just as important as its consummation in the tantric rite of sexual union in order to awaken the visionary propensities of tertöns. It is safe to say that it was central to how Tāre Lhamo and Namtrul Rinpoche developed a lasting partnership through which the visionary process continued to unfold.

Recalling the Beloved

Tāre Lhamo and Namtrul Rinpoche complement their past-life recollections, which connect them across time, with reminiscences of each other in this life that bridge the spatial distance separating them.[94] These passages are articulated in sentimental terms. One of the most lyrical occurs in Namtrul Rinpoche's ninth letter, where he openly expresses his affection for his beloved (here: *brtse grogs*). It features an eight-syllable meter, structured first in verses of three lines and then in couplets, as Namtrul Rinpoche begins to echo Tāre Lhamo's preference for folk song styles. In the first part the syllable *so* augments the meter without adding semantic meaning, and my translation uses "oh" in some lines to mirror its effect. The content is suggestive of an Amdo love song, literally "songs of the [mountain] pass" (*la gzhas*), named after the locus of amorous exploits and containing praises of the beloved.[95] While starting out with a classic Indian image of fertility, the bee and lotus, Namtrul Rinpoche otherwise places his reminiscences of Tāre Lhamo in the landscape of Golok amid the grasslands and snow mountains. The first half of his ninth letter reads:

Shall I also sing a song?

Dharma valley, oh, the auspicious jewel land,
Happy flowers, oh, in a lotus grove of delight,
Quivering hum, oh, it belongs to the little bee.

Melodious song, oh, recurring strum of the lute.
Sweet dew, oh, enjoy the extract of honey,
Yes, little bee, *a bu lo lo wo*!

Quivering hum, oh, through this sweet melody,
I refresh the memory of my affectionate friend.
I cannot help, oh, but hum a tune!

Singing this song, it reaches the snowy peak.
Snowy peak, oh, how could it possibly tremble?
Sweetheart, my mind is more firm than that.

Singing this song, it reaches the depths of the lake.
Verdant lake, oh, how could one possibly judge its depth?
Sweetheart, my devotion is more deep than that.

In past lives, deeds and aspirations were good.
At present, the shared coincidence is good.
Later come! Oh, the final aim is good.

The three goods, oh, aspirations and wishes fulfilled.
Friend, I am [caught] on the iron hook of your loving affection.
My three gates, oh, I delight to see you amid the crowd.

First and foremost, the inner and outer elements,
Second, the power of prior vows and aspirations.

Because of my faithful and yearning beloved,
How could I dare to be apart from you, friend?

Do I cherish the eyes on my face that let me see?
You, dear friend, [I cherish] more than that.

Do I cherish the heart that upholds the mind?[96]
You, dear friend, [I cherish] more than that.

When the wildflowers bloom across the grasslands,
The beautiful form of my beloved comes to mind.

When the cuckoo bird emits a melodious call,
The musical speech of my beloved comes to mind.

When sun rays shine at the break of morning's dawn,
The affectionate mind of my beloved comes to mind.

Splendor of high peaks, though I've seen hundreds, thousands,
You are the queen of the snowy [range], none higher.

At this juncture, due to the oaths of the past,
I promise to honor you always and forever.

I feel shy to say any more than that.
That's the point, darling, nothing else.

Though fatigued, the distance is not far.
Whatever the means, it's certain we will meet.

Only friend, whose mind is stable as the snow mountain,
Please remain within the radiant bliss of [my] heart.[97]

In this letter, Namtrul Rinpoche conveys in no uncertain terms how much he cherishes Tāre Lhamo, conveying the depth and unwavering nature of his affection. Moreover, he uses springtime imagery from the grasslands of Golok such that the sights and sounds of everyday life recall the beloved; a sense of optimism prevails.

In passages like these, Tāre Lhamo and Namtrul Rinpoche play off two related connotations of the Tibetan term for memory. The term *drenpa* (*dran pa*) means "to remember" or "to call to mind" as well as "to miss."[98] In a technical sense, the same term is used in reference to meditation practice, translating the Sanskrit *smṛti*. Buddhist notions of memory derive from what Collette Cox calls an "interrelated semantic complex" in which the term *smṛti* in Sanskrit refers to a "mode of attentiveness" as a technique in meditation, often translated as "mindfulness" and "recollection," and also can refer to the recollection of past lives.[99] Tibetan usage of the term *drenpa* encompasses this semantic complex and adds an affective dimension. In everyday usage, to recall a person or place frequently connotes missing them, as in "I miss [my] homeland" (Golok dialect: *pha yul dran gi*).[100] Tāre Lhamo and Namtrul Rinpoche use *drenpa* both for their affective reminiscences of the beloved and for their visionary recollections of past lives and the location of future treasures. As a result, these two types of memory play off each other throughout the correspondence, indicating a common medium through which they articulate love for each other and a sense of joint destiny.

Using the various connotations of *drenpa*, Tāre Lhamo and Namtrul Rinpoche effectively blur the lines between the prophetic and personal dimensions of their courtship on numerous occasions. A poignant example can be found in Namtrul Rinpoche's eleventh letter, which is akin to a song of remembrance (*dran glu*). It starts out with remembrances of their lives together as Yuyi Thortsug and Sarasvatī in a divine realm and as Karmavajra and Kālasiddhi in Nepal, followed by references to their seven lifetimes together in Tibet.[101] In elaborating their activities across those seven lives, Namtrul Rinpoche goes on to use a common form of ornamentation found in folk songs, verbal figures (*sgra rgyan*) involving phonemic repetition (*zung ldan*).[102] Here he repeats the term for memory (*dran*) at the end of successive lines, which I transpose to the start of the line for emphasis in the translation.[103] The main section of the letter consists of a long string of sacred sites across the Tibetan plateau that Namtrul Rinpoche recalls as sites of their previous activities where treasures await them. These include Sheldrak in central Tibet, Lake Kokonor in northern Amdo, a cliff on the eastern edge of the Tibetan plateau in Gyarong, the turquoise lake at Nyenpo Yutse,[104] and Drakar Tredzong, which Tāre Lhamo mentioned in her first letter and from which point we join his letter:

> Recalling Drakar Tredzong, the site of awakening,
> Recalling the cave of flowers at that mighty fortress,
> Recalling the treasure gate and auspicious white conch,
> Recalling the many cycles of profound ḍākinī treasuries,
> Now I also recall the aspiration of the father Padma.
> Recalling the treasure certificate of protectors and lords of mantra,
> I especially recall the entrustment to [us] pair of friends.
> I specifically recall yearning for [my] affectionate beloved.
> This is the convergence of deeds, coincidence, and aspirations,
> Even more happy than journeying to a lovely place.
> The etchings on my skull are becoming clearer,
> My joyful faith and longing are becoming stronger,
> This is the destiny of the succession of previous lives.
> Of course, affectionate beloved, heart companion,
> [You are my] spiritual support, impossible to forget.
> Jewel of the heart, don't have an attitude of separation,
> It's not possible to be separated; [we] have Padma's wish,
> [We] have the blessings of the sublime protectors and lamas,
> [We] have the companionship of the ḍākinīs and heroines,
> [We] have the power of dharma protectors and guardians.[105]

In this passage, Namtrul Rinpoche rehearses a number of their future treasure sites, staking a personal claim to remembering special features and markings at each place as well as occasions in the past when they made aspirations together.[106] Upon recalling the entrustment by Padmasambhava to the "pair of friends" (*grogs zung gnyis*) in a past life, he shifts to recalling her as the beloved and invoking their yearning and longing to be together in this life. By doing so, he skips across the centuries in between and effectively blurs the line between their prophetic mission and their personal affection. This increases his visionary capacities—the "etchings on his skull" (*thod pa'i ri mo*) becoming clearer—and also his love for Tāre Lhamo, expressed as "joyful faith and longing" (*yid dga' ba'i dad 'dun*). Within these intimate expressions, he invokes destiny (*bskos thang*) as a force from their past lives that will reunite them in this one, showing how inextricably the prophetic and personal dimensions of their courtship are linked in their letters.

In this passage, we can also observe the cultural and emotional resources the couple generated as they forged their union. In personal terms, while referring to her as his "affectionate beloved" (*byams brtse gdung*) and "heart companion" (*snying gi grogs*), Namtrul Rinpoche calls Tāre Lhamo his "spiritual support" (*sems kyi rten*), and elsewhere she uses the same expression to refer to him.[107] This term could also be glossed as mental or psychological support and, following its usage, he affectionately asks her not to think that they can remain separated for long. From this and other passages, it is evident how much their affection sustained them as a couple, serving as mutual supports and providing encouragement to persist in pursuing their shared mission. Complementing this, in prophetic terms, Namtrul Rinpoche invokes a host of transempirical forces as further support: the wishes of Padmasambhava, the blessings of lamas, the companionship of ḍākinīs, and the power of dharma protectors (*chos skyong*) and guardians (*srung ma*).

In a more subtle instance when the lines between love and destiny are blurred, Namtrul Rinpoche repeats the term for spiritual or mental support later in the correspondence, in an affectionate ditty within his nineteenth letter. Here I translate the term as "support for mind" to keep as close as possible to the terse meter of six syllables per line, which becomes increasingly difficult as the lines progress. Lending the passage a pulsing rhythm, each line starts with the phonemic repetition of the first two syllables:

Love love—aim of [my] heart,
Joy joy—vine of [my] mind,
Dear dear—gleam of [my] heart,
Kind kind—I don't dare part.
Yearn yearn—sole support for mind.
Match match—shared deeds and wishes.
Steady steady—sole steadfast friend.

Beauty beauty—recalling [your] fine face,
Sweet sweet—recalling [your] lovely speech,
Clear clear—recalling [your] wise mercy,
Recall recall—I won't forget [your] words.
Joy joy—showing the play of four joys.
Bliss bliss—wisdom of bliss-emptiness.
Arise arise—it arises in mind.
When when—my hope to meet [you],
Again again—it's vivid in mind.
Sad sad—words of affection.
Write write—I set down what arose.[108]

In affectionate terms, Namtrul Rinpoche positions Tāre Lhamo as the focal point or aim of his heart (*snying gi gtad so*) and as his mental support from whom he dares not part and whom he eagerly seeks to meet again. She is also his "steadfast friend" (*gtan gyi grogs*), whose beautiful visage, sweet speech, and wise mercy (*mkhyen brtse*) he recalls. His affection is mixed inextricably with their previous deeds and aspirations (here translated as "wishes" for the sake of meter) and the tantric idioms of the four joys and bliss-emptiness, referencing sexuality in the context of treasure revelation. Though these references are made in passing, it is clear that Namtrul Rinpoche's affection is bound up in the larger vision of their shared mission, derived from their visionary recollections of deeds and aspirations made together across lifetimes and the tantric practice of sexual union that facilitates the revelation process. Here, once again, the line gets blurred between the personal and prophetic dimensions of their courtship, indicating that both are integral to their relationship.

Snow Lion and Mountain Peak

Moving on to the third mode in the interplay between love and destiny, there is another type of destiny invoked in their letters that is tied even more closely to their affective bond in this life. At one point, Namtrul Rinpoche conjures up the term "worldly legacy" (*srid pa'i bkod thang*) to refer to the mutual compatibility and reliance between pairs of things in the natural environment.[109] As the correspondence progresses, he repeatedly

3.3 Mural painting of Gesar's warriors, flanked by a snow lion and other creatures.

uses folksy pairings between animals and their natural habitat, like a snow lion and a mountain peak, to express in naturalistic terms that the two are destined to be together in this life. While also employing these animal metaphors, Tāre Lhamo adds other imagery drawn from everyday sights on the grasslands of Golok, such as berries growing on a juniper branch. In doing so, they complement prophetic assertions regarding their inseparability across lifetimes with naturalistic metaphors of mutual reliance. This suggests a this-worldly compatibility that has nothing to do with the prophetic entrustment by Padmasambhava to reveal treasures. Instead they invoke a different notion of fate (*las dbang*), a term that in the years following their correspondence became a favorite in Tibetan pop songs about romantic love.[110] As deployed by Tāre Lhamo and Namtrul Rinpoche toward the middle of the correspondence, it is still suggestive of a karmic connection but no longer tied to their identity as tertöns, or Buddhist masters for that matter.[111]

Midway through the correspondence, Namtrul Rinpoche launches into a series of letters using pairings of animals deemed to be "inseparable" ('bral med) from their natural habitat, most commonly the striped tigress in a sandalwood forest, the gold-eyed fish in a turquoise lake, and the snow lion in its mountain abode. These are folk motifs that can be traced as far back as the eleventh century to the songs of Milarepa.[112] A good example is two verses from his eighteenth letter, in which he depicts the snow lion as inseparable from its mountain abode and the gold-eyed fish as inseparable from the turquoise lake:

"Peak" . . . though I've seen hundreds of thousands,
The one supreme peak is the regal sapphire mountain,
None other than you, stomping ground of the snow lion.
Peak and snow lion cannot be separated; it's past karma.

"Lake" . . . though I've seen hundreds of thousands,
The one supreme lake is the invincible turquoise lake.
None other than you, swimming hole of the gold-eyed fish.
Fish and lake cannot be separated; it's past karma.[113]

In these two verses, Namtrul Rinpoche gives two analogies for his bond with Tāre Lhamo. Both involve the connection between an animal and its habitat, which are deemed inseparable due to past karma, or more literally "deeds of the past" (sngon gyi las). In this case, Namtrul Rinpoche positions himself as the animal, snow lion and gold-eyed fish, and Tāre Lhamo as the habitat, the mountain peak and turquoise lake. Not just any peak or lake will do. There is only one unique habitat, the supreme peak and supreme lake, that is the destined home for these creatures. In this way, Namtrul Rinpoche emphasizes the naturalness of their union and their special compatibility, while also complimenting Tāre Lhamo as supreme among all other women.

In addition to emphasizing the inevitability of their union, these folksy pairings provide them with an indirect way to query and reassure each other of the constancy of their affection. Elsewhere in the correspondence, in his twelfth letter, for example, Namtrul Rinpoche describes the precariousness of their quest if one of them should falter.[114] As the landing pad of the bronze-breasted vulture, the white boulder must not wobble.

As the swimming hole of the gold-eyed fish, the turquoise lake must not fluctuate in water level. And as the stomping ground of the mighty lion, the snow mountain must not tremble. These images once again suggest the naturalness of their union, but there is a twist. The habitat must stay constant in order for the animal to make its way there safely. Coming in his twelfth letter, prior to their first meeting, this may be a way for Namtrul Rinpoche to ask Tāre Lhamo if her intentions are resolute before he ventures to Markhok to meet her and her relatives. Here again he assumes the position of the animal preparing to make the journey to its natural habitat.

Namtrul Rinpoche returns again and again to pairings between animals and their natural habitat to anticipate their meeting and characterize their growing commitment. His thirteenth letter has an anticipatory tone, with each of the animals displaying their special attribute on the way to their habitat:

> Beloved, vine of mind, great affectionate companion,
> I offer auspicious words and good tidings at setting forth.
>
> Stay well, invincible turquoise lake of wealth!
> Gold-eyed [fish] with six fins, setting out across the ocean,
> Flaunts its skills in the middle of the vast ocean.
> Without delay, fish and lake shall happily meet.
>
> Stay well, Indic fortress of sandalwood forest!
> Powerful red tigress, setting out for the meadows,
> Flashes its six stripes on a grassy hilltop overlook.[115]
> Without delay, tiger and forest shall happily meet.
>
> Stay well, pristine snow mountain!
> Splendid snow lion, setting out for the craggy peaks,
> Unfurls its turquoise mane atop the dark boulder.
> Without delay, snow lion and white peaks shall happily meet.
>
> Stay well, dear friend, jewel of my heart!
> Lowly me, Drime Lodrö, setting out to your homeland,
> With good intention to benefit the teachings and beings,
> Without delay, you, friend, and I shall happily meet.[116]

In a use of parallelism typical of Tibetan folk songs, previously discussed in reference to Tāre Lhamo's song of marvels, here Namtrul Rinpoche provides three analogies for their impending meeting; the last in this series of stanzas provides the referent. Just as the gold-eyed fish and turquoise lake, the tigress and sandalwood forest, the snow lion and craggy peak will meet without delay, so too will Namtrul Rinpoche and Tāre Lhamo. As he says in the final line, "Without delay, you, friend, and I shall happily meet." Characterizing the journey through these animals, he conveys a sense of fortitude and prowess.[117] Though he refers to himself as "lowly" (*dman phran*), it seems like a lighthearted remark to offset the series of mighty animals in whose image he casts himself as he sets forth to meet her. Through these animals, he projects an epistolary persona as a heroic figure.

In Amdo love songs and a related genre called simply the "compatible friend" (*rogs mthun*, alt: *rogs 'then*),[118] pairings drawn from the natural world are used to express the close connection between lovers and a relationship of dependence.[119] This can be seen clearly in a different set of naturalistic images used by Tāre Lhamo to depict their inseparability and mutual reliance. The most striking passage occurs in her twenty-fifth letter in the style of the "compatible friend," employed by lovers who are involuntarily separated.[120] This style is related to Amdo love songs but features a distinct meter of seven syllables, beginning with a monad followed by three dyads.[121] The following passage also features a Tibetan formulation of phonemic repetition, using the duplication or triplication of word stems that Géza Uray suggests intensifies the tone.[122] In the translation, I attempt to keep the lines as close in syllable count to the original as possible and mirror the word order so as to give the reader some sense of the rhythm in the Tibetan.[123] Notice how Tāre Lhamo explicitly correlates each member of the pair with one of them:

Turquoise dragon, clap clap you clap.
Rain clouds in sky, thick thick I'm thick.

Golden hillside, firm firm you're firm.
Grasses on top, grow grow I grow.

River water, flow flow you flow.
Gold-eyed fish, zoom zoom I zoom.

Juniper branch, grow grow you grow.
Berries at the tip, ripe ripe I'm ripe.

Lady friend for life, think think you think.
Kindness indeed, guard guard I guard.

. . . We two friends are inseparable.
Isn't that so, Tsebo lo lo?[124]

This is a delightful ditty that depicts their inseparability in a playful tone. Despite the prophetic cast of their correspondence as a whole, Tāre Lhamo is whimsical enough to depict herself as a ripe juniper berry and flirtatious enough to signal her readiness to be with Namtrul Rinpoche as a cloud ready to produce rain at his thunderclap (personified above as a turquoise dragon). These are humanizing moments in their correspondence, where they present themselves simply as man and woman. Nyingpo Tsering, who identified the genre of this song and performed it for me *a cappella*, glossed its meaning in romantic terms as an expression of being unable to live without the beloved.[125] The grasses cannot take root without the hillside, the fish cannot survive without water, and juniper berries cannot grow anywhere but on a juniper branch. The letter ends with her explicit statement of their inseparability—"we two friends are inseparable" (*rogs 'u gnyis 'bral med do*)—followed by a colloquial expression, "Isn't that so?" (*de 'u red*). She closes the passage affectionately with her nickname for Namtrul Rinpoche followed by cooing sounds: "Tsebo lo lo."[126]

Lest the reader think that this reliance is a gendered expression of female dependence on a man, let me highlight another example that reverses the relationship and shows that voice rather than gender determines the expression of reliance. The convention is for someone (man or woman) to state in the first person, "I rely on you" rather than "You rely on me." This meaning is clear in Tāre Lhamo's twenty-seventh letter, which consists of an extended duet between Tsebo and Tarpo, where she places the following in the voice of Namtrul Rinpoche:

For the able-bodied white snow lion,
Without snowy peak, there's nowhere to stand.

For the gold-eyed fish with six mottled fins,
Except in a lake, there's no way to survive.

For me, Pema Lodrö, steadfast in intent,
Without you, friend, it's impossible to live.[127]

In this passage, with its standard use of parallelism, it is clear that each animal relies on its habitat in the same way that Namtrul Rinpoche (here: Pema Lodrö) relies on Tāre Lhamo to thrive. Given that they use these images in a similar way, I read these pairings from the natural environment as a vehicle through which the two characterize their emerging partnership as based on steadfast commitment and mutual reliance. Elsewhere, in Namtrul Rinpoche's fourteenth letter, to emphasize the steadfastness of beloved and lover, he characterizes the snow mountain, turquoise lake, and sandalwood forest as "stable and steady" (*rtag brtan*) and their respective inhabitants—snow lion, gold-eyed fish, and striped tigress—as "changeless" (*'gyur med*).[128] Promising in this way that he has not changed his mind, he ends this letter requesting her to be as "unshakable" (*g.yo med*) and "steadfast" (*brtan*) as Mount Meru, thereby requesting her steadfastness and comparing her to the sacred center of the Buddhist cosmos to which he journeys on pilgrimage as he sets off to meet her in Markhok.

Just as affection enhances their visionary capacities, here the language of steadfastness encourages them to take the risk of coming together as a couple with no external authorities to sanction their union. Once the effects of liberalization reached Tibetan areas in the early 1980s, Tāre Lhamo and Namtrul Rinpoche did receive legitimizing prophecies from a number of the surviving lamas and cleric-scholars in the region. However, during the period of their correspondence, prior to that, they had to marshal trans-empirical authorities within the Tibetan Buddhist imaginaire to sanction their union, including Padmasambhava and a host of divine forces, such as the ḍākinīs and protectors. In addition, they reassured and supported each other by using folk song idioms to articulate their ongoing commitment to converge in one household and thereby indicate and reinforce their intention to form a lasting partnership.[129] Thus they created a vision of mutual reliance that encompasses the conventional terms of the reliance of husband and wife for livelihood or family matters, except that their stated aim is a grander destiny, conceived within a treasure idiom as a means to revital-ize Buddhism at this critical historical juncture.

Is This Love?

Tāre Lhamo and Namtrul Rinpoche became committed in a lifelong part-nership based on the emotional bond forged in their epistolary exchanges. They articulate this commitment in various ways beyond naturalistic images of mutual reliance and their encouragement to stay steadfast. One striking idiom, which harkens back to the importance of memory in the correspondence as a whole, involves the term "unforgettable" (*brjed med*). Passages employing this term suggest the enduring nature of their bond—not altogether unlike the Nat King Cole song of that name linking memory to undying love.[130] Here is an example from Namtrul Rinpoche's seventh letter. It refers to Tāre Lhamo by the exalted epithet "queen of reality" (*chos nyid dbang mo*) and the more amorous term "sweetheart" (*snying sdug*):

> Sweetheart, companion with shared karma and aspirations,
> Once again, I recall the Queen of Reality, dear to [my] heart.
> Even if [my] body is ill and [my state of] mind is miserable,
> In [my] thoughts, the beloved companion is unforgettable.
>
> Imagine if [we] were to reside in the same place,
> Imagine if [we] could ask about [each other's] health,
> Imagine if we could converge in one household.[131]

In contrast to the prophetic thrust of the correspondence as a whole, here a more personal aspiration for their partnership is invoked, the simple plea-sures of domesticity.

The emphasis on "recalling" and "not forgetting" throughout the cor-respondence is accompanied by a pledge of fidelity, indicating that they intend to forge a lasting partnership and that their bond goes well beyond an instrumental liaison to awaken the propensity for treasure revelation.[132] Toward the end of the correspondence, Tāre Lhamo swears her constancy of affection even in the face of death:

Congenial friend, I recall [our] connection.
Of course, I remember, congenial heart friend.

I could never forget [your] love and affection.
[My] mind is unwavering, stable as a mountain.

Even if I die, still [this] will not change.
Isn't that it, constant and worthy companion?

Ah! Just so, the mind is untainted by sadness.
[Such] words of promise, I hide in the heart.[133]

In this passage from her twenty-fourth letter, Tāre Lhamo expresses her constancy in no uncertain terms, declaring her unwavering mind to be as stable as a mountain, echoing Namtrul Rinpoche's request for her to be stable as Mount Meru. Even in the face of death, she pledges not to forget the love and affection of her "congenial friend" (mthun grogs), a term of endearment that emphasizes mutual compatibility.[134] At the end of this letter, she calls Namtrul Rinpoche the "companion who accompanies [me] in every moment" and wishes for them not to be separated even for an instant "in this life and in all the succession of [our] lives."[135]

In passages of this nature, Tāre Lhamo and Namtrul Rinpoche invoke something akin to romantic love. Romantic love is generally regarded as a phenomenon that emerged among the European bourgeoisie starting in the late eighteenth century, in which bonds of mutual affection between two individuals replaced economic and social ties between two families as the centerpiece of marriage. Central to romantic love, as discussed by Anthony Giddens, is the self-reflexive creation of a "mutual narrative biography" by two individuals who understand themselves to be uniquely compatible, completing each other in some fundamental way, and who see that unique compatibility as the basis for a lifelong partnership.[136] The emphasis on narrative as a key feature is of special interest to us here, given the connection between storytelling and agency discussed in the previous chapter in relation to cultural trauma.

Whether or not one agrees that romantic love is specifically modern, it is telling that, due to the devastation of traditional social networks during the Maoist period, Tāre Lhamo and Namtrul Rinpoche engage in precisely what Giddens suggests: "an emotional reconstruction of the past in order to project a coherent narrative of the future."[137] Recall that Tāre Lhamo's first marriage was arranged on her behalf by her principal teacher, Dzongter Kunzang Nyima, and older brother, Wangchen Nyima. In the absence of such external guideposts, Tāre Lhamo and Namtrul Rinpoche had to invent the terms of their partnership, drawing on cultural resources to reconstruct a useable past and invent a new future, including treasure lore, tantric practice, and folk idioms. Together, through the dialogue enacted in their correspondence, they created a narrative of past lives to link them to seminal times and places in the history of Buddhism and Tibet. The meanings engendered in that process made it possible to imagine their future as a couple whose revelations could help regenerate Buddhism in Golok and beyond. Just as with narrating cultural trauma, the self-reflexive project of romantic love required Tāre Lhamo and Namtrul Rinpoche to actively construct a narrative to make meaning out of the past and imagine a future. The narrative established in the correspondence interweaves love and destiny into a joint mission and lifelong partnership, integrating their private affections as a couple and public identities as tertöns.

Where the bond between Tāre Lhamo and Namtrul Rinpoche differs from romantic love is the way they distinguish their own affection and longing from emotional attachment, which has a negative connotation in Buddhist doctrine and could be regarded as a corollary to the need for emotional fulfillment associated with romantic love. In a key moment of self-definition, Tāre Lhamo makes clear how their relationship should be understood, and it precludes "attachment to worldly activities in saṃsāra" and "the confusion of inner emotions" without demeaning in any way the potential for creative collaboration in the context of a lifelong partnership.[138] In the process, she articulates a kind of love, not tainted by negative emotions. Perhaps due to local gossip in her homeland, Tāre Lhamo seems particularly on guard against any presumption that she might be operating under the influence of mundane desire by pursuing Namtrul Rinpoche. In a passage from her fifteenth letter, Tāre Lhamo emphasizes that their proposed union is *not* motivated by personal need or desire:

Not leaving out of lack of food and clothes,
Not roaming because I failed as a householder,[139]
Not cast aside for lack of affection from kin,

Not tossed away because a relationship didn't work out,
Not distracted by actions of the eight [worldly] concerns,[140]
Not thinking of destroying enemies and protecting friends,
Not attached to worldly activities in saṃsāra,
Not deceived due to the confusion of inner emotions,
I am [bound by] the visionary prophecy of glorious Padma!
The time for the oath of the mother ḍākinīs has come![141]

This passage signals a confident moment of self-representation in which Tāre Lhamo defines who she is and is not. In the Tibetan verse above, *min* signals the negative of the verb "to be" in the first person (which I translate simply as "not") and appears at the end of each line until the last two lines. This creates a certain cadence and rhythm that is broken abruptly at the end, when Tāre Lhamo switches to a declaration of who she is, using the verb *yin* to affirm "I am" and the true rationale of her actions.[142] The effect is to underscore the contrast between worldly preoccupations and her prophetic destiny with Namtrul Rinpoche.

This passage stands out stylistically for its use of slang and semantically for its earthy content. In no-nonsense terms, Tāre Lhamo gives various mundane reasons a mature woman in her early forties might seek a new companion: destitution, failure, or rejection. She denies each of these as her own rationale, yet still shows a kind of realism in her assessment of what others might think. To borrow Dondrup Gyal's expression in relation to the Sixth Dalai Lama's love songs, this passage is "grounded in real life."[143] Indeed, her first use of the term *saṃsāra* (*'khor ba*) here refers to her status as a householder over the previous two decades, not lifetimes in cyclic existence. But failure as a householder is not the reason for her aspiration to change residence and move to Nyenlung, nor are various forms of rejection, put unceremoniously as "cast aside" (*phud pa*) or "tossed away" (*'thor ba*). Her patent denial of a previous failed marriage is particularly poignant, given that her first husband died after being imprisoned in the late 1950s. In this passage, Tāre Lhamo sends an unequivocal message: in seeking a partnership with Namtrul Rinpoche, she is not motivated by attachment.

Tāre Lhamo's statement sheds much light on the nature of love in a revelatory context. While their mutual reliance may be infused with affection, because they are Buddhist masters, there is no room (at least rhetorically) for attachment to worldly concerns. The last lines in her series of "not" statements underscores this point. Tāre Lhamo proclaims that she is beyond attachment or deception, generated by the *kleśas* or negative emotions (*nyon mongs*). She thereby invokes a classical Buddhist framework in which attachment and confused emotions are expressions of self-clinging (*bdag 'dzin*) and run counter to the altruism befitting religious figures. In contrast, Tāre Lhamo asserts her own motivation in authoritative and incontrovertible terms within the Nyingma tradition, as fulfilling the prophecy of Padmasambhava, who entrusted the couple with treasures in a former lifetime, and the oath of the ḍākinīs, who are said to protect treasures until the predestined tertöns arrive to retrieve them. This does not read as an attempt to elide the mutual statements of affection found throughout the correspondence; rather, it places their personal bond squarely within the prophetic context of their shared revelatory mission.

Sarah Jacoby has done groundbreaking work regarding the question of love in treasure revelation, and a number of her findings on the topic are instructive. Just as Tāre Lhamo is careful in the passage above to place her aspiration to join in one household with Namtrul Rinpoche within a prophetic framework, rejecting emotional attachment or worldly concerns as a motivation, Jacoby demonstrates how Sera Khandro created a strict opposition in her autobiographical writings between carnal lust (*'dod chags*), a *kleśa* or negative emotion conducive to further enmeshment in saṃsāra, and love or affection (*brtse ba*), which in religious contexts between teacher and disciple can be conducive to liberation.[144] Jacoby emphasizes the mutuality of the consort relationship between Sera Khandro and Drime Özer, highlighting the ways they assisted each other in healing from illness, revealing treasures, and gaining liberation through the tantric rite of sexual union.[145] In doing so, she has been able to effectively overturn the prevailing assumptions about the consort relationship in Buddhist tantra—as an entirely instrumental liaison in service of (male) liberation—and retrieve from the literary record a noteworthy place for love in treasure revelation.[146]

That said, we should retain a measure of caution in deploying the term "love" in this context. While parallel to romantic love in their creation of a "mutual narrative biography" as the basis for a lifelong partnership, the affection shared between Tāre Lhamo and Namtrul Rinpoche in their courtship and correspondence departs from this model in important ways, not only by distinguishing the motive for their proposed union from attachment to worldly concerns but also in circumventing modern notions of the autonomous individual.[147] Throughout the correspondence, Tāre Lhamo and Namtrul Rinpoche remained deeply embedded in their religious and cultural contexts, drawing on long-standing understandings of personhood and rebirth within a Buddhist framework and also the well-developed lore of the treasure tradition. They represented their identities as an amalgamation of many lifetimes, reconstructing their past lives together as a couple linked to specific and pivotal moments in Buddhist and Tibetan history. By establishing this connection with the distant past in the continuity of their very persons, not as individuals but as a couple conjoined across lifetimes, Tāre Lhamo and Namtrul Rinpoche were able to envision a future engaged in treasure revelation and, through that, revitalizing the Buddhist teachings after a period of rupture.

It is important to highlight, then, that their emergent sense of agency as a couple depended on their connections to specific figures in the distant past and to transempirical forces integral to treasure lore. This point echoes the observation made by Gyatso about the importance of "connections" in the lives of treasure revealers as well as Jacoby's insight into treasure revelation as an "interdependent process."[148] By claiming access to authoritative sources through visionary modes of memory and their articulation in prophecy, Tāre Lhamo and Namtrul Rinpoche sanctioned their own future union and revelations within their epistolary exchanges. For this reason, their connection to each other and to figures of the distant past, as established in the correspondence, can be seen as central to their sense of agency as a couple, later expressed in their prolific religious activities during the 1980s and '90s and in their hagiographic portrait as a couple in *Jewel Garland*. In navigating the constraints and uncertainties of their historical moment, Tāre Lhamo and Namtrul Rinpoche show considerable resourcefulness in constructing a shared narrative as a couple and articulating a vision for the future.

Partners in Dance

Their agency as a couple is nowhere more prominent than in references to sexuality. Indeed, the final synthesis of the interplay of love and destiny in their correspondence can be found in passages referencing the tantric rite of sexual union. Tāre Lhamo and Namtrul Rinpoche exchanged erotic innuendos and descriptions of internal processes in the subtle body that give rise to realization and activate the revelatory process. In several passages, for example, playful images of fertility—such as a bee circling a lotus in order to extract its nectar—give way to tantric scenes of union and the resulting experience of "bliss-emptiness" (*bde stong*).[149] In others passages, they describe the practice of *caṇḍālī* or "inner heat" (*gtum mo*), which can be practiced alone or with a consort,[150] as the means to transform the subtle body and unlock the "treasure gate" (*gter sgo*), thereby accessing memories of teachings received in the distant past from Padmasambhava. In their epistolary exchanges, Tāre Lhamo and Namtrul Rinpoche depict the tantric rite, both explicitly and implicitly, as the culmination of their courtship and a recognizable feature in the revelation process in accord with traditional treatises on the topic.[151]

One passage in particular stands out for the way that it characterizes the emerging couple as "partners in dance" (*gnyis 'gros*). It features a series of images that depict their courtship and its consummation as a seamless progression, pointing beyond the correspondence itself to their future collaboration in the process of treasure revelation. In what follows, I do a close reading of this passage to elaborate on how the whole arc of their courtship and its consummation can be read as a catalyst to the visionary process and thereby showcases their agency as a tantric couple. This will also serve to recap an earlier point that love can play a distinctive role in the process of treasure revelation alongside sexuality. That said, sexuality is accorded a special place in the correspondence as the very force that can unleash their destiny. In his final letter, Namtrul Rinpoche attributes to their practice of the tantric rite of sexual union special powers—purifying illness and obstacles, overcoming adversity, enhancing health and wealth—as well as the capacity to activate the revelatory process and herald good fortune for Buddhism and the Tibetan people.

The passage depicting the couple as "partners in dance" comes from late in the correspondence, the twenty-second of Namtrul Rinpoche's letters, and offers a vibrant depiction of their courtship and its consummation. Specifically, it involves a progression through four stanzas featuring different pairs of creatures and people, described as "partners in dance," that illustrate how their relationship moves along a continuum from playful flirtation to the revelation of treasures via tantric techniques.

In the divine path of the sky above,
A pair of little black protective ravens
Glide and flutter as partners in dance,
Squawking good news back and forth:
[Their] aim is the red cliff palace
To become inseparable friends in this life.

Amid a river—pure, vast, sparkling, cool,
A pair of gold-eyed fish swoosh [their] fins,
Flaunting their agility as partners in dance:
[Their] aim is the invincible turquoise lake
To become inseparable friends in this life.

On the golden highway of Achen,[152]
A pair of supreme adepts, male and female,
Quiver in postures as partners in dance:
[Their] aim is the sacred land of Utsang[153]
To become inseparable friends in this life.

In the Zalmo [Range] of Do Kham in the Land of Snow,
A pair of friends with shared karma and aspirations
Reveal treasures as partners in dance:
[Their] aim is the land of Dhumathala[154]
To become inseparable friends in all lives.[155]

This passage uses the parallelism particular to Tibetan folk song styles, whereby a series of verses provide analogies with the referent revealed in the final verse. Here the referent is certainly Tāre Lhamo and Namtrul Rinpoche as the "pair of friends" in the Zalmo Range of Do Kham or eastern Tibet.[156] In successive verses, Namtrul Rinpoche articulates their pursuit of a shared aim, synthesizing images from the natural environment with the tantric rite of sexual union and prophetic idiom of treasure revelation. In each case, their aim involves a common destination, conjoining as a couple to become inseparable in this life and (in the final verse) in all lives.

Through these analogies, Namtrul Rinpoche depicts their courtship and its consummation as a fourfold process of dialogue, sport, sexual union, and revelation. Taking the verses as a progression, the first can be read as an allusion to the dialogue enacted in the process of exchanging letters. Two black ravens glide and flutter in the sky, exchanging news back and forth, on their way to a common destination. Their dialogue as "partners in dance" establishes the destination and ensures their flight in tandem. This progresses to sport and play, figured as fish swimming side by side, flaunting their skills as they swoosh through the water. Given the use of parallelism in Tibetan folk songs, making each of the preceding verses into analogies for the final referent (the couple themselves), the dialogue of the ravens and the play of the fish suggest the process of courtship in the letters. In these images, one can recognize the mutuality of their partnership, expressed in the ability to make a journey together toward a shared destination, sharing news and flaunting their skills along the way.

Elsewhere Namtrul Rinpoche refers to this play as "the sport of attraction" (*'dod pa'i sgyu rtsal*). This term appears in his first letter and introduces an erotic element at the very outset of their correspondence. Significantly, he credits Tāre Lhamo—as well as the process of letter writing itself—with the power to conjure this sport. Here is a more complete version of his request for her to send more letters, mentioned briefly at the outset of this chapter:

> If it arises in the mind of the lady of bliss-emptiness,
> Skilled in inciting the wisdom expanse of the four joys,
> With the iron hook that conjures the sport of attraction,
> Please send letters [continuously] like the flow of Ganges water
> Or like the dance of the sun and moon in the sky.[157]

In this ornate poetic passage, Namtrul Rinpoche places the sport of attraction firmly within the process of letter writing. For him, Tāre Lhamo holds an iron hook capable of conjuring attraction and wields it through composing letters.[158] As a complement to love in a romantic key elsewhere in the correspondence, here the sport of attraction suggests the erotic aspect of their courtship.[159] In flirtatious moments, they turn to Indian erotic motifs, as when Tāre Lhamo writes of "flashing sidelong glances" (*zur mig g.yo*)—traceable to the coquettish language of the eyes in Indian literature[160]—or when Namtrul Rinpoche describes himself as a peacock dancing with delight at receiving her first letter. Tāre Lhamo reciprocates that image when she describes Namtrul Rinpoche as a peacock "flaunting its plumage in a sphere like a parasol, / its dazzling form with the grace of a blooming hollyhock."[161] In such terms, the two conceive of their dialogue as a sport and mutual provocation, inspiring affective responses and ultimately spurring each other into action. Given the way they "flaunt" (ngom pa) their literary and visionary talents, one can detect an emergent sense of agency as a couple, constructing their epistolary personae in tandem and creating a mutual narrative across lifetimes.

At various points in their correspondence, Tāre Lhamo and Namtrul Rinpoche explicitly link the sport of attraction to tantric practices. As we have seen, in the passage in which Namtrul Rinpoche introduces this term, he associates Tāre Lhamo with "bliss-emptiness" (bde stong) and the skill to incite the "four joys" (dga' bzhi).[162] This is a veiled reference to the tantric rite of sexual union, in which a consort (usually cast in gendered terms as female) aids the practitioner (implicitly male in much of tantric literature) in eliciting the four joys,[163] a series of blissful states that culminate in a dissolution of duality into bliss-emptiness or sahajānanda, "spontaneously arisen bliss."[164] By linking the sport of attraction with the four joys, Namtrul Rinpoche indicates that inciting passion in the amorous play of courtship is an important precursor to their anticipated practice of this tantric rite, while instigating a visionary process in their letters.

This link between sport and sexuality can be seen clearly by returning to the passage on "partners in dance," which proceeds from courtship to its consummation. The third verse depicts the sexual union of male and female yogic adepts (rnal 'byor pho mo) conjoined quivering in postures (gom stabs g.yo). This image evokes an authoritative model for their anticipated practice, called simply "union" (sbyor ba) in Tibetan or "union between a couple" (yab yum zhal sbyor). When the verses are read as a sequence, this yogic practice is cast as the precursor to treasure revelation. In the final verse, their courtship reaches its fruition in the revelations of treasures, based on their shared karma and aspirations from previous lifetimes. Thus the elements of their partnership depicted in this passage follow a progression from dialogue and sport in their courtship to sexuality and revelation in its consummation. In the treasure tradition more generally, sexuality is ascribed the power to unlock the tertön's visionary potential and awaken the capacity to reveal treasures. These treasures in the form of esoteric Buddhist teachings, in turn, serve as the basis for founding new religious lineages.

According to the Third Dodrupchen, a native of Golok and the previous incarnation of Tāre Lhamo's own teacher Rigdzin Jalu Dorje, the tantric rite of sexual union allows tertöns to gain access to treasures, hidden in the deep recesses of their minds by Padmasambhava.[165] Alongside the physical treasure hidden in the Tibetan landscape—which could be as simple as a rock with a seed syllable emblazoned on it or as elaborate as a casket containing images, scrolls, and relics—the true hiding place of a treasure teaching is a special locus within the mind itself, which Dodrupchen refers to alternately as the "luminous innate awareness" ('od gsal gnyug ma'i rig pa) and the "sphere of luminosity" ('od gsal gyi khams).[166] With these terms, he emphasizes a sphere of the mind that is distinct from ordinary consciousness, such that treasures remain impervious to the winds of karma across lifetimes. To access treasures so concealed requires "the spontaneously arisen bliss . . . which can be produced by a special consort who has made the appropriate aspirations in the past, and who is to become the key to accomplishment."[167] In other words, the tantric rite of sexual union facilitates the four joys and thereby provides access to the special hiding place of treasures in the deep reaches of the mind.

In their correspondence, Tāre Lhamo and Namtrul Rinpoche refer to tantric practices to accomplish this in several ways. For example, in his third letter, Namtrul Rinpoche mentions "the profound dharma of Anu[yoga], the shortcut of [union with] a consort that liberates through touch," an explicit reference to the tantric rite, displaced to their previous lives as Yeshe Tsogyal and Namkhai Nyingpo.[168] Tāre Lhamo is more reticent about mentioning sexuality and describes treasure revelation through the practice of caṇḍālī, which can be done individually or with a partner. Witness Tāre Lhamo's description of the revelatory process as a result of this practice:

Within, the mind itself becomes naturally radiant awareness.
Meeting one's original face as awareness, the effortless ground,
Awakening the protector Padma's aspiration and entrustment,
The body's nāḍī and prāṇa blaze [with] the blissful heat of caṇḍālī.

The nāḍī knots at the five cakra sites release;
The sky-gate of symbols opens; letters manifest in space;
Nectar pools [in] the vase that grants glory of deathless life;
Visible, gross symbolic forms emerge from the sky.[169]

3.4 Padmasambhava and Yeshe Tsogyal in union, statue on Namtrul Rinpoche's reliquary.

This passage describes the revelation of treasures through the practice of caṇḍālī, as a result of which the knots in the nāḍīs, or channels of the subtle body, that ordinary constrict the flow of prāṇa, or vital breath, are released at their gathering points, or cakras, in the body. This opens the "sky-gate of symbols" (*brda nam mkha'i sgo*), a metaphorical way to describe accessing the locus in the mind where treasures are hidden. From there, letters and gross symbolic forms emerge, by which Tāre Lhamo likely refers to the symbolic script (*brda yig*) of the ḍākinīs that requires decoding in a further stage of the revelation process. According to Namtrul Rinpoche, throughout their twenty-two years together, the couple took turns revealing symbolic scripts and decoding them for each other.[170]

In his twenty-fifth and final letter,[171] Namtrul Rinpoche provides a similar description that portrays the practice of caṇḍālī, but firmly locates it within the context of sexual union. In more detail, he describes the generation of heat through the "sun of caṇḍālī" (*gtum mo'i nyi ma*) in order to melt the bindu or essential drop (*thig le*) at the crown of the head, referred to as the "nectar moon" (*bcud zla ba*). Blazing and dripping (*'bar 'dzag*) is then said to release the knots in the nāḍīs at the cakra centers and to "fully rouse bliss and joy through great passion."[172] This process is once again said to unlock the treasure gate in the deep reaches of the mind; as Namtrul Rinpoche avows, "without effort the treasure gate spontaneously opens."[173] Beyond the reference to "great passion" (*chags chen*), it becomes clear that sexual union is involved by the end of the passage, where Namtrul Rinpoche gleefully proclaims: "Hail to you, the beloved, sublime bliss-emptiness, / And to me, the playful vajra engaged in intercourse."[174] In tantric code, the vajra refers to the male sexual organ, while the term "intercourse" (*chags spyod*) refers explicitly to sexuality.

This bold passage at the end of the correspondence anticipates Tāre Lhamo's arrival at Nyenlung. It is part of a "song of joyous tidings" (*dga' skyid gtam gyi glu gzhas*) to welcome her and celebrate that they can finally converge in one household.[175] The letter has a festive tone, with a playful use of phonemic repetition and onomatopoeia, opening with "the pulsing dance of father warriors [that] beats and beats" and "the songs intoned by mother warriors: *sha ra ra*."[176] Banners swirl, music plays, rainbow clouds gather, and an auspicious rain falls on flowers that jingle *si li li*. The focus of the song is an offering of liquor, a customary way in Tibetan culture to greet a guest upon arrival. Yet the liquor of this song occupies another register as well.

He describes it as "supreme elixir" (*bdud rtsi mchog*), the "great substance symbolizing method and wisdom" and "the liquor of we two friends who have never parted."[177] The compound "method and wisdom" (*thabs shes*) is a standard referent for male and female partners who engage in the tantric rite of sexual union. In this way, the liquor to greet Tāre Lhamo is correlated to both the elixir consumed in the context of a tantric rite of initiation and the sexual fluids of the tantric couple in union.[178]

Namtrul Rinpoche goes on to attribute to this elixir—standing for their tantric practice of sexual union—a range of powers. Three—healing illness, enhancing longevity, and realization itself—are standard benefits ascribed to sexuality in a tantric context.[179] Yet Namtrul Rinpoche elaborates to include features specific to treasure revelation and more. Here is his list, using a cyclic repetition of the term for liquor (*chang*) in each line, by which he welcomes her in the form of the goddess Sarasvatī as a guest and defines a host of benefits from their joining together as a couple:

In the first season of coincidence,
You, goddess Sarasvatī, assemble with an array of gods.
Supreme elixir mixed of thousands of grains and juice,
This great substance symbolizing method and wisdom
Is the liquor at the festival when you arrive here.
It is the liquor to inquire about your health.
It is the liquor to merrily enjoy this festival of delight.
It is the liquor for the vajra feast of great secret mantra.
It is the liquor of indestructible life and changeless form.
It is the liquor with blessings by father lamas of the three lineages.
It is the liquor with siddhi of the divine protector *yidams*.
It is the liquor with the activity of mother ḍākinīs of three sacred places.
It is the liquor with the power of divine dharmapālas and guardians.
It is the liquor that accomplishes the intention of the protector Padma.
It is the liquor that engages the profound and extensive dharma treasures.
It is the liquor that reaches the lofty heights of gods on the side of virtue.
It is the liquor that stoops to the level of unworthy evil spirits.
It is the liquor that accomplishes mind's desires without exception.
It is the liquor that clears away all kinds of adversity and stains.
It is the liquor of we two friends who have never parted.
It is the liquor without contradiction to the samaya vow.

It is the liquor that dispels obstructing conditions without exception.
It is the liquor that guides those with a connection to the Glorious Mountain.[180]
It is the liquor that pacifies illness, evil spirits, obstacles, and the eight fears.
It is the liquor that expands life, merit, glory, and wealth.
It is the liquor that brings all saṃsāra and nirvāṇa, the cosmos, under
    one's sway.
It is the liquor that fiercely cuts the ten fields of enemies.
Tasting this liquor gives rise to a majestic form.
Consuming this liquor gives rise to melodious speech.
Drinking this liquor gives rise to bliss in the mind.
Partaking in this liquor enhances the qualities of realization.
Enjoying this liquor releases the three nāḍīs at the five cakras.
Tasting this liquor gives rise to the wisdom of bliss-emptiness.
The qualities of this liquor are indescribable.[181]

This can be read as a potent representation of their agency as a couple, attributing to the consummation of their union in the form of the "great substance symbolizing method and wisdom" many powers, both apotropaic and soteriological. On the apotropaic end of the spectrum, he attributes to the liquor (and hence their union) the capacity to dispel adversity, impurities, and obstructing conditions as well as to fulfill the mind's desires without exception. He also attributes to it the power to accomplish a standard set of four ritual actions (*las bzhi*) in Buddhist tantra: pacifying illness, obstacles, and fears; enhancing life, merit, glory, and wealth; holding sway over the cosmos, all of saṃsāra and nirvāṇa; and subjugating the ten fields of enemies. Adding to its potency, multiple forces are distilled into this liquor: the blessings of lamas, the intention of Padmsambhava, the activities of ḍākinīs, and the power of the protectors.

On the soteriological side, the liquor (and hence their union) promises to liberate the fixation of mind into a realization of bliss-emptiness. In reference to sexuality in a tantric context, enjoying this liquor is said to "enhance the qualities of realization," "release [knots in] the three nāḍīs at the five cakras," and "give rise to the wisdom of bliss-emptiness."[182] The soteriological promise is not only for themselves; at the end of the letter, Namtrul Rinpoche extends this benefit to "all beings who are connected, whether through good or bad karma."[183] It is on their behalf that he addresses his closing aspiration by wishing, "may we stir the depths of saṃsāra" and "may we be able to lead them to the land, Ngayab Palri," the pure land of Padmasambhava.[184] In this passage, their union is cast not only as a powerful force in the world to accomplish aims and defeat enemies but also as a vehicle for liberation for themselves and others.

This is a remarkable testimony to their union and correspondingly their sense of agency as a couple by the end of their epistolary courtship. In fact, it would be difficult to find terms in which to articulate the benefits of sexuality in a tantric context that were stronger than the range of apotropaic and soteriological powers ascribed here. Notably, treasure revelation is linked to these benefits, given that the liquor, standing for their union, "accomplishes the intention of the protector Padma," i.e., Padmasambhava, and "engages the profound and extensive dharma treasures."[185] Put another way, the potency of their union is inextricably bound to the intentions of Padmasambhava for them to reveal "profound and extensive" (*zab rgyas*) teachings together as treasures. In celebration, Namtrul Rinpoche gleefully states: "Hoist the victory banner of the Buddha's teachings! / The sun of happiness shines for all, / Pacifying strife, the damage of degenerate times."[186] Here he depicts Tāre Lhamo's arrival at Nyenlung as heralding no less than a new era of happiness for all (presumably Tibetans) in which the Buddhist teachings can once again proliferate (presumably through their own revelatory activities), thereby putting an end to the strife and damage of the turbulent decades of the Maoist period.

Just as I began this chapter by remarking on the sense of optimism projected in these letters through images of fertility and new possibilities, here let me close by highlighting the remarkable degree of agency expressed in their correspondence. Despite the devastation of the preceding decades, Tāre Lhamo and Namtrul Rinpoche roused a tremendous sense of inspiration and confidence through their epistolary exchanges, generating a mood of affection, intimacy, and mutual reliance while articulating a vision for their future religious activities. In synthesizing love and destiny in their correspondence, they forged a lifelong partnership, which provided both the context for their prophetic revelatory activity and the domestic setting for their enduring personal bond. Along the way, they kindled and flaunted their literary and visionary talents, constructed a shared narrative across lifetimes, launched the revelatory process by identifying the sites of their treasures, marshaled an array of transempirical forces to sanction their union, envisioned the transformative impact of their partnership as a force in Tibetan history, and created the foundation for their prolific revelations, frequent teachings, and extensive travels.

What comes through so vividly in the correspondence is the joint nature of their endeavor. Generally speaking, treasure revelation relies on the collaboration between male and female partners. While Nyingma lamas routinely marry and have children, since lineages of transmission for their esoteric teachings are often passed through the family, sexuality has a special place in treasure revelation, enabling the tertön to access teachings from the distant past in the deep reaches of the mind. This means that, with few exceptions,[187] tertöns have revealed treasures in tandem with a partner, though typically only one member of the pair gets the credit for a specific treasure cycle, even in the rare case of a tertön couple.[188] Tāre Lhamo and Namtrul Rinpoche are distinctive in that their treasures are considered to be jointly revealed and collected together into a single treasure corpus, and their example brings to the fore the agency of a tantric couple. Whereas such collaboration is usually elided or minimized, in textual sources by and about Tāre Lhamo and Namtrul Rinpoche, their partnership is highlighted and made a central aspect of their public religious identity.

Now that we have glimpsed the enormous possibility that Tāre Lhamo and Namtrul Rinpoche sensed at this pivotal moment of Tibetan history, we need to explore in more detail the way that they conceived of their capacity for action at the end of the Maoist period. We have yet to discern how the two confronted certain challenges to coming together as a couple, such as state restrictions on travel, the reluctance on the part of Tāre Lhamo's relatives to allow her to leave Markhok, and Namtrul Rinpoche's recurrent bouts of illness. More importantly, for a culturally nuanced account of agency, their construction of a shared mission must be placed firmly within a Buddhist explanatory framework, including the tensions posed between historical contingency and their sense of shared destiny. How did Tāre Lhamo and Namtrul Rinpoche construct a sense of destiny together in a way that left room for human initiative in confronting the challenges to their union and the contingencies of their historical moment? The next chapter explores this question in continuing to read from the rich and variegated archive of their correspondence.

FOUR

Emissaries of Padmasambhava

Tibetan Treasures and Healing Trauma

IN THEIR CORRESPONDENCE, while forging a personal bond replete with affection, Tāre Lhamo and Namtrul Rinpoche never lose sight of their prophetic mission. Envisioning a future vocation together as tertöns or treasure revealers, they express their duty to rescue Tibetans from the strife of degenerate times and to heal the damage to Buddhism in the wake of the Cultural Revolution. In one of her letters, Tāre Lhamo conveys their joint mission in prophetic terms as follows:

> You, the sublime son of good family and pure origin,
> And I the mantra-born woman, Devī, the two [of us],
> In order to rescue [beings] from the strife of degenerate times,
> We have been appointed by the protector Orgyan Padma.
> Awakening together [past] deeds, aspirations, and the entrustment,
> It is [our] promise to guide all mother beings.[1]

In this verse, Tāre Lhamo articulates their role as emissaries appointed by Padmasambhava (here: Orgyan Padma), the eighth-century Indian master whom Tibetans view as a second Buddha and credit with a seminal part in bringing Buddhism to Tibet.[2] From the twelfth century onward, the treasure tradition consolidated around Padmasambhava as the source of Nyingma scriptures and sacra to be revealed during times of strife and decline as a source of renewed teachings and blessings.[3] Adopting the language of the degenerate times (*dus snyigs ma*), which has permeated treasure lore, Tāre Lhamo expresses a heroic sense of duty to rescue Tibetans from the devastation caused by the Maoist period, when most visible signs of Tibetan culture, including Buddhist institutions, were destroyed.

However, their correspondence makes no mention of those tumultuous events, apart from veiled references to degenerate times and the influence of barbarians and demons. In their letters, as in *Spiraling Vine of Faith*, any specific reference to mistreatment suffered or destruction witnessed is omitted. These facts would have been risky to set down on paper in case their correspondence was intercepted, though they also could have been edited out when the letters were published.[4] Either way, the effect is parallel to that in Tāre Lhamo's hagiographic portrait—self-censorship emphasizes the heroic nature of their public personae. In their correspondence, Tāre Lhamo and Namtrul Rinpoche never present themselves as victims and always remain focused on the greater good of the Tibetan people. This is significant, given that traumatization is related to feelings of helplessness and overwhelm. Instead Tāre Lhamo and Namtrul Rinpoche consistently demonstrate a sense of resourcefulness, generating emotional resources through their personal bond and drawing on cultural resources from treasure lore to construct a shared narrative through which to envision revitalizing Buddhist teachings and institutions. Their sense of agency as a couple, which develops throughout the correspondence, is central to their aim to heal the devastation of collective trauma.

Instead of documenting the destruction of the Maoist period in testimonial fashion, Tāre Lhamo and Namtrul Rinpoche reached into the depths of Tibetan history to restore a sense of continuity with the past. In the verse above, she describes "awakening together [past] deeds, aspirations, and the entrustment," referring to their own deeds and aspirations (*las smon*) from past lives as well as the entrustment (*gtad rgya*) of treasures by Padmasambhava. In her language, the past is presented as a living force that remains dormant in the form of karmic latencies and buried treasures, but once activated, can operate causally on the present. In other words, the couple draw on the distant past not as the recorded events of history with which to re-create a sense of Tibetan identity, but rather as a resource that they can summon to shape events in the present and immediate future.

Tāre Lhamo and Namtrul Rinpoche evoke the distant past to enable them to "heal the damage to the teachings and beings" (*bstan 'gro'i rgud gso ba*), whereby "teachings" implicitly refers to Buddhism and "beings" contextually refers to Tibetans in the region of Golok and beyond. On numerous occasions in the correspondence, in prophecies and bardic verse, they use the language of "healing" (gso ba) and "rescuing" (skyob pa) beings as well as "victory" (rgyal kha) over demonic and barbaric forces. So far, in analyzing their letters, we have explored the interplay between the prophetic and personal dimensions of their courtship in ornate poetic and folk song styles, analyzing gestures of praise and deference, expressions of affection and their function in stimulating visionary recollections, and erotic motifs anticipating their practice of the tantric rite of sexual union. Now, in the first half of this chapter, we turn to the more declarative genres of prophecy and bardic verse to examine the heroic features of their epistolary personae as constructed in the correspondence. Their prophecies feature a metaphor of healing by which the revelation of treasures—as unsullied teachings and blessings from the very origins of Buddhism in Tibet—promises to reestablish cultural continuity after the prohibition of Buddhist practice for almost twenty years. In this sense, Tāre Lhamo and Namtrul Rinpoche saw their roles as emissaries of Padmasambhava to be central to the healing process in the wake of the Cultural Revolution.

Complementing this metaphor of healing, bardic verse employs the language of victory over demonic and barbaric forces, heralding the sun of Buddhist teachings rising once again to bring about the good fortune of Tibetans. Both prophecies and bardic verse have a declarative tone, invoking the power of Padmasambhava and Gesar as well as transcendent beings such as ḍākinīs and protectors, to effect the very healing and victory described therein. When writing in these genres, Tāre Lhamo and Namtrul Rinpoche claim the capacity to intervene in the very course of history through their revelations, yet also position themselves as intermediaries who merely invoke sources of power and authority beyond their own capacity for action. This poses a dilemma for their agency as a couple, discussed in this chapter with respect to Buddhist notions of causation.

Tāre Lhamo and Namtrul Rinpoche acknowledge the challenges and contingencies of their historical moment in the late 1970s, the topic of the second half of this chapter. As early as her first letter, Tāre Lhamo suggests a variety of forces at work in the unfolding of events: the power of aspiration, the fickleness of coincidence, their merit from past lives, the possibility of ritual intervention, Padmasambhava's handiwork in the distant past, and the uncertain timing of their union. A discussion of these factors and their bearing on the couple's future course of action continues throughout the letters. Along the way, Tāre Lhamo and Namtrul Rinpoche share candid statements about the very human dilemmas confronting them, which delayed their union by more than a year: health problems, seasonal weather, the opinions of relatives, and state restrictions on travel. In their assessment of these obstacles and their strategies for surmounting them, they again show resourcefulness as they openly confront uncertainty. Although destiny is invoked, nonetheless there is a strong sense of contingency, and, importantly for our discussion of agency, the possibility for the couple themselves to influence the outcome of events.

This chapter argues that in their correspondence, along similar lines as their later hagiographic portraits by Pema Ösal Thaye, Tāre Lhamo and Namtrul Rinpoche created a redemptive narrative through which they envisioned suturing the rupture in Tibetan cultural and religious practices. The narrative is redemptive first and foremost by making meaning out of the otherwise senseless and overwhelming loss of Tibetan leaders, religious and political, who died in prison during the social transformation of the late 1950s, and the destruction of the vestiges of Buddhist institutions as symbols of the "four olds" during the Cultural Revolution.[5] By encapsulating these events in veiled references to degenerate times, Tāre Lhamo and Namtrul Rinpoche were able to frame the period as a temporary aberration in an otherwise morally constituted Buddhist cosmos, subsuming the violence and destruction into a Buddhist master narrative as the work of demonic and barbaric forces. The narrative is also redemptive since the degeneration of the present calls forth the very revelations needed to overcome it and thereby, in the logic of the treasure tradition, restore the Buddhist teachings and the good fortune of Tibetans.

Tāre Lhamo and Namtrul Rinpoche performatively speak into existence a dramatic historical shift. In terms of narrating an alternative history, or what Chakrabarty calls "subaltern pasts,"[6] on the one hand, they draw on the ascribed power of transempirical forces from the distant past to help them to navigate the contingencies of their historical moment and actualize their shared mission to revitalize Buddhist teachings, practices, and institutions. And on the other hand, they symbolically restructure historical events by incorporating a period of collective trauma into a Buddhist master narrative. In the process, Tāre Lhamo and Namtrul Rinpoche assert interpretive control over events and create a shared narrative within which to imagine the transformative impact of their own future revelatory activities. This narrative allowed them, in the 1980s and '90s, to galvanize Tibetans in Golok and beyond in the restorative work of rebuilding Buddhist institutions.

Subaltern Pasts and Agency

To reflect on agency in light of Tāre Lhamo and Namtrul Rinpoche's prophetic role as tertöns, I would like to invoke a conundrum regarding the recovery of minority voices raised by Dipesh Chakrabarty. How can one recover subalterns as subjects of their own history if they themselves do not claim agency and instead deflect the credit for their actions to transempirical beings or processes? With reference to the Santal rebellion of 1855 against British colonial domination, Chakrabarty poses the dilemma thus: "What does it mean, then, when we both take the subaltern's views seriously—the subaltern ascribes the agency for their rebellion to some god— and want to confer on the subaltern agency or subjecthood in their own history, a status that the subaltern's statement denies?"[7] Like the Santal leaders Chakrabarty references, Tāre Lhamo and Namtrul Rinpoche would have been subaltern with respect to the colonial state but elite within their own local contexts. Moreover, they invoke a host of transempirical beings and processes as the driving force of history, including prophecies by Padmasambhava, the oath of ḍākinīs, the influence of protectors, the workings of karma, the binding nature of their own tantric commitments across lifetimes, and the process of treasure revelation itself.

Within sources by and about Tāre Lhamo and Namtrul Rinpoche, as considered in this book, Buddhist explanatory devices such as karma and prophecy tend to deflect agency to the distant past, when deeds were done or words uttered that have a determining effect on the present. For example, in chapter 2, I noted how Pema Ösal Thaye uses karma to narrate the events of recent history, specifically to frame the "extremely turbulent" decades between 1959 and 1978 in *Spiraling Vine of Faith*. In doing so, he both stakes a claim to agency on behalf of Tibetans and relegates their active role in determining events to their unspecified deeds as a collective in the past. In chapter 3, I discussed how Tāre Lhamo and Namtrul Rinpoche drew on cultural resources to construct a shared narrative across lifetimes and sanction their union. They did so through evoking the prophetic authority of Padmasambhava and the backing of transcendent beings in the absence of other legitimizing authorities at the end of the Maoist period. This chapter explores further how their letters draw on the distant past as a force to be summoned in order to accomplish their aims, negotiating the contingencies of their historical moment within a Buddhist framework of causation.

In the treasure tradition more broadly, one can detect a fascinating interplay between the heightened agency of tertöns, who found new ritual cycles and lineages through their revelations, and their deflection of the credit for their activities and prolific writings to Padmasambhava. The innovative nature of treasure revelation—introducing not only fresh formulations of esoteric teachings and rituals but also new relics, pilgrimage sites, monastic institutions, and incarnation lines—is masked through a phenomenon I call the *rhetoric of destiny*.[8] Prophecies attributed to Padmasambhava are understood to propel major events in the lives of tertöns and specify the teachings hidden for them in the Tibetan landscape. To the extent that prophecies provide a "script for life," they threaten to subsume human agency.

So how do we recover subalterns as the subject of their own history, if and when they themselves deflect agency? In a sense, Chakrabarty's conundrum begs the question: do we accept the deflection of credit for the subaltern's actions at face value or investigate culturally specific strategies for representing agency? Instead of treating ascriptions of agency as assertions to be judged by the epistemic parameters of secular history, it may be more profitable to view them as representational strategies that intersect with culturally specific notions of personhood and causation and also rely on literary genres or oral frames of reference. If one seeks to "provincialize Europe," as Charkrabarty does, it would be ironic to require the subaltern to speak in terms of the autonomous subject of Western humanism and thereby, in the case of the Santal Rebellion of 1855, expect its leaders to take personal credit for inspiring an uprising. Rather, I suggest that we must become attuned to culturally specific strategies for articulating agency and the different subject positions that might be implied even though Chakrabarty might disapprove of this move as "anthropologizing" the subaltern.[9]

With respect to the correspondence between Tāre Lhamo and Namtrul Rinpoche, we need to consider the specific terms for ascribing agency operative in their letters, including Buddhist notions of personhood and causation as well as Tibetan genre conventions related to specific styles of versification.

The ascriptions of agency in the letters are patterned in what Sherry Ortner has termed "cultural schemas," i.e., patterns of action and interpretation that inform but do not wholly determine the decisions of actors within a given culture.[10] Tāre Lhamo and Namtrul Rinpoche marshal specific symbols, discourses, and authoritative paradigms in their correspondence to explain events, to conceive of possibilities, and to articulate a course of action. As will be chronicled in the second half of this chapter, their letters show how the couple navigates historical contingencies within a specifically Buddhist framework, providing a nuanced account of how Nyingma masters take into account the karma-based rubrics of causes and conditions (*rgyu rkyen*) along-side prophecy in assessing a course of action and its timing.

Specifically, I highlight the importance of genre to representing agency, given that there is no single authorial stance in the letters of either Tāre Lhamo or Namtrul Rinpoche that can serve as a "transparent expression" of a private and autonomous self. The previous chapter took stock of the range of authorial stances in their correspondence, which depend to a large extent on the style of versification used in a given letter or passage. As an example of how genre influences self-representation, consider the contrast between the declarative tone of prophecy and the authorial stance of a supplication, which highlights the anguish of the supplicant and calls on the compassion of a transcendent being. Starting with the latter, the passage below from Namtrul Rinpoche's seventh letter illustrates well their overarching reliance on Padmasambhava, but the way it is articulated betrays a sense of helplessness that is rare in their correspondence. Namtrul Rinpoche wrote this supplication while quite ill, according to the letter in which it is found, and directed it at Padmasambhava as an ongoing beneficent presence in Tibetan lives:

Without refuge or protector, we beings of degenerate [times],
Now, in an anguished lament, cry out to whomever,
Asking for refuge and protection for the destitute,
As the iron shackles of karma and kleśa tighten their grip.

Lord guru, liberate swiftly through your compassion
Those who are trapped in the prison of saṃsāra
And fettered by the noose of suffering.
Supreme teacher, apart from you, there is no refuge!
Padmākara, [we] have no other protector [but you].

4.1 Mural at Nyenlung of Padmasambhava flanked by Yeshe Tsogyal to the right.

Precious Lake-Born One,[11] whose kindness cannot be repaid,
From this time forward until attaining awakening,
Please accept me and bless me to be inseparable [from you].[12]

This supplication heightens a sense of anguish at a time when Namtrul Rinpoche was beset with illness and complained of a profuse nosebleed and high blood pressure. His appeal to Padmasambhava is only partly on his own behalf; from the very outset, he broadens its scope to include all beings who are destitute and trapped in saṃsāra. As so often is the case in hagiographic literature, here his supplication is immediately answered, within the same letter, in the form of a vision that Namtrul Rinpoche recorded. Although his supplication is directed at Padmasambhava, the one who appears in a vision to give him advice is Tāre Lhamo in the form of Sera Khandro, one of her previous lives. In a song of experience (*nyams mgur*), she advises him on how to regard illness as "the unimpeded display of awareness" (*zang thal rig pa'i rtsal*). Thus his supplication, rather than an expression of helplessness after all, becomes another way to call upon emotional and cultural resources through visions prompted by and shared within his epistolary exchanges with Tāre Lhamo.

Padmasambhava is a ubiquitous presence in the correspondence. Again and again, they refer to the oath (*tha tshig*), command (*bka'*), prophecy (*lung bstan*), destiny (*bkod thang*), inheritance (*pha phog bu*), and entrustment (*gtad rgya*) that they received from Padmasambhava as his specially appointed emissaries (*pho nya*). This indicates the degree to which the authority for their own prophecies and revelations relied on their connection to him, bound across lifetimes by his entrustment, their shared aspirations, and the tantric commitment of samaya. In contrast to the supplication above, the second example features the declarative tone of prophecy while positioning the status of their future revelations as the inheritance of Padmasambhava. This passage follows a cryptic description of the location for one of their treasure in Tāre Lhamo's sixth letter:

> Now, to obtain the inheritance of Padmasambhava,
> The time has come for the entrustment of [us] pair of friends.
> Now if we proceed according to his command, it is good.
>
> In the vast casket of the inner sanctum of the mind
> Is the heart certificate of the 100,000 mother ḍākinīs,
> Expressly the means to reverse the strife of degeneration.
>
> In a punctuation-free missive in ḍākinī script,
> Definitely there is a prophecy of the ḍākinīs.
> Friend, it is the key of the vidyādharas![13]

The tone of this passage conveys a sense of performative certainty and command. Tāre Lhamo expresses confidence that the time has come to awaken Padmasambhava's entrustment of treasures and follow his command in propagating the teachings contained therein. By doing so, the treasure, which she frames as "the means to reverse the strife of degeneration" (*snyigs ma'i ru 'dzing bzlog pa'i thabs*), can be revealed. While the source of their revelations is clearly given as Padmasambhava, in no uncertain terms, she asserts the resulting treasures as their own inheritance to be retrieved in order to redress the strife and degeneration of their specific historical moment.

In prophecy and bardic verse, declarative statements are part and parcel of genre conventions, providing a vehicle for more strident claims and declarations about the future. These genres routinely contain performative speech in Austin's sense, which does not merely describe future events but is understood to make them so through the utterance itself.[14] A prophecy by Padmasambhava as voiced through the tertön does not merely predict future events; it is understood to effect or set into motion those very events. Likewise, in their correspondence, bardic verse evocative of the Gesar epic summons or calls into existence victory over demonic and barbaric forces, invoking a host of transcendent beings and heralding the restoration of Buddhism. Through these genres, Tāre Lhamo and Namtrul Rinpoche position themselves as having special access to sources of authority and power, reached through visionary means and expressed as performative speech. While these sources involve transempirical beings or processes, in answer to Chakrabarty's conundrum, their agency can surely be identified in the artful deployment of preexisting cultural rubrics and assertion of their visionary talents.

Healing the Damage

Their appropriation of the language of degenerate times is central to the way that Tāre Lhamo and Namtrul Rinpoche frame recent history, integrating the traumatic events of the Maoist period into a Buddhist framework and master narrative. The notion of degeneration harkens back to a widespread Buddhist conception of time as a process of decline,[15] parallel to the Brahmanical schema of the four *yugas* or ages, which start with a golden age and devolve from there into the *kaliyuga*, the present time of strife and degeneration. In Buddhism, this golden age begins with the appearance of a buddha in the world and declines until the Buddhist teachings finally disappear; yet in the treasure tradition, this principle of temporal degeneration has been adapted in order to introduce a mechanism to restore Buddhist teachings and lineage blessings. In a long-standing trope of decline and revival, times of strife and calamity call for the beneficent intervention of Padmasambhava through the revelatory activities of one of his appointed emissaries.

Based on this, Tāre Lhamo and Namtrul Rinpoche propose to reach beyond the degenerate present and into the distant past in order to reveal pristine teachings and renewed blessings. In their treasure corpus, a text titled *A Concise Explanation of Treasures* (*Gter gyi rnam bshad mdor bsdus*) refers to the plight of the Tibetan people at the hands of "barbaric foreigners" (*mtha' mi kla klo*). Assuming the prophetic voice of Padmasambhava, it describes the horrors of the degenerate age in terms that closely resemble recent Tibetan history:

> In the future, at the very end of the degenerate era,
> Human life will shorten and the five poisons intensify,
> The scourge of plague, famine, and war will arise.
> Upholders of the teachings will dwindle,
> And harm will come from enemies of Buddhism.
> Whatever terrain [contains] broken samaya vows
> Will be fenced in by the laws of barbaric foreigners.
> Unparalleled by [any] event in the four times,
> The land of Tibet will be orphaned without a protector.
> As it becomes more feeble, what can be done?
> With no means of defense, perverted aims will ripen.
> With power unchecked, the side of virtue will decline.
> Demons of false views will be honored as high,
> Good conduct will be scorned, evil praised,
> And dharma practice hidden like robber's loot.
> Alas, the Tibetan people! Mercy![16]

After a general opening, referencing standard elements of the degenerate era, this prophecy focuses on the land of Tibet and the fate of its people. It juxtaposes virtuous Buddhists or "upholders of the teachings" (*bstan 'dzin*), whose numbers are dwindling, with "barbaric foreigners" and "enemies of Buddhism" (*bstan dgra*), who have turned social values upside down. This part of the prophecy fits neatly into definitions of the degenerate era, which include the "decline in view or outlook" (*lta ba'i snyigs ma*) as a standard element. Yet it also tacitly offers a social critique of state policy as unjust and morally illegitimate. Implicit references to the Maoist period can be seen in phrases such as "dharma practice hidden like robber's loot" that reference the nearly two-decade prohibition of the public observance of religion. The language of prophecy is deliberately vague, yet evocative enough for contemporaneous readers to recognize their own predicament within it.

In terms of representing agency, this prophecy would seem to evoke a sense of helplessness. The Tibetan populace is portrayed as "orphaned without a protector" and "fenced in by the laws of barbaric foreigners" with "no means of defense," thereby becoming destitute, weak, and feeble. This image is pitiful, and Padmasambhava himself proclaims: "Alas, the Tibetan people! Mercy!" With this, the stage is set for treasure revelation. And this is where agency can be recognized. Prophecies like this, found in treasure texts and placed in the authoritative voice of Padmasambhava, identify periods of turmoil and decline as the very moments when revelation is vitally needed. And they identify the treasures that will redress the horrors they evoke and the appointed emissaries who will reveal them.

In many ways, treasure revelation is ideally suited to suture the rupture in Buddhist institutions and practices from the Maoist period due to the enduring trope of decline and revival.[17] This trope can be traced to the origins of the treasure tradition in the eleventh and twelfth centuries, when revelations provided a means for the Nyingma or "old school" (*rnying ma*) to reassert themselves after a so-called "dark period" following the persecution of Buddhist institutions by the king Langdarma.[18] Treasures were declared to be pristine teachings, directly from the golden era of Tibet's imperial past, which allowed surviving lineages to compete with an influx of newly translated scriptures from India among the "new schools" (*gsar ma*) emerging during the later propagation of Buddhism in Tibet, from the late tenth century onward. Over the centuries, the "dark age" became transposed to different times and places, such that times of decline and strife became the very sign to activate Padmasambhava's benevolent foresight in the form of treasure revelation. The well-known *Chronicles of Padma* (*Pad ma bka' thang*), revealed in the fourteenth century by Orgyan Lingpa, for example, contains more than forty prophecies enumerating signs of degenerate times—invading armies, schisms, heresies, disease, famine, and such— that herald the moment for a tertön to appear and bring forth treasures.[19]

Treasure revelation promises to restore peace and prosperity and to revive Buddhist teachings. As a restorative force, treasures are repeatedly referenced by Tāre Lhamo and Namtrul Rinpoche as the means to "heal the damage to the teachings and beings" and "heal the damage of degenerate times" (*dus snyigs ma'i rgud gso ba*).[20] Namtrul Rinpoche elaborated on this point to me as follows:

> When overcome by the damage of degeneration (*snyigs ma'i rgud pa*)—whatever the nature of that damage may be—afterward successive tertöns will come to heal that damage. By virtue of their previous aspirations, tertöns emerge in order to heal the damage of degeneration. . . . The time period of healing the damage of degeneration is called a renewed propagation of the teachings (*bstan pa yang dar*).[21]

The language of the degenerate times provides a ready-made rubric to encompass a variety of calamities that beset Tibetans as a collective. The so called "five degenerations" (*snyigs ma lnga*) include the perennial catastrophes of plague, famine, and war as well as more insidious forms of degeneration, such as a breakdown of values and loss of faith in the Buddhist teachings.[22] Any one of these signs of degeneration can be transformed into a redemptive moment for the activation of Padmasambhava's beneficence through the revelation of treasures, promising a period of revitalization. The treasure tradition thus contains within it the vocabulary to encompass social and political calamities and thereby integrate them into the flow of Buddhist history.

In the wake of the Cultural Revolution, Tāre Lhamo and Namtrul Rinpoche had recourse to these resources from treasure lore in order to respond to the devastation of their own times. In reference to early literary trends in the post-Mao era, Ban Wang observes that scar literature and the "search for roots" movement stemmed from a lack of consensual symbolic resources among Han Chinese, prompting the writing of memoirs, family sagas, and regional lore to articulate and recover the past. However, the situation for minorities in the PRC was somewhat different. Tibetans did not lack mythic tropes and religious symbols, which in Wang's estimation serve as "vital resources . . . to tell stories, make sense of experience, sustain cultural continuity, and above all, write history."[23] What Tibetans had left after the destruction and violence of the Maoist period were precisely those cultural resources from myth, ritual, and literature still held in living memory by those raised prior to the late 1950s. And out of such resources, Buddhist masters like Tāre Lhamo and Namtrul Rinpoche imagined and inaugurated cultural renewal.

This integration of cultural devastation within the flow of Buddhist history could be regarded as part and parcel of constructing subaltern pasts and healing from collective trauma. In their epistolary exchanges, Tāre Lhamo and Namtrul Rinpoche subsume the period symbolically in veiled references to "the damage of degeneration" (*snyigs ma'i rgud pa*), "strife" (*ru 'dzing*), "a dark age" (*mun pa'i bskal pa*), and persecution by "barbaric foreigners" and "vicious demons" (*bdud ma rung*). This allowed them to imagine their own revelations as a counterforce. Note the following aspiration, in which Tāre Lhamo gives voice to the prospect of cultural renewal in her twenty-second letter:

> To conquer the foreigner's machine and tame by whatever means
> Those who harm the dharma teachings of sūtra and tantra,
> May [we] pacify [this] dark age of suffering!

> To kindle the lamp of the teachings in the snowy land,
> And foster auspicious glory in every direction—
> The welfare of Tibet and deeds in accord with dharma—
> Accomplishing all virtue and goodness in this life and the next,
> May [we] gain dominion over profound treasures![24]

By correlating recent history with a "dark age of suffering" (*sdug mun pa'i bskal pa*) in the first verse, Tāre Lhamo can imagine, through the rubric of decline and revival within the treasure tradition, "pacifying" (*zhi ba*) anti-Buddhist forces in order to rekindle the Buddhist teachings in the snowy land of Tibet. In the next verse, she envisions a future of "auspicious glory" (*bkra shis dpal*), and according to the workings of karma, her aspiration becomes a seed for that future. In the last line, treasure revelation is the means by which she suggests that they can accomplish these aspirations. Here as elsewhere in the correspondence, she and Namtrul Rinpoche symbolically encompass traumatic events as symptoms of dark and degenerate times, which can be reversed through the activation of Padmasambhava's beneficence.

By bracketing off the Maoist period in this way, Tāre Lhamo and Namtrul Rinpoche are able to create a redemptive narrative wherein their own revelations promise a reversal of the fate of Tibetans and provide the means by which the restoration of Buddhism can take place. The language of healing can be found in numerous statements throughout the correspondence, promising to "heal the damage to the teachings and beings," "heal the damage of degenerate times," and "heal the demise and misery of destitute Tibetans" (*bod phongs rgud nyam thag gso ba*).[25] This is ultimately a promise to restore Buddhism to the Tibetan plateau and promote the good fortune and welfare of the Tibetan people as a corollary. They also use the language of "rescuing" beings and "pacifying" negative forces. In all this, they take a heroic stance as a tantric couple, who can save sentient beings from suffering and guide them to liberation.

Healing and restoration are made possible, in etic terms, by the narrative integration of the period of collective trauma. On the importance of memory and narrative, Rubie Watson has noted, "constructing the new is deeply embedded in reconstructing the old," such that "alternative remembrances" shared through unofficial channels under state socialism and colonial conditions can become the rallying points for a collective to move forward.[26] For Tibetans at the end of the Maoist period, the pressing issue was not restitution per se, but the restoration of meaning in order to move forward as a people under the continued conditions of colonialism and state socialism, albeit with an increasingly neoliberal articulation by Deng Xiaoping and his successors. Even without a testimonial to the atrocities they underwent or witnessed, the symbolic restructuring of historical events in their correspondence facilitates the healing process as a means to reestablish "connections among remembered past, lived present, and anticipated future," to borrow Susan Brison's felicitous phrasing.[27] To the extent that their construction of the distant past impels a particular future, within the prophetic idiom of treasure revelation, we can see the importance of constructing subaltern pasts outside the limits of official state history for healing cultural trauma.

This healing occurs through access to undamaged sources of Buddhist teachings and blessings brought about by the revelation of treasures. In this emic sense, treasure revelation provides a means to forge continuity with the distant past by producing vital artifacts, scriptures and relics traced to the early propagation of Buddhism in Tibet. Through asserting their direct connection to events during the imperial period in central Tibet and the reign of Gesar in Golok and northern Kham, both regarded as golden ages in Tibetan history, Tāre Lhamo and Namtrul Rinpoche locate continuity in the form of their treasure revelations. This continuity serves as the basis for the

4.2 Gilded statue of King Gesar of Ling at the Gesar Palace in Darlag.

restorative work promised in their correspondence: revitalizing Buddhist teachings, practices, and institutions in Golok and neighboring areas.

A Heroic Song

Their deflection of agency does not prevent Tāre Lhamo and Namtrul Rinpoche from striking a heroic stance in their letters as the ones able to bring forth the very means by which to "heal the damage of degenerate times." In fact, this is one of the continuities between their hagiographic portraits by Pema Ösal Thaye and their own self-representations and epistolary personae constructed in the correspondence. The striking differences that otherwise result from narrative voice make it all the more noteworthy.

Tāre Lhamo and Namtrul Rinpoche draw on the warrior tradition of Golok and its martial imagery in order to retrieve a source of indigenous Tibetan power. Let me provide two striking samples of bardic verse from their correspondence, starting with a passage dubbed "a heroic song" (*dpa' glu*) in a style evocative of the Gesar epic.[28] It can be found in Tāre Lhamo's fifteenth letter, written at the time of Namtrul Rinpoche's visit to Markhok. In forceful language, the passage summons the power to vanquish enemies and obstacles, and it illustrates how Tāre Lhamo conceived of their courtship as integral to the revival of Buddhism:

> [This] is a heroic song to conquer the enemy, hatred:
> A song to heal the damage of degenerate times,
> A song to vanquish conditions of disease, plague, and famine,
> It is the song Hūṃ to expel unruly demons!
> It is a song to lasso valuables, auspiciousness, and luck,
> A song to increase life, merit, and the domain of power,
> A song to spread the precious teachings of Buddha, the protector,
> A song to remove the gloom of countless [negative] conditions,
> A song to gather the lord king, ministers, and retinue of subjects,
> A song to convene the monastic assembly,
> A song to spread the teachings of the sublime Śākyamuni,
> A song to increase the profound nectar of Padma, the protector,
> A song to recall karma and aspirations of previous lives,
> A song to recall the seven lives of us two as companions,
> A song for coincidence to click [into place] from actions done,
> A song of abundant fortune for the time, today,
> A song to recall counsel from a loving friend
> [And] to recall amorous words upon parting![29]

Note the martial tone, employing the language of conquest and exorcism, which is tempered toward the end as Tāre Lhamo recalls her "loving friend" and "amorous words upon parting." As a "heroic song," it claims the power to accomplish a variety of things, set into motion by the song as performative speech: to heal the damage of degenerate times, to vanquish negative conditions, to promote long life and prosperity, to spread the Buddhist teachings, and to recall her loving friend. By placing these items side by side, the song suggests a link between their proposed union, the propagation of Buddhism, and the welfare of local Tibetans. This passage is distinctive in that it does not call on transcendent beings to carry out these actions; the utterance of the song itself, including the potent seed syllable Hūṃ, promises to do so.

As another example, in her tenth letter, Tāre Lhamo likewise utilizes bardic verse to issue forceful declarations about the revitalization of Buddhism in a duet she composed between Padma and Devī. Devī as transliterated into Tibetan was the name that her scribe used to sign a number of her letters, representing the Sanskrit for the second half of her name, "Lhamo," meaning "goddess" (*lha mo*), and Padma refers to Namtrul Rinpoche's name in religion as a youth, Pema Drime Lodrö. (Due to its frequent use as an abbreviation for Padmasambhava, I use "Padma" as the standard spelling for this Sanskrit term when it stands alone and "Pema" to reflect its pronunciation when it is embedded in longer Tibetan names.) According to its colophon, the duet was staged as a performance for her retinue of disciples during Sagadawa (*Sa ga zla ba*), the month celebrating the Buddha's *parinirvāṇa*, in the earth sheep year of 1979, placing it toward the middle of their correspondence but prior to Namtrul Rinpoche's visit to Markhok. This duet starts with images of fertility (bee and lotus, the peacock flaunting its plumage) and affective language, with Devī expressing a mood of sorrow (*skyo ba*) while remembering the words of her friend. For Padma, in turn, sorrow is cleared away by the recollection of her visage, like the brilliance of the moon, and he encourages her by suggesting that their aspirations to be together will soon be fulfilled. After its opening, the letter employs an eight-syllable meter typical of folk song styles in the region, and the imagery and martial tone take on a resonance with the Gesar epic.

As it progresses, the letter strikes a triumphal tone and stakes a claim for the efficacy of speech in a way that is particular to bardic verse throughout their correspondence. This passage and others from her tenth letter were identified for me by Nyingpo Tsering of the Gesar Research Institute at Qinghai Nationalities University as bardic verse in the style of the Gesar epic. We join the letter at a celebratory moment declaring good fortune and involving the warriors of Gesar's kingdom of Ling, the ḍākinīs and wisdom deities, as well as gods and spirits associated with the Tibetan landscape:

> At a time of plentiful good fortune, the month's start,
> To open the maṇḍala of the profound path of secret means,
> Friend, the lineage of many vidyādharas, are arranged in rows,
> And the powerful warriors of great Ling perform the dance.
> Hundreds of thousands of mother ḍākinīs sing songs of praise.
> Above, the wisdom deities disperse [blessings to] consecrate.

In between, all eight classes [of gods and spirits] provide aid.
Below, the earth lords and nāgas spread luck and fortune.
The great kings of the four directions protect and nurture.

This is a song to eat the lungs and hearts of vicious demons,
Enemies that harm the dharma, the teachings of Buddha.
In order to heal the demise and misery of destitute Tibetans,
This is a song to swirl the lasso at auspiciousness and fortune.
This is a song to gather whatever deeds have been undertaken.
Retinue of chief, ministers, and subjects, remain here now;
The time has come to bring down the eighteen fortresses.[30]
Coincidence falls [into place] without obstructing conditions.
Instigate the joy of dharma, the teachings of Buddha![31]

This song has a declarative tone; its words both summon a host of power-ful forces and invoke the very outcome it depicts. Like "words of truth" (Skt.: *satyavacana*, Tib: *bden tshig*) and "prophecy" (Skt.: *vyākaraṇa*, Tib.: *lung bstan*), the utterance is framed as the very means to make it so. Note the language of demons and enemies in a line that proposes to destroy anti-Buddhist forces: "This is a song to eat the lungs and hearts of vicious demons, / Enemies that harm the dharma, the teachings of the Buddha."[32] This fierce language, while it shares a certain resonance with wrathful Buddhist tantric practices, is distinctive to the Gesar tradition. For exam-ple, "piercing the hearts and lungs of vindictive enemies" can be found in a smoke purification offering (*bsangs mchod*) composed by the nineteenth-century Nyingma master Ju Mipham, which invokes the power of Gesar, his steed, and his ministers in order to defeat enemies and swiftly accom-plish aims.[33] However, this is not put in the form of an aspiration, using the formula "May it be so" (*shog*, alt: *'gyur cig*), as in the passage cited above when Tāre Lhamo wishes: "May [we] pacify [these] dark times of suffer-ing!" There is a notable difference between the open-ended optative mood of aspiration, as in "may it be so," and the declarative manner of an invoca-tion, as in "the time has come to," that summons with a sense of immediacy the power of transcendent beings to intervene in human affairs.[34]

In terms of narrating recent history, Tāre Lhamo's references to demons (*bdud*) and enemies (*dgra*) that harm the Buddhist teachings are euphemistic ways to characterize state policy as anti-Buddhist. The use of euphemism can be regarded as a strategic method of oppositional history that is heavily coded and placed within a genre that leaves its referent ambiguous. With respect to Mongolian literature under Soviet rule, Caroline Humphrey refers to the strategic use of cultural codes as "evocative transcripts," which are not so much hidden as encrypted within discourses and "*intended* to elicit or evoke a particular interpretation beyond the surface meaning" without the risk of directly expressing critique.[35] Within treasure lore and the Gesar epic, there is a ready-made vocabulary to communicate such messages and to integrate turbulent historical periods into wider mythic and historical frames of reference. Tāre Lhamo and Namtrul Rinpoche appropriate that vocabulary in order to making meaning of the past and envision a future involving their own efforts as a couple in effecting the revitalization of Buddhism.

In Tāre Lhamo's words, "In order to heal the demise and misery of destitute Tibetans, / this is a song to swirl the lasso at auspiciousness and good fortune."[36] The song calls forth a host of powerful forces, including the blessings of tantric deities and the aid of various classes of gods and demons, to bring about the auspiciousness and good fortune it describes. Tāre Lhamo proclaims that the opportunity for the restoration of Buddhism is now made possible. It is a "fortunate time" celebrated by the dance of Gesar's warriors and the songs of the ḍākinīs. In its declarative tone, bardic verse plays an important role in balancing out the diverse authorial stances found in their correspondence and contributing to the heroic aspect of their epistolary personae.

If the Garuḍa Can Fly

Despite the prophetic thrust of their correspondence and the declarative passages analyzed above, there is a keen awareness of the contingencies of their historical moment. At various points, Tāre Lhamo and Namtrul Rinpoche assess the challenges facing them in actualizing their shared destiny, illuminating once again the human side of this tantric couple. At this point, we turn to and examine their negotiation of these challenges, including their deliberations over causes and conditions within a Buddhist framework of action, the ritual prescriptions they suggest to overcome obstacles, and their careful consideration of timing. This will allow us to understand better how Tāre Lhamo and Namtrul Rinpoche ascribe agency in their correspondence in culturally specific terms. We also continue with the plot of the letters and observe the culmination of the correspondence as Tāre Lhamo prepares to leave Markhok and join Namtrul Rinpoche at Nyenlung. Stylistically, they utilize folk song styles, using various meters of verse to create a sense of urgency.

An acknowledgment of their historical context can be detected throughout the correspondence, tempering their sense of optimism with realistic assessments of the complications facing them. In recognition of the challenges ahead, Tāre Lhamo issues a call to action in her second letter. Framing it as a "song of marvels," she invokes a sense of possibility as well as adverse conditions to be surmounted.[37] In its entirety, it reads:

Aho! Mirror of [my] heart,
[Open] your ears and listen to this.
Ala! Dear friend, I sing a song of marvels:

On stalks of *bodhi*, the root of mind,
If the crops of virtue are not ripe,
It's difficult for black-headed Tibetans to be happy.[38]

If the snow lion doesn't emit its valiant roar,
It's difficult to subdue the lowland beasts;
Now's the time to unfurl [its] mighty turquoise mane.

If the young garuḍa won't spread [its] sturdy wings,
It's difficult for us birds to reach the heavens
[In] a flight path so far across the lofty sky.[39]

Ala, how wondrous! Long life!
May your teachings spread far and wide.
May there be auspiciousness.[40]

In this rousing song, Tāre Lhamo projects a sense of optimism that is tempered by her use of the conditional in each stanza. For example, in the first stanza, the happiness of Tibetans is said to be difficult to achieve if the crops of virtue are not ripe. This evokes a Buddhist causal framework, referencing a standard image related to the effects of karma, the ripening of fruit ('bras bu smin pa). In Buddhist doctrinal texts, intentional action is commonly depicted as a seed that inexorably bears fruit (Skt: phala, Tib: 'bras bu). With reference to karma, there seems to be no question for Tāre Lhamo that Tibetans are virtuous; indeed, she anchors their virtue ontologically in bodhi, or awakening, as the root of mind. Nonetheless, the reversal of Tibetan fortune is a matter of timing: whether or not the crops of virtue are ripe.

In the next stanza, she declares that the time has come to surmount adverse conditions. The snow lion and garuḍa are long-standing symbols of power in Tibet, which appear in the songs of Milarepa,[41] and Tāre Lhamo marshals them here to depict a latent power available to Tibetans. The capacity to overcome present challenges already exists; it simply needs to be roused and harnessed. From its mountain peak, the snow lion need only roar to subdue the beasts below. According to the poet Drukmo Kyi, with this image, she asks Namtrul Rinpoche to begin teaching.[42] Similarly, from its nest, the garuḍa—a mythical bird of Indic origin that is born full grown—need only spread its wings to fly. Without this show of strength, Tāre Lhamo seems to suggest, it will be difficult to overcome immediate challenges and reach their lofty aims. In her assessment of the historical moment, it is time for action. Despite an acknowledgment of contingencies, the overall tone is optimistic and galvanizing.

On a personal level, Tāre Lhamo and Namtrul Rinpoche faced numerous challenges. One of the uncertainties negotiated in the letters had to do with whether Namtrul Rinpoche would join Tāre Lhamo in Markhok or she would join him at Nyenlung. To complicate matters, Namtrul Rinpoche fell ill intermittently during this period, making travel all the more difficult. Other challenges had to do with the ruggedness of the terrain between them and weather conditions, such as heavy snow on the mountain pass or high waters of the Do River that prevented travel at certain times of the year. In addition, their letters contain tacit references to state policy restricting travel across province borders and the reluctance of her relatives to see her depart for Nyenlung.

A certain sense of caution can be detected in Tāre Lhamo's letters midway through the correspondence, as they arrange Namtrul Rinpoche's visit to Markhok to meet her relatives. Their first encounter, documented in her fifteenth letter, is dated to the hare month of the earth sheep year (1979).[43] From the content of this letter, I would venture that Tāre Lhamo went out a distance to welcome Namtrul Rinpoche in advance of his formal reception by her relatives.[44] In Tibetan areas, it is a common to send a welcoming party to greet a high lama, and this pretext would have allowed the future couple a private initial encounter. But it seems that Tāre Lhamo suddenly got cold feet, concerned about gossip. In that letter, she apologizes for her awkwardness:

> Friend, recalling many amorous words upon departure.
> Though suitably sad, there was no choice but to go. . . .
> Imagining there would be local gossip, I did not ask you to stay.
> Reflecting that the road is long, I did not ask you to go back.
> Thinking of the great physical hardship, I did not dare.[45]

This passage refers to a direct encounter between Tāre Lhamo and Namtrul Rinpoche outside the scope of the letters. She apologizes, stating she did not dare to ask him to stay for fear of gossip or to ask him to return home because of the long and difficult journey. Nevertheless, in the letter, she goes on to provide directions and encourages him by suggesting that he will be guided by dharma protectors (chos skyong), local guardians (srung ma), and "war gods" known as drala (dgra bla) and werma (wer ma). These latter categories of deities can be found in the Gesar epic and remain part of the visionary world of tertöns in Golok. Tāre Lhamo also recounts a vision she had in which Namtrul Rinpoche appeared to her in the form of a werma with a broad smile, riding on a horse in the sky, a portent of his imminent arrival.[46]

It appears that Namtrul Rinpoche did not feel well prior to his journey to Markok and encountered bad weather along the way. The topic of his ongoing illness first emerges in his seventh letter, in which he complains of a nosebleed and high blood pressure, and becomes an issue in his fifteenth letter, when it almost prevents him from journeying to Markhok. Illness arises again in his twenty-first letter, prompting a teaching on dependent origination and the illusory nature of phenomena.[47] Jewel Garland reports that, on their way to Markhok, Namtrul Rinpoche and his attendant Gelek Nyima unexpectedly got caught in a blizzard and were about to turn back.[48] However, after Namtrul Rinpoche supplicated local protectors, they noticed large hoofprints that packed down the snow enough for them to proceed. A passage from his fifteenth letter gestures to the difficulties of travel and also how he imagined overcoming them:

Though [my] physical elements are disturbed, I do not despair.
With the forceful gait of my horse, Öchung Kyangbu,
Though the peaks rise higher and higher, I do not give up.
Though the river has swollen more and more, I do not cower.
Though the weather blizzards, I'm not distressed.
Isn't it my wish to meet [my] companion? It is just so.[49]

This brief but compelling passage shows how Namtrul Rinpoche summoned the confidence to move forward. He bases this confidence on the strength of his horse, and its name appears to be a reference to the Gesar epic.[50] Stylistically, the passage juxtaposes a series of physical and environmental challenges with Namtrul Rinpoche's resolve. Four of the lines are structured around concessive particles (*kyang* and *yang*), with the challenge he faces given in the first half in a five-syllable description, followed by a quick three-syllable flourish to end on an upbeat note by indicating his refusal to give in to despair.

Namtrul Rinpoche's pledge of persistence depicts agency of a very human sort, paralleled elsewhere in their correspondence. Later in the same letter, he affirms the importance of never giving up, stating: "The Do and Mar [valleys] are close together. / But even if I had to circle the world, / Even if my body were exhausted, I would have no regrets!"[51] This sentiment is echoed when Tāre Lhamo later writes in his voice, "In order that the teachings of the Buddha do not disappear, / At the risk of one's life, by carrying the burden of benefiting others, / I wear the strong armor of resolve."[52] In this spirit, with a vision of the greater good, Tāre Lhamo and Namtrul Rinpoche confront and overcome personal hardships.

There is also a good deal of levity to be detected amid these challenges. After Tāre Lhamo apologizes for her bashfulness and reticence in their first encounter, Namtrul Rinpoche teases her:

I am grateful that you came to receive me in person.
How wonderful that you looked [for me] with squinting eyes!
When you did not speak, I thought: What's the matter?
I wondered: Did you not recognize me?
A la la, just kidding about all that![53]

This is a wonderfully intimate moment, where Namtrul Rinpoche brings a touch of humor to referencing the awkwardness of their initial meeting.

The interjection, *a la la*, indicates "joyful surprise" and signals a switch in mode from his mock queries to the disclosure of his teasing.[54]

Tāre Lhamo faced her own problems. The prospect of her leaving for Nyenlung to be with Namtrul Rinpoche initially met with resistance from her relatives. This was confirmed orally by Jamyang Nyima, the current head of Tsimda Gompa, who told me that her relatives had been reluctant to see her depart.[55] At one point, Tāre Lhamo summarizes her own dilemmas as follows:

> First is forceful policy of the Chinese authorities.
> Second is the chatter among country folk.
> Third is sharp dissent from the old aunties.
> If the felicitous means to benefit beings doesn't occur
> And if the coincidence for [our] union is reversed,
> I suppose it will not work out.[56]

Here in her fifteenth letter, Tāre Lhamo complains of the obstacles stacked against their union and expresses personal disappointment at the lost opportunity to be of benefit if their plans are reversed. As it turned out, in the 1980s, as restrictions on travel eased, Tāre Lhamo made annual trips to her homeland with Namtrul Rinpoche and continued to act as the spiritual leader of Tsimda Gompa, the monastery her father founded in Markhok.[57]

There is a down-to-earth quality to these exchanges, in the way they share personal challenges and joke together, which is so recognizably human. Despite the overall prophetic cast of the correspondence, passages like these illuminate the idiosyncrasies and challenges of an actual tantric couple, having to do with both personal and historical factors. Through these and other passages discussed below, we can glimpse the language in which they discussed pursuing their aims, particularly their deployment of the term "coincidence" (*rten 'brel*), which relates to whether or not the causes and conditions for their aspirations and shared destiny would come together.

Contingency and Coincidence

Discerning the notions of causation operative in the correspondence will allow us to see more clearly how the rhetoric of destiny—as mobilized by the

future couple—does not imply strict determinism. Instead, in their correspondence, Tāre Lhamo and Namtrul Rinpoche describe how causes rooted
in the distant past operate in coordination with other factors, leaving ample
room for human initiative. Here I am interested in their own deployment of
Buddhist rubrics in a strategic way to make sense of their historical moment
and retrieve agency in the wake of cultural trauma. Just as in the use of collective karma in *Spiraling Vine of Faith* to narrate the turbulent decades of the
Maoist period, here Tāre Lhamo and Namtrul Rinpoche adapt long-standing
Buddhist models to their own particular situation.

In its classical formulation in Buddhism, causation does not involve a
deterministic correlation of a single cause to a single result. Rather, the
Sanskrit term, *pratītyasamutpāda*—often translated as "dependent arising"
or "dependent origination"—describes a process whereby a primary cause
and multiple supporting conditions come together to produce a given phenomenon.[58] A seed alone cannot produce a sprout; other factors are necessary, such as earth, moisture, and sunshine. The abbreviated Tibetan for this
term, *tendrel* (*rten 'brel*), which I translate as "coincidence," retains this classical definition, but its colloquial usage adds other connotations.[59] Outside
of a scholastic milieu and doctrinal discussion of causation, in colloquial
usage, *tendrel* has the sense of "fortune or auspiciousness."[60] This meaning
is connected to the phrase *tashi tendrel* (*bkra shis rten 'brel*), or "auspicious
coincidence."[61] No longer neutral as a theory of causation, when modified
by *tashi* or "auspicious" (*bkra shis*), *tendrel* signals the advent of good fortune,
when causes and conditions come together in a felicitous manner. Tibetans
say there is "good tendrel" upon observing auspicious signs, such as the
appearance of a rainbow or the call of a cuckoo bird. Indeed, one of the contemporary definitions is "an omen or portent of things to come."[62]

In the context of treasure revelation, *tendrel* is mainly used to assess
whether or not the factors necessary for a specific revelation are coming
together fortuitously.[63] Despite prophecies, visions, and past-life recollections that confirm Padmasambhava's bequest of treasures to a tertön,
the success of any given revelation is never guaranteed. The possibility of
interference in the process is ever present, and any mistake in executing
prophecies or ritual protocols regarding the extraction of a treasure can
lead to disaster.[64] Until Tāre Lhamo's arrival at Nyenlung is imminent, the
couple is preoccupied with whether or not the tendrel for their revelations will "click" or fall into place,[65] in other words, whether or not the

appropriate conditions will come together to facilitate their union and revelatory activities.

In their correspondence numerous comments reflect their concern about tendrel. When things seem to be going well, Namtrul Rinpoche states cheerfully, "The coincidence for accomplishing our aspirations is falling [into place]."[66] When things are not going well, Tāre Lhamo worries, "Although the coincidence is good for many endeavors, / At present, vicious heretics obstruct us."[67] Again and again, they return to the topic of tendrel to assess whether or not the circumstances are ripe for them to take action. Toward the end of their correspondence, tendrel is also used to convey a sense of urgency, as when Namtrul Rinpoche urges Tāre Lhamo on by saying, "coincidence clicks, but not for long."[68]

In drawing on tendrel as a Buddhist theory of causation with its distinctively Tibetan connotations, Tāre Lhamo and Namtrul Rinpoche concentrate on the interaction of causes (rgyu) and conditions (rkyen). This allows them to negotiate between the karmic momentum of the past (providing the causes) and historical contingency (proving the conditions). They repeatedly refer to past deeds (sngon las) and aspirations (smon lam) performed together in previous lifetimes as a mean to assert the karmic momentum behind the unfolding of events. Modulating these causes are immediate circumstances ('phral rkyen), which can provide favorable conditions to facilitate a desired course of action or obstacles that impede the fulfillment of their aims. The term I am translating "immediate circumstances" highlights the temporary and incidental nature of conditions as opposed to the more irrevocable nature of karmic causes, which endure in the mindstream across lifetimes until they eventually ripen. In this way, the rubric of tendrel accounts for both the enduring power Tāre Lhamo and Namtrul Rinpoche ascribe to the distant past and the challenges they recognize in their immediate circumstances.

Tāre Lhamo and Namtrul Rinpoche use the distinction between causes and conditions in order to gain leverage over their present challenges and obstacles. Anchoring their aspirations in the distant past as karmic causes, they thereby define them as a force that can impel but not wholly determine their future. By contrast, they reckon the obstacles facing them to be immediate circumstances, temporary and mutable. The implication is twofold. First, deeds and aspirations in that distant past are credited with greater weight than obstacles in the present. Second, because of their contingent nature, immediate circumstances are subject to remedial action and ritual intervention. For this reason, they can be placated or eliminated, as when Tāre Lhamo exclaims, "By that, immediate conditions will be pacified—there is certain to be good fortune!"[69] By invoking the karmic momentum of the past and prescribing rituals to reverse immediate circumstances, Tāre Lhamo and Namtrul Rinpoche generate a sense of agency together.

The letters are replete with ritual prescriptions, through which Tāre Lhamo and Namtrul Rinpoche seek to bring about the appropriate conditions for their union and revelatory activities. These ritual prescriptions are central from the outset of their correspondence, as evidenced in prophecy contained in Tāre Lhamo's first letter:

> Through the power of our aspirations,
> If coincidence [makes it] possible to meet,
> In the powerful monkey year [1980–81],
> At the eastern turquoise peak's lakeshore,
> Sacred site of the Eight-Command Sādhana,
> If we are able to make aspirations together,
> We will awaken the entrustment as a couple.
> If we reach ten million feast offerings—
> The material arrangement of five gems[70]
> Along with gold, silver, copper, and iron—
> We will have the fortune for coincidence to converge.
> At the meditation site of White Cliff Monkey Fortress,
> Are yellow scrolls of the one hundred thousand ḍākinīs.[71]

This passage contains a set of ritual prescriptions and a prophecy about a treasure awaiting them at Drakar Tredzong, or White Cliff Monkey Fortress.[72] It illustrates the efficacy they attribute to aspirations and ritual activity as factors to awakening their visionary capacities. In addition, it shows how central coincidence, or tendrel, is to their understanding of the unfolding of events. Tendrel governs whether or not they will meet as well as whether or not they will retrieve their treasures. Yet it is also subject to ritual manipulation, by which they can create the appropriate conditions to facilitate the revelatory process.

The importance of performing rituals drawn from the repertoire of Buddhist tantra, particularly feast offerings (tshogs mchod) and mantra recitations (*sngags bzla*), is evident throughout the letters. Early in the correspondence, in his third letter, Namtrul Rinpoche offers his own ritual prescription. He recommends that they perform a feast offering to the ḍākinīs and accumulate 100,000 recitations of a formula known as the "essence of tendrel" (*rten snying*).[73] He credits the mantra with overcoming "external conditions of barbarians" (*phyi rkyen kla klo*) and "internal conditions of torpidity" (*nang rkyen 'ol le*) as well as repairing breaches in samaya.[74] About the feast offering, he states, "If performed, [it] awakens the power of [past] deeds, aspirations, coincidence, and the entrustment."[75] Significantly, these are the very causal factors that need to be unleashed to activate the revelatory process, indicating how rituals serve as a preparatory stage, helping to awaken the latent seeds of karma and aspiration and creating the appropriate conditions. This verse continues by naming the treasure site as a turquoise lake in the east: "At a turquoise lake in the east, encased in a jewel casket / Is *Profound Nectar of Bliss Emptiness: The Secret Path of the Four Joys*. / When the time comes, a prophecy of the mother ḍākinīs [will appear]."[76]

4.3 Nyenpo Yutse mountain range in Jigdral County of Golok.

This description refers to one of two sacred lakes, Shimtso and Ngöntso, at Nyenpo Yutse, a sacred mountain range in eastern Golok that served as an important treasure site for the couple. As we will see in the next chapter in a reading of *Jewel Garland*, their revelations of treasures typically occur at previously established sacred sites and are preceded by a feast offering, which fosters favorable conditions.

There are dozens of ritual prescriptions in their correspondence, which include a range of activities understood to create favorable conditions for their future revelations, such as supplications, feast offerings, and purification practices. Here is a sampling: 100,000 recitations of the *Seven Line Supplication* (*bdun tshig*) and 10,000 recitations of *Spontaneous Fulfillment of Wishes* (*bsam pa lhun grup*)—both supplications to Padmasambhava—plus 100,000 feast offerings to the ḍākinīs; 10 million approach and accomplishment (*bsnyen sgrub*) recitations of Vajrakīla and petition offerings (*gsol mchod*) to the ladies of glorious mantra (*dpal sngags kyi bdag mo*); 10 million feast offerings of the three roots (*rtsa gsum*), 100,000 petition offerings to the ladies of glorious mantra, the purification practice of Vajrasattva, and smoke offerings (*bsangs*) to the lords of the land (*gzhi bdag*).[77]

In the account that opened this book, we can see how the couple attributes efficacy to ritual action, which gives them the confidence to overcome challenges. Recall that Tāre Lhamo sent Namtrul Rinpoche a ritual that she composed to dispel his ongoing bouts of illness, accompanied by a protection circle (*srung 'khor*) and strands of her own hair as a gift. In a rare prose section of her twenty-second letter, she recounts a vision in a dream in which a ḍākinī appeared as a messenger for one named "Tshe," requesting a protection circle from among her own treasures and seven strands of her hair in order to "reverse immediate circumstances" (*'phral rkyen bzlog*).[78] A protection circle consists of one or more mantras and designs to ward off obstacles, such as obstructing spirits or demonic forces, and the strands of hair would have been considered relics with apotropaic powers by virtue of their association with her. In addition, the letter contains a short ritual practice of wrathful Mahāvairocana, which she composed expressly for Namtrul Rinpoche, and she ascribes to its mantra the power to "pacify illness, demons, evils, and obscurations" (*nad gdon sdig sgrib zhi*). Following this, in verse she states confidently, "I believe we can definitely pacify immediate circumstances."[79] This statement demonstrates the efficacy they attributed to rituals to overcome adverse conditions, an important resource with which to negotiate contingencies and bolster a sense of confidence in preparation for pragmatic action.

Irreversible Momentum

Tāre Lhamo and Namtrul Rinpoche use the distinction between causes and conditions to summon causes rooted in the distant past as an inexorable force to trump the conditions obstructing them in the present. Here destiny itself serves as an important cultural resource that they mobilize based on Buddhist notions of karma and the prophetic orientation of the treasure tradition. Their correspondence contains a number of terms suggestive of destiny. The most common throughout is *kalwa* (*skal ba*), which I translate as "fortune" and more literally means "portion," as in one's lot in life. This term is regularly used in phrases like "based on merit, it is our fortune to meet,"[80] by which Tāre Lhamo and Namtrul Rinpoche assure each other that their proposed union will go forward based on virtuous deeds and aspirations in their past lives together. A related term that regularly appears means "inheritance" (*pha phog bu*), indicating a bequest (*phog*) by one's father (*pha*). In their usage of this term, Tāre Lhamo and Namtrul Rinpoche refer to their inheritance from Padmasambhava in the form of treasures that he bequeathed to them.[81] Another term, which I translate as "legacy" (*bkod thang*), is more difficult to pin down.[82] In its usage in the correspondence, the term indicates some kind of birthright or heritage, as in the phrase "worldly legacy," which describes the natural compatibility between animals and their habitat. It is also used more pointedly to refer to the legacy from the past in karmic terms, as when Tāre Lhamo states, "I recall the legacy of deeds from past lives."[83] Referring to Namtrul Rinpoche, she also uses this term to suggest Padmasambhava's determinacy in their union: "The support, the method companion, is the legacy of Padma."[84] Here "method companion" refers to the male consort in the context of the union of "method and wisdom" (*thabs shes*) in a tantric partnership.

This set of terms suggests how Tāre Lhamo and Namtrul Rinpoche view the indebtedness of the present to causal factors in the past. A cluster of causal factors are repeated throughout their correspondence, neatly brought together in the following verse by Tāre Lhamo:

Deeds of prior lives, oh, at Utsal Serkhang,
Profound command, oh, its initiation bestowed again and again.
Deeds and aspirations, oh, [we] have the coincidence to meet.
Profound command, oh, its flowers descend together.
Guardian Padma, oh, his entrustment and aspiration are sewn.[85]

Tāre Lhamo employs a folk song style featuring the syllable *so* after the third syllable of each line (translated above as "oh"), which serves to punctuate the first words of each line, emphasizing "deeds of prior lives" (*las skye sngon*), "profound command" (*bka' zab mo*), "deeds and aspirations" (*las smon lam*), and "Guardian Padma" (*mgon pad ma*). Here as elsewhere in the letters, the deeds and aspirations of the couple in past lives constitute the driving force for their present lives. It is due to that previous karma that the "coincidence to meet" (*'dzoms pa'i rten 'brel*) exists at all. The "profound command," important enough to be repeated twice in this short passage, refers to speech of Padmasambhava (here: Guardian Padma), understood to carry the force of "words of truth," which, once uttered by a worthy individual, are infallible and thereby set into motion the actions they describe.[86]

The scene conjured above is that of a tantric initiation bestowed by Padmasambhava. At that time, the passage states that Padmasambhava made aspirations and performed the entrustment. The entrustment is the *sine qua non* of treasure revelation, the moment in which he designates the disciple who will reveal, in a future lifetime, the set of tantric rituals and esoteric teachings given during the initiation.[87] These factors—deeds and aspirations on the part of the couple and the command and entrustment of Padmasambhava—constitute the prevailing portrayal of the legacy of the past in the correspondence. They can also been seen in Namtrul Rinpoche's third letter, which vividly depicts the scene of a tantric initiation during the eighth century on the occasion when they locate the prophetic entrustment:

At the profound, secret, eternal, and glorious palace of Samye,
The master [Padmasambhava] and disciples, lord and subjects,
Assembled for a feast of vidyādharas and ḍākinīs.
Do you recall the samaya of the initiation, aspiration, and entrustment,
When the elixir was distributed at [this] festival of great secret dharma?

Illustrious disciple Chokgyur Nupban Namkhai Nyingpo
And Yeshe Tsogyal, who attained the *dhāraṇī* of total recall,
Actualized bliss-emptiness, the wisdom of the four joys,
[Through] the profound dharma of Anu[yoga], the short cut
Of [union with] a consort that liberates through touch,
Sublime path of means to ripen the illusory body into divine form.

Do you recall the conferral of the fine vase of profound elixir?
The Great Orgyan, Lord of Victors, Great Holder of Gnostic Mantras,
[Thereby] bestowed the garland of eternal, adamantine command.
Please protect the samaya unimpaired over all lifetimes like an eye.
May we be forever blessed not to be separated, even for a moment.[88]

In ornate poetic style, typical of his early letters, Namtrul Rinpoche recounts
his visionary recollections of a gaṇacakra feast and tantric initiation at Samye,
the first Buddhist temple constructed in Tibet, in which Padmasambhava plays
a legendary role. In this context, the couple in their past lives as Yeshe Tsogyal
and Namkhai Nyingpo received the aspiration and entrustment by Padmasambhava for their treasures in this life. Moreover, they are depicted as engaging in the tantric rite of sexual union, referred to as "the profound dharma
of Anu[yoga], the short cut / of [union with] a consort that liberates through
touch."[89] To seal their destiny, Padmasambhava (the Great Orgyan) conferred
elixir from the initiation vase and bestowed the "garland of eternal, adamantine command."[90] Note the gravity of this command as a causal factor in their
union; it is described as "eternal" and "adamantine" and thus incontrovertible.

The final factor that contributes to the force of the distant past, mentioned in the passage above and referenced on other occasions in their correspondence, is the potency ascribed to the samaya vow taken during a tantric
initiation. Simply put, when Tāre Lhamo and Namtrul Rinpoche accepted
their assignment to reveal treasures in past lives, they made the tantric commitment of samaya in order to receive the "eternal, adamantine command"
from Padmasambhava. In his fifth letter, Namtrul Rinpoche writes:

Inseparable through all times and lives, conjoined by samaya,
Affectionate friend, in the confluence of joy and happiness,
Now, at this time, in the Zalmo Range of Do Kham,
Together [let us] awaken [past] deeds, aspirations, and the entrustment.[91]

In this passage, he credits the force of their samaya—a tantric vow that entails, among other things, an oath of fidelity to the master presiding over the initiation—with creating their bond together, "inseparable through all times and lives" (*dus skye kun mi 'bral*). Tāre Lhamo makes a similar point when she compares them to "inseparable twins" and "relatives of one samaya,"[92] referring to the notion that the participants in the same tantric initiation are rendered "brothers" and "sisters" by the force of their vows of commitment to the same tantric master. This vow, if maintained without corruption, is said to retain its potency over time, whereas Padmasambhava's entrustment as well as their own past deeds and aspirations together remain dormant until activated. For this reason, at one point in the correspondence, Namtrul Rinpoche uses the image of a "golden thread of samaya" (*dam tshig gser gyi skud*) to characterize their unbroken connection across lives.[93] In the final line of the verse above, he urges Tāre Lhamo to awaken the entrustment, past deeds, and aspirations through their union, suggesting that the latent potential requires activation by them as a tantric couple.

In one poignant passage, Tāre Lhamo ascribes irreversibility to the samaya vow and their aspirations made in previous lifetimes, casting them as far more powerful than the obstacles confronting them. It is the clearest statement in their correspondence of the power of the past to determine the course of the future, found in a passage composed in Namtrul Rinpoche's voice:

> The profound samaya of the past is irreversible.
> The Tsangpo River does not flow uphill.
> An avalanche doesn't go back up a mountain.
> The cool north wind doesn't change course.
> The oath of the ḍākinīs cannot be reversed.
> Friend, our aspirations cannot be reversed.
> We have the fortune of karma and coincidence converging.[94]

In the face of the contingencies of their historical moment, Tāre Lhamo attributes an irreversible momentum to the distant past. This momentum is likened to an incontrovertible law of nature in successive metaphors: a river flowing downstream, an avalanche tumbling down the mountainside, and the direction of the north winds. In this way, their inheritance from the distant past, and in particular their samaya vow as well as the oath of the ḍākinīs, is deemed to be more powerful than the obstacles confronting them. Tāre Lhamo thereby asserts the primacy of destiny in order to imagine overcoming adverse conditions that might otherwise have seemed insurmountable.

In the context of their correspondence, destiny serves as a resource that Tāre Lhamo and Namtrul Rinpoche *actively* marshaled in order to overcome challenges. As described in the previous chapter, in their epistolary exchanges, they constructed a shared narrative and mission by spurring each other to remember their past lives and the locations of treasures, thereby mapping the course of their future activities. In addition, it was up to Tāre Lhamo and Namtrul Rinpoche to devise a course of action, take remedial action to address obstacles, discern the appropriate time to act, and risk censure in order to join together and pursue their vocations as emissaries of Padmasambhava. I propose that the rhetoric of destiny as invoked in the letters—rather than promoting passivity associated with determinism or foreclosing agency through its deflection to transempirical beings or processes—in fact galvanized Tāre Lhamo and Namtrul Rinpoche into action to seize the moment when the circumstances were ripe.

A Perfectly Auspicious Time

From the outset of their correspondence, at the end of the Maoist period, the couple sensed that the time was right for their union and career together as tertöns. In her second letter, Tāre Lhamo encourages Namtrul Rinpoche to make a show of strength and to begin teaching the dharma, using folksy images of the snow lion unfurling its turquoise mane and a garuḍa spreading its wings. His second letter, translated below, echoes her initial sense of urgency by citing how short-lived a window of opportunity can be. Within the rubric of tendrel, a sense of timing is key. This is part of a process that takes discernment to know when to wait and when to act. For example, midway through the correspondence, Tāre Lhamo cautions Namtrul Rinpoche to be patient, and later, in their final exchanges, Namtrul Rinpoche urges Tāre Lhamo into action. Toward the end of their correspondence, the two traded short, spirited passages to assess their circumstances, determine the best course of action, and ultimately seize the moment when the time was right.

Tendrel is linked to timing in their correspondence by the suggestion that it is fleeting. If action is not taken at the right moment, the opportunity could be missed. Already in Namtrul Rinpoche's second letter, we get a sense of how tenuous he deemed the situation in his call for swift action:

E ma! The profound extract
Of Padma, the Lord of Victors,
Supreme heart essence of ḍākinīs,
Is the wish-fulfilling jewel that heals
Damage to the teachings and beings.
Coincidence clicks, but not for long:
Heya, just at the present moment!
After, we speak of good fortune.[95]

In this passage, Namtrul Rinpoche highlights the fleeting nature of tendrel. A sense of urgency is conveyed by the use of a more compact meter of seven syllables, rather than his usual preference for nine syllables in many of his letters, especially toward the beginning of the correspondence when his tone is more formal. Namtrul Rinpoche uses the exclamatory "E ma!" and "Heya"—calling sounds, according to Dondrup Gyal—to heighten his appeal for action.[96] What is at stake? Tendrel indicates favorable circumstances for revealing their treasures, here called the "profound extract" (*zab bcud*) of Padmasambhava and "heart essence" (*snying bcud*) of the ḍākinīs. Namtrul Rinpoche suggests that they should act first and talk later, though as it turned out, their proposed union was delayed for more than a year.

After their meeting in Markhok, Tāre Lhamo and Namtrul Rinpoche discussed the issue of timing in short but earnest statements. These letters may have been exchanged in close proximity while Namtrul Rinpoche remained in Markhok, helping to explain their more brisk and informal style.[97] In his seventeenth letter, Namtrul Rinpoche broaches the topic again, suggesting early winter as a possible time to move ahead with their plans, stating emphatically, "Not long from now, the time will come for traveling!"[98] In response, Tāre Lhamo asks him to be patient and wait. Appealing to the implicit language of karma—planting seeds as causes and harvesting fruits as results—she cautions him not to shake off the fruits too early. This passage from her eighteenth letter puts off their union until after the new year:[99]

The tree has sprouted shoots, *lo lo bo.*
Don't shake off the fruits too early.
Next year or thereafter, in early summer,
When water-laden clouds shower rain, *tha la la!*
Branches of juniper bushes, *ya la la!*
Melodious call of the cuckoo, *kyu ru ru!*
When the turquoise dragon's thunder rolls, *di ri ri!*
These are natural guests, not invited by [past] deeds.
When karma and coincidence converge, it is like this.[100]

This song evokes images of early summer to both entice Namtrul Rinpoche with the promise of the fruit, once ripe, and ask him to be patient. Tāre Lhamo's use of onomatopoeia at the end of several lines gives the passage an energetic and playful mood.[101] She evokes the alpine meadows of Golok with juniper bushes and the call of the cuckoo as signs of spring or early summer, highlighting the multiplicity of factors that must converge to bring about new beginnings. Moreover, she describes the arrival of spring as a natural occurrence, when causes and conditions converge. Tacitly, she suggests that the two of them cannot force the situation.

As their epistolary exchanges progress, there is a growing sense of urgency. To convey this, Namtrul Rinpoche brings the meter down to only six syllables, consisting of three dyads that create a brisk rhythm. To intensify the tone, he uses phonemic repetition of adjacent syllables, here the first two syllables of each line.[102] In my translation, to capture the rhythm of this passage, I preserve the repetition of the initial syllable in most lines as well as the structure of semantic dyads. Where I change the word order, it is to keep the translation down to six syllables per line. In his twenty-fourth letter, Namtrul Rinpoche urges Tāre Lhamo to make the journey to Nyenlung soon:

Dear, dear, vine of [my] mind,
Received [your] note and gift.
Joy, joy, words can't express.
I miss, life mate, miss you.
Soon, soon, can you travel?
Myself, I am hopeful![103]

This passage speaks for itself. Namtrul Rinpoche must have just received word that Tāre Lhamo had decided to make the journey to Nyenlung soon. As a result, he expresses excitement and expectancy. As best as I can tell, this comes after her twenty-fifth letter, a short one in which she indicates that despite the gossip among her country folk and their reluctance to see her go, her greater mission to work for the welfare of others and obligation to maintain her samaya must prevail. She also indicates her readiness, using phonetic repetition in a passage cited in the previous chapter in which she compares herself to a juniper berry, pronouncing: "ripe, ripe, I'm ripe."[104]

When Tāre Lhamo's arrival is imminent, urgency turns into jubilance. In his twenty-fifth letter, Namtrul Rinpoche conveys a sense of celebration in a passage that highlights the impending fulfillment of their aims:

> Friend, we two fulfill our aims today,
> Kindness of the wish-fulfilling three roots!
> For this life and next, joy starts today!
> Auspicious coincidence clicks today!
> True words to fulfill aims realized today!
> The sun of bliss and joy shines today![105]

The quick beat of his previous six-syllable meter is no longer evident, but there is still a sense of immediacy. Stylistically, Namtrul Rinpoche achieves this through the repetition of "today" in five of the lines above.[106] The tone is one of celebration, and a later section of the same letter, discussed in the last chapter, features male warriors dancing, female warriors singing *sha ra ra*, banners swirling, rainbows appearing, and rain jingling *si li li*. This devolves into a drinking song related to the custom of offering liquor upon the arrival of a guest, and I suspect that this letter may have been presented to Tāre Lhamo on her arrival, as it is tagged a "song of joyful tidings."

At the very end of this letter, Namtrul Rinpoche declares victory in no uncertain terms. This is not just a personal victory over obstacles to their union, but the victory of Buddhism over demonic forces and the pacification of the strife associated with the degenerate times.

> Today is a perfectly auspicious time!
> Victory over demonic forces in battle today![107]

The golden sun rises in the heavens.
The conch moon appears at mid-sky.
A rain of dharma falls to the earth.
Hoist the victory banner of dharma,
The teachings of the Buddha!
The sun of happiness shines for mother beings,
Pacifying strife, the damage of degenerate times.
A joyous truth, the coincidence to meet.
Now, each person sing a joyful song![108]

In this passage, Namtrul Rinpoche declares the day to be a "perfectly auspicious time" as the coincidence to fulfill their aims has arrived. This is a victory not just for them but for all beings, as it portends a "rain of dharma" in the form of their treasure revelations. It is for this reason, I surmise, that he exclaims: "Hoist the victory banner of dharma!" The victory is for Buddhism itself and for all Tibetans, auguring a new era of happiness.

It is significant that Namtrul Rinpoche depicts Tāre Lhamo's arrival at Nyenlung as a victory for Buddhism. For the couple, who as tertöns cast their own activities in cosmic terms, her arrival signaled the beginning of their activities to "heal the damage of degenerate times." Through their correspondence, Tāre Lhamo and Namtrul Rinpoche asserted interpretive control over personal and historical challenges by subsuming these into a Buddhist framework as barbaric and demonic forces characteristic of dark times. When they achieved their aims in an immediate sense through Tāre Lhamo's arrival, they connected this triumph in their personal lives to the prospect of the revitalization of Buddhism as a whole. If the passage above is any indication, at the cusp of cultural and economic liberalization in the post-Mao period, Tāre Lhamo and Namtrul Rinpoche were filled with optimism and poised for action, ready to tap into the deep well of the Tibetan past to retrieve sources of authority and continuity with which to restore Buddhist teachings, practices, and institutions.

In exploring their rich and variegated correspondence, we have seen a wide range of registers through which Tāre Lhamo and Namtrul Rinpoche constructed the past and envisioned the future. A close reading of select passages, in this chapter and the previous one, has shown the formality of extended praises and elaborate gestures of deference, the playfulness of short ditties and love songs expressing affection, the performative certainty of their prophetic voice, the intimate humor following their first awkward encounter, flirtatious moments using coded references to the tantric practice of sexual union, assertive statements of self-definition, heroic songs that summon transcendent beings to subjugate demonic and barbaric forces, and urgent calls for action once the timing finally seemed right. Across fifty-six letters, Tāre Lhamo and Namtrul Rinpoche forged a personal bond and shared narrative, creating a script for their religious activities that they lived out during their teaching career together. In the 1980s and '90s, their literary vision took shape in action as the couple visited the sites described in their prophecies to discover and disseminate their treasures, restored Buddhist institutions and practices in Golok and neighboring areas, and consecrated anew Tibetan people and places through their extensive ritual activities.

How did their public personae and agency as a tantric couple, which emerged over the extended dialogue of their correspondence, get translated and transformed within the genre of namthar? The life story of Namtrul Rinpoche, *Jewel Garland*, in which Tāre Lhamo serves as a joint protagonist, builds on and differs from their extended dialogue in their correspondence in important ways. Their identity as a tantric couple, as constructed in the correspondence, continues to inform their public personae, creating a distinctive hagiographic narration of their religious career together in which the couple appears to speak and act in concert. Yet there are certain differences in returning to the idealization of hagiography narrated in the third person. Whereas their correspondence reveals multiple facets of their relationship, ranging from prophetic to personal, *Jewel Garland* leaves out the personal side of their lives altogether. Gone are the human touches revealed in their letters: the personal affection they shared, the obstacles they faced, and the way that they forged an enduring partnership. Instead, *Jewel Garland* focuses on their public activities: meetings with dignitaries, pilgrimage tours, large-scale rituals, and public teachings. Excerpts from their correspondence are included, but the passages focus on the couple's public personae in terms of their past-life recollections and prophetic statements about future treasures. Moreover, while the specter of obstacles is palpable in their correspondence, apart from inclement weather and illness, *Jewel Garland* presents their activities as by and large unimpeded.

Despite these differences, we nonetheless witness how Tāre Lhamo and Namtrul Rinpoche enacted the healing process proposed in the correspondence, and the heroic stance in their letters continues in their hagiographic representation, though with some gendered inflections. The next chapter turns to their activities in the post-Mao era and how these are represented in *Jewel Garland*. In 1980, Tāre Lhamo journeyed to Nyenlung to settle there with Namtrul Rinpoche until her death in 2002. During the 1980s and '90s, the couple played an active role in building projects for monasteries, temples, and stūpas in and around Golok while disseminating their own revelations and those of her father, Apang Terchen, and introducing new ritual programs throughout the region. From their home base at Nyenlung, they traveled and taught extensively throughout Golok and neighboring areas and as far away as Lake Kokonor, Rebkong, and central Tibet.

FIVE

A Tantric Couple

The Hagiography of Cultural Revitalization

FROM 1980 FORWARD, the life stories of Tāre Lhamo and Namtrul Rinpoche are synthesized in *Jewel Garland: The Liberation of Namtrul Jigme Phuntsok*. From the moment that Tāre Lhamo first appears in the work, in many ways, it becomes the hagiography of a tantric couple. This occurs early on in the context of their courtship and correspondence. The story of Namtrul Rinpoche's past lives, prophecies at birth, early training, and activities during the Maoist period takes up the first twenty-seven pages of *Jewel Garland*, only a quarter of the whole. Next, the period 1978–80 is covered by passages excerpted from their correspondence, alongside prophecies by other religious figures confirming their union that were likely gathered over time. These excerpts and prophecies take up twenty pages, another quarter of the work. In this section, Tāre Lhamo's voice emerges in a way that never occurs in her own namthar. She is given pride of place, with excerpts from ten of her letters to lead off the section, and excerpts from three of Namtrul Rinpoche's letters follow thereafter.[1] From that point forward, for the second half of the work, the couple serve as joint protagonists in a way that is unprecedented in Tibetan literature.

This portrayal constitutes a significant departure from genre conventions, which customarily focus on the life story of a single person—not more than one, let alone a couple. Though biographical compilations for religious and family lineages do exist, the entries for individual figures tend to be discrete.[2] There are cases in which a Tibetan couple occupies center stage

5.1 Namtrul Rinpoche and Tāre Lhamo on their peacock throne at Nyenlung. Original photographer unknown.

for a number of episodes, particularly with respect to accounts of treasure revelation, such as in the namthar of female Bön tertön, Dechen Chökyi Wangmo (b. 1868), and the auto/biographical writings of Sera Khandro.[3] Yet this is not quite the same as featuring a tantric couple as the protagonist for the greater part of a namthar. Through this distinctive narration, *Jewel Garland* highlights the collaboration of Tāre Lhamo and Namtrul Rinpoche in contributing to the revitalization of Buddhism in Golok and neighboring areas. For the most part, they function as a unit, sometimes even speaking prophetically in one voice and sharing the same visionary experiences. Their hagiographer, Pema Ösal Thaye, depicts Tāre Lhamo and Namtrul Rinpoche throughout the 1980s and '90s revealing treasures, bestowing tantric initiations, establishing ritual practices at various monasteries in the region, and constructing stūpas and temples.

In a salient assertion of their agency as a couple, the chronicle of their life in *Jewel Garland* begins with the following statement: "From that point forward, the Eminent Couple, the pair of defenders of the teachings and beings, having converged in one seat, together awakened the karma, aspirations, and coincidence in order to heal the extensive damage of degenerate times."[4] Three different terms are used to emphasize the joint nature of their endeavors: couple (*yab yum*), pair (*zung*), and together (*mnyam du*). It makes Tāre Lhamo and Namtrul Rinpoche joining together as a couple in "one seat" (i.e., a shared residence) pivotal to their ability to awaken the causal forces necessary in order "to heal the extensive damage of degenerate times" (*snyigs dus kyi rgud pa mtha' dag gso*). Through this statement, echoing the language found in their correspondence, the reader is prepared to view the account of their activities together as enacting the very healing mentioned, repairing the extensive damage to Buddhist institutions and Tibetan culture during the Maoist period. The language of healing or restoration (*gso ba*) can be found elsewhere in *Jewel Garland*.[5] In addition to their prolific revelations, Pema Ösal Thaye credits the couple with inspiring the construction of more than a thousand stūpas and an unspecified number of temples as well as burying hundreds of treasure vases (*gter 'bum*) at sacred sites "in order to restore the potency of the earth" (*sa bcud gso*).[6] The abbreviated namthar by Abu Karlo, *Jewel Lantern of Blessings*, published four years later in 2001, presents their stūpa construction at vital geomantic points (*sa gnad*) in similar terms: "for the purpose of healing the damage to the environment and its inhabitants" (*snod bcud kyi rgyud pa gso phyir*).[7] In published accounts of their religious activities together in the post-Mao era, the metaphor of healing continues to be central, particularly in relation to a ritual process of transforming and rehabilitating the Tibetan landscape.

As a corollary, I introduce the notion of *connectivity* as a key rubric in the healing of cultural trauma. In my usage, connectivity has a temporal dimension involving the integration of past, present, and future into a coherent narrative and a spatial dimension in terms of repairing connections in the social body and remaking the Tibetan landscape as Buddhist. The previous two chapters examined the temporal dimension of connectivity in Tāre Lhamo and Namtrul Rinpoche's construction of a shared narrative across lifetimes in their correspondence, linking their identities as well as their future revelations to seminal moments in the history of Buddhism and Tibet. This chapter focuses on the spatial dimension of repairing social networks and spatial associations, as represented in *Jewel Garland* through their revalatory and ritual activities in the post-Mao era. This is akin to what David Germano has discussed in his essay "Re-membering the Dismembered Body of Tibet," which traces the activities of the internationally renowned Khenpo Jigme Phuntsok (1933–2004), the Nyingma master largely responsible for restoring and bolstering monastic scholasticism in northern Kham. As the founder of Larung Buddhist Academy in Serta with well over ten thousand monks and nuns, the late Khenpo was a pivotal figure in revitalizing Buddhism in Tibetan areas of the PRC and a focal point for the contemporary treasure movement that included Tāre Lhamo and Namtrul Rinpoche. Germano characterizes his activities as a "treasure-driven resuscitation" that had the effect of "reconstituting and reconnecting the extended cultural body of Tibet."[8]

Such a process of ritual transformation, based on the prowess of tantric masters, echoes the long-standing practice of Buddhicization, whereby the Tibetan landscape and indigenous mountain deity cults have been integrated into Buddhist hierarchies through a "conversion" or "taming" (gdul ba) process.[9] Such a process effected through temple building can be traced to myths surrounding the imperial period, when Buddhism first entered Tibet and Songtsen Gampo is reported to have constructed a series of temples to suppress the Tibetan landscape, represented in the form of a supine demoness.[10] Since then, a parallel conversion process has involved the visionary talents of Buddhist masters, who identify sites associated with indigenous territorial deities (gzhi bdag) as the abodes of tantric ones. Indeed, the original usage of the term "mandalization" by Toni Huber referenced this process of converting sacred sites by overlaying Buddhist associations and spatial hierarchies onto them.[11] Since cultural and economic liberalization reached Tibetan areas of the PRC in the early 1980s, Buddhist masters have reclaimed the Tibetan landscape and its people through a comparable process enacted in rituals of consecration and tantric initiation.

Instead of the typical language of "conversion" or "taming," however, in Jewel Garland, Pema Ösal Thaye characterizes the couple's activities as forging "connections" ('brel ba). During their frequent pilgrimage cum teaching tours, Tāre Lhamo and Namtrul Rinpoche are shown establishing two types: "dharma connections" (chos 'brel) with a growing community of disciples and "place connections" (gnas 'brel) with sacred sites in Golok, greater Amdo, central Tibet, and China proper. Jewel Garland thereby situates the couple at the hub of a network of people and places, concentrated in Padma and Serta counties but radiating from there throughout Golok, reaching eastward as far as Dzamthang, southward into Kandze, northward as far as Rebkong, and westward into central Tibet. Given the historical context,

I suggest that such connectivity, in its temporal and spatial dimensions, represents the reintegration of Buddhist systems of meaning and Tibetan social formations that serve to repair the effects of anomy (loss of meaning) and atomy (rupture in social networks)—modes of cultural and social disintegration accompanying the systematic attacks to the "old society" during the Maoist period.[12]

The connections Tāre Lhamo and Namtrul Rinpoche forged through their ritual activities, as represented in *Jewel Garland*, position the couple at the nexus and pinnacle of a web of connectivity. This can be considered part of the process of mandalization, used by Charlene Makley to characterize the revitalization of Tibetan culture in the post-Mao period, but in slightly different terms. In her study of the Great Monastic Dance at Labrang Tashi Khyil in Amdo, Makley highlights the reassertion of "lay-monastic masculine alliances" through rituals to tame or subjugate the earth (*sa gdul*), which thereby assert a "countergeography" against the Chinese discourse of a multiethnic state and its positioning of minority "nationalities" (Ch.: *minzu*) at the periphery of Han modernity.[13] By contrast, here a tantric couple occupies the center of the maṇḍala, and the metaphor of healing emphasizes how their ritual activities remake the world as Buddhist.

In most episodes in *Jewel Garland*, Tāre Lhamo and Namtrul Rinpoche serve as joint protagonists. More precisely, the protagonist of the second half of *Jewel Garland* is the "eminent couple" (*skyabs rje yab yum*), a salient fusion of their identities. This term has two components: *yab yum*, referring to the union of male and female as "method and wisdom" (*thabs shes*) that is so iconic in Buddhist tantric art and ritual, and the term *kyabje*, literally the "lord of refuge" (*skyabs rje*), an epithet affixed before the name of a high-ranking lama and usually translated for a male referent as "His Eminence." I will use "Eminent Couple" as a translation rather than "Their Eminences" in order to highlight the yab-yum depiction.

While their hagiographic construction as joint protagonists has certain gendered complications, *Jewel Garland* presents a striking narrative of cultural revitalization with a tantric couple at the center of the action. In reading from this namthar and drawing on field research, I present Tāre Lhamo and Namtrul Rinpoche as part of a synergistic nexus of Nyingma lamas, traveling and teaching side by side in the 1980s and '90s. In addition, I demonstrate that the connectivity forged through their revelatory and ritual activities is central to the restorative or healing process in *Jewel*

Garland and functions as the very mechanism by which Tāre Lhamo and Namtrul Rinpoche reconstitute the landscape of Golok and Tibetan communities in Buddhist terms.

Gender in Hagiography

While portraying the couple as joint protagonists, Pema Ösal Thaye may inadvertently position Tāre Lhamo in a supporting role in partnership with Namtrul Rinpoche. This issue arises in the portrayal of their union in prophecies included in *Jewel Garland*. As mentioned, the twenty-page section that introduces Tāre Lhamo into the namthar begins with excerpts from her letters, totally almost ten pages or half of the section.[14] Following this is a sequence of oral prophecies by local Nyingma masters that describes the benefit to Namtrul Rinpoche of his union with Tāre Lhamo. Each has a slightly different gendered inflection, while cumulatively serving as important confirmations of the legitimacy of their union. For example, in a prophecy delivered orally by Lama Pelo,[15] she is predicted to be Namtrul Rinpoche's "karmic consort over successive lifetimes" (*tshe rabs las kyi gzung ma*) and the "intermediary key" (*bar gyi lde'u mig*) that will enable him to reveal treasures.[16] Here, Tāre Lhamo is positioned in the supporting role of a female consort (*gzung ma*) and an aid to his activities, rather than as an active partner in the revelatory process.

By contrast, Sera Yangtrul Tsultrim Gyatso (alias Rigdzin Sang-ngak Lingpa) prophesized the following during a personal encounter with Namtrul Rinpoche: "I had a vision of [the protectress] Tseringma, in which your constant companion across lifetimes has been Tāre Lhamo. Based on this prophecy, if you two converge together, it is certain to accomplish great benefit for the teachings and beings."[17] This statement more closely approximates the couple's own conception of their union, as found in their correspondence, by referring to Tāre Lhamo as his "constant companion across lifetimes" (*tshe rabs gtan gyi grogs*). More equitably, it suggests that great benefit will result if they join forces. Yet there is a subtle, contextual difference. In their correspondence, Namtrul Rinpoche is also her constant companion, referred to as her "method companion" (*thabs grogs*) and "legacy" (*bkod thang*) from Padmasambhava.[18] In the context of their epistolary exchanges, they serve as spiritual supports (*sems kyi rten*) for each other. Also contained in *Jewel Garland* are more formal written prophecies, including a "treasure certificate" (*gter gyi kha byang*) by Garra Gyalse Pema Tsewang (b. 1927)[19] and an excerpt from a prophetic certificate (*lung byang*) by Apang Terchen. The first focuses on Tāre Lhamo without reference to Namtrul Rinpoche, as a "smiling tigress named Tā" (recall that Tāre Lhamo was born in the tiger year) about whom he predicts: "If one meets with her, the two benefits [of self and other] are accomplished / and the hundred gates of magnetizing activity will open."[20] Though focused on Tāre Lhamo, this prophecy nevertheless casts her in gendered terms, whereby her agency is harnessed as a support for the activities of an unnamed male partner. The second, by her father, Apang Terchen, foretells a "method and wisdom pair named Abhaya and Tāre"[21] who will "spread treasure teachings, old and new, in the ten directions."[22] Here the Sanskrit term *abhaya,* meaning "fearless" (Tib.: *'jigs med*), indicates someone with the name Jigme as his daughter's future partner. In this case, Tāre Lhamo is envisioned in a yab-yum relationship with more parity, the emphasis being on the wide reach of her joint activities in partnership with a male figure. Notably, Namtrul Rinpoche adopted the name Namtrul Jigme Phuntsok only after his union with Tāre Lhamo, possibly in order to fulfill this crucial prophecy by her father.[23] Prior to that, his name in religion was Pema Drime Lodrö, or in its longer version, Pema Drime Ösal Lodrö Thaye. Here we can sense the complex negotiation of their relative status, whereby Namtrul Rinpoche's identity is derivative in part of Tāre Lhamo's own, yet he is given priority within the structuring of their hagiographies.

This section also contains recorded visions and letters by Namtrul Rinpoche, which are geared toward sanctioning their union as the handiwork of destiny, yet once again tacitly place Tāre Lhamo in a gendered role as his destined consort. The first vision involves Gesar, who appears in armor and instructs Namtrul Rinpoche to pick a *ghanta* or bell (*dril bu*) from among many, at which point one ghanta rises in the air, blazing with light, and lands on Namtrul Rinpoche's lap, then suddenly turns into Yeshe Tsogyal.[24] A ghanta is a symbol for the feminine principle of "wisdom" (*ye shes*) and the female partner in tantric pairings, while the *vajra* or ritual scepter is a symbol for the masculine principle of "method" (*thabs*) and the male partner. Though no interpretation is offered in the namthar, the reader is to understand that Namtrul Rinpoche's destined consort is an emanation of Yeshe Tsogyal.

In another vision, Namtrul Rinpoche sees Padmasambhava and Yeshe Tsogyal in union, but Yeshe Tsogyal appears sad. When asked the reason, she responds that she worries about Namtrul Rinpoche's recurring illness and plans to appear in person to nurse him back to health. As we have seen, Namtrul Rinpoche's health was a major concern in the couple's correspondence and remains so in *Jewel Garland* (as indeed throughout his life), and one of the benefits ascribed to a female consort is to extend the life of a male lama. Here the reader is not left to guess the meaning; it is given in Namtrul Rinpoche's own voice in response to a query from among his retinue to whom he recounted the vision. He states, "This is a sign that later I will converge together with a genuine emanation of [Yeshe] Tsogyal, Khandro Tāre Devī."[25] Though subjective in nature, nevertheless this vision and its interpretation in *Jewel Garland* carry authority as a prophetic statement about the future. Once again, Tāre Lhamo is positioned as a support, here explicitly for his health and longevity.

Despite the gendered role she is assigned, one must marvel at the prominence given to Tāre Lhamo in her entrance into *Jewel Garland*, which takes up a full twenty pages. Such a large pause in the flow of the narration, with prophecies and visions inserted, signals the importance of the event. There are other passages in *Jewel Garland* where Tāre Lhamo occupies the center of the narrative, as when Pema Ösal Thaye acknowledges that rumors circulated about her being a tertön in her own right, before she and Namtrul Rinpoche began widely disseminating their treasures together.[26] Moreover, twice during the narration of their lives together, as discussed later in this chapter, Namtrul Rinpoche is depicted offering a maṇḍala to Tāre Lhamo, on one occasion requesting her to share the yellow scrolls of a treasure cycle and on another to propagate a specific tantric liturgy or sādhana. In the context of broader representational practices in Tibetan literature, which tend to elide the role of women in the lives of male religious figures, it is exceptional that Tāre Lhamo plays such a prominent role in *Jewel Garland*. This is particularly the case given the "eminent couple" at the center of the narrative.

The Tibetan term *yab-yum* used to characterize the couple throughout *Jewel Garland* emphasizes their complementarity as a pair, yet its deployment can also reflect a gendered hierarchy. The term *yab-yum*, which I translate "couple," refers to male and female partners in a tantric context, conveying a sense of two-as-one. As distinct yet merged partners, conceived in heterosexual terms, the yab-yum is a functional unit in Tibetan liturgical materials as when applied after the name of the central deity of a visualization. For example, Vajrasattva when depicted in union with Vajraṭopa can be referred to by the epithet "the Vajrasattva couple" (*Rdor sems yab yum*), though it is often translated loosely as "Vajrasattva and consort," eliding the nature of yab-yum as a complementary pair. The signification of two-as-one with the term *yab-yum* does not necessarily connote "equality" in a second-wave feminist sense, since the name of the more prominent member, usually male, is given first to stand for the couple as a whole. In iconographic depictions of deities in union, moreover, the male typically faces the viewer while the female, often smaller in size, is draped around his neck, so much so that the female "half" of the couple can appear as a mere appendage to the male. Since images of this nature are the inspiration for visualization practices and a model for human relations, they raise salient issues about gender in relation to tantric partnerships.

Given this background, the epithets used in *Jewel Garland*—the "Eminent Couple" and a variant that could be translated as something like the "Dharma Lord and Lady" (*chos rje yab yum*)—underscore their partership as the basis of their religious activities and tacitly designate Namtrul Rinpoche as the principal. When referred to on his own, he is either "His Eminence" (*skyabs rje*) or the "Dharma Lord" (*chos rje*), followed by the reflexive particle *nyid*, meaning in this context "himself," emphasizing that he is acting alone on a particular occasion. Meanwhile, Tāre Lhamo is referred to consistently by the epithet "Supreme Khandro" (*mkha' 'gro mchog*), in *Spiraling Vine of Faith* and when she stands alone in *Jewel Garland*. Since generally the yab-yum is named after the principal member of a couple, whether human or divine, this suggests that Namtrul Rinpoche occupies that role in *Jewel Garland*. That said, I have seen a reference to the "Tāre Lhamo couple" (*Tā re lha mo yab yum*) listed at a pilgrimage site at Tashi Gomang in Padma County, Tāre Lhamo's homeland, figuring her as the principal member. Given this discrepancy, it may be that the figure listed as the principal, in their case, varies according to location: she in her homeland, he in his homeland. As a work sponsored by Nyenlung Monastery and published in Serta County, overall *Jewel Garland* seems to privilege Namtrul Rinpoche's role in the relationship. Yet Pema Ösal Thaye never goes as far as Abu Karlo in consigning her to the role of female consort. Instead they remain a yab-yum pair throughout. In this light, it makes sense that Tāre Lhamo only stands alone in her newest namthar by Rigdzin Dargye, who hails from her homeland in Markhok of Padma County and is a cleric-scholar affiliated with Tsimda Gompa, the monastery that her father founded.

Masculinizing Thaumaturgy

There are numerous episodes in which Namtrul Rinpoche comes to the fore in the narration of *Jewel Garland*, particularly those related to his own visions and miracles as well as passages concerning his recurring bouts of illness. It makes sense that the visions recounted in *Jewel Garland* would be Namtrul Rinpoche's own, particularly those that occurred in his youth, since the work is labeled as his namthar, subtitled "The Liberation of Namtrul Jigme Phuntsok." Recall that in 1960, during widespread famine when he was just a teenager, Namtrul Rinpoche had a vision of Yeshe Tsogyal, who warned him of bad times ahead and offered assurances that he would be spared the worst.[27] As an adult, in addition to visions included in the narration of Tāre Lhamo's entrance into *Jewel Garland*, there is one extended visionary sequence in which Yeshe Tsogyal appears to him in the midst of a rainbow dome, surrounded by a retinue of ḍākinīs. The vision includes a series of exchanges between Namtrul Rinpoche and ḍākinīs in her entourage, including a female nāga who gives him a symbolic certificate and various treasure substances.[28]

Throughout *Jewel Garland*, Namtrul Rinpoche plays the role of thaumaturge, despite comparable miracles by Tāre Lhamo in oral accounts and in *Spiraling Vine of Faith*. For example, when a man on the brink of death approached the "eminent couple" for help, it is Namtrul Rinpoche shown performing the knife healing: a miraculous cure that involves making an incision in order to excise the sickness, only performed by someone considered to be a *drupthob* or tantric siddha (Skt.: *siddha*, Tib: *grub thob*).[29] I heard a comparable story of Tāre Lhamo performing a knife healing by drawing a design on the hand of an old woman and making three incisions, though it is not recorded in *Jewel Garland*.[30] On another occasion, Namtrul Rinpoche is credited with averting the danger posed by a rockslide by singing a song of experience (*nyams mgur*):

In the wood rat year [1984], when the Eminent Couple departed for Serta, a torrent of water suddenly flooded the road. Since many rocks and boulders [also] rolled down [the hillside], their vehicle could not pass. At that time, the supreme Dharma Lord composed a song of experience and exclaimed, "Do you want to obstruct the presence of a tantric adept?" [After that] the vehicles were able to go around without any harm or difficulty whatsoever, and [they] were easily able to continue with their travels.[31]

This is not so very different from a miracle found in *Spiraling Vine of Faith* in which Tāre Lhamo stops a rockslide with a simple gesture of her hand. Where she used a gesture, he used an utterance, and such tales showcase their tantric prowess. While the second half of *Jewel Garland* mainly focuses on their activities together and only includes a few miracle tales, these few are for the most part attributed to Namtrul Rinpoche.

There is at least one story that could be read as a contest of masculinities, where it becomes clear that thaumaturgy would have been expected of Namtrul Rinpoche. This comes through in a passage where he is shown controlling the weather after being teased by Geluk monks during a visit to Drakar Tredzong for having to wait out a storm. Here is the episode:

Then, as the Dharma Lord and Lady were about to depart for the county seat of Shingho in Qinghai,[32] a fierce rainstorm broke out. The valley floor filled with water, making it impossible to clear the Hang-nge river. The lamas and monks of Tredzong Monastery said teasingly, "If you Nyingma have the power to stop rain, we can see you off this morning." The master replied, "Oh, that's easy!" Merely by focusing his mind, the sky became perfectly clear, and the river diminished. That morning, on the way back to the county seat of Shingho, after traversing [the river], the master said [to others in their entourage], "You should try to reach home by five o'clock. At that point, I will dispatch the rains." In accordance with his statement, at five o'clock, heavy rains once again descended, and there was no longer any way to clear the swelling river.[33]

As recounted in the passage above, Namtrul Rinpoche rises to the monks' challenge with an air of assurance, stopping the rains just long enough for the couple's entourage to descend through the rugged gorge and cross the river safely. I read this as a contest in masculinities to the extent that the monks, when teasing the Nyingma couple, prompt Namtrul Rinpoche specifically to defend their honor by producing a miracle.

Given the centrality of Tāre Lhamo's own miracle tales in oral accounts and *Spiraling Vine of Faith*,[34] it is surprising that supranormal feats of thaumaturgy and ritual prowess are for the most part attributed to Namtrul Rinpoche in *Jewel Garland*. Yet there is one prominent exception, which credits her with healing powers. When Namtrul Rinpoche fell severely ill toward the end of 1980 and beginning of 1981, a cohort of local tertöns intercede on his behalf, performing rituals and spontaneously revealing treasures in order to provide a cure. For example, Pema Tumpo—better known to English-speaking audiences by his tertön name, Kusum Lingpa—performed a propitiation of local female protective deities in order to dispel obstacles and established a cycle of ḍākinī teachings.[35] On this occasion, Payul Chagme Rinpoche revealed a "mind treasure" (*dgongs gter*) that contained medical rituals from among Namtrul Rinpoche's own "treasure allotment" (*gter skal*) from Yarlung Sheldrak in central Tibet.[36] Sera Yangtrul performed a similar feat when "from midair without any support, [he] received a treasure casket and many pills" to clear away the illness.[37] In addition, Khenpo Jigme Phuntsok sent a letter confirming that Namtrul Rinpoche should remain steadfast for a long time as the defender (*dpung gnyen*) of the teachings and beings, accompanied by an image of the protector, Amitāyus.[38]

Despite the aid of other Nyingma masters, Tāre Lhamo is highlighted in the narrative of his illness as the one who effected a cure through ritual means when Namtrul Rinpoche hovered on the verge of death. Gathering a group of monks and disciples for a gaṇacakra feast, she performed a ritual for "averting [the call] of the ḍākinīs" (*mkha' 'gro'i sun bzlog*):

With a gathering of monks and disciples, [she] offered an extensive and profound gaṇacakra, reciting [the liturgy for] "averting the call of the ḍākinīs."[39] The master was quite ill, and his whole body grew freezing cold. When he was no longer able to speak, the Supreme Khandro became restless. While calling out the master's name, she waved a [longevity] arrow three times, and slowly he came back to consciousness. When he had just [regained] the ability to speak and move, he recounted, "Many ḍākinīs welcomed me with various instruments and melodies along a silk cord and a rainbow path dangling in the sky. You waved the arrow with silk [ribbons] and cut the rainbow path and silk cord. Though the ḍākinīs were not pleased, since returning, I am now free of injury." At that time, the down feathers of a white eagle fell like snow on the whole house, outside and inside. A mist of fragrance descended. A dome of rainbow light formed. Many such auspicious signs occurred.

Here Tāre Lhamo is credited with bringing Namtrul Rinpoche back from the verge of death through her ritual prowess. Upon regaining consciousness, he attributes his recovery to her ritual action, cutting the pathway by which he was being led to the ḍākinī realms, a departure that would signify his passing into *parinirvāṇa*. It seems to take a ḍākinī on earth to bring a lama back from the call of the ḍākinīs in more ethereal realms. In her ability to reverse the death process, Tāre Lhamo performs one of the long-standing roles of a female consort: extending the life of a male Buddhist master. Yet this does not diminish the miraculous nature of the account, signaled by the auspicious signs that followed: eagle feathers falling like snow, a mist of fragrance, and rainbow light.

As another twist in the gendered narration of *Jewel Garland*, even when agency is credited to the couple in an episode, occasionally the outer frame subsumes that action into the enlightened activity of Namtrul Rinpoche. For example, in 1991 representatives from Shukjung Monastery reportedly arrived at Nyenlung with a prophecy that the Gödem tulku would protect the monastery from a flood. Rigdzin Gödem, the founder of the northern treasure tradition, is counted among Namtrul Rinpoche's past lives at the outset of *Jewel Garland*. In response, the couple issued "a prophecy that the Gesar of Ling performance from the Eminent Couple's own treasure corpus, if performed, has the ability to reverse those conditions," refering to the threat of flood. As a result, the performance troop was readily invited to Shukjung Monastery.[40] Next, speaking in one voice, the couple warned the troupe, which they duly dispatched from Nyenlung on the rough road to nearby Shukjung: "Along the way there, you should not get distracted even for a moment from the inseparability of your own mind with that of the teacher."[41] Moreover, they tied protection cords on the performers and their horses and tossed rice as blessings. On the way, a fierce hailstorm beset the group, and lightning struck nearby. Though some of the performers panicked, after Namtrul Rinpoche suggested they stop and make further aspirations, they arrived safely with drenched clothing and completed the performance. Accordingly, the following year when the Do River flooded, *Jewel Garland* triumphantly reports that Shukjung Monastery remained unharmed and credits its safety to the "compassionate activity of the Master himself" (*rje nyid kyi thugs bskyed 'phrin las*). In the concluding refrain, we can see that somewhere along the line, Tāre Lhamo's contribution got lost, although she also warned the traveling dance troupe, blessed them in their journey, and contributed to the potency of their Gesar treasure, all constituent features of the salvific nature of the tale.

These examples shows an underlying tension in which *Jewel Garland* serves as Namtrul Rinpoche's authorized life story, yet for the most part he shares center stage with Tāre Lhamo. One can detect a conundrum in representation, whereby gender norms dictate that Tāre Lhamo serve in a supporting role but her prominence in the discovery and dissemination of their treasures is well beyond the scope of a typical consort. Perhaps for this reason, the action mainly centers on the two as a couple, an indication of the extent to which they functioned as genuine partners in their religious careers. Though gendered in selection and presentation, miracle tales are comparatively few in *Jewel Garland*. For the most part, it presents a record of their accomplishments as a tantric couple in revealing treasures, presiding over large-scale ritual occasions, and playing a significant role in reviving Buddhist teachings, ritual programs, pilgrimage sites, and monastic institutions in Golok and neighboring areas during the post-Mao era.

Nexus of Nyingma Masters

Prior to recounting their accomplishments, in its narration of the early 1980s, *Jewel Garland* depicts the further teachings that Tāre Lhamo and Namtrul Rinpoche received from older Nyingma masters who survived the Maoist period and, in the process, charts their rise to prominence during the early years of the post-Mao era. In the late 1950s, when so many prominent religious figures were imprisoned and public religious observances were curtailed, Tāre Lhamo had just entered her twenties, and Namtrul Rinpoche was only a teenager. Thus, in order to ensure the continuity of transmission for particular esoteric cycles, *Jewel Garland* shows them recapitulate as a couple the training they received individually in their youth. It thereby contextualizes them within a synergistic network of Nyingma masters whose activities are shown to be loosely coordinated and mutually supportive. Their interaction with figures such as Khenpo Jigme Phuntsok,

Pema Tumpo, Sera Yangtrul, Dola Chökyi Nyima, and Payul Chagme also affords *Jewel Garland* the opportunity to record further prophecies to legitimate their union and authorize them to teach as a couple.

Jewel Garland records that Khenpo Jigme Phuntsok "took them on as his students with great affection and gave them many dharma teachings that ripen and liberate."[42] In 1980, he bestowed the initiation for the entire treasure corpus of Apang Terchen, Tāre Lhamo's father, and in 1986, cycles from the treasure corpus of Lerab Lingpa, regarded as one of Khenpo Jigme Phuntsok's previous lives.[43] Additionally, in the early 1980s, Sera Yangtrul bestowed the transmission for his entire treasure corpus on Tāre Lhamo and Namtrul Rinpoche; Thubten Trinle Palzangpo bestowed an empowerment of Yeshe Tsogyal and teachings on Dzogchen or "the great perfection" (*rdzogs pa chen po*); and Kachö Wangmo, another female tertön of Tāre Lhamo's generation, gave them teachings related to Buddha Palmo (*Sangs rgyas dpal mo*).[44] As late as 1990, Dola Chökyi Nyima bestowed the treasure corpus of his father, Dudjom Rinpoche Jigdral Yeshe Dorje, to the couple in its entirety and authorized them to transmit it far and wide.[45] It was around this time that Tāre Lhamo garnered international attention by recognizing Dola Chökyi Nyima's son as the reincarnation of Dudjom Rinpoche.[46] In addition to their own treasures and Apang Terchen's corpus of revelations, the treasure corpus of Dudjom Rinpoche constitutes one of the main lineages that Tāre Lhamo and Namtrul Rinpoche held and propagated.[47]

As a record of their receipt of teachings and authorization to disseminate them, *Jewel Garland* emphasizes their legitimacy as Nyingma lineage holders and the continuity of transmissions being passed down to them. This was critical for those cycles of teaching for whom they have been considered lineage holders, particularly the treasure revelations of Apang Terchen, which Tāre Lhamo received from her father when she was young. Khenpo Jigme Phuntsok conferred the reading authorization for the entirety of Apang Terchen's treasures to them, depicted in formal and elaborate terms as follows:

> During the same year [1980], in the presence of a cohort of lamas with the Sublime Khenchen foremost among them, the crown jewel wielding the saffron victory banner [of monasticism], they requested him to bestow the nectar of oral instructions that ripens and liberates for the entirety of the profound treasures of the great tertön [Orgyan] Trinle Lingpa [a.k.a. Aphang Terchen], who was in

actuality the lord of secrets, a magical emanation of the three secrets of the victorious lord Padmākara. At that time, Khenchen Rinpoche said, "In the past the precious lama and great tertön said to me: 'In the same way that I am now bestowing the empowerment on you, in the future, you should bestow [it] on others.' Although my vision is fading, you the couple are surely fortunate individuals, great beings who are emanations. From this time forward, you will accomplish great blessings for the benefit of the teachings and beings. Of this I am certain. Having completed the recitations, perfectly confer this empowerment." With great affection, he bestowed the initiation, reading authorization, and esoteric instructions as well as the subsequent teachings as if filling a vase to the brim. [In this way] he entrusted [them] with the bequest.[48]

In this passage, Khenpo Jigme Phuntsok (referred to as the "Sublime Khenchen" and "Khenchen Rinpoche") bestows the corpus of Apang Terchen and also authorizes them to confer it on others. The completeness of the transmission is emphasized, including the initiation (*dbang*), reading authorization (*lung*), oral instructions (*man ngag*), and subsequent teachings (*rgyab chos*). The image of "filling a vase to the brim" suggests their full and unadulterated receipt of the transmission. Moreover, in the last phrase, the term that I translate as "bequest" (*pha nor bu*) denotes the family jewels (or valuables) passed down as patrimony. The use of this term evokes the family lineage that Khenpo Jigme Phuntsok returned to Tāre Lhamo in the form of her father's treasure corpus. From that point forward, she and Namtrul Rinpoche served as the main lineage holders for this tradition. There is no doubt in this passage of the importance given to ensuring the continuity of Nyingma teachings and also the authorization of the couple as lineage holders for Apang Terchen's treasures in particular.

Indeed, *Jewel Garland* goes to extra lengths to legitimate Namtrul Rinpoche as a holder of Apang Terchen's lineage. Since Nyingma lineages, and particularly treasure teachings, are routinely passed through the family, there is little question of Tāre Lhamo's authority as a lineage holder for her father's treasure corpus. But for Namtrul Rinpoche, the situation would be different. An open-ended prophecy attributed to the fifteenth-century tertön Pema Lingpa is glossed to refer to Namtrul Rinpoche as follows: "At the site of vajra essence, profound treasures, / when unveiled by one named Dorje, / will be employed as the glory of one named Mati."[49] The glosses provided in *Jewel Garland* specify the one named Dorje to be Pawo Chöying Dorje

5.2 The couple with Khenpo Jigme Phuntsok, seated in the center. Original photographer unknown.

(a.k.a. Apang Terchen), the treasure teachings to be *White Lotus Garland of the Great Compassionate One* (*Thugs chen pad dkar 'phreng ba*), a ritual dedicated to Avalokiteśvara, the bodhisattva of compassion, and the one named Mati or Lodrö in Tibetan (*blo gros*) to be Namtrul Rinpoche, whose name prior to his partnership with Tāre Lhamo was Pema Drime Lodrö.

A reinterpretation of another prophecy illustrates the creative adaptation by Nyingma masters in adjusting traditional lineage formation schemas to fit the exigencies of their time. A prophecy by Dzongter Kunzang Nyima was reinterpreted by Khenpo Jigme Phuntsok to refer to Namtrul Rinpoche in lieu of Wangchen Nyima, one of Apang Terchen's sons.[50] The prophecy itself is rather obscure; without mentioning Apang Terchen's treasures, it references a "powerful monkey youth" (*rtsal ldan sprel gyi gzhon nu*) who lassoes a tigress—lining up with the animals associated with Namtrul Rinpoche's birth year in the Tibetan calendrical cycle (wood monkey) and Tāre Lhamo's own (earth tiger).[51] Given its placement in *Jewel Garland*, it may imply that Namtrul Rinpoche replaces a role as a principal lineage holder originally slated for Wangchen Nyima. Beyond this, *Jewel Garland* makes a point of stating that the couple received letters and oral encouragement from numerous religious figures to propagate the profound treasures of Apang Terchen.[52] Specifically mentioned is the key figure Sakya Trizin—now living in Dehradun, India—who was recognized at an early age as the reincarnation of Apang Terchen, despite his status as head of the Sakya lineage.[53]

In its account of the 1980s, *Jewel Garland* highlights their participation in activities that constellated around Khenpo Jigme Phuntsok, a charismatic leader and tertön based in Serta who emerged as a towering figure in the revitalization of Buddhism in the post-Mao era. Tāre Lhamo and Namtrul Rinpoche participated in his large-scale Kālacakra initiation in 1986, joined his entourage of 10,000 on a historic 1987 pilgrimage to Wutai Shan—the Buddhist pilgrimage site in Shanxi Province where the couple also revealed treasures, and accepted places of honor at the head of the assembly during the 1989 consecration of stūpas and public teachings at Larung Buddhist Academy.[54] *Jewel Garland* reports that Khenpo Jigme Phuntsok sat at the head of the section for saffron-robed monastics, Namtrul Rinpoche at the head of the section for white-robed yogins, and Tāre Lhamo at the head of an assembly of nuns, suggesting the positions of honor the couple were given on public occasions.[55]

In *Jewel Garland*, Pema Ösal Thaye emphasizes the role that Khenpo Jigme Phuntsok played in launching their teaching careers, confirming them as tertöns and encouraging them to teach widely. During the Kālacakra initiation in 1986, after rumors had circulated that Tāre Lhamo was a tertön,[56] he pulled the couple aside and pronounced: "In the past, Jamyang Khyentse Wangpo invested Chokgyur Dechen Lingpa as an authentic tertön. Similarly, I also invest you, the couple, as authentic regents of Orgyan Padma. Henceforth you should compose many treasure teachings."[57] By proclaiming them to be "authentic regents of Orgyan Padma" (Padmasambhava) as a couple—the term *yab-yum* is used here—Khenpo Jigme Phuntsok is shown directly authorizing Tāre Lhamo and Namtrul Rinpoche together as tertöns.

That same year, *Jewel Garland* highlights a meeting that Tāre Lhamo and Namtrul Rinpoche had with the Tenth Paṇchen Lama, the most prominent

Buddhist master within Tibetan areas of the PRC at the time, during his historic visit to Serta. The namthar reports his authorization of the couple to teach as follows: "Over many of our lifetimes, we have never been separated. You two should bestow as many initiations and instructions to others as possible."[58] Moreover, on their return from Wutai Shan, Khenpo Jigme Phuntsok is reported to have said, "Now the pair of you should travel extensively to such places as Lake Kokonor, Drakar Tredzong, and the white snow mountains of [Amnye] Machen."[59] These moments of authorization are presented as a turning point in their career, which had previously been restricted to travels and teachings closer to home in Serta and Padma counties, and sanction their pilgrimages and teaching tours from the late 1980s forward. Beginning in 1987, *Jewel Garland* depicts Tāre Lhamo and Namtrul Rinpoche routinely traveling on long pilgrimage tours with an entourage to discover and disseminate their own treasures and to propagate those of Apang Terchen.

5.3 Long-standing treasure site at Drongri in Serta, covered in prayer flags.

Revelations on Pilgrimage

In *Jewel Garland*, the narration of their revelations begins in the iron monkey year (1980) at the "treasure gate of golden Drongri Mukpo." This is a sacred mountain that serves as the local territorial deity of Serta, also understood to be an emanation of the dharma protector Mahākāla,[60] and had been an active treasure site for preceding generations of tertöns. At a power spot halfway around the mountain, they offered a seven-day gaṇacakra feast and from its southern face extracted a treasure whose purport was to "lastingly stabilize the lotus feet of all the holders of the [Buddhist] teachings of Tibet."[61] Not much detail is given about the revelation process, except for the appearance of symbolic script on the face of a zi-stone casket (*gzi sgrom*),[62] from which they set down a sādhana of Mandāravā, the Indian consort of Padmasambhava. In this episode, the very first of their recorded activities together, *Jewel Garland* asserts the broader significance of the couple's treasure revelations in fostering the restoration of Buddhism in the form of a sādhana to secure the longevity of the "holders of the teachings" (*bstan 'dzin*), Buddhist masters who survived the Maoist period. This echoes an episode in *Spiraling Vine of Faith*, described in chapter 2, when Tāre Lhamo revealed a long life sādhana and bestowed it on the "defenders of the teachings and beings" in 1978.[63]

Overall, *Jewel Garland* portrays pilgrimage, treasure revelation, and feast offerings as intertwined in the activities of Tāre Lhamo and Namtrul Rinpoche, suggesting the ritual context for treasure revelation and the importance overall of ritual to the representation of their restorative efforts. For example, in their second revelation, which took place at Nyenpo Yutse, a sacred mountain range and pilgrimage site in Jigdril County of Golok, they extracted a "lake treasure" (*mtsho gter*) from one of its two sacred lakes, Shimtso and Ngöntso, and then performed a feast offering (*tshogs mchod*) in gratitude to the nāga king associated with the lake. Yet it appears that they were only able to extract a portion of their treasure allotment, a jewel casket described as "sealed by the hand of master Padma," foregrounding the claim that treasures are concealed by Padmasambhava himself or alternatively Yeshe Tsogyal.[64] Pema Ösal Thaye notes that their treasure allotment also included a crystal stūpa, which they were not able to obtain due to "circumstances of time and place, such as not completing the number [of recitations] for the gaṇacakra," harkening back to the contingencies involved in treasure revelation discussed in the previous chapter.[65] Nonetheless, this is an apt illustration of how *Jewel Garland* situates their revelations in the context of pilgrimage and in conjunction with feast offerings. No mention is made of the contents of the treasure, only the miracle following it: "Although it was winter, the ground heated up, storm clouds slowly gathered, and a rain of flowers fell. A variety of flowers newly bloomed at the lakeshore. Many such auspicious signs occurred."[66]

Apart from presenting the ritual context, *Jewel Garland* does not provide much detail about the revelation process itself, whereas the wondrous signs that followed are vividly described. In response to their first revelation, the sacred mountain Drongri Mukpo is said to have turned the color of crystal, and at the conclusion of their feast offering, "on the refined golden peak of the treasure site, Drongri Mukpo, spheres of rainbow light filled the whole sky, atmosphere, and ground as if the sun blazed with hundreds of thousands of dazzling light rays, a colorful offering lamp that shone forth in the sky for two days and nights without end. There were many wondrous auspicious signs like that, established as an appearance in common for hundreds of people [as far away as] Dzamthang, Golok, and Serta."[67] In line with the presentation of miracles in *Spiraling Vine of Faith*, Pema Ösal Thaye emphasizes the common perceptions (*mthun snang*) among bystanders who witnessed these signs, often those traveling with them on pilgrimage. Yet here he stipulates that the signs were visible from farther afield, indeed counties away.

On these pilgrimages to sacred places within and beyond Golok, *Jewel Garland* sometimes shifts the epithet used for its protagonists from the "eminent couple" to the "couple with entourage" (*yab yum 'khor bcas*). The "couple with entourage" never becomes an agent in the way that the "eminent couple" remains through most of the narrative. Instead, the members of the entourage serve as participants in rituals led by the couple and witnesses to the wondrous signs that accompany their revelatory activities. The frequent mention of their travels with an entourage highlights the mandalic framework in which Tāre Lhamo and Namtrul Rinpoche's activities are represented. The yab-yum couple and entourage are a maṇḍala in motion, traversing the landscape of Golok and beyond. Indeed, the term for entourage literally means "circle," and it is the same word used in the Tibetan for *maṇḍala*, combining the words for "center" (*dkyil*) and "circle" ('khor), indicating a center point and the periphery around it. By depicting Tāre Lhamo and Namtrul Rinpoche as a "couple with entourage," *Jewel Garland* fashions a maṇḍala in the very narration of their activities with the couple at its center.

In this mandalic framework, the reader is positioned as part of the entourage, accompanying Tāre Lhamo and Namtrul Rinpoche on pilgrimage to witness wondrous signs associated with their deeds, through which Pema Ösal Thaye seeks to engender faith. The episodes chronicling their travels on pilgrimage provide a snapshot summary of each event: where they went and what they did, almost in list fashion, followed by wondrous signs, at times described in more detail than the event itself. These signs belong to a stock set as old as Buddhism itself—rainbows appearing, flowers falling from the sky, fragrance permeating the air—or, more creatively, statues trembling and rolling their eyes. At one point, following a series of wonders accompanying their 1992 pilgrimage to central Tibet, Pema Ösal Thaye states, "through [witnessing their] various signs of accomplishment, even the logician is set onto the path of faith."[68] I take this to mean that even the most rational (perhaps even skeptical) person would be moved by witnessing the wonders accompanying the couple's deeds.

In line with its emphasis on establishing connectivity, *Jewel Garland* depicts the "place connections" Tāre Lhamo and Namtrul Rinpoche forged during their pilgrimage tours with previously established sacred sites (*gnas chen*), harvesting their associations and sometimes adding new ones. Their local treasure sites would be well known to any informed reader native to Golok and neighboring areas. Both Drongri in Serta County and Nyenpo Yutse in Jigdral County are established pilgrimage sites and domains of territorial deities for the areas surrounding them, regarded as ancestral progenitors of local clans. Drongri is associated with the origins of the Washul clan in Serta, and Nyenpo Yutse with the three major clan divisions in Golok.[69] Moreover, both are long-standing sites of treasure revelation by masters from the previous generation, including Dzongter Kunzang Nyima and Apang Terchen. Harvesting and reactivating the previous associations of sacred sites is a salient feature of the pilgrimages and revelations represented in *Jewel Garland*, and reminiscent of Germano's characterization of the "treasure-driven resuscitation" of Buddhism in the post-Mao era.

At Tashi Gomang, a sacred site long associated with Padmasambhava, Tāre Lhamo and Namtrul Rinpoche add a new association, identifying one of the hillsides behind the monastery as a treasure site connected with the legendary king Gesar of Ling. Prior to this revelation, the main attractions at Tashi Gomang have been a "self-arisen" (*rang byung*) stūpa and footprints in rock attributed to Padmasambhava and Yeshe Tsogyal.[70] Here, as elsewhere, *Jewel Garland* provides little details about the process itself, stating only that in 1985, in the midst of offering an extensive gaṇacakra feast, they identified a Gesar treasure site, setting down a catalogue of its contents.[71]

Only in their abbreviated namthar, *Jewel Lantern of Blessings* by Abu Karlo, is there an explicit statement about the process of treasure revelation between the couple, particularly the phase of transcribing or more literally "setting down" (*gtan la pheb*) a revelation. In a general statement about their revelatory activities, Abu Karlo writes:

> In this life, the great tertön couple perfected in mind the secret pith of all the intentions of the Buddha in their entirety without relying on training in hearing, contemplating, and [practicing] austerities. Fully awakening the entrustment [of Padmasambhava], they caused treasure teachings such as precious earth treasures, mind treasures, and pure visions to burst forth from the expanse of the sky treasury. That is to say, based on the symbolic script of Namtrul Rinpoche, the Supreme Khandro would set down a text, or else, based on the symbolic script of the Supreme Khandro, Namtrul Rinpoche would easily elucidate a text. [In this way] the profound dharma in approximately thirteen volumes[72] of the noble method-and-wisdom couple is distinct from [that of] other tertöns. It has special qualities: its meaning is profound, [expressed] in beautiful language, and its blessings are great, [placing] accomplishment near at hand.[73]

In the opening statement, Abu Karlo clearly shares the stance of studied reverence found in *Spiraling Vine of Faith* and *Jewel Garland* by declaring that Tāre Lhamo and Namtrul Rinpoche have perfected the pith of all the Buddhist teachings. Moreover, if one fills in the blanks a bit, he seems to suggest that tertöns, by virtue of their illustrious past lives and visionary talents, are exempted from the rigorous training needed to perfect the Buddhist path. This is an important caveat, given that their religious training was interrupted at an early age. Though more explicit than *Jewel Garland*, Abu Karlo still does not give much away about treasure revelation as a visionary process. Nonetheless, he does emphasize their distinctive style of collaboration as a couple, describing how one of them would first received a symbolic script—as an earth treasure, mind treasure, and pure vision—and then the other one would decode it and elucidate it in textual form. This process of taking turns in receiving the symbolic script and decoding the treasure was reiterated to me by Namtrul Rinpoche on at least one occasion.[74]

Lest we imagine his reticence has to do with secrecy, Pema Ösal Thaye does not even elaborate on the revelation process when chronicling the only public treasure (*khrom gter*) recorded in *Jewel Garland*, also in 1985, when Tāre Lhamo and Namtrul Rinpoche returned to Tashi Gomang. This event came just before their public recognition as tertöns by Khenpo Jigme Phuntsok. *Jewel Garland* recounts, "Thereafter, [they] visited the sacred site Tashi Gomang. At the site of Gesar, king of *dralas* [lit. war gods], in the midst of a crowd of many hundreds of people, they received as treasure a nine-pointed vajra made of various types of precious substances, called 'the vajra that binds by oath the gods and demons.'"[75] It is not so unusual for ritual implements like a nine-pointed vajra to be revealed as treasures, yet *Jewel Garland* presents few details about this public feat. The reader is left wondering which one of them retrieved the vajra and from where at Tashi Gomang.

Public revelations are more typically recorded in the namthars of tertöns as spectacular achievements. In a comparable revelation, witnessed by a crowd that include the King of Dege, the namthar of the nineteeth-century tertön Chokgyur Lingpa (abbreviated: Chokling) recounts, "Chokling opened the rock and extracted a vajra, leaving it half out and half in just for show."[76] This feat, narrated as a playful demonstration of tantric prowess, precedes the extraction of the actual treasure casket with which he later blessed the crowd by touching it to their heads. This event is situated after Chokgyur Lingpa's public recognition as a tertön and portrays a certain showmanship in treasure revelation. No such bravado can be detected in *Jewel Garland*'s narration of their one and only public treasure, though Pema Ösal Thaye does credit the couple with a high degree of tantric prowess in their possession of a ritual scepter capable of binding gods and demons, invoking Padmasambhava's demon-taming activities in the eighth century. This is a curious omission, given the emphasis on miracles in *Spiraling Vine of Faith* and wondrous signs in *Jewel Garland*.

One wonders whether a modernist sensibility caused Pema Ösal Thaye to tone down the most spectacular element of treasure revelation. Is he really concerned with logicians (*rtog ge ba*), or might this stand for a novel sensibility among the newly educated laity within his intended readership?

The extraction of a treasure is certainly a miraculous feat, wherein a tertön is said to place his or her hand into sheer rock to open the "treasure gate" (*gter sgo*). But so are hand- and footprints in rock, and Pema Ösal Thaye does not shy away from recording miracles of this nature. This reticence could also explain his presentation of miracles and wondrous signs as "perceived in common" rather than venturing a claim of miracles as empirical facts. Of course, there could be more practical considerations at work. Pema Ösal Thaye confessed to me at one point that he did not accompany the couple on their travels and thus could not report on these events first-hand.[77] This may also account for the brevity of episodes and lack of details related to the revelation process.

In its narration of their activities in the late 1980s, *Jewel Garland* portrays pilgrimage as the tertön couple's modus operandi and the mechanism by which they extend their sphere of influence beyond Golok. While they continued to reveal treasures locally—at Drongri, Nyenpo Yutse, and also Shukjung—*Jewel Garland* shows them traveling farther afield to reveal treasures and make "connections" to sacred sites. The namthar highlights their participation in the large-scale pilgrimage led by Khenpo Jigme Phuntsok in 1987 to Wutai Shan, the abode of Mañjuśrī, the bodhisattva of wisdom, in China. But Pema Ösal Thaye does not portray them as merely part of the entourage. Rather, the couple remains at the center of the narration, which highlights their own visions and revelations at Wutai Shan and their conferral of those on a group of lamas and monks who had also joined the pilgrimage.[78] For example, while resting on the stone staircase at Phosatin (Ch.: Pusading), a major temple at Wutai Shan run by Tibetan Buddhists since the early Qing, the couple had a shared vision of a young Chinese girl with the syllable *hring* on her forehead who wrote symbolic letters (*brda yig*) on the palm of Namtrul Rinpoche's hand. From this, the couple established the sādhana cycle of Sarasvatī and bestowed its initiation to small parties of lamas and monastics while still at Wutai Shan.[79]

On their return trip, Tāre Lhamo and Namtrul Rinpoche made an extended pilgrimage to major sacred sites in Amdo and revealed treasures at Drakar Tredzong and Amnye Machen. The account of this trip repeats a set of characteristic features: feast offerings, treasure revelations, and wondrous signs. On the first stop, Lake Kokonor, they offered an extensive gaṇacakra feast, accompanied by wondrous signs like rainbow-colored lights on the lake and the sound of musical instruments in the sky. At the next stop,

Drakar Tredzong, they revealed "a mighty red casket as treasure and set down many profound teachings," including a Yeshe Tsogyal sādhana cycle.[80] Drakar Tredzong is a well-known pilgrimage site, a rocky mountain with many caves and a circumambulation route around its base. Though a Geluk monastery stands near the site, it has long-standing Nyingma associations, particularly caves where Padmasambhava and Yeshe Tsogyal are reputed to have practiced. For this reason, it has been a favorite hermitage for solitary adepts, including the early nineteenth-century yogin Shabkar Tsokdruk Rangdrol. On this segment of their pilgrimage, *Jewel Garland* employs the term "place connection" (*gnas 'brel*) to highlight the connectivity that the couple created with sacred sites in Golok, northern Amdo, central Tibet, and greater China. Once again, Pema Ösal Thaye places their revelation in a ritual context of pilgrimage but says little about the revelation itself.

Given that so many of the revelations mentioned in *Jewel Garland* are rituals dedicated to female figures like Sarasvatī and Yeshe Tsogyal with whom Tāre Lhamo is associated, it is worth considering whether this might have to do with her status as a female tertön. A ritual focus on female deities and enlightened women is remarkably prominent in their treasure collection (*gter chos*).[81] Four entire volumes are dedicated to Yeshe Tsogyal, Mandāravā, Tārā, Sarasvatī, Vārāhī, Krodhī, Kurukullā, and other lesser-known figures. In line with the gendered hierarchy in the textual corpus of Tāre Lhamo and Namtrul Rinpoche overall, standard ritual cycles pertaining to male tantric deities like Amitābha, Vajrasattva, and Vajrakīla come first, followed by cycles pertaining to the enlightened female figures listed above. Only after their treasure revelations proper do we find the couple's treasure certificates and ordinary compositions, including songs of experience (*nyams mgur*), supplications (*gsol 'debs*), confessions (*bshags pa*), aspirations (*smon lam*), and a cycle of advice (*gdams skor*). The twelfth volume is dedicated to Gesar; like their correspondence, it seems to be an addendum, not fully integrated within the hierarchical ordering and presumably a stand-alone text originally.

It would be difficult to say conclusively whether the predominance of female figures in their treasure corpus and highlighted in *Jewel Garland* is linked to gendered visionary proclivities or a gendered representation on Pema Ösal Thaye's part. On the one hand, the colophons of their treasures confirm that, just as Abu Karlo described above, Tarē Lhamo and Namtrul Rinpoche alternated in the roles of revealing the symbolic script and setting down the treasure. On the other hand, *Jewel Garland* seems to suggest Tāre Lhamo's special affinity for treasures related to female figures. Just prior to their first revelation at Drongri, it portrays Namtrul Rinpoche offering a maṇḍala to Tāre Lhamo to beseech her to show him the yellow scrolls for a treasure cycle related to Krodhī, a wrathful form of Vajrayoginī. Then, at her request, he set down a sādhana of Sarasvatī.[82] Later in the narrative, Pema Ösal Thaye shows Namtrul Rinpoche once again offering a maṇḍala to Tāre Lhamo, this time to request her to spread the sādhana of Tārā throughout Kham and Amdo.[83] In addition, *Jewel Garland* highlights the "Supreme Khandro" as the one to establish a one-month Tārā practice at Nyenlung and again later at Tsimda Gompa.[84] This suggests, at least to some degree, a link between Tāre Lhamo as a female tertön and her propagation of female deities, for some of whom, according to prophecies recorded in *Spiraling Vine of Faith*, she serves as the embodiment.

Connectivity to Central Tibet

The most extensive account of a pilgrimage in *Jewel Garland* chronicles their tour of Lhasa and environs in 1992, which Tāre Lhamo and Namtrul Rinpoche undertook with an entourage of disciples. The namthar dedicates twelve pages to the trip,[85] indicating the importance of the connections they made with sites in central Tibet associated with the imperial period and Nyingma masters of yore. In line with the overall style of the namthar, the narration is episodic, naming the sites they visited and the treasures they revealed, punctuated with visions, feast offerings, and wondrous signs. *Jewel Garland* highlights their revelations at Samye, the first Buddhist temple constructed in the imperial period and associated with the myth of Padmasambhava's taming of the gods and demons of Tibet. It also highlights their visits to Gangri Thökar, a former hermitage of Longchenpa Drime Özer near Shugsep Nunnery, and Tsogyal Latso, the lake associated with the birthplace of Yeshe Tsogyal, where there is a small nunnery. After their return to Golok, Tāre Lhamo and Namtrul Rinpoche continued to send financial support to the nuns at Tsogyal Latso.[86]

As elsewhere, treasure revelation takes place in a ritual context, and wondrous signs are central to the narration. At Samye, they extracted and set down several treasures during an extensive feast offered together with their disciples. While setting down a sādhana cycle of Hayagrīva, the horse-headed tantric deity, they heard the sound of a horse neighing, described as one of many "wondrous signs" (*ya mtshan pa'i rtags*) on that occasion.[87] There Tāre Lhamo and Namtrul Rinpoche also had a vision that Padmasambhava himself crowned them with tertön names, Ḍākki Tāre Dechen Gyalmo and Orgyan Jigme Namkha Lingpa respectively.[88] At Gangri Thökar, one or both of them had a vision of Longchenpa in which he gave them esoteric instructions to set down; the subject is not stated, and it is possible that the vision was Namtrul Rinpoche's alone. At Tsogyal Latso, after revealing elixir said to be Yeshe Tsogyal's breast milk (*mtsho rgyal nu chu*), they performed a seven-day Yeshe Tsogyal sādhana together with lamas and monastics at the site, during which a statue of Yeshe Tsogyal reportedly rolled its eyes.[89] Though it is not listed among their treasure sites, at the Jokhang Temple before the Jowo Śākyamuni, they offered a gaṇacakra feast together with "many thousands of faithful pilgrims from regions within Do Kham," during which they set down the *Secret Completion: Essence Sādhana of Great Orgyan*.[90] In his representation of their pilgrimage to central Tibet, Pema Ösal Thaye makes sure to link Tāre Lhamo and Namtrul Rinpoche with the charisma of past Nyingma masters and sacred sites dating back to the first propagation of Buddhism in Tibet.

The importance of this pilgrimage to the hagiographic construction of the couple in *Jewel Garland* cannot be underestimated. It places Tāre Lhamo and Namtrul Rinpoche at the very sites where events in the eighth century from which they derive their authority as tertöns are believed to have occurred. *Jewel Garland* highlights this in its representation of an initiation they bestowed at Samye, for which it states that people from various regions gathered around the "eminent couple" like a constellation of stars in the sky. This image suggests a mandalic arrangement with the yab-yum at its center and echoes a similar image in Tāre Lhamo's fourteenth letter, in which she imagines their future teaching career surrounded by constellations of disciples.[91] Of this event, *Jewel Garland* reports: "Everyone commented that they thought this was no different than when in the past the great master Padmākara bestowed the good fortune of profound secret elixir on the gathered assembly of his disciples; eyes streaming with tears of faith, many made [such] comments."[92] With this statement, *Jewel Garland* homologizes the ritual activities of the couple in disseminating their revelations to the original event in which they received teachings from

Padmasambhava (a.k.a. Padmākara) in previous lives as Yeshe Tsogyal and Namkhai Nyingpo. Through their pilgrimage to central Tibet and revelations there, they bridged both time and space to establish a vital connection to Tibet's imperial period and the sites associated with it. Moreover, they shared this sense of connectivity in the bounty of treasures they brought home and transmitted upon their return.

Overall, *Jewel Garland* emphasizes the links that Tāre Lhamo and Namtrul Rinpoche forged to well-known sacred sites. Thus, while excerpts from their letters showcase their temporal connections to historical and mythic figures, such as Padmasambhava and Gesar, the rest of the namthar focuses on the spatial connections that they made throughout the sacred landscape of Golok and beyond. A list of their treasure sites (*gter gyi gnas*) in the final pages includes major and minor sacred sites across ethnically Tibetan regions: Samye Chimpu, Gangri Thökar, Amnye Machen, Drakar Tredzong, Drongri Mukpo, Nyenpo Yutse, Dröphug Khandrö Duling, Tashi Gomang, Yangdzong, Shukjung Pema Bumdzong, Lake Kokonor, and Tsogyal Latso.[93] They are shown not only making "place connections" by visiting and revealing treasures but also "befriending" the protective deities of the regions, such as Nyenchen Thangla, who is depicted as serving as a visionary guide during their pilgrimage to central Tibet. Through their revelations, Tāre Lhamo and Namtrul Rinpoche created transregional linkages to reconnect, as Germano puts it, "the extended cultural body of Tibet."[94] This network of sites is further linked to their religious community through the dissemination of their treasures and the "dharma connections" they thereby create.

Ritual as Revival

Jewel Garland pronounces 1980 as the starting point for their joint teaching career, beginning with their transmission of the revelations of Tāre Lhamo's father. The namthar calls it a time of "good fortune and coincidence to propagate in the ten directions the transmission for instructions that ripen and liberate in the entirety of the profound treasures of Apang Terchen Orgyan Trinle Lingpa."[95] Despite the grandness of this claim, their teaching career began locally in Serta and Padma counties, the very places where Apang Terchen spent his days and remains well known. For the early 1980s, *Jewel Garland* chronicles their teaching at two monasteries in Tāre

Lhamo's own homeland of Padma County: Tsimda Gompa, founded by her father Apang Terchen, and Tashi Gomang, where another member of the Apang family was prominent.[96]

Through the record of this early local circuit, *Jewel Garland* inaugurates a paradigm for representing their pilgrimage cum teaching tours in general. In addition to pilgrimage, feast offerings, and treasure revelation, its features include conducting tantric initiations to groups of lamas and monastics at nearby monasteries, performing a public initiation (*khrom dbang*) for the general populace (*dmangs khrod*), and giving ethical advice to the laity. In Pema Ösal Thaye's presentation, their teachings frequently follow a pilgrimage, such as when they gave teachings in Machen, Gabde, and Padma counties after their pilgrimage to Wutai Shan, Lake Kokonor, and Drakar Tredzong. Nevertheless, in the following, I focus on how *Jewel Garland* presents the initiations and teachings they bestow, especially the way Tāre Lhamo and Namtrul Rinpoche made "dharma connections" with people in the region and established ritual cycles at numerous monasteries.

In 1985, Tāre Lhamo and Namtrul Rinpoche conducted their first large-scale rituals together at Tsimda Gompa, which *Jewel Garland* presents as a grand occasion, with lamas and monastics from more than fifty different monasteries in attendance.[97] On this occasion, the couple bestowed initiations and reading authorizations for the treasures of Apang Techen as well as for their own revelations. The size of this event is impressive, considering that Golok Prefecture as a whole by 1992 only had fifty-eight monasteries and, out of those, forty-three were Nyingma.[98] If one adds neighboring Serta County in Kandze Prefecture, there are an additional thirty monasteries in the vicinity as of 1995, all of which are Nyingma.[99] So it is certainly possible that out of seventy-four Nyingma monasteries in those counties, fifty were represented at this event. And, if accurate, it shows the regional importance of the couple during the early stages of the post-Mao era in no uncertain terms. Even if this is slight hyperbole, *Jewel Garland* nonetheless signals their prominence, which seems to be derivative of Apang Terchen's regional renown.

This event is also the first record of Tāre Lhamo and Namtrul Rinpoche transmitting their own treasures, and it is significant that they did so in the context of bestowing the complete treasures of Apang Terchen at the monastery that he founded. As his only direct descendant still living, Tāre Lhamo was the legitimate heir and lineage holder of his treasure corpus, and she vigorously promoted its transmission alongside Namtrul Rinpoche throughout their long teaching career. She would also have been the legitimate head of Tsimda Gompa, but forfeited the role when she left Markhok in 1980 to join Namtrul Rinpoche at Nyenlung.[100] Also, 1985 was the same year they revealed their one and only public treasure on record, and the year before they were authorized as tertöns by Khenpo Jigme Phuntsok. So Tāre Lhamo and Namtrul Rinpoche staked their own claim publicly to be tertöns, prior to gaining official recognition, and *Jewel Garland* is not shy about pronouncing this.

The account of their teachings at Tsimda Gompa makes a significant statement of the ritual agency of the couple, who not only give the transmission for treasure cycles together but also transform the status of thousands of people who attend their teachings. In general, *Jewel Garland* presents their tantric initiations as two-tiered events in which Tāre Lhamo and Namtrul Rinpoche bestowed an extensive series of transmissions to a gathering of lamas and monastics (*bla ser* or *bla grwa*) from various monasteries and afterward conferred a public initiation as a blessing for the local laity, here *The Swift Path: Sādhana of the Great Bliss Realm* (*Myur lam bde chen zhing sgrub*).[101] The namthar also sometimes presents these as occasions for bestowing specific vows, though tantric initiations always presupposes the samaya vow as the condition for attendance. In this episode, Pema Ösal Thaye reports that the "eminent couple" inspired more than three hundred to renounce and take novice ordination and four thousand to take *upāsaka* vows of anywhere from one to five precepts, while conveying ethical advice to the laity more broadly.[102]

The conferral of Buddhist precepts on the laity at this sort of large-scale gathering—and ethical reform more generally—have become common in recent decades, and after the almost twenty-year hiatus in public religious observances during the Maoist period, could be seen as part of a re-Buddhicization process in Tibetan areas. *Jewel Garland* describes the scene: "They exhorted [those in attendance] at length to adhere to virtue by protecting the lives of [beings] up to and including insects, regularly paying homage [to the Three Jewels], arranging [daily] water offerings, and to prevent, as much as possible, the sorts of activities that are discordant with the dharma, such as smoking, drinking alcohol, or harming the life of creatures: using pesticides, explosives, or snares and plucking the hair [of yaks]."[103] In this description, Tāre Lhamo and Namtrul Rinpoche ask the laity to perform simple acts of devotion and also to stop engaging in conduct "discordant with the dharma." (*chos dang mi mthun pa*). In the post-Mao era, this type of ethical exhortation, alongside mass vow-taking, has become a way to reassert the primacy of a Buddhist episteme in governing the values and lifestyles of Tibetans.

Such ethical prescriptions are connected with the way that karma is used to narrate recent history in *Spiraling Vine of Faith*, as highlighted in chapter 2. Take, for example, their advice not to pull out the hair from yaks. I was told that Tāre Lhamo determined that the karmic cause for people being dragged by the hair in struggle sessions during the Maoist period was the long-standing nomadic practice of pulling out the hair of yaks (instead of shearing them) to make the wool for yak-hair tents.[104] Thus their prescription to stop this has as much to do with compassion toward animals as with preventing the repetition of trauma. No mention is made of vows not to sell livestock for slaughter, which was vigorously promoted by Khenpo Jigme Phuntsok starting in 2000, and more recently efforts at ethical reform have morphed into a new set of "ten virtues" (*dge bcu*) promulgated by cleric-scholars at Larung Buddhist Academy in Serta.[105] Overall, ethical reform has been integral to the revitalization of Buddhism in Golok, and *Jewel Garland*'s description of their advice to the laity here is one of the few times any details are given regarding the content of what Tāre Lhamo and Namtrul Rinpoche taught, besides the names of rituals.

From 1985 forward, *Jewel Garland* depicts a centrifugal process, whereby Tāre Lhamo and Namtrul Rinpoche began to extend their sphere of influence beyond Serta and Padma to other counties in Golok and east into neighboring Ngawa Prefecture. That same year, they visited Soru village in Jigdril County and various monasteries in Ngawa, a prefecture east of Golok in Sichuan Province.[106] In narrating this eastward extension, *Jewel Garland* records the various "dharma discourses" (*chos bka'*) they gave and the many "dharma connections" (*chos 'brel*) they made. No details are given about the topics of their discourses; the emphasis instead is on the geographic sweep of their teachings and many connections to people and places along the way.

The term "dharma connections" is used frequently in *Jewel Garland* to denote the outcome of the couple's ritual activities. The namthar indicates that, at various stops along their travels, the couple made "dharma connections" with lamas and monastics as well as with the general public (*mang tshogs*). Verbs such as "give" (*gnang*) and "bestow" (*stsol*) are used, indicating a one-way or even top-down process. *Jewel Garland* never defines what it means by "dharma connections," though it quotes a prophecy that through them, Tāre Lhamo and Namtrul Rinpoche can lead disciples to Padmasambhava's pure land: "Opening the gates of the sky treasury of profound treasures, they will guide whoever is connected to Ngayab Palri," the pure land of Padmasambhava.[107] This statement highlights the couple's salvific powers beyond the confines of this life and indicates the soteriological import of such connections.

When I asked Namtrul Rinpoche how dharma connections were made, he responded that they occur through a request for teachings. His initial explanation was that "when lamas from various places come here to request teachings, [this] becomes a dharma connection."[108] However, he then broke down this general definition into different degrees of connections based on the category of teachings bestowed: outer (*phyi*) corresponds to public initiations given to the laity as the basis for faith, inner (*nang*) to esoteric teachings to lamas and monastics, secret (*gsang*) to practices done in retreat, and extra-secret (*yang gsang*) to instructions on Dzongchen or the "great perfection" (*rdzogs chen*), the highest teachings for the Nyingma tradition. According to this schema, the degree of connectivity corresponds to the level of teachings: the higher the teachings received, the closer the connection.

From his response, it becomes clear that dharma connections involve a teacher-student relationship, created in the context of esoteric teachings and rituals in which faith also plays a significant role. Namtrul Rinpoche's definition is reminiscent of the samaya vow, taken at tantric initiations, in which the disciple pledges allegiance to the presiding master. Through this vow, participants are ritually constituted in familial terms as siblings,[109] and a ritual community is formed in mandalic fashion on the basis of a shared allegiance. In pragmatic terms, such ritual activity has provided the means for Tibetans to recuperate from social disintegration and re-create the social web with Buddhist masters as the focal point.

Though surely central to Buddhist soteriology, these connections can also be read in this-worldly terms to signify the very means by which Tāre Lhamo and Namtrul Rinpoche reconstituted Tibetan communities in Buddhist terms. To the extent that *Jewel Garland* portrays the "eminent couple" as the centerpiece of large-scale ritual gatherings in which dharma connections are made, it participates in the mandalization process that repositions religious figures at the center and apex of Tibetan society. In episode after episode, Tāre Lhamo and Namtrul Rinpoche remake the world around them through ritual acts of consecration and initiation. People and places are transformed, gaining new identities, commitments, and connections.

Wherever they traveled, Pema Ösal Thaye also notes the rituals they established. At Soru village, for example, the couple newly established the *Sādhana of the Great Compassionate One, White Lotus in Hand* (*Thugs chen phyag na pad dkar gyi sgrub pa*), referring to Avalokiteśvara in the form of the "Great Compassionate One" (Skt.: Mahākāruṇika).[110] This text comes from Apang Terchen's corpus and is the most frequently mentioned public initiation and practice that Tāre Lhamo and Namtrul Rinpoche transmitted widely.[111] In their teachings and travels, Pema Ösal Thaye notes that they newly established this sādhana in the ritual programs at numerous monasteries, emphasizing their regional influence and promotion of Apang Terchen's treasures.

5.4 Performance of Drime Kunden outside of the main assembly hall at Nyenlung in 2007.

Once back at Nyenlung, *Jewel Garland* includes much more about the ritual programs they established than about their construction projects. In his summary of their activities there in the early 1980s, Pema Ösal Thaye states that the "eminent couple" newly established a variety of annual rituals: calendrical commemorations, a large-scale festival on the tenth of the month, a month-long Vajrasattva practice, the practice of the *Great Compassionate One*, and a summer retreat.[112] Though not mentioned, the annual events at Nyenlung gradually came to include performances from the Gesar epic, the namthar of Drime Kunden, and sacred dances ('*cham*).[113] In line with its presentation of their travels, *Jewel Garland* concentrates on the transformations that Tāre Lhamo and Namtrul Rinpoche effected. Through establishing ritual programs, they helped to restructure a Tibetan sense of time in Buddhist terms, since the liturgical calendar in turn regulates the rhythm of monastic life and the timing of local festivals.

In 1986, they extended their reach eastward, through teaching, revealing treasures, establishing liturgical practices, and contributing to construction projects. First they visited Shukjung, a small monastery along the Do River just past Dodrupchen, where they revealed a treasure at the "soul site" (*bla gnas*) of the protective deity Mayum Tenma. There they set down treasures related to the Medicine Buddha and the Goddess of Coincidence (Rten 'brel lha mo), and established the *Sādhana of the Ḍākinī's Secret Wisdom* (*Mkha' 'gro gsang ba ye shes kyi sgrub pa*).[114] From there, they proceeded farther east, along the river toward Dzamthang and north to Drakor Gompa, where they are credited with erecting a new assembly hall and establishing sādhanas of Red Tārā and the *Great Compassionate One, White Lotus in Hand*. Drakor Gompa is among the dozen monasteries for which Tāre Lhamo and Namtrul Rinpoche provided ongoing financial aid, spiritual guidance, and served as teachers.[115] Additionally, at that location, *Jewel Garland* states that the "supreme khandro" left her footprint in rock, which occasioned the construction of a demon-suppressing stūpa, eight smaller stūpas, and clay images of the Buddha.[116] Recounting such visits, *Jewel Garland* presents the very active role the couple took at the monasteries they visited: giving teachings, establishing liturgical practices, sanctifying the landscape through their presence, and instigating construction projects.

Pema Ösal Thaye seamlessly blends pilgrimage, revelation, and tantric initiations into the narration of the couple's return from Wutai Shan in 1987. After their pilgrimage to Lake Kokonor and treasure revelation at

Drakar Tredzong, on their way back through Golok, Tāre Lhamo and Namtrul Rinpoche began to confer the initiation and reading authorization for the Sarasvatī cycle they had just revealed at Wutai Shan. First, they visited and offered a feast at Amnye Machen, where they also "set down several profound teachings" (*zab chos 'ga' gtan la phab*) and bestowed the initiation for the Sarasvatī sādhana on a small group of students.[117] Next, they visited Tongkyab Gompa in Gabde County and "bestowed various dharma discourses that ripen and free to all the lamas and monastics," newly establishing the *Great Compassionate One, White Lotus in Hand* there.[118] On their way back through Padma County, they visited Dogongma and other monasteries in Markhok to confer the initiations for Sarasvatī and the Medicine Buddha before returning home for another treasure revelation and more teachings at Nyenlung.[119] Pema Ösal Thaye packs quite a remarkable year into a few pages as the couple traveled between pilgrimage sites from China proper through Amdo and into Golok.

Jewel Garland portrays the steady stream of their ritual activities during the late 1980s and thereby highlights their growing regional importance in Golok and neighboring areas. Having visited Machen, Gabde, and Padma counties in 1987, they returned to Padma County the following year after a jaunt farther afield to Dartsedo to attend a conference, in which the namthar reports they made "dharma connections" with lamas and tulkus in Kandze Prefecture as well as the local populace in nearby areas of Drango and Tawu counties, southeast of Serta, on the way home.[120] Back in Padma County, *Jewel Garland* returns to the steady flow of their ritual activities with more initiations at Tsimda and nearby Wangda monasteries before moving onto Serkhar in Dzamthang to newly establish the *Great Compassionate One, White Lotus in Hand* and give teachings to the general public.[121]

In 1989, Tāre Lhamo and Namtrul Rinpoche made local tours through Jigdril and Padma counties again in a whirlwind through which *Jewel Garland* displays their activities as a couple reaching their height. This time in Jigdril County, they visited the monasteries of Payul Tarthang and Dong Dzong Gompa, where they performed the initiation and reading authorization for the *Great Compassionate One, White Lotus in Hand* and established the sādhana as a regular practice.[122] Then, back in Padma County, they established an annual practice of the *The Swift Path: Sādhana of the Great Bliss Realm* and the one-hundred-day Tārā intensive at Wangda and Böpa monasteries, where they also constructed a stūpa and consecrated images.[123] While still in Padma County, at Utsa Gompa they gave "dharma discourses that ripen and liberate to all the lamas and monastics" and "spoke to the general public [for the sake of] dharma connections." Next, at Dumda and Getse monasteries they "bestowed various types of dharma discourses that ripen and liberate to all the monastics and laity."[124] The amount of their activity and the degree of repetition on these teaching tours is so high that Pema Ösal Thaye stops bothering to list what rituals and instructions the couple gave and simply distills the description to two main constituents: "dharma discourses" and "dharma connections."

In the early 1990s the flurry of activity continues, and *Jewel Garland* portrays Tāre Lhamo and Namtrul Rinpoche extending their sphere of influence northward into the Nyingma enclave around Rebkong, consolidating their religious community at Nyenlung, and continuing to tour locally in and around Golok. Their activities in the Rebkong area are more typical of the Buddhicization process in which Buddhist masters convert areas on the border of ethnically Tibetan regions to Buddhism by, among other things, banning animal sacrifice.[125] En route, Pema Ösal Thaye reports no less than 17,000 people attending their teachings at Tertön Chögar, a monastery in Hor township east of Tongde, and at Rongpo Monastery in Rebkong.[126] Although it is hard to imagine them drawing crowds of this number in a place at some remove from their home bases of Serta and Padma, clearly Pema Ösal Thaye wants to impress upon the reader their increasing renown and the grand scale of their activities. As further evidence, on this trip, he mentions that Tāre Lhamo and Namtrul Rinpoche ransomed the lives of and set free more than 100,000 animals. Thereafter, the narrative of their activities tapers off as it reaches 1995, the year *Jewel Garland* was composed.

Building Projects in Golok and Environs

Because of its focus on ritual, *Jewel Garland* presents scant details on the building projects Tāre Lhamo and Namtrul Rinpoche sponsored. For these we turn to other sources, including regional histories of monasteries in Golok and Kandze prefectures as well as interviews I conducted with Namtrul Rinpoche and the heads of several monasteries where the couple visited and acted as stewards, teachers, and patrons. These supplement *Jewel*

Garland as sources for their activities during the 1980s and '90s and help to round out a portrait of their contributions in concrete terms.

Beginning in 1980, Tāre Lhamo and Namtrul Rinpoche, along with another local Buddhist master, Rigdzin Nyima, took responsibility for the rebuilding of Nyenlung Monastery.[127] *The History of Nyenlung Monastery* credits these three as the impetus or "dominant condition" (*bdag rkyen*) in the reconstruction, highlighting their leadership in the process, and also credits the "faithful public" (*dad ldan mang tshogs*) among the local Rusarma clan as the "harmonious condition" (*mthun rkyen*).[128] This is a nod to collective agency that cannot be found in *Jewel Garland*, with its focus on the couple as principal agents in the revitalization process. But it was reiterated to me by Namtrul Rinpoche, who underscored the donation of labor by members of his clan (*tsho ba*) after everything had been "eradicated from the root" (*rtsa ba nas med par btang*) during the Cultural Revolution.[129]

Though Nyenlung had been fairly modest in scale prior to 1958,[130] nonetheless *The History of Nyenlung Monastery* records that its temples, main assembly hall, sacra, and monks' quarters had been destroyed during the Cultural Revolution.[131] Between 1980 and 1995, Tāre Lhamo and Namtrul Rinpoche rebuilt the large assembly hall, a small temple, a golden central image of Padmasambhava, more than ten other golden images, various physical supports made of medicine and clay, fifteen *thangkas* or scroll paintings (*thang ka*), stūpas and circumambulatory temples of various sizes, musical instruments, and more than one thousand volumes of scriptures.[132] In this list, emphasis is given to buildings as well as the sacra and scriptures installed inside them.

In the mid-1990s, a small pavilion with a peacock throne for two was constructed on the hillside above the monastery grounds, with an open front for public teachings. Tāre Lhamo and Namtrul Rinpoche began hosting an annual dharma gathering (*chos tshogs*) at Nyenlung in 1996, part of a centripetal process of consolidating their following there, not mentioned in *Jewel Garland* given that the narrative ends in 1995. The dharma gathering has been held annually ever since for approximately ten days during Sagadawa, the fifth month of the Tibetan calendar, with anywhere from one to several thousand monastics and laity in attendance.[133] Video footage from the late 1990s and early 2000s shows large crowds of Tibetan and Chinese disciples on this occasion.[134] When I attended in 2006, there were up to a thousand disciples gathered on the lawn below the teaching pavilion

5.5 Nyenlung Monastery as seen from the fields above the monastery in 2014.

for the opening ceremony and other public events. I present this in more detail in the epilogue in describing their ongoing community at Nyenlung after Tāre Lhamo's passing.

Construction has continued unabated at Nyenlung since the mid-1990s. Over the next decade, more buildings were added, including a school (*slob grwa*), two retreat centers (*sgrub grwa*), a study center (*bshad grwa*), a residence (*gzim khang*) for the couple, several temples (*lha khang*), and a meditation hall (*sgom khang*).[135] A guest house for visiting dignitaries was constructed in 2005, which contains a large hall downstairs used for teachings given to Chinese students. A new assembly hall designed to fit several thousand participants on ritual occasions was completed in 2007 in order to accommodate the swelling number of Chinese students who have flocked to Nyenlung in recent years. When I visited in 2011, a more elaborate study center was under construction and a Gesar temple had been added. By my last visit in 2014, another temple had been constructed on the top of the hill above the study center, this time a three-tiered structure representing Zangdok Palri (*zangs mdog dpal ri*), the pure land of Padmasambhava, and featuring shrines to Amitābha, Avalokiteśvara, and Padmasambhava on successive levels. In addition, several memorials have been added since Namtrul Rinpoche's passing: a gilded stūpa situated near the large stūpas toward the entrance of the monastery, where locals routinely gather to circumambulate; the pyre where he was cremated on the hill above their residence; and a novel memorial (*rjes dran*) structure composed of photographs behind windows above the pavilion. The structure has three tiers, mirroring the architecture of the Zangdok Palri, with each tier featuring larger-than-life photographs of Tāre Lhamo and Namtrul Rinpoche on all four sides.

The History of Nyenlung Monastery emphasizes continuity even though the character of Nyenlung has changed significantly. Founded in 1797 by Lama Sang-ngak, Nyenlung became affiliated with Katok under its branch Zhuchen Monastery, based on its use as a retreat hermitage for Namtrul Jigme Ösal Dorje, the third Namkhai Nyingpo incarnation of Zhuchen Monastery, who introduced the Katok ritual systems of Rigdzin Dudul Dorje and Rigzin Longsal Nyingpo.[136] The history declares that "the good custom of protecting the continuity of explanation and practice of the Buddha's stainless tradition of victorious Katok has remained until the present."[137] However, today Nyenlung includes a variety of Nyingma practices, with an emphasis on Tāre Lhamo's and Namtrul Rinpoche's own treasures and those of her father, Apang Terchen. For example, at one of two practice centers, housing ten monks for stays of three to twelve years, the monks complete preliminaries and practices associated with Longsal Nyingpo, the more widely practiced *Longchen Nyingthik*, and the "six dharmas" (*chos drug*) of Apang Terchen.[138]

Indicating the shift in ritual focus, the second retreat center, built after 2002 according to Tāre Lhamo's wishes, is dedicated mainly to the Varjasattva practice of Apang Terchen.[139] To presage this, *The History of Nyenlung Monastery* highlights a visit to Nyenlung by Apang Terchen for new year festivities in 1945, the year he passed away. The texts indicates that he stayed there "henceforth for the tendrel of accomplishing great benefit for the teachings and beings," and for that reason, "these days the activity of the three secrets of this master are propagated at this place."[140] Apang Terchen's visit was no doubt included in *The History of Nyenlung Monastery* for the express purpose of conferring legitimacy on the shift in liturgical practices.

Although the artwork for these structures had to be commissioned from elsewhere, Namtrul Rinpoche emphasized to me that the rebuilding process, in its initial phases, relied exclusively on local funds and voluntary labor. Moreover, he insisted that he and Tāre Lhamo never actively raised funds, nor did they accept money that came from slaughtering animals, which would have been tainted by unethical deeds. Instead, people contributed of their own accord, and this was sufficient to rebuild the monastery.[141] The local funding of monastery construction has been typical of the cultural revitalization process more broadly, according to Kolas and Thowsen, whose findings indicate that, despite government claims to have channeled money into monastery reconstruction, "local people and pilgrims provided the vast majority of funding."[142] More recently, since the late 1990s and early 2000s, a growing interest in Tibetan Buddhism among Han Chinese from China proper as well as Hong Kong and Taiwan has increased the funding base of monasteries and allowed for significant expansion projects beyond the basic facilities constructed in the early phase of revitalization efforts.

Beyond Nyenlung, Tāre Lhamo and Namtrul Rinpoche helped with the reconstruction of a number of other monasteries in the region. Foremost among these was Tsimda Gompa in Padma County, the monastery founded by Tāre Lhamo's father in 1925 and reopened in 1981.[143] While Tāre Lhamo was not officially the head as recognized by the county Religious Affairs Bureau, by virtue of residing in another province, she played an important role in its reconstruction. Jamyang Nyima, the acting head of Tsimda, credits Tāre Lhamo with rebuilding several prominent structures: the main assembly hall dedicated to Vajrasattva, a retreat center dedicated to ritual systems from her father's treasure corpus, and two stūpas, one for her mother and one for her son.[144] For more than two decades until her passing in 2002, the couple served as the principal teachers for Tsimda, had their own modest residence on the grounds, and visited annually to give teachings. Gesturing to its significance for them, Namtrul Rinpoche described Nyenlung and Tsimda as "two eyes" (mig gnyis), indicating that both monasteries had been integral to their religious activities and community.[145]

Tāre Lhamo and Namtrul Rinpoche served in a stewardship capacity for other monasteries. Their abbreviated namthar by Abu Karlo, *Jewel Lantern of Blessings*, mentions ten monasteries for which the couple were "stewards responsible for the teachings" (bstan pa'i khur chen bdag).[146] When I asked Namtrul Rinpoche for the names of these monasteries, in addition to Nyenlung and Tsimda, he listed several in Serta, including Zhuchen, Ragtram, Taktse, and Bumlung; two in Golok, Tagthok in Padma and Gangpa in Darlag; Drakor in Dzamthang in neighboring Ngawa Prefecture; plus one farther afield in Tsekhok County in Huangnan Prefecture of Qinghai Province.[147] As far as I have discerned, these monasteries represent institutional ties— such as to Zhuchen, where Namtrul Rinpoche served as a reincarnate lama, and two of its affiliate monasteries, Drakor and Taktse—or sites where the couple had a significant following and served as teachers to the head of the monastery. At these monasteries as well as others not listed, their stewardship consisted in one or more of the following: funding building projects, sponsoring rituals, establishing liturgical practices, and visiting regularly to give teachings.

Two concrete examples illustrate the constituent aspects of their stewardship. Located in Dzamthang, Drakor Gompa is a monastery with institutional ties to Namtrul Rinpoche as a branch of Zhuchen, and one of its heads, Yonten Palzang, was a close disciple of Tāre Lhamo.[148] He first met her when he was eighteen years old and quite ill. She provided him with medicine, performed rituals on his behalf, and conferred instructions on the nature of mind. During the Cultural Revolution, most of Drakor Gompa was destroyed except for one temple and a wall of maṇi stones. However, Yonten Palzang stayed nearby, consigned to manual labor and sometimes acting as a secretary (drung) for his work unit. In the early 1980s, he traveled to Tsimda Gompa to receive the treasure collection of Apang Terchen from Tāre Lhamo and Namtrul Rinpoche, and from that point forward he visited Tsimda and Nyenlung regularly.

At his invitation, the couple visited Drakor Gompa several times to give empowerments and teachings. In addition, they helped each year by donating 20,000 RMB to the monastery, providing ritual objects, sponsoring the summer retreat (yar gnas), and providing a stipend to each of its thirty monks. Moreover, Tāre Lhamo established a seven-day Tārā practice, which the monastery performs each year in August. Though Yonten Palzang has become too old to travel, many people from the village below Drakor Gompa visit Nyenlung regularly to receive teachings. When I joined the dharma gathering at Nyenlung in 2006, there was a group of approximately thirty monastics and laity from Dzamthang.

My second example, Abzö Gompa in Jigdril, indicates the reach of their stewardship beyond the monasteries on the list Namtrul Rinpoche provided. This may have been an oversight, as one of its two principal teachers, Jigme Wangdrak Dorje, remained close to Namtrul Rinpoche after Tāre Lhamo's passing. Jigme Wangdrak Dorje is Tāre Lhamo's cousin and the only one of four incarnations of her father, Apang Terchen, to be formally enthroned.[149] His own father, Gyurme Gyatso, was a drupthob or "accomplished one" and the brother of Apang Terchen. Jigme Wangdrak Dorje was recognized at an early age by Dzongter Kunzang Nyima and enthroned in central Tibet as the incarnation of Apang Terchen by Dudjom Rinpoche Jigdral Yeshe Dorje at the age of eight. In his youth, he joined Tāre Lhamo on a pilgrimage around Nyenpo Yutse and studied with Dzongter Kunzang Nyima at Rizab while she resided there. The buildings, texts, and sacra at Abzö Gompa were all destroyed in the Cultural Revolution, and although it reopened in 1982, I was told that it has not yet been rebuilt to scale.

Tāre Lhamo and Namtrul Rinpoche visited Abzö Gompa twice while touring Nyingma monasteries in Jigdril. In 1991, they bestowed a number of empowerments, including Vajrasattva, Kīla, and Gesar, to the monks of Abzö Gompa and nearby monasteries, such as Drasar and Jamda, who joined the gathering. In 1995, they visited again in order to consecrate a maṇi wall and perform rituals, including Avalokiteśvara in the form of the Great Compassionate One, Vajrasattva, Gesar, and One Thousand Buddhas. At that time, the couple donated several thousand yuan and fifty to sixty yaks to the monastery. Jigme Wangdrak Dorje regularly visits Nyenlung, witnessed at least one

5.6 Gesar Temple established by the couple at the base of Amnye Machen.

of their treasure revelations, and still wears a *zi* stone (*gzi*) around his neck that Tāre Lhamo revealed as a treasure in her youth and presented to him as a gift. Such gifts function as relics of contact and tokens of Tāre Lhamo's blessing, another way that connections between teacher and disciple are forged and fortified. In interviews, her close friends and disciples in Golok often spoke of gifts they received from Tāre Lhamo, like a set of rings in the shape of a bell and scepter given to a prominent government official in Tawu; a ring given to the grandparents of a family I stayed with in Padma County, placed in the maṇḍala offering on their shrine; or a zi stone worn by a good friend, added to the beads on her necklace, also in Padma.

To wrap up this discussion on their building projects, let me mention a significant project the couple undertook outside of the bounds of monastery reconstruction that reflects their broader interest in revitalizing Tibetan culture, and specifically the Gesar epic. At the base of the sacred mountain range Amnye Machen, Tāre Lhamo and Namtrul Rinpoche constructed a temple dedicated to Gesar, referred to as Ling Mountain Fortress of One Hundred Thousand Lotuses (*Gling ri pad ma 'bum rdzong*), today one of six state-recognized Gesar temples in Golok.[150] Unlike other Gesar temples that feature the king surrounded by his ministers, ladies, and generals, this one has a tantric flavor, with Gesar in the form of Hayagrīva as the central deity on the shrine and the Nyingma protectress Ekajaṭī by his side. Murals on walls to either side of the main shrine feature the local protector, Amnye Machen, and Gesar as king surrounded by his generals. Beyond this temple, Tāre Lhamo and Namtrul Rinpoche have promoted the regional lore of Gesar through their joint revelation of a volume dedicated to the Gesar epic and by founding a Gesar performance troupe in Serta in the late 1980s, which regularly has performed at Nyenlung and toured various other monasteries in Golok.[151] Indicating their stature with respect to reviving the Gesar epic, the couple served as guests of honor for a conference on the topic held in Serta around the year 2000.[152]

The building projects that Tāre Lhamo and Namtrul Rinpoche sponsored in Golok and environs indicate the regional nature of their sphere of influence. If we also take into account their revelation sites and teaching tours, as chronicled in *Jewel Garland*, that sphere significantly expands. Generally, the couple discovered treasures while on pilgrimage and thereby laid claim to treasure sites that span the sacred geography of Golok and neighboring Serta and also extend far beyond its borders northward into Amdo, westward into central Tibet, and eastward into Gyalrong and beyond that, to Wutai Shan in central China. Their teaching tours traversed a more circumscribed yet sizeable domain, consisting of their homelands of Serta and Padma counties and extending east into Jigdril and Dzamthang, north to Tawu, the prefecture capital of Golok, and beyond that into a Nyingma enclave near Rebkong in northern Amdo. Within these three sets of parameters—related to their building projects, treasure revelations, and teaching tours—their sphere of influence was predominantly regional, concentrated in Golok and surrounding areas, yet extending farther along certain trajectories.

At the Center of the Maṇḍala

Jewel Garland presents the couple's contribution to the revitalization of Buddhism as a ritual process through which Tāre Lhamo and Namtrul Rinpoche forged connections with people and places throughout Golok and neighboring areas. Within the web of connectivity that the narrative weaves, the yab-yum couple remains conspicuously at the center in a mandalic configuration that positions them as the focal point. In its presentation of their activities between 1980 and 1995, *Jewel Garland* depicts their entourage in a circle around them, traveling with the couple on pilgrimage, participating in rituals, and witnessing their revelations and the wondrous signs that accompany them. Beyond that, it records the sizeable number of participants, reaching from the hundreds into the thousands, including lamas and monastics from numerous monasteries in the region. Thus, in the assertion of a mandalic framework, *Jewel Garland* depicts both the couple and the audience for their teachings and ritual activities, who are thereby the beneficiaries of their efforts to "heal the damage of degenerate times."

Jewel Garland itself could be viewed as an agent in the mandalization process by positioning readers as witness to Tāre Lhamo and Namtrul Rinpoche's wondrous activities. As Charlene Makley has suggested, namthar as a genre of Tibetan literature has played a vital role in reconstituting Tibetan identity as grounded in faith during cultural revitalization in Tibetan regions.[153] First and foremost, hagiographic accounts like *Jewel Garland* reassert religious figures at the center and apex of Tibetan society and showcase their activities as the charismatic centerpiece of large-scale gatherings. In addition, and perhaps more subtly, namthar draws the reader into a Buddhist episteme and its presumptions regarding the ritual prowess and transformative powers of tantric masters. In this way, the genre recruits the reader as potential disciples into a mandalic framework centered around the ritual activity of Buddhist masters.

The appropriate disposition for the reader, as modeled by their entourage, is one of faith. For example, in the scene where Tāre Lhamo and Namtrul Rinpoche gave teachings at Samye, Pema Ösal Thaye depicts the audience with tears of faith streaming down their cheeks.[154] Such displays among the entourage and the wondrous signs following the couple's deeds are meant to cue the reader's own response. More pointedly, simply by virtue of reading the namthar and learning of the couple's activities, the reader enters into the web of connectivity centered around Tāre Lhamo and Namtrul Rinpoche and shares in the promise to be beneficiaries of their grace.

Pema Ösal Thaye narrates *Jewel Garland* in such a way as to forge a connection between the protagonists and its readers based on faith. His account begins with an image of the namthar as a seed planted in the field of faith. Through this image, Pema Ösal Thaye suggests that namthar itself is a primary cause for reawakening the faith of Tibetan people after the almost twenty-year hiatus of public religious observances during the Maoist period. Engendered by the teachings and activities of Buddhist masters like Tāre Lhamo and Namtrul Rinpoche and their representation in namthar, faith is the very means by which Tibetan communities have been and continue to be reconstituted in terms other than those provided by the Chinese state. Faith thereby has the capacity to restore systems of meaning and social networks temporally and spatially, within a mandalic framework grounded in a Buddhist episteme.

The genre of namthar positions Buddhist masters as Tibetan agents par excellence. *Jewel Garland* unequivocally shows Tāre Lhamo and Namtrul Rinpoche in leadership roles, galvanizing monastic and lay communities throughout Golok and northern Kham to recommit themselves to Buddhist practice, to rebuild Buddhist institutions and, in the process, to reassert their identity as Tibetans in Buddhist terms. In the narration of their activities during the 1980s and '90s, there is no deflection of agency, the narrative strategy so prevalent in their first-person voices of their correspondence and in the gendered telling of Tāre Lhamo's life in *Spiraling Vine of Faith*. Even though Namtrul Rinpoche on occasion comes to the fore in *Jewel Garland* as the thaumaturge, for the majority of the namthar, it is the "eminent couple" who acts, speaks, consecrates, initiates, builds, transforms, and reconnects Tibetan people and places. As a result, *Jewel Garland* presents a striking account of the agency of a Buddhist tantric couple as central figures in recent Tibetan history.

We have at last come full circle and can see the hagiographic lens that Pema Ösal Thaye crafted to portray this tantric couple. Through Tāre Lhamo's divinization as a ḍākinī-in-action in *Spiraling Vine of Faith* and her fusion of identity with Namtrul Rinpoche in *Jewel Garland*, they emerge as a formidable pair, capable of transforming the world around them. Comparing hagiographic and epistolary sources, we have witnessed how the vision that Tāre Lhamo and Namtrul Rinpoche constructed together in their correspondence, in the midst of historical uncertainties and personal challenges, came to fruition during their two decades of discovering and disseminating their treasures. Although the intimacies they shared in their epistolary exchanges cannot be found in their idealized portrait in *Jewel Garland*, their enduring bond is evident in their representation as a yab-yum couple at the center of the action. Tāre Lhamo and Namtrul Rinpoche enacted the very healing process that they envisioned in their letters, reinvigorating teachings and ritual systems through their revelations, overseeing and aiding in the reconstruction of monasteries, and reintegrating social networks through making connections to people and places.

Moreover, Pema Ösal Thaye reaffirms Tibetans as agents of their own history by highlighting the success of Buddhist masters in reconstituting Tibetan cultural worlds. While their activities in revitalizing Buddhism are emblematic of the efforts by Nyingma lamas in Golok and Buddhist teachers elsewhere on the Tibetan plateau, the crafting of their agency as a couple in *Jewel Garland* is distinctive, echoing the mutual narrative constructed in their correspondences and shared mission to "heal the damage of degenerate times." The heroic cast to their activities is made possible due to genre conventions specific to namthar narrated in the third person, allowing their hagiographer to elide the specter of the state with respect to both the destruction of the Maoist period and the neoliberal, development-driven agenda of the post-Mao era. By focusing instead on the ritual prowess of Tāre Lhamo and Namtrul Rinpoche in transforming Tibetan people and places, *Jewel Garland* narrates an alternative to official history, a subaltern past that is situated firmly within a Buddhist framework and positions Buddhist masters as the preeminent leaders of Tibetan communities. Alongside a nexus of Nyingma lamas in Golok, the accomplishments of Tāre Lhamo and Namtrul Rinpoche in revitalizing Buddhist practices and institutions, as presented in *Jewel Garland*, are a triumphal assertion of Tibetan agency in Buddhist terms.

Epilogue

The Legacy of a Tantric Couple

THERE IS NO published account of the final years that Tāre Lhamo and Namtrul Rinpoche spent together. The narrative in *Jewel Garland* ends in 1995, and their abbreviated namthar, *Jewel Lantern of Blessings*, published in 2001, adds little by way of a chronological record of their activities.[1] For this reason, during the summer of 2006, Namtrul Rinpoche agreed to dictate what might be considered the final chapter of Tāre Lhamo's life story, recounting events from 1996 to her passing away in 2002.[2] I had asked him to do this several times before, and he had made an excuse, saying, "I don't remember" (*mi dran gi*). On this occasion, he began in a similar vein, first by saying that he did not remember and then by questioning the value of adding more information to what has already been published in *Jewel Garland*. Since they continued to visit the same set of monasteries in a circuit well established by 1995, Namtrul Rinpoche averred that there was nothing new to say: "From 1995 up until now, there has not been anything new. What monasteries we visited in the past are in the previous namthar. Still today, I visit the same monasteries to give initiations and teachings. It is just as before."[3] This led him to question the whole enterprise of narrating the cyclical features of a life story, posing the rhetorical question, "If one writes about visiting a monastery once and thereafter many times again, year after year, what is the benefit?"[4] What was the nature of his hesitation? Was it a polite refusal to revisit the events of those years, suggesting that a detailed explanation would require too much effort? Or can his

Epi.1 Reliquary and shrine dedicated to Tāre Lhamo at Nyenlung Monastery in 2005.

response be read as a self-effacing gesture characteristic of the first-person voice in Tibetan?

I am tempted to conclude the latter, given his final statement on the matter, which downplayed the extent of their travels altogether: "Sometimes we traveled for part of the year and some years we did not travel at all. Most of the time, we stayed here [at Nyenlung]. A continuous stream of lamas and tulkus from hundreds of monasteries visited here for initiations from Khandro, and we hardly had time for a day of retreat or a day of rest. More and more of them would come and request initiation."[5] While this seems to deemphasize their regional teaching tours and devalue recounting its repetitive cycle, the final thrust actually moves in the opposite direction. Namtrul Rinpoche highlights the steady stream of distinguished visitors requesting teachings from Tāre Lhamo, gesturing to her prominence while deemphasizing his own. In his description, one can detect a shift in their late career together toward consolidating their religious activities and community at Nyenlung.

To situate his reply more precisely, I should add that Namtrul Rinpoche had already asked an assistant to retrieve calendars for the years 1996–2002—from the year after the narrative in *Jewel Garland* ends to the year that Tāre Lhamo passed away. Clearly this time he planned to describe the main events of those years and to use Tibetan calendars, in the form of contemporary paperback astrological charts, to prompt his memory. Since such charts are used to decide on auspicious times to schedule rituals and other ceremonial occasions, it makes sense that they would also be used to record those events. This suggests that the narration of autobiographical events may not be based on the selectivity inherent in memory, but involves a more deliberate act of crafting a self-representation in the process of reviewing notes.[6] Likely something comparable occurred in the composition of *Jewel Garland*, since Pema Ösal Thaye indicated to me that the narration for the 1980s and '90s came mainly from the couple themselves,[7] highlighting their own involvement in producing the authorized account of their religious career together. On this occasion, once the astrological calendars were brought out, I realized this was not going to be a spontaneous recitation. Namtrul Rinpoche wanted to consult the records.

Final Years Together

Starting with 1996, Namtrul Rinpoche began by listing the various monasteries the two of them had visited on their teaching tours. One by one, he flipped through the astrological charts for each year, scanning the pages for notes that he had made. As in *Jewel Garland*, the events he deemed worthy of mention were generally his travels with Tāre Lhamo and the large-scale rituals they performed together. Similarly, he focused his account of them as a couple—"the two of us" (*nged gnyis*)—with brief descriptions of events, noting only the date, place, and ritual conducted. What follows is a summary:[8]

In 1996, they visited Rebkong and bestowed initiations for sādhanas dedicated to Padmasambhava and Tārā to a group of more than 20,000. There they also issued ethical advice to the laity and conducted vows for the ethical precept not to kill, in this case, specifically livestock. That year, they visited Lhasa on pilgrimage and toured various monasteries in Padma and Jigdril counties on their return trip, bestowing initiations to lamas, monastics, and laity at Wangda, Minthang, Taklung, Tashi Gomang, and Tsimda monasteries.

In 1997, he said, they did not go anywhere, even though they received many invitations to travel, including invitations to China proper. That year, they focused instead on meditation and retreat. In this context, Namtrul Rinpoche mentioned that they did a six-month retreat every year, a detail not included in *Jewel Garland* but found in *Jewel Lantern of Blessings*.[9]

In 1998, they went to Shukjung Monastery and gave the empowerment of the Thousand Buddhas (*Sangs rgyas stong*), which was followed by a performance based on their own Gesar revelation. They also visited Rebkong. That year, Khenpo Chökyab grew ill.[10] Namtrul Rinpoche reported that the couple gave him a long life empowerment, and he recovered. During the fall, the Dudjom Rinpoche incarnation (that Tāre Lhamo had recognized) visited them, and they bestowed on him initiations for the sādhanas of Padmasambhava and Vārāhi. That year, Namtrul Rinpoche mentioned that they also conducted a dharma gathering, the first of which he estimated had occurred in 1996 (though he did not note it in his narration of that year or the following one).

For 1999, he stated, "we went to several monasteries, once again the same [as before]."[11] That year, they discerned the first signs of Tāre Lhamo's illness and visited a hospital in Barkam.

In accord with Namtrul Rinpoche's statement about the cyclic nature of their teaching tours, in his chronicle of the late 1990s, their later activities by and large follow a paradigm and territory already established in the late 1980s and early 1990s, except for the addition of their annual dharma gathering (*chos tshogs*) at Nyenlung.

For the year 2000, Namtrul Rinpoche began to narrate Tāre Lhamo's illness and death, concentrating on the various signs auguring the inevitability of her passing. Emphasizing again the joint nature of their activities, even visionary experiences, he reported that during their annual winter retreat that year they had a shared dream, "the dream of us two" (*nged gnyis kyi rmi lam*), which he described as "a dream that Khandro would not remain in this body much longer."[12] He also mentioned a prophecy of his own that when Tāre Lhamo reached the age of sixty-five, she would "rest in the *dharmadhātu*" (*chos dbyings su gzims*), one of several euphemistic ways of describing the death of a Buddhist master. The following year, on the road to Jigdril to visit a Tibetan doctor, vultures circled the car as they drove.

Mentioning that the vulture had been her "soul bird" (*bla bya*), Namtrul Rinpoche said he had thought it a bad omen, a sign that she would die soon. But to console her, he said instead that it was a good omen that her health would improve. In this interview, he also mentioned a prophecy by Apang Terchen that Tāre Lhamo would encounter twelve obstacles in her life, the last of which could not be reversed. These dreams, signs, and prophecies constitute the way that Namtrul Rinpoche chose to narrate and make sense of misfortune, coping with the loss of Tāre Lhamo through invoking the hand of destiny.

By 2001, she was diagnosed with an illness related to *bakan*, or phlegm (*bad kan*), one of the three humors in Tibetan medicine. Since Namtrul Rinpoche mentioned pain in her throat and trouble with her digestion, it may have been esophageal cancer (*bad kan gre thog*), a common diagnosis of fatal illness in Golok related to this humor.[13] Throughout the year, they tried both pragmatic and ritual means to reverse the course of her illness. They visited the hospital in Barkam again, and Namtrul Rinpoche also performed a long life empowerment on her behalf, although he knew it could not save her. During this period, Sakya Trizin and Dodrubchen Thubten Trinle Palzang as well as lamas from various monasteries in Golok did prayers for her long life. Tāre Lhamo herself ransomed and set free ten thousand yaks and sheep as a way to make merit, then went to Chengdu for further medical treatment. While she was in Chengdu, her conditioned worsened, and Namtrul Rinpoche said that they consulted medical experts from Beijing, America, and other places, to no avail.

Other mysterious signs portended her impending death. At one point, Namtrul Rinpoche said that music started to emanate from Tāre Lhamo's body, and soon thereafter they discovered a symbolic script on her arm. He grew sad, taking this to mean that "the time had come for Khandro to pass away" (*mkha' 'gro 'das ran*). Namtrul Rinpoche recounted that later the ḍākinīs came to fetch Tāre Lhamo, but she initially refused to join them. Then he had a dream that seven ḍākinīs came before him, asking him to let her go so that they could escort her to a pure land. At one point, he performed the ritual to avert the call of the ḍākinīs (*mkha' 'gro'i sun bzlog*), by which Tāre Lhamo is credited with saving his life in the early 1980s, but it only extended her life for a short while longer.

According to her "last testament" (*bka' chems*), composed by Namtrul Rinpoche to chronicle her passing,[14] Tāre Lhamo called together their close disciples, gave them parting advice, and requested that they "accomplish whatever her constant companion, the precious Supreme Incarnation and guru, commands and serve his three gates [of body, speech, and mind] however they are able."[15] The document uses language reminiscent of their correspondence, gesturing to their enduring nature of their bond. It also suggests her ongoing agency, through Namtrul Rinpoche's activities, in her first-person voice: "Effortlessly, I will [continue to] be of benefit to the teachings and beings [by virtue of] not being separated even for a moment from my constant, precious companion until attaining awakening. This is my aspiration and oath to the three roots, protectors, and Apang Terchen, in whom I take refuge."[16] These words confirm Namtrul Rinpoche's role in continuing their shared mission and highlight her ongoing impact through him.

On March 26, 2002, in her final hour, Tāre Lhamo lay down in a resting posture.[17] Many lamas, including Khenpo Jigme Phuntsok and Dodrubchen Rinpoche, called to recite prayers for her over the phone. Before she passed away, as recounted, she smiled and looked vibrant as if she were twenty years old. Then she exhaled. Her last testament reports: "At that moment, inside the building, there was a perfume scent, and rainbow clouds of various colors also appeared all around, inside and outside."[18] Since it was hot in Chengdu, Namtrul Rinpoche indicated that they could not leave her body in place to rest for several days, as is customary, and instead brought it back to Nyenlung, where many people visited to pay their respects. When it was cremated, her last testament reports that rainbow light filled the sky and pieces of vulture feather fell to earth.[19] The closing line, reminiscent of the hagiographic impulse to engender faith, states that these signs were "witnessed directly" (mngon sum du mthong) by the many Chinese and Tibetan disciples gathered there, inducing in them "a state of amazement and faith" (ngo mtshar zhing dad pa'i gnas).[20]

On the Anniversary of Khandro's Passing

In 2003, Namtrul Rinpoche composed a final letter, prior to the facimile reproduction of their correspondence in its entirety. The letter is addressed to Tāre Lhamo on the one-year anniversary of her passing into parinirvāṇa.[21] As a lament, it expresses his sorrow and how much he misses his "constant companion" (gtan grogs), meaning life partner. It begins by giving the setting, a commemorative service and feast offering held by their ongoing religious community:

On the twelfth day of the second month, the water sheep year (2003),
On the anniversary of my constant companion Khandro's passing,
During the commemorative feast offering to the ḍākinīs,
When thoughts arise of [your] loving speech at the time of death,
Unable [to hold back], I utter these sorrowful words of lamentation.[22]

Namtrul Rinpoche reminisces about her "loving speech" (byams brtse'i gsung) on her deathbed, and this gives rise to his "sorrowful words of lamentation" (smre sngags skyo ba'i tshig) to follow. The letter proceeds to supplicate Padmasambhava, Yeshe Tsogyal, and the dharma protectors and ḍākinīs to show compassion in the midst of his despair. Referring to their numerous past lives together bound by shared aspirations and oaths, Namtrul Rinpoche recalls the identity between Yeshe Tsogyal and Tāre Lhamo as follows: "Constant companion, Tsogyal in the guise of a woman, / Mantra-Born Lady, endowed with good qualities, Khandro Tāre, / Sustaining the union of method and wisdom [in realizing] bliss-emptiness."[23] After invoking their consort relationship, Namtrul Rinpoche expresses his grief as follows:

Reflecting on the circumstances, my grief swells,
Wondering why now and not later, in despair.
[My] constant companion, the Wish-Fulfilling Jewel, departed,
Leaving the old, ailing Namtrul behind.

In [our] retreat hut, pleasure grove of the vidyādhara's great bliss,
There's no occasion to awaken the mind seeking to end anguish,
There's no chance to be nurtured by [your] loving affection,
[Now that] suddenly [you] rest in the peaceful space of dharmatā.[24]

Despite their enduring bond across lifetimes, Namtrul Rinpoche expresses feeling left behind, full of sorrow that Tāre Lhamo is no longer with him in this life. While she rests in the "the peaceful space of dharmatā," they can no longer conjure "bliss-emptiness" together in their small retreat hut above their main residence at Nyenlung.[25]

In the course of expressing his despair, Namtrul Rinpoche reflects on the nature of impermanence, using naturalistic images such as the sun descending over mountains all too soon, wildflowers in mountain meadows that wilt when the winter frost sets in, and the body like a rainbow dissolving once the consciousness departs. All these become "teachers showing impermanence" (*mi rtag ston pa'i slob dpon*) to help reconcile himself to the loss. He returns to a number of images of fertility from their courtship: the cry of the cuckoo, the clapping of thunder, and flowers and vegetation in bloom. As before, these natural sights and sounds provide the occasion for him to "recall the loving affection" (*byams brtse rjes su dran*) of his constant companion. But in this case, there is no peacock showing off its feathers or bee circling the lotus, signaling the sport of attraction. Even so, in similar terms to the letters they exchanged during their courtship, Namtrul Rinpoche uses the medium of memory to assuage the sadness of separation.

Overall, this final letter is reminiscent of poignant departures in the lives of Tāre Lhamo's female antecedents, Yeshe Tsogyal and Sera Khandro. In Taksham Nuden Dorje's well-known version of her life, Yeshe Tsogyal cries out to Padmasambhava as he departs to ethereal realms, and he responds by emphasizing their inseparability, particularly if she can see with pure perception that everything arises as the guru.[26] In the auto/biographical corpus she authored, Sera Khandro likewise laments the passing of her destined consort and teacher, Drime Özer, who appears as a visionary apparition to console her.[27] In parallel fashion, but adding a gender reversal, Tāre Lhamo appears in the sky in response to Namtrul Rinpoche's expression of grief:

> From the murky depths of anguish and sorrow,
> Expressing [my] gloom, tears cascade in a constant stream.
> Distraught with grief, audibly wailing: alas!
> Unable to bear the situation, I let my personal flaws burst forth;
> Not knowing what to do, I almost lost consciousness.
>
> At that moment, in the vast, dazzling azure sky,
> Beneath a dome [made] of radiant rays of rainbow-colored light,
> Accompanied by the enchanting sound of lute music,
> And at the center of a coemergent gathering of ḍākinīs,

Hail, the beloved bestowing the wisdom of bliss-emptiness!
[My] constant companion, the precious Wish-Fulfilling Jewel,
Smiling with pleasure and passion, joyfully flashing sidelong glances,
Dancing beautifully with grace and suppleness,[28]
Delivered [this] advice in a pleasing, melodious voice.[29]

As a visionary apparition, Tāre Lhamo appears in ḍākinī fashion, amid rainbow lights and an entourage, to console Namtrul Rinpoche by emphasizing pure appearance (dag snang) and asserting their ultimate inseparability. What follows is her advice:

"Kye ho! Eternally kind guru and lord,
[My] precious, sole, constant companion across lives,
Your Eminence, the Supreme Incarnation and Wish-Fulfilling Jewel,
I cannot bear to be separated from you even for an instant.

Although the intimacy of our bond and affection cannot be reversed,
The nature of illusory phenomena is impermanent.
Kind one, who has intentionally not departed [from this life],
When the time for past karma [to ripen] comes, what is there to do?
Spiritual support, you remain nurtured by [my] affection.
Constant companion, we have not been separated for even an instant.

Rinpoche, don't let [your] mind grow weary with sorrow.
Train in [recognizing] all apparent phenomena as illusion.
The vajra of awareness, the stable and steady consummated nature,
Is not separate from the mind of me, Tāre . . .

Even when separated in the manner of relative appearances,
In the definitive truth, fundamentally, we have never been apart.
From your indestructible, original mind beyond measure,
I didn't go anywhere. There is nowhere else [for me] to go.

Within primordial dharmakāya, changeless great bliss,
Visualize all sights and sounds as the body of the wisdom ḍākinī;
Recite all sounds as the mantra of the ḍākinīs of great bliss;
Within the sole dharmatā, whatever thoughts arise,

Spontaneously realize [them] to be great nondual wisdom.
Within the unfabricated, self-arising, unimpeded, naked nature,
Leave it as is! [This is] the union of method and wisdom, bliss-emptiness.

A la la ho! Awareness in its own character.
E ma ho ya! The kindness of the glorious guru.
Within the wisdom of equality, abide in bliss.
Carefree and unrestrained, dwell joyfully.
In an effortless, self-arising state, rest free and easy.

Until enlightenment, there is no separation even for an instant.
Until the impure karmic manifestations of beings are exhausted,
For that long, we two, method and wisdom, as inseparable,
Effortlessly accomplishing the benefit of the teachings and beings.

When the three realms of saṃsāra are emptied, [our] wishes fulfilled,
The darkness of impure duality will be awakened on its own [to reveal]
Apparent phenomena of saṃsāra and nirvāṇa already perfected,
The ground of existence purified into the great equality. A la la!
Dear, dear, you and I are nondual, one taste."[30]

While addressing Namtrul Rinpoche as her guru, the visionary apparition of
Tāre Lhamo also plays the role of teacher by advising him on the ultimate
view of their nature as "nondual, one taste" (*gnyis med ro gcig*) and asserting
their inseparability on an ultimate level. She harkens to their karmic connection across lifetimes and also to the nature of mind as indestructible (*mi
shigs*) and beyond measure (*gzhal yas*), in which duality and hence separation is not possible. In line with pure appearance in the tantric view, next
Tāre Lhamo invites Namtrul Rinpoche to regard all sights as the body of the
wisdom ḍākinī, all sounds as the mantra of the ḍākinīs, and all thoughts as
nondual wisdom. In that way, she suggests that she will always be with him
in the sights and sounds of everyday life.

The letter ends by Namtrul Rinpoche describing how he and Tāre Lhamo
touched foreheads, a gesture of mutual respect and intimacy, and then her
image dissolved into light, transforming into a red sphere (Skt.: *bindu*, Tib.:
thig le) that melted into his heart. This ending is akin to tantric practices
in which the guru or deity visualized is dissolved into the heart center at

Epi.2 Sample of audio-visual materials produced by Nyenlung Monastery. Photograph by Corey Kohn.

the end of the practice. At that moment, Namtrul Rinpoche experienced "unobstructed awareness" (*zang thal rig pa*) beyond expression, and despair slipped from his mind.[31]

Like the Sun and Moon

In the years since Tāre Lhamo's passing, audio-visual materials produced by Nyenlung Monastery have continued to represent the couple as insep-arable. Nyenlung has produced official photographs of Tāre Lhamo and Namtrul Rinpoche together for display on shrines as well as cassette tapes and VCDs (video compact discs) with their photograph on the cover, con-taining devotional songs by and about the couple and video footage of their activities in the late 1990s. The lyrics are generally either composed by one of them for the other or dedicated to them as a couple, as the following refrain illustrates: "Jigme Phuntsok Rinpoche / Khandro Tāre Lhamo-la / Together, like the sun and moon, / You shine radiant light, pervading everywhere. / Ah, precious ones! / For you, this is a song from the depths of our hearts, / To you, the refuge and protectors of beings."[32] This song was played at the opening of the dharma gathering (*chos tshogs*) at Nyenlung, which I attended in 2006, suggesting that Tāre Lhamo has remained an object of veneration alongside Namtrul Rinpoche for their ongoing religious community.

A VCD compilation titled *Melodious Songs of Nyenlung* contains rare footage of Tāre Lhamo and Namtrul Rinpoche at the center of ritual activity together in a similar way to scenes depicted in *Jewel Garland*.[33] Containing a number of hagiographic features, the VCD begins with short summaries of their lives, read aloud from *Jewel Lantern of Blessings*. The narration is in both Tibetan and Chinese, indicating the importance of their growing community of Han Chinese followers; *Jewel Lantern of Blessings* itself was translated and published in a glossy Chinese version with photographs of the couple.[34] On *Melodious Songs of Nyenlung*, during the summary of their life stories, a slideshow of photographs shows the couple on pilgrimage at various sacred sites, including Wutai Shan, central Tibet, Lake Kokonor, and Nyenpo Yutse. In this way, it creates a visual pilgrimage as a synopsis of their activities in the 1980s and early 1990s, before portable video cameras became widely available in Tibet. Moreover, it highlights how their identity as a couple has remained central to their public representation.

In the late 1990s, *Melodious Songs of Nyenlung* contains actual video footage from their pilgrimage cum teaching tours and highlights their annual dharma gathering, which Tāre Lhamo and Namtrul Rinpoche began to host at Nyenlung Monastery in 1996. The footage shows an uncommon sight in Tibetan Buddhism—a tantric couple, seated side by side on thrones, presiding over ritual gatherings. These gatherings, large and small, illustrate the range of their activities and the revitalization of Buddhism in Golok in progress. A number of them take place in half-finished assembly halls or during consecration ceremonies for newly built structures. For example, Tāre Lhamo and Namtrul Rinpoche are shown conferring a tantric initiation in an unfinished assembly hall at Tashi Gomang; presiding over the consecration of the large stūpa at the county seat of Padma; visiting Chinese cities hosted by Han Chinese disciples; and giving transmissions for esoteric teachings to the young reincarnation of Dudjom Rinpoche. Raw footage is interspersed with devotional songs, performed by Namtrul Rinpoche's son,

Tulku Laksam Namdak, and accompanied by mandolin in the *dunglen* style (*rdung len*) popular in Amdo. In this way, footage from the late 1990s serves as an extension of the narration in *Jewel Garland*, focused on their activities as a couple.

In parallel fashion to hagiographic writing, by presenting the eminent couple at the center of ritual activity, audio-visual materials like the *Melodious Songs of Nyenlung* participate in the mandalization process, discussed in the previous chapter. In China, where television and newspapers are state-controlled, music videos on commercial and monastery-produced VCDs have become an important medium for minority self-representation.[35] Like the genre of namthar, monastery-produced VCDs create a mandalic framework in which Buddhist masters are the focal point of large-scale public gatherings and objects of veneration for the Tibetan (and Chinese) disciples constellated around them. Since the late 1990s and early 2000s, monastery-produced VCDs featuring devotional songs and chronicling the activities of Buddhist masters have become enormously popular, and they are routinely played in Tibetan areas in public and private settings alike.

In this vein, the representation of Tāre Lhamo and Namtrul Rinpoche as a tantric couple in *Jewel Garland* extended to audio-visual materials in the wake of Tāre Lhamo's passing. Even the VCD compilation chronicling Namtrul Rinpoche's 2004 solo pilgrimage, titled *A Compilation of Deeds That Naturally Liberates the Beholder*, bears a photograph of him with Tāre Lhamo on the cover and contains songs written by her.[36] A third compilation produced by Nyenlung in 2009, a DVD (digital video disc) set titled *Adamantine Songs, Meaningful to Hear and Behold*, likewise bears both their images on the cover.[37] It features excerpts from the couple's correspondence, performed by well-known singers like Sherten and Dartso with dunglen-style vocals accompanied by MIDI (musical instrument digital interface), and other devotional songs to the couple with photographs of them scattered throughout. These audio-visual materials indicate Tāre Lhamo's ongoing importance as Namtrul Rinpoche continued to forge an enduring lineage based on their joint treasure revelations. Moreover, the compilation titles suggest that the salvific benefits of their blessings are available through audio-visual materials, simply by seeing images of the couple and hearing songs by or about them.

Ongoing Community at Nyenlung

Namtrul Rinpoche started to travel again and teach regionally in 2004. With a sizeable entourage of several dozen Tibetan and Chinese disciples, he revisited sites along the pilgrimage route he had traversed with Tāre Lhamo over the years, including Payul Tharthang, Nyenpo Yutse, Tongkyab Monastery, and Amnye Machen in Golok and Drakar Tredzong in Amdo.[38] From there, with a smaller entourage, he visited Lhasa, Samye Chimpu, and Tsogyal Latso in central Tibet, and several Chinese cities. The sites closer to home became regular stops in his regional tours thereafter, including Shukjung, Tashi Gomang, Tsimda Gompa, and Wangda Gompa in Padma County. In addition, for almost a decade until his own passing, Namtrul Rinpoche continued to preside over the dharma gathering at Nyenlung, a vibrant annual event over ten days during the auspicious month of Sagadawa, the fifth month in the lunar calendar, in which the commemorative date of the Buddha's parinirvāṇa falls.

When I attended the dharma gathering at Nyenlung Monastery in June 2006, there were up to a thousand participants. Monks had traveled from as far away as Rebkong and lamas gathered from Serta and Jigril counties, while the Tibetan laity consisted mainly of locals, along with a group of thirty who had journeyed from Dzamthang. Almost half of those in attendance were Han Chinese disciples from various provinces of China, who began coming to Nyenlung in the late 1990s and early 2000s after having met Tāre Lhamo and Namtrul Rinpoche in Chengdu or heard about them from a friend. Quite possibly some first came to meet the other Jigme Phuntsok in Serta, Khenpo Jigme Phuntsok of Larung Buddhist Academy, and later made their way to Nyenlung.

Over the ten days of the 2006 gathering, Nyenlung Monastery became like a small village, with makeshift shops and restaurants in tents lining the road. Visitors crowded into every corner of the monastery: dignitaries stayed in the guesthouse constructed in 2005, Chinese disciples clustered in cabins rented from monks, and an empty storage room above the kitchen housed the thirty Tibetans from Dzamthang. The action alternated among the main assembly hall, the lawn where a teaching pavilion had been constructed for the couple, and a small courtyard beneath Namtrul Rinpoche's residence where he sometimes gave teachings from a window. This meant a steady flow of foot traffic between sites within the monastery, as different constituencies often attended different events. On most days, lamas and monastics gathered in the assembly hall for initiations and teachings while the Tibetan laity assembled on the lawn beneath the teaching pavilion to recite prayers.³⁹ Meanwhile, the Chinese disciples convened in the downstairs of the new guesthouse for teachings by Tulku Laksam, who is fluent in Chinese, or made offerings in a small temple across from the main assembly hall. At night, an intimate cluster of his entourage and close disciples gathered in Namtrul Rinpoche's quarters for a feast offering, and sometimes he gave Dzogchen teachings on the *Six Dharmas of the Profound Path* (*Zab lam chos drug*) from Apang Terchen's corpus to a small group who had completed their preliminary practices (*sngon 'gro*) and congregated in the courtyard outside. On several occasions, the whole group filled the lawn for teachings by Namtrul Rinpoche and also crowded into the assembly hall for two feast offerings and one public initiation.⁴⁰

Epi.3 Assembly of Tibetan and Chinese disciples during the annual dharma gathering at Nyenlung in 2006.

Altogether, the dharma gathering had a festival-like atmosphere. During prayer sessions on the lawn, as the liturgy was recited over the loudspeaker, children played, the elderly spun prayer wheels, and the youth strutted and gossiped. In the assembly hall, feast offerings began as solemn devotional occasions with speeches and praises given by Tibetan dignitaries and ended in a playful yet earnest scramble for handfuls of candy and bottles of soda, which had been blessed as offerings during the ceremony, distributed by the monks. One day was dedicated to the annual consecration of the monastery, when Namtrul Rinpoche visited all the shrine halls, stūpas, and small temples to bless them anew and re-sanctify each site. On this day, a stream of saffron and burgundy, the colors of Tibetan monastic garb, wended through the monastery grounds, followed by a stream of yellow robes, worn by the Chinese monks and nuns, while the laity, both Tibetan and Chinese, jostled on the roadside to catch a glimpse or snap a photograph of Namtrul Rinpoche.

Whereas Tibetan monks generally took precedence in the ritual arena, Chinese disciples were central in a procession during which they greeted Namtrul Rinpoche in groups organized by region, gathered under the banner of their province, and offered lavish gifts of statues, rugs, and maṇḍala plates. Namtrul Rinpoche later assured me that all twenty-two provinces of China were represented. There were also international representatives: one couple from Singapore and myself, the American researcher, bearing flags with our country names on them. (Regrettably, I had little forewarning and had only a ceremonial scarf and a modest offering in an envelope to present when my turn came.) This annual procession, which was captured on video during the late 1990s when Tāre Lhamo was still alive, has become a public demonstration of the couple's growing sphere of influence that regularly constellates at Nyenlung. The array of Chinese disciples demonstrates the increasing scope and importance of their lineage beyond the Tibetan plateau.

The following year, a new assembly hall was completed to house their rapidly growing community on such ritual occasions. Namtrul Rinpoche gave the transmission for the entirety of their treasure corpus and those of Apang Terchen and Dudjom Rinpoche to several thousand attendees over the course of ten days in June 2007. Video footage taken between 2007 and 2009 in *Adamantine Songs, Meaningful to Hear and Behold* shows the new assembly hall overflowing with Chinese disciples, appearing to significantly outnumber the Tibetans. During the late 2000s, prior to Namtrul Rinpoche's passing in 2011, the number of Chinese disciples swelled to more than ten thousand

Epi.4 Thrones in the old assembly hall at Nyenlung, of Namtrul Rinpoche, Tāre Lhamo, and Tulku Laksam (from left to right).

participating in several hundred dharma groups across China, with a dedicated space to assemble twice a month for feast offerings as well as for special holidays and occasional retreats.[41] In addition, according to Tulku Laksam, Nyenlung now has three subsidiary monasteries beyond the Tibetan plateau, two in the northeastern region of Dongbe and one in Gansu Province.[42]

Lineage Succession

In the years after her passing, when Namtrul Rinpoche taught and conferred initiations, right beside his throne stood Tāre Lhamo's own, no longer occupied.[43] Just as in ancient Indian art, the Buddha's empty throne signified the seeming paradox of his absence by virtue of attaining parinirvāṇa and his ongoing presence as an object of veneration for the early Buddhist community,[44] Tāre Lhamo's throne has signified both her absence and her ongoing presence at Nyenlung. According to her last testament, Tāre Lhamo pledged to stay forever by Namtrul Rinpoche's side, and it is for this reason, I was told, that her throne and the place in their quarters where she used to sit remained empty.[45] Even though Namtrul Rinpoche acquired a new consort, named Kunzang Drolma, she never occupied these seats of honor, nor did she preside over ritual occasions with him as Tāre Lhamo had throughout their teaching career together.[46] In Namtrul Rinpoche's public representation, in materials still produced by Nyenlung, Tāre Lhamo remains at his side. To the extent that he continued to propagate their treasures and those of her father, Apang Terchen, her legacy remained very much alive in him.

In order to construe himself as the legitimate heir to Apang Terchen's treasures, Namtrul Rinpoche appropriated certain aspects of Tāre Lhamo's identity. When I first met him in 2004, he wrote in my notebook: "Since it is stated that I myself am the reincarnation of Drime Özer and the action emanation of Apang Tertön, we two necessarily composed our treasure collection [together] and propagated its initiation and transmission."[47] Drime Özer was the son of the towering figure Dudjom Lingpa and a tertön in his own right, who also served as the destined consort and teacher of Sera Khandro, one of Tāre Lhamo's past lives. Namtrul Rinpoche's identification with Drime Özer is not mentioned in their correspondence or in *Jewel Garland* and, to my knowledge, this identification was first made public in *Melodious Songs of Nyenlung*, produced in 2003 after Tāre Lhamo's death. The voice-over follows his past life genealogy from *Jewel Lantern of Blessings*, the abbreviated namthar of the couple by Abu Karlo, and inserts an extra line not found in this 2001 publication that makes this identification.[48] While Namtrul Rinpoche's claim to be the reincarnation of Drime Özer is less well known,[49] his status as the activity emanation of Apang Terchen is more public and widely acknowledged. It is highlighted in his past life genealogy in *Jewel Lantern of Blessings* and in a short biography of Apang Terchen, published in 2000 alongside the biographies of other tertöns in a compilation on the Golok medical tradition, where Namtrul Rinpoche is named among four of Apang Terchen's emanations.[50] His public identity as an emanation of Apang Tertön is crucial, since it legitimates him as a lineage holder for the treasure corpus of Tāre Lhamo's father, customarily restricted to family descendants and incarnations.

As a further mechanism to ensure lineage succession, at the dharma gathering in 2006, Namtrul Rinpoche announced that his son from his first marriage, Tulku Laksam, is an incarnation of none other than Tāre Lhamo's

Epi.5 Namtrul Rinpoche with Tulku Laksam in 2005.

own son, who died during the Cultural Revolution.[51] This is a secondary identification for Tulku Laksam, who was recognized at a young age to be the incarnation of Namtrul Rinpoche's own teacher, Zhuchen Kunzang Nyima, associated with Zhuchen Monastery in Serta. This announcement and new past-life association show the importance of incarnation status and family ties to lineage succession in Golok and surrounding areas in northern Kham. By virtue of his status as Namtrul Rinpoche's son, Tulku Laksam is unquestionably the legitimate heir to the treasure corpus he revealed together with Tāre Lhamo. But it seems that only as the incarnation of the grandson of Apang Terchen can Tulku Laksam also be a legitimate heir to the lineage Tāre Lhamo held as Apang Terchen's daughter. This has become particularly important for lineage continuity since the passing of Namtrul Rinpoche in 2011.

Now in his mid-forties, Tulku Laksam serves as the head (*dgon bdag*) of Nyenlung Monastery and the lineage holder (*brgyud 'dzin*) for the teachings held by Tāre Lhamo and Namtrul Rinpoche, which include their own revelations and those of Apang Terchen.[52] Fluent in Mandarin, over the previous decade, Tulku Laksam had already taken over responsibility for teaching the growing number of Han Chinese disciples who visit Nyenlung regularly and sometimes reside there for months at a time. Since the early 2000s, he has regularly traveled and taught in Chinese cities, including Beijing, Shanghai, Chengdu, Guangzhou, Tianjin, Shenzhen, and Hong Kong, and more broadly in the provinces of Liaoning, Shandong, and Guangxi. He has also taught at a number of local monasteries where Tāre Lhamo and Namtrul Rinpoche regularly gave teachings, including Shukjung, Menthang, Drakor, Wangda, Tsimda, Raktram, and more. In this way, as their successor, he is following their footsteps along the well-trodden path of their regular teaching tours.

Namtrul Rinpoche continued to teach until he passed into parinirvāṇa on November 7, 2011, though he was quite ill during the final year of his life. When I last saw him in May 2011, after he had spent the winter in a hospital in Xining, he could not speak and received visitors by his bed to sit in silence with him for a period of time. Apparently he recovered enough to preside over the dharma gathering at Nyenlung that summer, but then his health deteriorated again in the fall. His longtime attendant, Gelek Nyima, reported that the doctors could not identify the source of his illness, but mentioned that there were issues with his liver (*mchin pa*) as well as the humor of wind (*rlung*), according to the Tibetan medical tradition.[53]

When I visited Nyenlung in the summer of 2014, Gelek emphasized to me the special quality of Namtrul Rinpoche's passing. Beforehand, he gathered his close disciples around him and gave them parting advice, emphasizing that they should think about the next life, not just this one, and think about others, not just oneself. When Namtrul Rinpoche passed away, he reportedly sat upright in meditation posture, with legs arranged like Padmasambhava (in royal ease) and arms crossed like Vajradhara, according to traditional iconography. According to Gelek's account, he spent seven days like this in *tukdam* (*thugs dam*), a state of deep meditative concentration understood to continue after biological death, thereby preventing the body from decaying. Over those seven days, as narrated by Gelek, the body shrank to two feet tall, fragrance pervaded the monastery, and rainbow light streamed out from the room. Tulku Laksam reportedly carried the body of Namtrul Rinpoche on a tray so that all who attended the cremation could witness the miracle, then placed it on the wood of the cremation pyre. During the cremation, many colored lights were said to shine forth.

Numerous lamas attended the cremation, along with hundreds of Tibetan and Chinese followers. After several days, they looked for pearl-like relics (*ring bsrel*) and any remaining bones in the ashes, which were used to make clay figurines (*tsha tsha*) to place inside a reliquary. According to his instructions, a number of these clay figurines were also placed in the lakes and rivers around the Tibetan plateau in order to bless each place and its inhabitants, whether animals, fish, or nāgas. Namtrul Rinpoche's reliquary was completed in 2012, and a large gilded stūpa in his honor was consecrated in 2013 during the annual dharma gathering at Nyenlung Monastery.

Today the reliquaries (*sku gdung*) of Tāre Lhamo and Namtrul Rinpoche are the central objects of veneration in a shrine room in the family compound at Nyenlung. Connected by a green cord that passes through the hands of statues on the altar between them, the two reliquaries stand approximately eight feet tall, gilded and covered in jewels. Between them is an elaborate shrine lined with statues of Padmasambhava and Yeshe Tsogyal, among other images, texts, and sacra. Daily offerings of water and butter lamps are made, and there are other signs of veneration, including a tiered maṇḍala offering filled with rice and jewels. This intimate shrine room has become a special place for small groups of visiting Chinese disciples to practice. In no uncertain terms, these reliquaries embody their ongoing presence at Nyenlung and connection, even beyond death, as a tantric couple.

But their stories do not end there. In 2010 Rigdzin Dargye, a high-ranking cleric-scholar from Tsimda Gompa, the monastery founded by Tāre Lhamo's father, visited India to supplicate Sakya Trizin to identify the reincarnation of Tāre Lhamo. Recall that Sakya Trizin is the head of the Sakya lineage while also being the earliest recognized reincarnation of Apang Terchen, thereby uniquely qualified to recognize her reincarnation. According to Rigdzin Dargye, he identified his own granddaughter, Jetsun Kunga Trinley Palter, born on January 2, 2007, as the reincarnation of Tāre Lhamo.[54] In a noncommittal vein, given her young age, the Sakya Trizin himself would neither confirm nor deny the recognition when asked in 2015.[55] Nevertheless, in a symbolic gesture to acknowledge this identification, Tulku Laksam visited Dehradun, India, in 2012 to present some of Tāre Lhamo's belongings to Sakya Trizin and his granddaughter.

Thus, in a fascinating twist on family lineage, it appears that Tāre Lhamo has taken rebirth in the family of her father's reincarnation. Yet this means that her own reincarnation will grow up far from Nyenlung and the activities of the lineage she established there with Namtrul Rinpoche. When I asked about lineage continuity, Rigdzin Dargye admitted that it would be up to her grandfather how the girl is trained. In turn, Sakya Trizin insisted that Jetsun Kunga Trinley Palter would receive an ecumenical training, including Nyingma teachings, as is customary for daughters in the Sakya family. Will she travel to Golok and northern Kham to visit the places where Tāre Lhamo lived and taught? Will she receive and hold the treasure corpus that her predecessor and Namtrul Rinpoche revealed together? Only time will tell. As the years progress, one wonders whether any other emanations of Tāre Lhamo will be identified closer to home and what implication that may have for carrying forward the couple's legacy.

Meanwhile, as this book went into publication, it was still too early for a reincarnation of Namtrul Rinpoche to be publicly identified. Yet it is noteworthy that, after six daughters, in 2014 Tulku Laksam finally had a son.[56]

Catalogue of the Letters of Namtrul Rinpoche

*Adamantine Garland: The Collected Letters by the Lord of Refuge,
Namtrul Jigme Phuntsok, to the Supreme Khandro Tāre Lhamo*

*Skyabs rje rin po che nam sprul 'jigs med phun tshogs kyis mkha' 'gro rin po che tā re de vī
mchog la phul ba'i zhu 'phrin phyag yig rnams phyogs bsdus rdo rje'i phreng ba*

Letter	Facsimile Edition	Paperback Version	Main Content
NJP 1	2.1–7.1	1.1–3.15	Praise of Tāre Lhamo and her Yeshe Tsogyal sādhana.
NJP 2	7.2–8.1	4.1–10	Verse about the healing power of treasures.
NJP 3	8.1–12.4	5.1–7.15	Past life recollection as Namkhai Nyingpo and Yeshe Tsogyal engaged in the tantric rite of sexual union. This letter is excerpted in *Jewel Garland* almost in its entirety.[1]
NJP 4	12.4–13.6	8.1–15	Prophecy of union between Yuyi Thortsug and Sarasvatī.
NJP 5	13.6–17.5	9.1–11.5	Summary of Namtrul Rinpoche's past life as the Prince of Jang, Yulha Thogyur, during the time of Gesar of Ling. This letter is excerpted in *Jewel Garland* in its entirety.[2]
NJP 6	17.5–19.2	11.6–12.5	Folk song about their connection across lifetimes due to stainless samaya and the aspiration of Padmasambhava. The first half of this letter is excerpted in *Jewel Garland*.[3]

(continued)

Letter	Facsimile Edition	Paperback Version	Main Content
NJP 7	19.2–25.6	13.1–16.17	Vision of Tāre Lhamo appearing as Dewe Dorje (a.k.a. Sera Khandro) to offer him advice on carrying illness onto the path.
NJP 8	25.6–26.4	17.1–8	Recollection of receiving teachings and practicing together as Mingyur Paldrön from Kham and Dudul Dorje.
NJP 9	26.4–32.5	17.9–20.10	The first half is a love song (la gzhas), and the second half contains a prophecy, marked with the orthographic feature indicating its status as treasure, called a tertsek (gter tsheg).
NJP 10	32.5–33.6	20.11–21.4	Affectionate words to the beloved (brtse grogs).
NJP 11	34.1–37.5	21.5–23.8	Recollection of past lives, including reference to seven lifetimes together in Tibet, and the locations of numerous treasure sites.
NJP 12	37.5–39.1	23.9–24.6	A happy song (bde skyid glu) containing folksy pairings of animals and habitats drawn from the Tibetan landscape.
NJP 13	39.2–41.2	24.7–25.11	Images of the gold-eyed fish flaunting its six fins, a tigress flashing its six stripes, and a snow lion unfurling its turquoise mane along the way to their respective habitats.
NJP 14	41.2–6	25.12–26.4[4]	Portrayal of habitats as "stable and steady" (rtag brtan) and their respective inhabitants— snow lion, gold-eyed fish, and grinning tigress—as "changeless" ('gyur med).
NJP 15	41.6–44.4	26.5–27.13	Passage in which Namtrul Rinpoche overcomes despair at his failing health and the rugged terrain on journey to Markhok.
NJP 16	44.4–6	27.14–17	Marked with tertsek, this consists of a single verse hailing primordial buddhahood when clouds disperse.
NJP 17	44.6–45.5	27.18–28.6	Praise of Tāre Lhamo's body, speech, and mind.
NJP 18	45.5–48.2	28.7–29.16	Song of remembrance and praise of Tāre Lhamo, emphasizing their inseparability.

Letter	Facsimile Edition	Paperback Version	Main Content
NJP 19	48.2–50.5	30.1–31.11[5]	Inseparability of snow lion and mountain peak, gold-eyed fish and turquoise lake, tigress and sandalwood forest, framed as "fate" (las dbang), followed by an affectionate ditty.
NJP 20	50.6–52.2	31.12–32.10	Prophetic letter with symbolic script (brda yig), recalling their past lives as Yulha Thogyur and Metok Lhadze and indicating the site of a treasure awaiting them in Gyalrong.
NJP 21	52.3–54.4	32.11–33.17	Illness as a teaching on dependent origination and illusion.
NJP 22	54.5–56.6	34.1–35.7	Images of inseparability as "partners in dance" (gnyis 'gros).
NJP 23	56.6–58.2	35.8–36.4	Namtrul Rinpoche asserts his identity as an emissary (pho nya) of Padmasambhava and life force (srog shing) of the Buddhist teachings.
NJP 24	58.3–59.2	36.5–14	A note urging Tāre Lhamo to come quickly, containing tantric imagery and possible references to one or more past lives.[6]
NJP 25	59.3–67.3	36.15–41.14	A song of joyous tidings (dga' skyid gtam gyi glu gzhas) to celebrate Tāre Lhamo's arrival. I consider this to be the last actual letter by Namtrul Rinpoche in the correspondence.
NJP 26	67.4–68.5	41.15–42.10	Addendum attributed to the ḍākinīs, which contains a ritual prescription and predicts a treasure.[7]
NJP 27	68.5–70.3	42.11–43.9	Addendum with prediction by Yeshe Tsogyal concerning their propagation of the treasures of Apang Terchen.
NJP 28	70.3–72.3	43.10–44.13	Addendum tagged as a symbolic certificate (brda byang) predicting that the time has come to propagate Apang Terchen's treasures.
NJP 29	72.4–73.3	44.14–45.5	Addendum heralding auspiciousness, again tagged as a symbolic certificate.
NJP 30	181.1–188.4	—	Addendum to the whole collection of letters, written to Tāre Lhamo in 2013 on the anniversary of her passing.[8]

Catalogue of the Letters of Tāre Lhamo

Garland of Lotuses: The Collected Letters by the Mantra-Born One,
Khandro Tāre Lhamo, to the Supreme Namtrul Jigme Phuntsok

Sngags skyes mkha' 'gro rin po che tā re de vīs nam sprul rin po che 'jigs med phun tshogs
mchog la phul ba'i zhu 'phrin phyag yid rnams phyogs bsdus pad ma'i phreng ba

Letter	Facsimile Edition	Paperback Version	Main Content
KTL 1	76.1–78.1	47.1–48.3	Prophecy locating a future treasure, dated to the seventh day of the hare month in the earth horse year (1978). The entire letter is excerpted in *Jewel Garland*.[1]
KTL 2	78.2–78.6	48.4–11	A song of marvels (*kha mtshar glu*) in three stanzas using images of the snow lion and youthful garuḍa.
KTL 3	78.6–79.2	48.12–15	Short aspiration prayer for the welfare of Tibetans, dated to the thirteenth day of the sheep month in the earth horse year. The entire letter is excerpted in *Jewel Garland* and also translated as the dedication for this book.[2]
KTL 4	79.2–80.5	49.1–17	Another song of marvels, dated to the eight day of the dog month in the earth sheep year (1979).
KTL 5	80.5–82.2	50.1–16	Letter containing flirtatious language, erotic images, and tantric elements, dated to the tenth day of Sagadawa (*sa ga zla ba*) in the earth sheep year.

(continued)

Letter	Facsimile Edition	Paperback Version	Main Content
KTL 6	82.2–83.4	51.1–16	Prophecy about a treasure to the north at Trachugmo Pass. All but the opening lines are excerpted in *Jewel Garland*.[3]
KTL 7	83.4–84.1	52.1–6	Confession of recollecting her inseparable companion one hundred times a day with increasing yearning and affection.
KTL 8	84.1–86.3	52.7–53.16	Folk song with images of fertility that shift into a tantric milieu.
KTL 9	86.4–87.4	54.1–13	Past lives at Rasa Tsuklakhang among five heroes (*dpa' bo lnga*); refers to Namtrul Rinpoche as Atsara Sale and sprout of the Nuden tulku. First half excerpted in *Jewel Garland*.[4]
KTL 10	87.5–92.4	55.1–58.2	Duet between Padma and Devī with parts in bardic verse, dated to the fifteenth day of Sagadawa in the earth sheep year and performed for her retinue of disciples.
KTL 11	92.4–93.4	58.3–14	Tagged as ḍākinī symbols (*mkha' 'gro'i brda*) and marked with *tertsek* (*gter tsheg*), this letter contains a ritual prescription to pacify immediate conditions, dated to the twenty-first day of the fifth month in the earth sheep year. Six lines of this letter are excerpted in *Jewel Garland*.[5]
KTL 12	93.4–94.6	58.15–59.12	Marked with tertsek, this cryptic letter is framed as the symbolic music of ḍākinīs predicting a treasure at Amnye Machen (here Magyal Pomra). The main prophecy section is excerpted in *Jewel Garland*.[6]
KTL 13	94.6–97.2	59.13–61–3	A song like a circling bee articulating destiny through images of regeneration. Five lines toward the end, Tāre Lhamo references their past lives together and entrustment by Padmasambhava; these are excerpted in *Jewel Garland*.[7]

Letter	Facsimile Edition	Paperback Version	Main Content
KTL 14	97.2–99.2	61.4–62.10	Tagged as a song of sorrow (*skyo ba'i glu*). Tāre Lhamo confesses to being weary, yet envisions their future propagating the dharma at the center of crowds likened to constellations of stars. Dated to the twenty-fifth day of the ox month in the earth sheep year.
KTL 15	99.2–110.1	62.11–69.10	This long letter contains diverse content: a heroic song in bardic verse, a short list of obstacles to their union, a recorded vision of a *werma* (*wer ma*), Tāre Lhamo's assertion of being free from worldly concerns, and a series of past life memories recounted in Namtrul Rinpoche's voice. Dated to the eighth day of the hare month in the earth sheep year, it references their initial meeting.[8]
KTL 16	110.1–112.4	69.11–70.19	A song about preparing for the journey, using saddle imagery, as Namtrul Rinpoche prepares to meet her relatives.
KTL 17	112.4–122.3	71.1–76.18	Marked with tertsek, this is another long letter containing two more past lives together in India, an homage to Apang Terchen, and a prophecy about a treasure with ritual prescriptions. Tāre Lhamo also expresses regret at her lack of accomplishments. Five passages from this letter are excerpted in *Jewel Garland*, represented as her direct speech during Namtrul Rinpoche's visit.[9]
KTL 18	122.4–127.5	77.1–80.1	Marked with tertsek and tagged as a song called "Fortress Garland of Flowers" (*rdzong me thog 'phreng ba*),[10] this letter starts with Tāre Lhamo imagining herself with Namtrul Rinpoche together in various settings in India, Tibet, and China, and then shifts into a setting from the Gesar epic.
KTL 19	127.5–128.3	80.2–8	A short letter contrasting conceptual obscurations with the unobscured expressive power of Samantabhadra.
KTL 20	128.3–129.4	80.9–81.4	A playful articulation of view, expressing the difference between renunciation and equanimity.
KTL 21	129.4–131.5	81.5–82.10	Marked with tertsek, this letter contains ritual prescriptions to reverse obstacles.

Letter	Facsimile Edition	Paperback Version	Main Content
KTL 22	131.5–136.6	82.11–85.13	Tāre Lhamo sends a protection circle and seven strands of her hair to reverse immediate conditions. The second half of the letter is marked with tertsek and contains a short liturgy. Dated to the twentieth day of the hare month in the earth sheep year.
KTL 23	136.6–137.2	85.14–17	Marked with tertsek, this letter contains a prophecy about treasure in Gyalrong, which is excerpted in *Jewel Garland*.[11] Dated to the twenty-eighth day of the dragon month in the sheep year.
KTL 24	137.2–138.4	86.1–18	Tāre Lhamo expresses the constancy of her affection.
KTL 25	138.5–140.1	87.1–17	Song of the "congenial friend" (*rogs mthun*), containing images of mutual dependence and inseparability.
KTL 26	140.1–144.4	88.1–90.16	Tāre Lhamo wishes Namtrul Rinpoche to be free of illness and provides him with a recipe for medicine. The final portion of the letter is marked with tertsek.
KTL 27	144.4–159.1	91.1–100.19	Dated to the eighth day of the horse month in the earth sheep year,[12] this letter contains a prophecy marked by tertsek, followed by an extended duet between Tsebo and Tarpo.[13] Three passages are excerpted in *Jewel Garland*.[14]
KTL 28	159.1–3	101.1–5	A song of remembrance in seven lines.[15]
KTL 29	159.4–165.2	101.6–104.16	The letter begins by emphasizing their inseparability and goes on to enumerate a series of past lives and locations of treasures.[16]
KTL 30	165.2–167.5	105.1–106.12	A song expressing good fortune with flourishing vegetation as the habitat for the tigress and fruit for the monkey to enjoy, alongside other naturalistic pairings.
KTL 31	167.6–180.4	106.13–114.17	This appears to be another duet, here with ten distinct entries, which continues through the end of Tāre Lhamo's letters.[17]

Abbreviations

COD   *Cloud Offerings to Delight the Vidyādharas and Ḍākinīs: The Liberation of Namtrul Jigme Phuntsok and Khandro Tāre Lhamo.* Pad ma 'od gsal mtha' yas. *Skyabs rje nam sprul rin po che 'jigs med phun tshogs dang mkha' 'gro tā re lha mo mchog gi rnam thar rig 'dzin mkha' 'gro dgyes pa'i mchod sprin.* Chengdu: Si khron mi rigs dpe skrun khang, 1997.

JG   *Jewel Garland: The Liberation of Namtrul Jigme Phuntsok.* Nam sprul 'jigs med phun tshogs kyi rnam thar nor bu'i do shal. In Pad ma 'od gsal mtha' yas 1997.

SVF   *Spiraling Vine of Faith: The Liberation of Khandro Tāre Lhamo.* Mkha' 'gro tā re lha mo'i rnam thar dad pa'i 'khri shing. In Pad ma 'od gsal mtha' yas 1997.

PTC   *The Profound Treasure Corpus of Orgyan Jigme Namkha Lingpa and Ḍākinī Tāre Dechen Gyalmo.* Nam sprul 'Jigs med phun tshogs and Mkha' 'gro Tā re lha mo. *O rgyan 'jigs med nam mkha' gling pa dang ḍāk ki tā re bde chen rgyal mo rnam gnyis kyi zab gter chos.* Facsimile edition in 12 volumes. Gser rta: Snyan lung dgon, n.d.

NJP   *Adamantine Garland: The Collected Letters by the Lord of Refuge, Namtrul Jigme Phuntsok, to the Supreme Khandro Tāre Lhamo.* Nam sprul 'Jigs med phun tshogs. *Skyabs rje rin po che nam sprul 'jigs med phun tshogs kyis mkha' 'gro rin po che tā re de vī mchog la phul ba'i zhu 'phrin phyag yig rnams phyogs bsdus rdo rje'i phreng ba.* Gser rta: Snyan lung dgon, c. 2003-4.

KTL   *Garland of Lotuses: The Collected Letters by the Mantra-Born One, Khandro Tāre Lhamo, to the Supreme Namtrul Jigme Phuntsok.* Mkha' 'gro Tā re lha mo. *Sngags skyes mkha' 'gro rin po che tā re de vīs nam sprul rin po che 'jigs med phun tshogs mchog la phul ba'i zhu 'phrin phyag yid rnams phyogs bsdus pad ma'i phreng ba.* Gser rta: Snyan lung dgon, c. 2003-4.

JLB   *Jewel Lantern of Blessings: An Abridged Biography of the Tertön Couple, the Lord of Siddhas Zhuchen Namtrul and Khandro Tāre Dechen Lhamo.* A bu dkar lo. *Gter ston grub pa'i dbang phyug gzhi chen nam sprul dang mkha' 'gro tā re bde chen lha mo zung gi mdzad rnam nyer bsdus byin rlabs nor bu'i sgron me.* Xining: Mtsho sngon nang bstan rtsom sgrig khang, 2001.

EGT *The Emanation of Green Tārā.* Mkhan po Rig 'dzin dar rgyas. Untitled and unpublished manuscript that begins *De yang rje btsun sgrol ma ljang mo'i thugs kyi rnam sprul,* received from the author in Gser rta in 2014.

KD *Brief Account of Khandro's Departure.* Nam sprul 'Jigs med phun tshogs. *Mkha' 'gro sku gshegs pa'i lo rgyus mdor bsdus.* Unpublished account of Tā re lha mo's last testament and death, received from the author at Snyan lung dgon in 2004.

HN *History of Nyenlung Monastery.* Krung go'i bod rig pa zhib 'jug lte gnas kyi chos lugs lo rgyus zhib 'jug so'o, etc. *Snyan lung dgon gyi lo rgyus.* In *Khams phyogs dkar mdzes khul gyi dgon sde so so'i lo rgyus gsal bar bshad pa thub bstan gsal ba'i me long.* Beijing: Krung go'i bod kyi shes rig dpe skrun khang, 1995.

HT *The Concise History of Tsimda Monastery.* 'Jam dbyangs nyi ma. *Rtsis mda' dgon pa'i lo rgyus mdor bsdus.* Unpublished manuscript, received from the author at Rtsis mda' dgon in 2006.

Notes

Introduction: Journey to Golok

1. Mgo log as a region shares much culturally, historically, and linguistically with its neighboring regions, such as Gser rta, and prior to 1950 Rnying ma figures traveled between Pad ma and Gser rta frequently, as this was the domain of their religious affiliation and extended community of followers. For this reason, my usage of "Mgo log" in this book often denotes a broader cultural zone than its current prefecture borders within Qinghai Province.

2. This account, from Tā re lha mo's twenty-second letter (KTL 22: 134.4–5), is discussed in more detail in chapter 4. The Tibetan for this phrase reads: *nga rang 'bral ba skad cig kyang med par 'grogs* (*nga rang* is left out in the translation).

3. Mkhan po 'Jigs med phun tshogs (1933–2004) was the charismatic founder of Serta Larung Buddhist Academy of the Five Sciences (Gser thang bla rung dgon rig lnga'i nang bstan slob grwa), commonly referred to as Bla rung sgar. On this important figure, see Germano 1998, Terrone 2010a, and Gayley 2011. Both figures were active in Gser rta County in Sichuan Province.

4. For a nuanced discussion of the healing power attributed to sexual union in Tibetan biographical literature, see Jacoby 2014a, especially chapter 4.

5. I use "modern Tibet" in the title of this book and in this introductory chapter to refer to the culturally Tibetan areas of central Tibet, Khams and A mdo, more in line with diaspora Tibetans' usage of the term than with political configurations within the People's Republic of China (PRC), which delimit Tibet as the Tibetan Autonomous Region (TAR). I do so only because English readers will be most accustomed to this usage, not to stake any claim to this as historically accurate, either personally or on behalf of the figures studied in this book. Otherwise, I use "Tibetan areas of China," since Mgo log Prefecture does not fall within the TAR, but lies on the eastern part of the Tibetan plateau in Qinghai Province.

6. Here I give Tā re lha mo's age according to Western convention; in subsequent chapters, when reading from their life stories and letters, I provide ages according to the Tibetan convention, which counts someone's age by the year they are entering. So a child is considered to enter their first year (age one) at birth.

7. NJP 1: 3.4–4.1.

8. Pad ma (Ch.: Banma) lies in Mgo log (Ch.: Guoluo) Prefecture of Qinghai Province, while Gser rta (Ch.: Seda) lies in Dkar mdzes (Ch.: Ganzi) Prefecture of Sichuan Province and has a number of variant renderings: Gser rta, Gser thar, Gser thang, and Gser ljongs. I phoneticize Pad ma as "Padma" when it stands alone or exists in the name of the Indian tantric master, Padmasambhava. When it forms part of a longer Tibetan name, I phoneticize it as "Pema," as in Pema Ösal Thaye (Pad ma 'od gsal mtha' yas) according to Tibetan pronunciation.

9. His full name is A phang gter chen O rgyan 'phrin las gling pa, alias A phang dpa' bo Chos dbyings rdo rje. There are various spellings for his family name: A phang, A pang, and A paṃ. I provide more context regarding her father and family lineage in chapter 1.

10. Her first husband was Mi 'gyur rdo rje (1934–59), locally known as Sprul sku Mi lo, the son of her principal lama, Rdzong gter Kun bzang nyi ma (1904–58), who himself was the grandson and speech emanation of his grandfather, Bdud 'joms gling pa (1835–1904), one of the great "treasure revealers" or *gter ston* of Golok.

11. Her three brothers were 'Gyur med rdo rje (b. 1928), Dbang chen nyi ma (b. 1931), and Thub bstan chos kyi nyi ma (b. circa 1939). See chapter 1 for more information regarding their incarnation status.

12. On this figure, see chapter 1, note 22.

13. There is no record of a formal marriage ceremony between Tā re lha mo and Nam sprul rin po che in their hagiographic corpus; nonetheless, due to their long partnership in which they resided together for more than twenty years at Snyan lung dgon, I refer to their union loosely as a marriage, to clarify that it was the second for both of them.

14. In his youth, at the age of eight by Tibetan reckoning, Nam sprul rin po che was recognized as the fourth Nam mkha'i snying po incarnation of Gzhu chen dgon in Gser rta County. For this reason, in Tibetan, the prefix of his name is spelled *nam sprul* rather than the more commonplace *rnam sprul*.

15. For an overview of treasure revelation, see Gyatso 1993 and 1996, Thondup 1997, Doctor 2005, and Gayley 2008.

16. KTL 15: 99.6. See chapter 4 for a discussion of the metaphor of healing in their correspondence.

17. Treasures in the form of hitherto unknown scriptures and relics, said to be hidden throughout the Tibetan and Himalayan landscape and traced to the distant past, most frequently to Padmasambhava or a comparable figure in the imperial period, have been revealed since at least the twelfth century. See Gyatso 1993: 98 note 2 and Doctor 2005: 198 note 14 for names of other figures credited with concealing treasures.

18. On the historicity of Padmasambhava and his activities in Tibet, see Kapstein 2000.

19. The policy of "reform and opening" (*gaige kaifang*) officially commenced with the 3rd Plenary Session of the 11th Central Committee of the Communist Party of China in December 1978. The impact of those reforms was not felt in Tibetan areas until the early 1980s.

20. Germano 1998: 90.

21. As discussed in chapter 5, they did this with the help of Rig 'dzin nyi ma, a Rnying ma master who had used the site as a retreat hermitage and remained close to Nam sprul rin po che throughout his life.

22. See note 37 below.

23. The earliest version of their corpus of treasure revelations and writings is *O rgyan 'jigs med nam mkha' gling pa dang dākki tā re bde chen rgyal mo rnam gnyis kyi zab gter chos* (abbreviated PTC), a facsimile edition in traditional *dpe cha* format and *dbu med* script in twelve volumes. There is a new paperback version, published together with A phang gter chen's corpus of treasures, which includes their correspondence and more recent writings by Nam sprul rin po che: *Khyab bdag gter chen bla ma 'ja' lus pa dpal mnyam med nam mkha' gling pa rin po che dang mkha' 'gro rin po che tā re lha mo zung gi zab gter nam mkha' mdzod kyi chos sde* in 14 volumes (Chengdu: Si khron mi rigs dpe skrun khang, 2013).

24. Published by their home institution, Snyan lung dgon, this volume in a facsimile edition contains two separate collections of their respective letters, *Skyabs rje rin po che nam sprul 'jigs med phun tshogs kyis mkha' 'gro rin po che tā re de vī mchog la phul ba'i zhu 'phrin phyag yig rnams phyogs bsdus rdo rje'i phreng ba* (abbreviated NJP) and *Sngags skyes mkha' 'gro rin po che tā re de vīs nam sprul rin po che 'jigs med phun tshogs mchog la phul ba'i zhu 'phrin phyag yid rnams phyogs bsdus pad ma'i phreng ba* (abbreviated KTL). The volume contains fifty-six actual letters and several addenda, including four treasure certificates at the end of the first collection and a letter that Nam sprul rin po che wrote to Tā re lha mo after she passed away in 2002 at the end of the volume as a whole. I discuss the contents, numbering, and dating of the letters in more detail in chapter 3; see also appendices A and B. Their correspondence is included as volume 12 in the new paperback version of their corpus of treasure revelations and writings. See note 23 above.

25. I discuss audio-visual sources produced by Snyan lung dgon in more detail in the epilogue.

26. Academic monographs focused on specific historical Tibetan Buddhist women—rather than the separate but related topic of feminine symbolism in Buddhist tantra—include Edou 1995, Schaeffer 2004, Diemberger 2007, and Jacoby 2014a. Notable too are groundbreaking anthologies by Willis 1989, Gyatso 2006, and Karma Lekshe Tsomo 2014; translations from the Tibetan of the life stories and/or teachings of exemplary Buddhist women include Sangye Khandro 1998, Padmakara Translation Committee 2002, and Harding 2003b and 2011. Panels on "Writing Tibetan Women" and "Female Lives and Narratives in Tibet: New Materials and New Perspectives" at the American Academy of Religion conference in November 2013 and 2015 respectively showcased several promising projects in process that will no doubt add to this list in future years.

27. Rita Gross coined the term "androcentric record-keeping" (1993: 20) to refer to the tendency for Buddhist women tend to disappear from the historical record.

For an example from the Bdud 'joms family lineage, to which Tā re lha mo had close connections, see note 81 below.

28. This trend can already be detected in articles by Antonio Terrone that mention Nam sprul rin po che as a *gter ston* of importance in the region while omitting mention of Tā re lha mo altogether (2008: 97 and 100) or relegating her to the role of consort (2010b: 391).

29. The Tibetan term *mkha' 'gro ma* translates the Sanskrit *ḍākinī* and refers to a category of nonmonastic female religious specialists. *Mkha' 'gro ma* typically live either as recluses or as the consorts of male lamas, particularly in the Rnying ma sect, and Tā re lha mo herself played both of these roles at different times in her life. While some *mkha' 'gro ma* serve as Buddhist teachers, rather than traveling widely and presiding over large-scale rituals as male lamas do, *mkha' 'gro ma* tend to give esoteric teachings in private to small groups of disciples. They are usually locally known and revered, but only occasionally enter the annals of history.

30. Tā re lha mo is mentioned in an appendix of *gter ston* in *Hidden Teachings of Tibet* (Tulku Thondup 1997: 201); in David Germano's essay, "Re-membering the Dismembered Body of Tibet: Contemporary Tibetan Visionary Movements in the People's Republic of China," in *Buddhism in Contemporary Tibet* (Germano 1998: 91); and in the epilogue of Jacoby 2014a: 320–21. Two other contemporary female *gter ston* discussed in academic writings to date are Mkha' spyod dbang mo in Span Hanna 1994 and Mkha' 'gro Chos spyan in Schneider 2015.

31. His name is Sangs rgyas pad ma bzhad pa, the son of Bdud 'joms rin po che's own son in Mgo log, named Mdo bla Chos kyi nyi ma. See http://www.nyingma .com/artman/publish/dudjom_yangsis.shtml.

32. SVF was excerpted and reproduced in its entirety in *Sngags pa'i shes rigs dus deb* 5:1 (2003): 117–32.

33. Michael Sheehy, "The Bibliographic Scope of Buddhist Women Literati in Tibet," paper presented at the panel "Female Lives and Narratives in Tibet: New Materials and New Perspectives," American Academy of Religion conference, Atlanta, November 21–24, 2015. In this anthology by Larung Buddhist Academy, titled *A Garland of White Lotuses: The Liberation [Stories] of the Great Holy Women of India and Tibet* (*'Phags bod kyi skyes chen ma dag gi rnam par thar ba pad ma dkar po'i phreng ba*), SVF was again excerpted and reproduced almost in its entirety (vol. 12: 121–54), but retitled *The Ladder Traversing to Akaniṣṭha: The Liberation of Khandro Tāre Lhamo* (*Mkha' 'gro tā re lha mo'i rnam thar 'og min bgrod pa'i them skas*). This change reflects how her *rnam thar* is titled in the 2013 paperback edition of their collected works (see note 23 above). Volume 12 contains the *rnam thar* for two other identifiably contemporary female masters, Rta mgrin lha mo (1923–79), a student of the Rnying ma master Nyag bla Byang chub rdo rje, and Rje btsun ma Mu med ye shes mtsho mo (b. 1966, abbreviated Rje btsun ma Mu mtsho), who is the niece of Mkhan po 'Jigs med phun tshogs and currently lives and teaches at Larung Buddhist Academy in Gser rta. In this anthology, the biographies of Tibetan women are generally labeled as either *rnam thar* and *lo rgyus*. In the last several volumes, there are also *gtam rgyud* related to female classes of Tibetan deities as well as *'das log* accounts. My thanks to Michael Sheehy for sharing the *dkar chag* for this collection with me. A sixteenth volume addendum further elaborates the life story of Rje btsun ma Mu med ye shes mtsho mo;

my appreciation to the TBRC for allowing me access to scans for the entire anthology.

34. Even Tulku Thondup, who is a relative of Nam sprul rin po che, lists Tā re lha mo alone in his appendix of *gter ston* in *Hidden Teachings of Tibet* (1997: 189–201).

35. JG 60.11–61.7. In chapter 1, I discuss the importance of family to lineage succession in the Rnying ma school of Tibetan Buddhism and to the treasure tradition within that.

36. JLB 2.12–13, A bu dkar lo et al. 2000: 213, and *Snyan mo lung gyi sgra dbyang* (VCD 1 of 2) 12: 50–53 respectively. I discuss these identifications, their sources, and significance at more length in the epilogue. *Jewel Garland* (published in 1997) makes oblique reference to his past life identification with A phang gter chen, using the Sanskrit, Dharmadhātu Vajra, which translates Chos dbyings rdo rje. However, Nam sprul rin po che's identity as his activity emanation only gets brought to the fore and made more explicit in later publications.

37. In Tibetan, these sources are, respectively, *Mkha' 'gro tā re lha mo'i rnam thar dad pa'i 'khri shing* (abbreviated SVF) and *Nam sprul 'jigs med phun tshogs kyi rnam thar nor bu'i do shal* (abbreviated JG) as composed by Pad ma 'od gsal mtha' yas in *Skyabs rje nam sprul rin po che 'jigs med phun tshogs dang mkha' 'gro tā re lha mo mchog gi rnam thar rig 'dzin mkha' 'gro dgyes pa'i mchod sprin* (abbreviated COD) and published in 1997.

38. SVF 160.5–6. This office is given as: *Rdzong srid gros rig gnas dpyad gzhi u yon lhan khang.*

39. *Gter ston grub pa'i dbang phyug gzhi chen nam sprul dang mkha' 'gro tā re bde chen lha mo zung gi mdzad rnam nyer bsdus byin rlabs nor bu'i gron me* (abbreviated JLB) is a shorter and derivative hagiography by A bu dkar lo, which has been translated into Chinese and English in publications by Snyan lung dgon. The English translation of his work by Tulku Thondup never gained a readership, but its companion Chinese translation has been reproduced numerous times in unofficial publications by Snyan lung Monastery and circulated widely among their Han Chinese disciples. The Chinese title is *Nianlong shangshi fumu renboqie lüezhuan*, which roughly translates as *A Brief Biography of the Precious Nyenlung Teaching Couple.* Other published sources, which include biographical accounts and selections from their teachings, are now available in Chinese: *Nianlong shangshi fumu guang zhuan: Wugou moni baoman* and *Yanjiao Huibian: Erli renyun moni baoman* (published by Snyan lung dgon, c. 2009).

40. See JLB 15.3 and 23.12–24.6.

41. See note 39 above and the epilogue for a further discussion of this and other Chinese-language sources about Tā re lha mo and Nam sprul rin po che.

42. This new *rnam thar* remains untitled and unpublished; I will refer to it as *The Emanation of Green Tārā* (abbreviated as EGT) based on its first line, which identifies Tā re lha mo as the mind emanation of her namesake. The Tibetan reads: *De yang rje btsun sgrol ma ljang mo'i thugs kyi rnam sprul.* I make a detailed comparison of these three sources in "Gendered Hagiography in Tibet: Comparing Clerical Representations of the Female Visionary, Khandro Tāre Lhamo" in *Buddhist Feminism(s) and Femininity*, ed. Karma Lekshe Tsomo (Albany: State University of New York Press, forthcoming).

43. Mkhan po Rig 'dzin dar rgyas is a high-ranking monk from Rtsis mda' dgon, the monastery founded by Tā re lha mo's father in Pad ma County, who currently serves as the *dge bskos* at Larung Buddhist Academy in Gser rta. He kindly shared with me over the years an alternative perspective of Tā re lha mo's youth than available in the official account by Pad ma 'od gsal mtha' yas, who is based in Gser rta, and put me in contact with old women who lived through the Maoist period with Tā re lha mo.

44. Janet Gyatso had obtained a copy of *Spiraling Vine of Faith* from Gene Smith at the Tibetan Buddhist Resource Center.

45. The abbreviated accounts of Ye shes mtsho rgyal and Se ra mkha' 'gro excerpted in *Spiraling Vine of Faith* are discussed in more detail in chapter 1.

46. On sources for Ye shes mtsho rgyal's life, see Gyatso 2006, and on the life of Se ra mkha' 'gro—also known as Dbus bza' mkha' 'gro, Bde ba'i rdo rje, and Kun bzang bde skyong chos nyid dbang mo—see Jacoby 2010, 2014a, and 2014b.

47. Ekvall 1968.

48. Prior to this, the largest library of Tibetan texts in North America, the Tibetan Buddhist Resources Center (TBRC) in Cambridge, MA, had only a partial collection of their corpus retrieved several years earlier by Susan Costello.

49. My colleague for this journey was Sarah Jacoby, who was also beginning field research in the region.

50. The title of A phang gter chen's corpus is *Rgyal dbang pad ma'i rgyal tshab o rgyan phrin las gling pa'i zab gter nor bu'i phreng ba* (published by Snyan lung dgon in 16 volumes, n.d.).

51. During field research, Nam sprul rin po che sometimes wrote messages in the notebook I brought to all our interviews. In one memorable interview, when I asked about how he and Tā re lha mo dealt with obstacles, he composed a Vajrakīla practice on the spot, using the formal stationery of Snyan lung dgon. His composition is marked with *gter tsheg*, the orthographic feature indicating its status as treasure.

52. Bkra shis sgo mang is a Rnying ma monastery in Pad ma County, Tā re lha mo's homeland.

53. As Edward Said has pointed out, the idea of the "Orient" as open to researchers from the "Occident" emerged through a power differential in the context of imperialism, and its legacy continues today (1979).

54. *Snyan mo lung gi sgra dbyangs*, set of 2 discs, produced by Snyan lung dgon, c. 2003 (no ISRC number).

55. *Mdzad bsdus mthong tshad rang grol*, set of 2 discs produced by Snyan lung dgon, c. 2006 (no ISRC number).

56. On various occasions, I was introduced as the disciple of Nam sprul rin po che, and to the extent that I observed and participated in rituals over which he presided, as the grounds for attendance, I was constituted as such. When I contacted lamas and laity in Pad ma County and elsewhere for interviews, a number of them remembered me from Bkra shis sgo mang and agreed to speak with me partly on that basis.

57. Kolas and Thowsen survey these representations in the media in the introduction to their collaborative study, *On the Margins of Tibet: Cultural Survival on the Sino-Tibetan Frontier.* The content of this paragraph is indebted to their work, except where otherwise noted.

58. The term "cultural wasteland" can be found in exile Tibetan statements quoted in Kolas and Thowsen 2005: 5. The broader point derives from Benno Weiner, "The Development and Composition of Cultural Revolution-era Factionalism in the Tibetan Autonomous Region" (unpublished paper).

59. On the ideological nature of historiography, see Guha 1982 and Powers 2004.

60. In the words of Kolas and Thowsen, such representations are "unfair to all the Tibetans who have contributed to the rebuilding of religious sites, supported the use of Tibetan in the schools, and involved themselves in contemporary Tibetan literature and the arts" (2005: 173).

61. Tsering Shakya 2008: 83. Contemporary literary production by Tibetans exists within a delicate balance between publishing opportunities and censorship and reprisals against authors who publish politically sensitive content. Nonetheless, Lauran Hartley and Patricia Schiaffini-Vedani have called literary magazines a "proxy public forum" in which writers find "creative ways to negotiate their literary freedoms amidst these limits of permissible discourse" (Hartley 2008: xvi).

62. Good examples of this trend are anthologies edited by Barnett and Schwartz 2008 and Tuttle 2011.

63. Hartley and Schiaffini-Vedani 2008.

64. I have begun this work related to contemporary works of advice to the laity in Gayley 2011 and 2013.

65. Ahearn 2001: 112.

66. In conceiving of agency within the framework of constraints and resources, I am also influenced by the work of Anthony Giddens in *Central Problems in Social Theory: Action, Structure and Contradiction in Social Analysis* (1979).

67. For a critique of agency along these lines, see Salgado 2013.

68. Goldstein and Kapstein 1998.

69. While not intending "hagiography" as a translation for *rnam thar*, I refer to the life stories of Tā re lha mo and Nam sprul rin po che as hagiographic representations in order to highlight the features of idealized third-person accounts, like *Spiraling Vine of Faith* and *Jewel Garland*, which share much with how Patrick Geary discusses medieval Christian hagiographic literature (1996). I discuss this point in more detail in the next chapter.

70. Chakrabarty 2000: 97–113.

71. Chakrabarty 2000: 100.

72. In discussing karma as a framing device for this period, I draw on Erving Goffman's rubric of "frame analysis" in which humans create meaning out of events and actions, which otherwise lack inherent meaning, through the application of frameworks that he defines as "schemata of interpretation" (Goffman 1974).

73. Based on the old "talking cure," storytelling provides an active way to make meaning and come to terms with trauma, colonial violence, and social suffering (Visser 2015; see also Das and Kleinman 2001). A pioneer in the study of trauma narratives, Judith Herman posits that healing requires "the reconstruction of a system of belief that makes sense of her undeserved suffering" (1997: 178), since the arbitrary quality of traumatic experience calls into question a victim's sense of a predictable world order. The healing process occurs by integrating traumatic events into a cohesive narrative.

74. I borrow the term "interethnic domination" from Stevan Harrell (1995), who uses it to characterize minorities in China vis-a-vis the Han dominated state.

75. Jackson 2002: 15.

76. This term was first coined in Huber 1999 to describe the visionary transformation of sacred mountains from abodes of indigenous local deities into pilgrimage sites for circumambulating the maṇḍala of a Buddhist tantric deity.

77. In Makley's words, "Storytelling about trulku lives in a variety of contexts thus positioned Tibetan selves as grounded in *dapa*, or 'faith'—that is situated within the patrifilial mandalic sphere of trulkus' benevolent and powerful protection" (2007: 96).

78. Prevalent in China until recently, VCDs provide a similar viewing experience to DVDs, through the video quality is not as high. For a study of monastery-produced VCDs, see Gayley 2016.

79. A monk affiliated with Dung dkar dgon, Pad ma 'd gsal mtha' yas works at the Bureau of Culture, History, Education, and Health (*Rig gnas lo rgyus tshan slob 'phrod rten mthun tshogs su u yon ltan khang*) at the county seat in Gser rta, Dkar mdzes Prefecture, Sichuan Province. He has published numerous hagiographies and local histories through the Sichuan Minorities Publishing House and written miscellaneous articles on Tibetan culture, arts, translation, and religion as well as works of poetry.

80. 'Ju skal bzang heads the Nationalities Language Government Office (*Mi rigs skad yig bya ba'i gzhung las khang*) in Rta'u, the capital of Mgo log Prefecture, Qinghai Province.

81. Note, for example, in the genealogy of Bdud 'joms gling pa's family lineage in *Yab mes rigs 'dzin brgyud pa'i byung ba mdor bsdus tsam brjod pa* (Pad ma 'od gsal mtha' yas 2003), his three consorts are only mentioned in relation to the parentage of his eight prominent sons; his four daughters remain nameless even though they are identified as *mkha' 'gro ma*. The consorts of many of his sons go unnamed within their biographical sketches, except for the famous Se ra mkha' 'gro, a teacher in her own right whose autobiographic corpus has been studied by Sarah Jacoby (2010, 2014a, and 2104b). Several are recovered in the next generation in the birth account of Bdud 'joms gling pa's grandchildren. As the generations get closer to the present, the names of more women in the family are included. See my post on the Tibetan Buddhist Resource Center website: http://about.tbrc.org/whos-who-in-the-dudjom-lineage.

82. I discuss the difference between forms of collective trauma, both social and cultural, in chapter 2.

83. Such statistically oriented work on the revitalization of Buddhist monasteries, Tibetan education, and other quantifiable aspects of Tibet's civilizational inheritance has already been ably charted by Kolas and Thowsen in *On the Margins of Tibet: Cultural Survival on the Borderlands* (2005).

84. The study of colonialism has demonstrated the insidious way that dominant systems of meaning tend to become internalized over time by subordinated groups, which Ashis Nandy has eloquently termed the "intimate enemy" (1988). As Tsering Shakya has discussed, more than sixty years of Chinese colonial occupation has resulted in the "dislocation of identity and traditional epistemology" (2008: 61).

85. Personal communication from Lung dkar mkha' 'gro ma, July 2006.

86. For example, Allione 1984, Willis 1989, Havnevik 1999, Harding 2003b, Schaeffer 2004, Gyatso and Havnevik 2006, Diemberger 2007, and Jacoby 2014a.

87. See Quintman 2014: 20–27 for a helpful summary of how approaches to the study of Tibetan life writings intersect with recent trends in the study of hagiography more broadly.

1. Daughter of Golok: Tāre Lhamo's Life and Context

1. As will be recounted later in this chapter, the first was Khra dge slong Tshul khrims dar rgyas, a monk of local renown, who confided this to her during a *khecarī* empowerment, and the second was Bde ba'i rdo rje, alias Se ra mkha' 'gro, a female *gter ston* of the preceding generation.

2. The prophecy is translated below and also includes her identification with the tantric deity Varjavārāhī and the female *gter ston* of the previous generation, Se ra mkha' 'gro (SVF 1997: 132.5–10).

3. *Mkha' 'gro tā re lha mo mchog gi rnam thar dad pa'i 'khri shing* was published together in a single paperback volume with *Nam sprul 'jigs med phun tshogs kyi rnam thar nor bu'i do shal* in Pad ma 'od gsal mtha' yas 1997. As mentioned in the introduction, it was excerpted and reproduced in its entirety in a journal issue of the Sngags mang Institute dedicated to the lives of exemplary Rnying ma women, *Sngags pa'i shes rigs dus deb* 5:1 (2003): 117–32, and also in *'Phags bod kyi skyes chen ma dag gi rnam par thar ba pad ma dkar po'i phreng ba* (vol. 12: 121–54) under a different title. In this version, her life is intertwined with those of her female antecedents, Ye shes mtsho rgyal and Se ra mkha' 'gro, as detailed in this chapter. Only in the newest version of her life story by Rig 'dzin dar rgyas, as yet unpublished when this book went to press, does Tā re lha mo emerge as the solo protagonist of her life story.

4. On sources for Ye shes mtsho rgyal's life, see Gyatso 2006. And on the life of Se ra mkha' 'gro—also known as Dbus bza' mkha' 'gro, Bde ba'i rdo rje, and Kun bzang bde skyong chos nyid dbang mo—see Jacoby 2009/2010, 2014a, and 2014b.

5. In *Jewel Lantern of Blessings*, A bu dkar lo likewise weaves their lives together, although their joint activities as a couple in the post-Mao era appear in her portion of their *rnam thar*.

6. Scholars concerned with the cross-cultural study of personhood, such as Wimal Dissanayake, define the "self" as "the imaginary register consisting of identifications, narratives, formulations, and images" that produce an "imaginary singularity" (1996: x). With a belief in past lives and the philosophical doctrine of "no self" (*anātman*), one wonders if there is an "imaginary singularity" as suggested by Dissanayake in Buddhist hagiographic sources, or if personhood would be better described as composite, relational, and interdependent.

7. See Gyatso 1999: 179 and 219 and Jacoby 2014a: 12 ff.

8. Even in the newest and yet to be published version of her life story by Rig 'dzin dar rgyas, where Tā re lha mo serves as the central protagonist on her own without

an elaborate past life preamble or a hagiographic coupling with Nam sprul rin po che, she is thoroughly embedded in her local context, interacting with members of her own clan, the Song yul, and various families in her homeland throughout her youth. In contrast to published hagiographic and epistolary sources that are the focus of this book, her representation there is more akin to the "relational autonomy" discussed in Jacoby 2015.

9. Regarding the ḍākinī as a symbol in Buddhist tantra, see Aziz 1989, Willis 1987, Herrmann-Pfandt 1990, Shaw 1994, Campbell 1996, Gyatso 1998, and Simmer-Brown 2001.

10. For example, Gyatso 1998, Schaeffer 2004, and Jacoby 2014a.

11. The social construction of Tibetan biographies, composed over time among religious communities, has recently been thematized in Quintman 2014 and Holmes-Tagchungdarpa 2014.

12. This issue is explored in chapter 5 along similar lines to David Germano's argument about how treasure revelation enabled a "re-membering" of Tibet in the post-Mao era, and thereby a reconstituting of Tibetan time and space (1998).

13. In this chapter, I leave out the names of her friends and family who shared stories about Tā re lha mo during the period between the late 1950s and the death of Mao in 1976 and references to those who confided any other information about politically sensitive issues.

14. A phang reflects his family name (alternatively rendered as A pang and A paṃ). This was a prominent family in which his father was a local chieftain (dpon po) and his brother 'Gyur med rgya mtsho was an accomplished master, according to a personal communication from A phang gter chen's nephew and one of his reincarnations, 'Jigs med dbang drag rdo rje, in May 2006. The Mgo log sman rtsis rig pa'i lo rgyus gives his birth year as 1895 and parents' names as A phang bsod rdor and Ma sgron (A bu dkar lo et al. 2000). His full name is A phang gter chen O rgyan 'phrin las gling pa, alias Dpa' bo Chos dbyings rdo rje.

15. The first child died at birth.

16. In 1945, when A phang gter chen passed away, Tā re lha mo would have been eight by Western count. Her age is recorded as nine in Spiraling Vine of Faith, due to the Tibetan method of reckoning that counts a newborn as already one year old. Unless otherwise indicated, I follow the Tibetan convention in my translation and analysis. The unusual feat of a father-daughter revelation is mentioned in a short biography of A phang gter chen in Mgo log sman rtsis rig pa'i lo rgyus. A bu dkar lo et al. 2000: 211. A more detailed account can be found in the unpublished manuscript of The Emanation of Green Tārā, which I am abbreviating EGT, by Rig 'dzin dar rgyas.

17. Three incarnations of the Third Rdo grup chen were recognized: Yar lung Bstan pa'i nyi ma, Rig 'dzin 'Ja' lus rdo rje, and Thub bstan 'phrin las dpal bzang po, who currently lives in Sikkim and regularly visits his home monastery.

18. Rdzong gter Kun bzang nyi ma, alias Rig 'dzin Nus ldan rdo rje (1904–58).

19. Sprul sku Mi lo is the local abbreviation of his name, Sprul sku Mi 'gyur rdo rje, alias Pad ma 'od gsal snying po.

20. Personal communication by Pad ma theg mchog rgyal mtshan, July 2006.

21. On the emanations and scions of Bdud 'joms gling pa, see Pad ma 'od gsal mtha' yas 2003. I have traced the scions of Bdud 'joms gling pa according to this

work in a paper titled, "All in the Dudjom (*Bdud 'joms*) Family: Overlapping Modes of Authority and Transmission in the Golok Treasure Scene," presented at the annual meeting of the American Academy of Religion, November 7–10, 2009. More recently, it has been published as a series of blog entries on www.tbrc.org.

22. His name was Dbang phyug rdo rje (alt. Dbang grags rdo rje). According to 'Jam dbyangs nyi ma at Rtsis mda' dgon pa, he was nicknamed Sprul sku Rna bo.

23. *Jewel Garland* notes that Nam sprul rin po che was arrested much later in 1969 but only held in prison for two months before being released.

24. Rig 'dzin dar rgyas shared a number of these tales with me over the years, based on recorded interviews with locals in Smar khog, and gave me a draft version of the new *rnam thar* in June 2014 that has rendered some of them in literary form.

25. Personal communication by 'Jam dbyangs nyi ma, the acting head of Rtsis mda' dgon, May 2006.

26. Mdo li nyi ma (b. 1946), alias Dpal don 'grub 'phrin las rnam rgyal, was the son of the Gter chen Bsod nam lde'u btsan and Se ra mkha' 'gro's daughter, Mgar bza' Chos dbyings sgrol ma (alt. Chos dbyings sgron ma); a short biographical sketch is available in Pad ma 'od gsal mtha' yas 2003: 71.16–72.6. Pad ma 'od gsal mtha' yas confirmed that Tā re lha mo also had revealed treasures with Mdo li nyi ma when I met with him in May 2007. Rig 'dzin dar rgyas also confirmed their revelations together and characterized their relationship as tantric consorts (*yab yum*).

27. Rig 'dzin dar rgyas described this account in an interview in May 2007. It appears in a slightly different form in EGT.

28. I was told this by an elderly member of the Thar ba family in May 2006. Mdo li nyi ma's brief biography states that he was rumored to have departed for the land of the khecarīs during the period of the Cultural Revolution without leaving behind his body (Pad ma 'od gsal mtha' yas 2003: 72).

29. The description of Tā re lha mo's living conditions in this paragraph is derived from a conversation with members of the Thar ba family in May 2006.

30. SVF 142.1–5. These have been incorporated into her joint corpus of treasure revelations, shared with Nam sprul rin po che.

31. On the life and revelations of Mkha' spyod dbang mo, see Span Hanna 1994.

32. Don grub dbang rgyal and Nor sde 1992: 106.

33. Personal communication from Nam sprul rin po che, May 2007. This meeting is evident in the letters themselves, and his journey to meet Tā re lha mo for the first time is also depicted in JG 41.5–15.

34. Their building projects and teaching tours will be discussed in more detail in chapter 5.

35. For a discussion of the significance of this pilgrimage and the revelation of treasures outside of culturally Tibetan regions, see Germano 1998.

36. The six sites include: (1) Seng 'brug stag rtse in Dar lag; (2) Rma yul ge sar rig gnas tshog pa in Dga' bde; (3) Rdi mda' dgon in Pad ma; (4) Pad ma lha rtse in Pad ma; (5) Gling ri padma 'bum rdzong pa in Rma chen; and (6) Rma stod hwa hri zha in Rma stod. The fifth is the temple Tā re lha mo and Nam sprul rin po che constructed near A myes rma chen. Personal communication by Nor sde, May 2006.

37. Personal communication by Nor sde, May 2006.

38. I discuss her illness and the final years of her life in more detail in the epilogue.

39. The description of Tā re lha mo's final activities in this paragraph is derived from an extensive interview with Nam sprul rin po che in July 2006, summarized in the epilogue.

40. The Mgo log dialect shares more with that of its nomadic neighbors in Sichuan Province than the dialect of the settled farming communities in the northern part of Qinghai. Linguistically, Tibetans distinguish between the nomadic dialect ('brog skad) spoken in the southern part of present-day Qinghai Province—Mgo log and environs—and the agrarian dialect (rong skad) spoken among Tibetans in the northern part of Qinghai. Related dialects extend beyond these present-day prefecture borders to regions in Sichuan Province: south into Gser rta, west into Rdza chu kha, and east into Rnga ba.

41. Pirie 2005: 5.

42. A discussion of the origins of the Mgo log clans and their divisions can be found in the Mgo log lo rgyus deb ther in one of two chapters dedicated to clan genealogy (Don grub dbang rgyal and Nor sde 1992: 115–32.) A different version is found in the rnam thar of Mdo mkhyen brtse Ye shes rdo rje 1997: 3–24. See also Rock 1956: 123–29 for yet another variation of this tale. The social formations among nomads in Mgo log and A mdo are usually regarded as tribal groupings based on common ancestry, actual or mythic (see Eckvall 1968: 28–29). I use "clan" to characterize these social formations, captured by the Tibetan terms tsho ba and sometimes also sde ba, in lieu of the term "tribe," which can convey a derogatory association with the primitive.

43. On Golok as a clan confederation, see Rock 1956, Carrasco 1959, Clarke 1992, and Pirie 2005. The Annals of Golok History portrays Golok as successful in resisting domination by outside forces, but also repeatedly embroiled in internal disputes and wars over territory (Don grub dbang rgyal and Nor sde 1992: 33). Though Mgo log was never united politically, its clans formed alliances that allowed them to resist, for the most part, outside control from the Dga' ldan pho brang in central Tibet, Muslim overlords to the north, and the Republican-era authorities in Sichuan. Notably, the Xining-based Muslim warlords, Ma Qi and Ma Bufang, made a number of incursions into Mgo log in the 1920s and '30s and faced fierce resistance (Alak Tsayu Tenzin Palbar 1997: 25–26). This is significant because it suggests how for centuries Mgo log remained a distinctive region on the margins and largely independent of competing state interests.

44. Information available from the Mtsho sngon bod brgyud nang bstan gyi dgon sde (published in 2005) indicates the prevalence of Rnying ma monasteries in each county as follows: 20 out of 23 in Pad ma, 7 out of 11 in Gcig sgril, 8 out of 11 in Dar lag, 4 out of 11 in Dga' bde, 5 out of 7 in Rma chen, and 6 out of 6 in Rma stod. See Don grub dbang rgyal and Nor sde 1992: 102–5 for data on the affiliations of Rnying ma monasteries with monastic seats in Khams.

45. To the south, in Gser rta County, all the monasteries belong to the Rnying ma sect, and there was much cross-fertilization in the treasure scene between Gser rta and Pad ma historically. When considering the Mgo log treasure scene below, I include Gser rta County, which, though part of Sichuan Province, shares much culturally and linguistically with the rest of Mgo log. This monastery later became associated with the Jo nang school and it remains so today; currently its name is

A skyong rgya dgon Nges don rtag brtan bshad grub 'phel rgyal gling. See Don grub dbang rgyal and Nor sde, *Mgo log lo rgyus deb ther* (1992: 118).

46. See note 21 above.

47. This account can be found in *The Concise History of Tsimda Gompa* (*Rtsis mda' dgon pa'i lo rgyus mdor bsdus*), abbreviated HT, an unpublished document I photocopied from the current monastery head, 'Jam dbyangs nyi ma. The full name of the monastery is Rtsis mda' bkra shis dga' 'khyil gling.

48. Personal communication by 'Jam dbyangs nyi ma, May 2006.

49. A phang gter chen has four incarnations, among them Nam sprul rin po che (JG 5–6 and JLB 2.12–13). A short biography of A phang gter chen in *Mgo log sman rtsis rig pa'i lo rgyus* gives these four as Sa skya gong ma chen po Aḥ yu vajra, the birth name of the current Sakya Trizin; Sprul sku bu lo, the son of a Golok chieftain; Sprul sku Tshe bo, alias 'Jigs med dbang brag rdo rje, the nephew of A phang gter chen; and Nam sprul rin po che (A bu dkar lo et al. 2000: 213). This identification also appears prominently in A bu dkar lo's 2001 *rnam thar* of the couple, *Jewel Lantern of Blessings*, and more obscurely in *Jewel Garland*, which was published in 1997.

50. This information can be found in *The Concise History of Tsimda Gompa*. Additionally, in reference to his first child, a short biography of A phang gter chen states, "The reincarnation of Phuntsok Jungne, anointed a mahāsiddha, was born but did not survive" (*grub chen sku bar phun tshogs 'byung gnas kyi yang srid cig 'khrung kyang sku tshe mtha' ma 'khyol*, A bu dkar lo et al. 2000: 213).

51. A 'dzoms 'brug sprul 'Gyur med rdo rje. A 'dzom 'brug pa was a Klong chen snying thig lineage master, whose encampment was known as A 'dzom chos sgar in Khams. He passed away in 1924, and Tulku Thondup records his principal reincarnation as 'Brug sprul rin po che in a brief account of his life (1996: 228–29).

52. Wa shul dpon bla bsod nams 'gyur med gyi yang srid Dbang chen nyi ma; his tertön name was Gter chen Sgrib bral rig pa'i rdo rje.

53. Mdo rin po che Khams gsum zil gnon dgyes pa rdo rje'i yang srid Thub bstan chos kyi nyi ma. Mdo rin po che Khams gsum zil gnon dgyes pa rdo rje (1890–1939) was the grandson of Mdo mkhyen brtse Ye shes rdo rje, born to his son and lineage holder Rig pa'i ral gri. This identification was not accepted by the family of Mdo mkhyen brtse, according to the *rnam thar* of Mdo Zla gsal dbang mo by Thub bstan chos dar in *Mdo mkhyen brtse ye shes rdo rje'i gdung rgyud rim byon gyi rnam thar* (Mi nyag: Tibetological Publishing House of China, 2008).

54. SVF 1997: 132.5–10. The term I translate "celestial realms" is *mkha' spyod zhing*, the land of the khecarīs.

55. Note that the term for "secret consort" (*gsang yum*) often implies a wife or lifelong partner. As an example, Tā re lhamo's mother, Dam tshig sgrol ma, was herself considered to be a speech emanation (*gsung sprul*) of Ye shes mtsho rgyal (SVF 131.5–6). Within the Rnying ma tradition, there seems to be no problem with more than one person, even mother and daughter, being emanations of the same figure. After all, in the life story of Ye shes mtsho rgyal, revealed by Stag sham nus ldan rdo rje, Ye shes mtsho rgyal promises to bring forth myriad emanations in each generation.

56. Janet Gyatso (2006: 13) emphasizes the importance of identification with Ye shes mtsho rgyal as a means to recognize exceptional Tibetan women as follows:

"There can be no question that the story of Ye shes mtsho rgyal not only provided for Tibetans a template for the ideal female religious life, it also created a reference point for the identification and legitimation of female hierarchs and masters. One of the few ways to recognize a talented woman in Tibetan religious society has been to declare her an emanation of Ye shes mtsho rgyal."

57. SVF 131.4–132.1. A series of prophecies follows in SVF 132.1–17.

58. While it is not uncommon in Golok for a Buddhist figure to have overlapping past-life identities, it is unusual for those identities to crisscross gender. Most frequently in Tibetan areas, though there seems to be no doctrinal rationale for this, religious figures maintain the same gender across lifetimes. Of course, there are notable exceptions, such as Ma gcig lab sgron, reputed to be the reincarnation of an Indian monk, or Klong chen pa Dri med 'od zer and his reincarnations, who trace their past lives to Pad ma gsal, the reputed daughter of the Tibetan king Khri srong lde'u btsan. These cases are unusual, and it is especially rare to hear of a male Tibetan monastic taking rebirth as a woman.

59. On the date of Se ra mkha' 'gro's passing, see Jacoby 2009/2010. Tashi Tsering provides the dates 1892–1940 for Se ra mkha' 'gro, based upon a biography written by Bya bral rin po che (www.tbrc.org). *Spiraling Vine of Faith* gives the date as 1937 in an effort to harmonize her death with the birth year of Tā re lha mo.

60. In *Khra dge slong tshul khrims dar rgyas kyi gsung rtsom gces bsgrigs*, the foreword provides a short biography of Khra dge slong life and gives his dates as 1866–1937 ('Ju skal bzang 2000: 1–17).

61. There is a phenomenon known as *ma 'das pa'i sprul sku*, a reincarnation appointed prior to death, that could account for this situation in emic terms. That said, I have not heard this term used in reference to Tā re lha mo. *Spiraling Vine of Faith* lists the death of Se ra mkha' 'gro as 1937 in order to avoid this discrepancy, though its reproduction in the 2013 paperback addition of the couple's treasure corpus and in *'Phags bod kyi skyes chen ma dag gi rnam par thar ba pad ma dkar po'i phreng ba* (vol. 12: 121–54) corrects the date to 1940.

62. SVF 134.2–153.2.

63. There are at least two other Se ra mkha' 'gro emanations, including Rdzong gter Kun bzang nyi ma's daughter Lha lcam Chos kyi sgrol ma (Pad ma 'od gsal mtha' yas 2003: 73) and Bya bral rin po che's daughter Sarasvatī (Tulku Thondup 1996: 297). See the epilogue to Jacoby 2014a for a complete list. There are also at least two other Khra dge slong incarnations, including Tulku Thondup, who resides in Cambridge, MA, and A khu Chos dbyings, who resides in Rta'u, the prefecture capital of Mgo log (personal communication from these two figures).

64. The genre of *rnam thar* contains various types of life writing that differ in style and content. For an overview, see Gyatso 1998: 6–8 and 101–23. Life stories may also be called *rtogs brjod* or "expressions of realization" (Skt.: *avadāna*). While *rtogs brjod* can refer to secular biographical works, *rnam thar* remains the principal genre label for rendering the lives of Buddhist saints in Tibet.

65. As Janet Gyatso puts it, *rnam thar* "share the presumption—or at least the suggestion—that the protagonist reached full liberation" (1998: 103).

66. Despite overlaps and commonalities between biographical and autobiographical writing, Janet Gyatso highlights one crucial difference: "The self-written life

account, due to powerful constraints in Tibetan linguistic convention on how one should talk about oneself, typically exhibits a studied diffidence, whereas the life written by someone else typically exhibits an equally studied reverence" (1998: 105).

67. Geary 1996: 15. On the comparative usage of the term "saint," see Hawley 1987 and Kieckhefer and Bond 1988. On the *gter ston* as a category of saint, see my introduction to Harding 2003.

68. This salvific power can manifest in the ascribed efficacy of their prayers and ritual performance as well as the blessings understood to emanate from relics and other objects associated with them. See Geary 1978, Tambiah 1984, and Strong 1987.

69. Schaeffer 2004: 51.

70. Quintman 2014, especially chapters 4 and 5.

71. According to from Pad ma 'od gsal mtha' yas, in writing *Spiraling Vine of Faith*, he particularly sought out elders in the community in and around Gser rta who were considered to be reliable authorities, including the personal attendant of Tā re lha mo's family when she was a child (personal communication, June 2006).

72. LaFleur 1987: 220–24. LaFleur prefers the term "sacred biography" to "hagiography" in his essay.

73. This claim comes in the authorial statement in *Jewel Garland* but arguably pertains to the volume as a whole. He insists that he records what was recounted to him without distortion by exaggerating or minimizing (*sgro bskur*) and without deceit (*zol sbyor*), bias (*phyogs zhen*), or adulation (*bstod 'dod*). See JG 4.5–10.

74. See Hawley's introduction to *Saints and Virtues* (1987) and Eliade's chapter on "Archetypes and Repetition" in *The Myth of the Eternal Return* (1954).

75. See Jacoby 2009/2010, which focuses on the extensive version of Se ra mkha' 'gro's autobiography, a manuscript in more than 400 folios, titled *Dbus mo bde ba'i rdo rje'i rnam par thar pa nges 'byung 'dren pa'i shing rta skal ldan dad pa'i mchod sdong.*

76. The well-known version of the life of Ye shes mtsho rgyal, *Bod kyi jo mo ye shes mtsho rgyal gyi mdzad tshul rnam par thar pa gab pa mngon byung rgyud mangs dri za'i glu phreng* by Stag sham Nus ldan rdo rje 1972, has been translated in Padmakara Translation Group 2002 and Keith Dowman 1996.

77. For a study of Chos kyi sgron ma's life and incarnation line, see Diemberger 2007.

78. Schaeffer 2004; 132, 180, 184.

79. Suzanne Bessenger suggests that her *rnam thar* may have been one of the first instances of claiming emanation status for a Tibetan woman as a female tantric deity. She details how Bsod nams dpal 'dren's "divine status" (2010: 43) as the emanation of Vajrayoginī and her associated form, Vajravārāhī, is emphasized in the opening lines, statements attributed to Bsod nams dpal 'dren, and posthumous visions of her by her husband Rin chen dpal. See her "Echoes of Enlightenment: The Life and Legacy of Sonam Peldren" (Ph.D. diss,, University of Virginia, 2010).

80. Diemberger 2007: 151. Though Chos kyi sgron ma's *rnam thar* does not have a comparable prophetic cast, her hagiographer continually reminds the reader of the exalted status of the heroine as an emanation of Vajravārāhī, through epithets such as "the emanation body" (*sprul ba'i sku can*), "the wisdom ḍākinī" (*ye shes mkha' 'gro*), and simply Rdo rje rnal 'byor ma (Skt.: Vajrayoginī), the female deity of which Vajravārāhī is one form. These reminders are reinforced by legitimating

statements by male figures peppered throughout, most importantly her identification as Vajravārāhī by both Bo dong phyogs las rnam rgyal and Thang stong rgyal po (185 and 223). According to Diemberger, later sources make a past life connection between Chos kyi sgron ma and Bsod nams dpal 'dren (257), and Bessenger explores this issue further in 2010: 258 ff.

81. SVF 135.2–4. That her hagiographer does not feel the need to describe these "faults" implies a well-established negative stereotype of women. Since her hagiographer is a monk, such a stereotype may well derive from long-standing misogynist depictions of women in Buddhist monastic literature. For early examples in Buddhist monastic literature from India, dated to the post-Aśokan period, see Wilson 1996. Schaeffer discusses this issue in Tibetan literary contexts in 2004: 92 ff.

82. The historicity of Ye shes mtsho rgyal has yet to be established. For an examination of the evolution of her life story, see Gyatso 2006.

83. This identification is made explicit in Rig 'dzin dar rgyas' new life story of Tā re lha mo, currently in the process of being finalized.

84. In her youth, up through the age of eighteen, her principal epithet is the "supreme maiden" (*sras mo mchog*); after that point, it switches to the "supreme khandro" (*mkha' 'gro mchog*).

85. We must be careful how we understand this multivalent symbol in relation to the lives of actual historical Tibetan women. As the editors of the volume *Immaculate and Powerful: The Female in Sacred Image and Reality* (Atkinson et al. 1985) pointed out long ago, positive female religious symbols do not automatically imply a high standing for women in society; rather, such symbols serve as resources that must be appropriated by situated actors. In other words, religious symbols that valorize the feminine, in and of themselves, tell us nothing about the status of women in a given social context; one must inquire into how such symbols are appropriated—whether by or on behalf of particular women.

86. As non-monastics, *grub thob* or *mkha' 'gro ma* may or may not be considered emanations of past masters and frequently have not received scholastic training in the monastery.

87. SVF 106.8–12.

88. At the end of the text she is also characterized as the "magical emanation" (*sgyu 'phrul*) of Vajravārāhī (SVF 157.8–10).

89. The two accumulations are merit (Skt.: *puṇya*; Tib.: *bsod nams*) and wisdom (Skt.: *jñāna*; Tib.: *ye shes*); the two obscurations are emotional obscurations (Skt.: *kleśāvaraṇa*; Tib.: *nyon mongs pa'i sgrib pa*) and cognitive obscurations (Skt.: *jñeyāvaraṇa*; Tib.: *shes bya'i sgrib pa*).

90. Between the past life genealogy (JG 5.11–6.7), which is a formal list in verse form, a text called "The Garland of Births Supplication: A Beautiful Strand of Lotuses" (*Sku 'phreng gsol 'debs pad ma'i phreng mdzes*), and the short account of his predecessor's life (JG: 8.10–9.6), there are approximately three pages of prophecies regarding Nam sprul rin po che's status as an emanation of Nam mkha'i snying po and Rig 'dzin rgod ldem.

91. JG 19.13–20.9. I take *dung* to mean *dung phyur* or "one hundred million."

92. The creation stage (*bskyed rim*) and completion stage (*rdzogs rim*) practices are detailed in Harding 1996.

93. This distinction is based on whether the revelation is understood to primarily derive from the deep reaches of the mind or from a location in the Tibetan landscape, where it was reportedly hidden by Padmasambhava or Ye shes mtsho rgyal. The process of revelation and the way these categories overlap will be discussed in chapter 3. See Doctor 2005 for an extensive typology of treasures.

94. Later in the chapter, I will discuss a moment in *Spiraling Vine of Faith* that could be identified as Tā re lha mo's liberation, but it is displaced to a vision and does not highlight her own achievement in the same way.

95. Like her identification with female tantric deities, Tā re lha mo's past lives as the merchant's daughter and Gaṅgādevī can be traced to her primary identification with Ye shes mtsho rgyal. Conze identifies Gaṅgādevī as the Goddess of the Ganges, citing Maitra, Vogel, and Coomaraswamy for evidence of the Gaṅgā as a river goddess (1968: 173 note 2). However, this figure is described in *Prajñāpāramitā* literature as Gaṅgādeva *bhaginī* (Tib.: *sring mo gang gā'i lha mo*), indicating the name of a woman rather than a goddess (Kimura 1990, 4: 189–92 and Harrison 1987: 88 note 9). On this figure, see also Paul 1985 and Sunim 1999.

96. While *Spiraling Vine of Faith* alludes to these figures, it does not mention that the transformation of the merchant's daughter and Gaṅgādevī into bodhisattvas and future buddhas entails a sex change. In the *Aṣṭasāhasrikā Prajñāpāramitā Sūtra*, the daughter of a merchant and her retinue of five hundred female attendants magically transform into men immediately following the Dharmodgata's prediction of their future buddhahood (Paul 1985: 115–34), and in the Gaṅgādevī chapter of the *Mahāprajñāpāramitā Sūtra* and the *Aṣṭasāhasrikā Prajñāpāramitā Sūtra*, the Buddha predicts that Gaṅgādevī will be reborn male in the next life (Paul 1985: 180–84; Conze 1973: 219–21; Kimura 1990, 4: 189–92; and Conze 1975: 422–23). In both cases, according to a common trope in Mahāyāna literature, sexual transformation is depicted as a prerequisite to entering buddha fields, which acknowledges women's aspiration to strive for buddhahood but denies the possibility of realizing that goal in a female body. These Mahāyāna literary figures may be somewhat ironic choices as female antecedents for Tā re lha mo (and for Ye shes mtsho rgyal before her) because their gender is explicitly disavowed through their sexual transformation.

97. Recall that she is a "joint emanation" of Se ra mkha' 'gro (female) and Khra dge slong (male), and others of her past lives crisscross gender boundaries as well. A combination of male and female figures are listed in an excerpted "garland of lives" (*skye phreng*), which covers the millennium between Ye shes mtsho rgyal and Se ra mkha' 'gro by mentioning only six of her previous lives. Following Ye shes mtsho rgyal, her lives include: Ne'u chung at the time of the legendary king Ge sar; the female siddha Lakṣmīṅkarā in India; a "conch bearer" named Vajradeva to the north; a learned man named Sīla in eastern Tibet; two other figures who are difficult to place geographically, Dpal kyi blo gros and Bshad sgrub bstan pa'i nyi ma; and finally Se ra mkha' 'gro, referred to by the name Sukha (the Sanskrit for *bde ba* in Bde ba'i rdo rje). While Ye shes mtsho rgyal, Ne'u chung, Lakṣmīṅkarā, and Se ra mkha' 'gro are well-known female figures, the other names are more commonly male but not easily identifiable. An almost entirely different list is given in the abbreviated *rnam thar* of Tā re lha mo and Nam sprul rin po che, *Jewel Lantern of Blessings*, published in 2001 by A bu dkar lo. It repeats several past identifications, including Ye shes mtsho rgyal,

Ne'u chung, and Se ra mkha' 'gro, while adding four female antecedents (Karmadevī in India, Kālasiddhi in Nepal, Ma cig Zhi ba mtsho in Zangs ri, and a Mi 'gyur dpal sgron from Khams) and one male antecedent (Bdud 'dul rol ba rtsal to the south in present-day Bhutan). It is unclear what to make of this inconsistency, other than that Tā re lha mo's past life genealogy is somewhat indeterminate beyond her identification with Ye shes mtsho rgyal, Ne'u chung, Khra dge slong, and Se ra mkha' 'gro. Her correspondence with Nam sprul rin po che adds other past life associations beyond these, to be discussed in chapter 3.

98. Townsend, "Buddhism's Worldly Other: Secular Subjects of Tibetan Learning," in a special issue of the journal *Himalaya* on "The Secular in Tibetan Cultural Worlds," *Himalaya* 36, no. 1 (2016): 130–44, co-edited by Nicole Willock and Holly Gayley. This point was also raised by Alison Melnick in her paper at the 2015 American Academy of Religion conference (see note 99 below).

99. Alison Melnick, "Female Authority and the Lives of Women in Eighteenth-Century Tibet: Reading Hagiography as History," a paper presented in the panel "Female Lives and Narratives in Tibet: New Materials and New Perspectives," American Academy of Religion conference, Atlanta, November 21–24, 2015.

100. Jacoby 2014a: 80–91. Jacoby emphasizes that the inspiration for this opening can be traced to the well-known *rnam thar* of Ye shes mtsho rgyal, revealed by Stag sham Nus ldan rdo rje.

101. Stag sham Nus ldan rdo rje 1972: 134.1–137.3. Much of the sixth chapter of *Bod kyi jo mo ye shes mtsho rgyal gyi mdzad tshul rnam par thar pa gab pa mngon byung rgyud mngas dri za'i glu phreng* (134.3–136.3) is excerpted verbatim in SVF 107.13–109.8.

102. Se ra mkha' 'gro's abbreviated autobiography is titled *Ku su lu'i nyams byung gi gnas tshul mdor bsdus rdo rje'i spun gyis dris lan mos pa'i lam bzang* (Se ra mkha' 'gro Bde ba'i rdo rje 1978, 4: 103–29). The text is excerpted verbatim starting on 104.3 and ending on 128.5, omitting the opening verses and colophon. For a study of Se ra mkha' 'gro's full-length autobiography, see Jacoby 2014a. Note that in *Spiraling Vine of Faith*, Se ra mkha' 'gro is referred to by her aliases, Bde ba'i rdo rje and Kun bzang bde skyongs chos nyid dbang mo.

103. Taking up two pages in *Spiraling Vine of Faith*, it functions as a mnemonic of sorts, reminding readers of the highlights of Ye shes mtsho rgyal's life, and would be incomprehensible to someone not already familiar with her story. Mentioning her so-called "eight trials" (*dka' ba brgyad*) in passing, the verses focus instead on her "signs of accomplishment" (*grub rtags*).

104. SVF 108. 12. According to Jigme Linpga 2007, the *vidyādhara* with mastery over life (*tshe dbang rig 'dzin*, abbreviated in the excerpted prophecy as *tshe'i rig 'dzin*) is the second in four stages of accomplishment as a vidyādhara, signifying the attainment of the path of seeing, the third of the five paths and equivalent to the first *bhumī*.

105. Stag sham Nus ldan rdo rje 1972: 136.2 and SVF 109.6–7.

106. SVF 109.8–14. One might wonder if this perspective is offered in order to assure the reader of Tā re lha mo's own parity with Nam sprul rin po che, though he is primarily identified as an emanation of Nam mkha'i snying po rather than Padmasambhava himself. Sarah Jacoby suggests that in a comparable statement in Se ra

mkha' 'gro's autobiographical writings, "equality" (*mnyam pa*) should be viewed as mutuality rather than equal status between tantric partners (2014a: 287 ff).

107. For an overview of the genre of *mgur*, see Jackson 1996.

108. Gyatso 2006: 1.

109. The female *gter stons*, Jo mo sman mo and Kun dga' 'bum pa, are both identified with Ye shes mtsho rgyal in their short biographies in Kong sprul's *Gter ston brgya rtsa'i rnam thar*: 'Jam mgon kong sprul Blo gros mtha' yas 2007–8, 1: 538–43 and 547–49 respectively. See Jacoby 2014a and Schneider 2015 on Se ra mkha' 'gro and Mkha' 'gro Chos spyan respectively.

110. This literally reads "the land of Tibet and the world, upper, middle, and lower" (*bod yul 'dzam gling stod smad bar*). I take the emphasis to be the three domains of cultural Tibet, whereby "upper" refers to western Tibet (*Mnga' ri*), "middle" to central Tibet (*Dbus gtsang*), and "lower" to eastern Tibet (*Mdo khams*).

111. Stag sham Nus ldan rdo rje 1972: 135.4–6 and SVF 108.13–109.2.

112. See Monson 2013 and Jacoby 2014b. Bibliographic information for this text can be found in note 102 above.

113. For this, I would refer the reader to Jacoby 2009/2010, 2014a, and 2014b.

114. Se ra mkha' 'gro's past life genealogy is given briefly in the opening lines of her autobiography as excerpted in *Spiraling Vine of Faith*. While they share a common identification as emanations of Ye shes mtsho rgyal, the list of figures contains several names that do not match those claimed for Tā re lha mo, including Ut pal ma, Ro lang bde rol, and Byang chub sgron. See SVF 110.16–111.1.

115. Stag sham Nus ldan rdo rje 1972: 134.2–3 and SVF 107: 13–14.

116. SVF 142.6.

117. Her long autobiography takes a different approach by opening with an extended account of how Ye shes mtsho rgyal and other female figures from the same period manifested as precursors to Se ra mkha' 'gro. See Jacoby 2014a: 80–91.

118. For the fascinating details of this and other portions of Se ra mkha' 'gro's life, see Jacoby 2009/2010 and 2014a.

119. Sarah Jacoby describes how Se ra mkha' 'gro's "self-deprecating comments . . . occasion responses from many other human and superhuman figures who defend and encourage her," thereby asserting the validity of her actions through the voices of others. Jacoby 2014a: 132 ff.

120. Schaeffer 2004: 131–32.

121. SVF 116.3–4.

122. SVF 117.4–8.

123. Jacoby discusses moments like this in Se ra mkha' 'gro's autobiographical writings as follows: "Thematizing her 'inferior female body' is more than an internalization of the misogynist views of her social milieu because it has the subversive effect of occasioning responses from others that articulate highly positive views of women. I suggest that this dual tone of Se ra mkha' 'gro's repeated laments about her female body are intentional; by drawing attention to her 'inferior' status as a woman, she both mitigated others' potential criticism and defended herself in writing from the charge of overestimating her social status and religious authority" (2009/2010: 128–29).

124. The response from Yum chen mo can be found in SVF 117.11–119.4, and the line translated here comes from SVF 118.12–4. I use "coincidence" to translate

rten 'brel, shorthand for *pratītyasamutpāda* (*rten cing 'brel bar 'byung ba*), but carrying other valences as well in colloquial speech and in the treasure tradition. The valences of this term and my choice of translation are discussed in chapter 4.

125. When the reader finally arrives at the story of her birth, A phang gter chen is given pride of place, referred to as "the undisputed great tertön, a renowned emanation" (*rtsod med yongs grags kyi sprul pa'i gter chen*), and his robust past life genealogy is inserted, accentuating his stature (SVF 133.1–11).

126. SVF 134. 12–4.

127. SVF 136.14–137.8.

128. SVF 138.1–5.

129. SVF 135.2–8.

130. SVF 135.8–15. The source of the passage is not given.

131. SVF 136.6–9. This is the only prophecy recorded in *Spiraling Vine of Faith* to associate her with Ne'u chung.

132. SVF 137.9–15.

133. SVF 138.8–139.4. As mentioned in note 63, the identification for Lha lcam Chos kyi sgrol ma with Se ra mkha' 'gro can be found in Pad ma 'od gsal mtha' yas 2003: 73.

134. I discuss Nam sprol rin po che's youth more in the next chapter.

135. This vision can be found in SVF 153.8–154.5.

2. Local Heroine: The Hagiography of Cultural Trauma

1. Ban Wang 2004: 100, drawing on Walter Benjamin's famous analysis of the "Angelus Novus" in "Theses on the Philosophy of History" in Benjamin 1969.

2. SVF 140. 3–8 and 142: 7–13. The person being rescued in the latter episode is given as Mgar ra rgyal sras. This is likely the same figure mentioned in *Jewel Garland* and discussed in chapter 5, i.e., Pad ma tshe dbang (b. 1927), the son of Mgar ra rgyal sras Pad ma rnam rgyal (A bu dkar lo et al. 2000: 246–49).

3. Jackson 2002. See my discussion of his views in the introduction.

4. I have seen this term in other contemporary works by Pad ma 'od gsal mtha' yas, such as his *rnam thar* of Rdzong gter Kun bzang nyi ma, where he proposes that the purpose of narrating a *rnam thar* is "the restoration of faith in followers" (*rjes 'jug dad pa'i gsos*). Pad ma 'od gsal mtha' yas 2000: 105.

5. Trauma, according to Judith Herman, "overwhelms systems that give people a sense of control, connection and meaning" (Herman 1997: 33). The "blow to the psyche" that occurs in individual trauma has been compared by Kai Erikson to the "blow to the basic tissues of social life" in collective trauma, including the social fabric and shared cultural values (1995: 187). See also Bessel van der Kolk 1996: 279.

6. Smelser 2004: 38.

7. Ban Wang 2004: 113–14. On the Cultural Revolution as trauma, see also Dittmer 1991 and Choy 2008. One could argue that all Tibetans had left during this period was their "culture's repertoire of representational and expressive means," but they

were not allowed to utilize these publicly until the 1980s, following liberalization in the economic and cultural arenas. I discuss how Tā re lha mo and Nam sprul rin po che draw on their cultural repertoire in subsequent chapters.

8. De Vries 1996: 400.

9. Kay Schaeffer and Sidone Smith note that it took thirty years for testimonials about the Holocaust to "reach a discursive threshold of intelligibility" and "unifying discursive framework" to become part of public discourse (2004: 19–23). For this reason, the authors of *Cultural Trauma and Collective Identity* (in particular, Alexander 2004) make a mistake when they suggest that trauma narratives should be a prerequisite for identifying a cataclysmic event as collective trauma. Groundbreaking research by Judith Herman and others suggests otherwise, that narratives signal the process of healing from trauma.

10. Das and Kleinman 2001: 3.

11. Makley 2007. It would be difficult to estimate the number of *rnam thar* chronicling the lives of contemporary religious figures that have been published by Tibetans within the PRC in recent years, as many are produced and distributed locally through monasteries. More widely distributed in Mgo log are collections and edited volumes that recover the histories of local lineages and abbreviated life stories of local masters of the previous generation and beyond. See for example, Pad ma 'od gsal mtha' yas 2003 and A bu dkar lo, Dung gces, and Gsang bdag tshe ring 2000.

12. SVF 140. The Tibetan reads: *rkyen ngan grogs su khug.*

13. SVF 139.16–17. The Tibetan reads: *dus kyi yo lang drag pos skyid sdug sna tshogs 'dres mar snang . . .*

14. A number of exile testimonials testify to the initial hesitation that ordinary Tibetans feel at narrating their own lives. See for example prefaces by the author in Palden Gyatso 1997, Hortsang Jigme 1998, and Tubten Khétsun 2008.

15. See Gyatso 1997.

16. The definition for the term *zhwa nag* in the TTC reads: "a classification assigned to an elevated figure, namely a criminal charge or bad reputation" (*nyes ming ngam / ming ngan gzugs su bkod pa'i don*). I translate *gzugs* as "elevated figure," as it denotes the honorific for "body," thereby implying a person of high standing. The accompanying example suggests the innocence of such figures: "A black hat was placed on a virtuous person" (*mi dkar po la zhwa nag g.yogs pa*). Other unrelated definitions refer to the ritual use of a black hat in sacred dances (*'cham*) and its reference to the Bka' brgyud hierarch, the Kar ma pa, who is the bearer of a black ceremonial crown reputedly made of ḍākinī hair (TTC 2407).

17. Horlemann attributes the sharp decline in livestock and unprecedented famine to "a combination of negligence, mismanagement, and the establishment of unviable agricultural state farms and factories" (2002: 248).

18. Horlemann 2002: 248.

19. On the relative prosperity of nomadic pastoralists in Golok, see Eckvall 1968: 94–97.

20. Tsering Shakya 1999: 267. His account is based on a biography of the Tenth Paṇ chen bla ma that was published following his death in 1989 by the Oriental Publishing House in Beijing and then withdrawn from circulation in the wake of the Tiananmen Square protests that same year.

21. Ibid., 271. In 1962, during a time when top leadership was open to criticism, the Paṇ chen bla ma issued a 70,000-Character Petition to the Central Committee in which he complained about the "endangering of Tibetan people as a nationality" due to the decline in population, imprisonment of young men, and the repression of Buddhism. See Tibet Information Network 1997. The Paṇ chen bla ma was purged in 1964 and did not reemerge in public again until 1978.

22. The impact of the Great Leap Forward and the magnitude of the famine was not known until the 1980s, when census information first became available. Scholars disagree on the death toll, and diverse positions are summarized in Yang 2008.

23. Li and Yang 2005.

24. Yang 2008.

25. SVF 140.9–10. The Tibetan reads: *ri thang kun tu mi ro dang rta ro gcal du bkram.*

26. One can only detect that Tā re lha mo spent much of her twenties and thirties tending livestock and performing manual labor from the contexts evoked in several scenes; there is just one explicit reference to her life during that time as a herder (*phyugs rdzi*). See SVF 144.1.

27. Tubten Khétsun 2008: 142. Sparrows were regarded as problematic because they ate grain seeds, but it was not adequately understood that they mainly consumed insects. In an attempt to bolster grain production, sparrows were chased away and their nests destroyed. Of course, the irony of this ill-conceived campaign was that the attack on sparrows led to an increase in the locust population, compounding the problems of grain shortfalls provoked by collectivization and the Great Leap Forward (Shapiro 2001).

28. Tsering Shakya 1999: 321.

29. SVF 140.15–141.9.

30. See McGranahan 2010.

31. See Goldstein 1999 and Shakya 1999. A photograph taken in September 1966 of the Jo khang Temple in the heart of Lha sa vividly illustrates its desecration, showing smashed religious paraphernalia strewn across the courtyard. This photograph was first published in Woeser's book, *Forbidden Memory: Tibet During the Cultural Revolution.* It has been reproduced on http://voyage.typepad.com/china/2007/04/tibet_during_th.html and in Tubten Khétsun 2008: 172.

32. Don grub dbang rgyal and Nor sde 1992: 106. These monasteries, referred to as the "eight great monasteries" (*dgon pa che gras brgyad*), were Dpal yul dgon pa, Rwa rgya dgon pa, Khra gling dgon pa, Snyan mo dgon pa, Shar 'od dgon pa, Stong skyabs rdo kha dgon pa, Yar thang rgya dgon pa, and Drub chen dgon pa. The decision to reopen select monasteries occurred at the provincial level by the Northwest Minorities Affairs Council.

33. Ibid., 106.

34. Knight 2006 and Link 2000.

35. In describing scar literature, Ban Wang has noted the impulse toward "recovering and recreating alternative, livable histories" in an "outpouring of fiction works that address the remembrance of things past—personal incidents, family sagas, local traditions, and regional lore—that testified to memory as a way to fill the gaps left by the official history" (2004: 108).

36. This Tibetan term was coined by Go po Lin in the journal *Light Rain* (*Sbrang char*) in 1989 (Tsering Shakya 2008: 75). For a brief overview of Tibetan scar literature, see Tsering Shakya 2008.

37. On the topic of Tibetan life writings in English, see McMillin 2001.

38. For example, see Tubten Khétsen 2008.

39. The birth of exile testimonials gives some clue to their purport, given their genesis in refugee camps along the Indian border, where interviews with refugees were first organized in 1959 to be compiled and submitted as evidence to the International Commission of Jurists in 1960 (McMillin 2001: 131). This work of gathering oral testimonials and histories has continued up to the present through the Oral History Project at the Library of Tibetan Works and Archives in Dharamsala, India, founded in 1976, and testimonials for human rights claims have also continued.

40. For example, see Palden Gyatso 1997: 232.

41. SPV 140.4–5. The Tibetan reads: *spyi mthun las kyi dbang gis yul khams yongs la mu ges ha cang gdung ba.*

42. JG 17.11–12. The Tibetan reads: *bod lcags byi lor spyi mthun las kyi dbang gis yul khams spyi dang bye brag kun la mu ges gzir.*

43. SVF 145.10–11. The Tibetan reads: *gangs ljongs bsod nams kyi mkha' la yang dar bstan pa'i nyi gzhon shar ba.*

44. Note that there is no comparable end frame for this period in *Jewel Garland*.

45. The Tibetan term for the Cultural Revolution, *rig gnas gsar brje*, appears once in *Spiraling Vine of Faith* (SVF 140.15).

46. In Tibetan contexts, the balance of one's good and evil deeds is said to be reckoned by Yama, the "lord of death" (*gshin rje*), who determines whether the consciousness ascends to the higher realms of rebirth to become a god, demigod, or human or descends to the lower realms to become an animal, hungry ghost, or denizen of hell. These realms are graphically depicted in the Wheel of Existence (Skt.: *bhavacakra*; Tib.: *srid pa'i 'khor lo*), a mural routinely found at temples on Buddhist monastery grounds in Tibetan areas. Teiser 2007 has recently traced the history of iconographic depictions of the *bhavacakra*.

47. McDermott 1976.

48. On the modernist deployment of "national karma" in Southeast Asia, see McDermott 1976.

49. See Almond 1998: 84–90 on the variety and range of Victorian reactions to the doctrines of karma and rebirth. Wimal Dissanayake makes a similar point in Ames 1994: 271–78.

50. For Peter Berger, the threat of anomy is a social concern "endemic to the human condition," such that a foundational project for any human society is constructing a "meaningful order," or nomos, which is at once a social order and cosmic order. In his view, religion offers a "sacred canopy" to stave off the threat of anomy and chaos by investing the social order with meaning and legitimating it through divine or transcendent authority. Religion plays an important shielding role during times of upheaval and misfortune for both individuals and society by offering "a plausible theodicy" such that "entire collectives are thus permitted to integrate anomic events, acute or chronic, into the nomos associated with their society" (1990: 58ff.).

51. Keyes 1983.

52. See Weber 1958: 121 and Berger 1990: 67.

53. One cannot underestimate the importance of maintaining systems of meaning in the face of tragedy; as Clifford Geertz suggestions, the loss of meaning is no less than the "greatest of human fears" (1973: 83–85).

54. Indeed, there were armed insurrections throughout A mdo and Khams resisting the Chinese occupation during the mid-1950s.

55. I employ the Tibetan rendering for Tā re lha mo's age as given in *Spiraling Vine of Faith*. In Tibetan, age is counted by the year that a person is entering rather than the year that he or she just completed. So when Tā re lha mo is twenty-two in the Tibetan rendering, she is twenty-one by the international standard, and the year is 1959. Likewise, when she is forty-one in the text, the year is 1978.

56. SVF 139.16–140.3.

57. SVF 140.5–6. The Tibetan reads: *mi 'dzad nam mkha' mdzod la mnga' dbang bsgyur ba'i grub thob mo*. This could also refer to her mastery of a tantric ritual to garner wealth.

58. One difference is that the term *siddha* is a Buddhist paradigm that connotes tantric mastery in human terms, whereas her status as a *mkha' 'gro ma* emphasizes her divinization as an emanation of female deities.

59. SVF 140.3–8.

60. SVF 140.8–15. In my translation, I left out the phrase *phyi nang* (outer and inner) describing the five ḍākinīs, as it is unclear to me what it adds to the scene. For a discussion of the outer, inner, and secret dimensions of the ḍākinī as a symbol in Tibetan Buddhism, see Simmer-Brown 2002.

61. It strikes me that the interpretation of the vultures as the five ḍākinīs is integral to the story, rather than a gloss by her hagiographer, and I heard a similar account recounted by locals in Pad ma during field research.

62. SVF 141.9–13.

63. This example would entail a transformation of the emotional state of fear (Skt.: *bhaya*, Tib.: *'jigs pa*) into the aesthetic experience of apprehension (Skt.: *bhayānaka*, Tib.: *'jigs rung nyams*).

64. This would entail a transformation of the emotional state of amazement (Skt.: *vismaya*; Tib.: *ngo mtshar ba*) into the aesthetic experience of wonder or marvel (Skt.: *adbhuta*; Tib.: *rmad byung nyams*).

65. The portrayal of amazement in relation to faith can be traced in Buddhist literature back to the *Jātakamālā* of Ārya Śūra, a Buddhist classic in courtly Sanskrit depicting the past lives of the Buddha, in which his virtuous conduct across lifetimes is repeatedly hailed as a source of amazement. The *Jātakamālā* has been translated by Peter Khoroche, who dates Ārya Śūra to the fourth century C.E., in *Once the Buddha Was a Monkey* (1989).

66. Iser 1980: 86–103.

67. Ibid., 93.

68. JG 17.14–15. The Tibetan reads: *khyed la gnas skabs sdug bsngal tsam snang yang nga ni khyed dang skad cig tsam la yang 'bral ma myong*. The whole episode can be found in JG 17.11–18.6.

69. JG 22.11–12. The Tibetan reads: *nyi ma sprin las grol ba bzhin btson nas thar*. The whole episode, including the prophecy from the ḍākinī, takes place in JG: 20.9–22.12.

70. JG 24.14–25.9.

71. JG 18.12–19.12.

72. JG 27.1–7.

73. Rig 'dzin rgod ldem is renowned for founding the tradition of "northern treasures" (*byang gter*). He is also a figure in the past life genealogy of both Nam sprul rin po che and A phang gter chen, Tā re lha mo's father.

74. This episode, from the prophecy by Rig 'dzin rgod ldem through to the statement about the harvest, is found in JG 25.17–26.16.

75. There are four miracles comparable to those in *Spiraling Vine of Faith*, which contain parallel themes. They start in 1974, after he turns thirty years old by Tibetan reckoning, already toward the end of the Maoist period.

76. JG 22.13–23.2. The Tibetan for this is: *nam mkha' mdzod sngags kyi byin rlabs*. This may be the same ritual referenced in the parallel episode in *Spiraling Vine of Faith* discussed above.

77. In this rather idiosyncratic story, Nam sprul rin po che and his attendant perform a gaṇacakra feast associated with *gcod* practice, and *Jewel Garland* notes that vultures that were emanation of the five ḍākinīs arrive to consume the offering (JG 25.9–16).

78. JG 23.11–24.2. I discuss the parallel episode in *Spiraling Vine of Faith* in more detail later in this chapter.

79. Tshul khrims blo gros, *Snyigs dus bstan pa'i gsal byed gcig bu chos rje dam pa yid bzhin nor bu 'jigs med phun tshogs 'byung gnas dpal bzang po'i rnam thar bsdus pa dad pa'i gsos sman* in *Chos rje dam pa yid bzhin nor bu 'jigs med phun tshogs 'byung gnas dpal bzang po'i gsung 'bum* (Hong Kong: Xianggang xinzhi chubanshe, 2002), 3: 364–418. The narration for this period begins on 385.9 and the miracle tale summarized in this paragraph can be found on 385.21–386.15. By contrast, the Chinese version of Mkhan po 'Jigs med phun tshogs's life story, by Mkhan po Bsod dar rgyas, does reference collective karma but also makes more direct statements about the period. See Ganpu Suodajie, *Xueyu dashi jinmei pengcuo fawang zhuang/His Holiness Jigme Phuntsok Rinpoche: A Biography* (Taipei: Zhonghua minguo xuema bala rongsan chengfalin foxuehui, 2001). The English translation of this source can be found online, and the relevant section is: www.khenposodargye.org/2013/03/biography-of-h-h-jigmey-phuntsok-dharmaraja/21.

80. A bu dkar lo, *Gter ston grub pa'i dbang phyug o rgyan sku gsum gling pa'i rnam thar mdo tsam brjod pa ma tshogs rig 'dzin bzhad pa'i rang gdangs* (Zhang kang then mā dpe skrun khang, 2003). Chapter 7 of his *rnam thar* (102–11) is dedicated to this period and has three parts: his maintenance of the bodhisattva vow, his surreptitious practice of the dharma, and his prophetic statements about the future.

81. The information in this paragraph and the next comes from Thub bstan chos dar, *Mdo zla gsal dbang mo'i rnam thar* in *Mdo mkhyen brtse ye shes rdo rje'i gdung rgyud rim byon gyi rnam thar gsal ba'i me long* (Mi nyag: Khrung go'i bod rig pa dpe skrun khang, 2008). My thanks to Gene Smith for giving me a copy of this book. I assisted Ravenna Michalsen with a translation of Mdo zla gsal dbang mo's *rnam thar* for her M.A. thesis, "Daughter of Self-Liberation: Lineage Position and Transmission in the Namthar of Do Dasel Wangmo" (2012), under my supervision at the University of Colorado Boulder. Since then, her *rnam thar* has been translated by Sarah Schneider

in *Luminous Moonlight: The Biography of Do Dasal Wangmo* (Pagosa Springs, CO: Machig Publications, 2013).

82. Thub bstan chos dar 2008: 399.7–9. The Tibetan reads: *khong ni skyes bu dam pa'i rigs su gnas pa dang 'khor 'das mnyam nyid du rtogs pa'i gang zag yin pas bden med sgyu ma lta bu'i chos gang gis kyang gnod pa ga la srid do.*

83. This is a translation by Sarah Jacoby from her article, "Relational Autonomy in the Life of a Contemporary Tibetan Ḍākinī," *Revue d'Etudes Tibétaines* 34 (December 2015): 79–113, about Mkha' 'gro rin po che, based on interviews with her over a period of some years and her short biography as found in Pad ma 'od gsal mtha' yas, *Mdo khams rgyal mo tsha ba rong gi bai ro'i sgrub phug ngo sprod mdor bsdus* (2006). The information in this paragraph is based on Jacoby's article.

84. Tshul krims blo gros 2002 and A bu dkar lo 2003.

85. The newest and unpublished version of Tā re lha mo's life by Rig 'dzin dar rgyas contains far more miracles, more than forty in a single section on "The Manner in Which [She] Displayed the Outer Signs of Accomplishment and Accepted Fortunate Ones [as Followers]" (*grub pa'i rang rtags phyi ru ngoms te skal ldan rjes su 'dzin tshul*) in EGT 9.10–15.10. Because these miracle tales span her entire youth, rather than being clustered to represent the years 1959–78, they do not function in the same way as in *Spiraling Vine of Faith*.

86. EGT 9.35–41.

87. SVF 141.13–142.1.

88. Personal communication from members of the Thar ba family, May 2007.

89. SVF 142.17–143.3.

90. SVF 143.11–17.

91. Although this is the only episode in *Spiraling Vine of Faith* in which Tā re lha mo appeared in the visions of others, it is not an anomaly. An aged doctor in Pad ma County, who spent eighteen years in a Chinese prison, shared with me his account of visiting with Tā re lha mo at night in dreams and keeping relics (a strand of her hair and a gold ring given by her) as a source of solace during those long years. This is recounted in my contribution, "Modern Miracles of a Female Buddhist Master," in *Figures of Buddhist Modernity*, ed. Jeffrey Samuels, Justin McDaniel, and Mark Rowe (Honolulu: University of Hawai'i Press, forthcoming).

92. See previous discussion of the Anti-Sparrow Campaign earlier in this chapter. The local rodent, *a 'bra*, has been a persistent problem in the grasslands of Mgo log. For more details on state policies regarding the *a 'bra*, see Horlemann 2002.

93. SVF 140.15–141.9.

94. SVF 116.2–117.10. This episode was discussed in chapter 1.

95. SVF 142.5–7.

96. For various perspectives on the samaya vow, see chapter IV of *Buddhist Ethics* (Jamgön Kongtrul Lodrö Tayé 1998: 215–306).

97. Germano 1998: 70.

98. SVF 145.5–10.

99. See Tsering Shakya 2008: 75–76.

100. The characterization of her body as indestructible would seem to be sufficient to "explain" this miracle. Nevertheless, a preamble to the story credits her

survival to a protective amulet especially for lightning (*thog srung*) copied from yellow scrolls and offered to her by Mkhan po 'Jigs med phun tshogs in 1978.

101. Personal communication from Rig 'dzin dar rgyas, May 2007. This episode can also be found in EGT 13.31–33. The practice of *gtum mo* outside in frigid temperatures is reminiscent of the test undertaken by those who complete the traditional three-year retreat. Reportedly, retreatants don a wet cotton sheet and demonstrate their master of the practice by drying it overnight.

102. In Buddhist iconography and narratives, the denizens of hells are graphically portrayed being boiled alive in cauldrons, pierced by sharp weapons, and attacked by ghoulish creatures of all sorts. In Tibet, such depictions would be widely known through images of the Wheel of Existence (*srid pa'i 'khor lo*) and through '*das log* accounts of Tibetan revenants who return from traveling in the realms beyond death. On the former, see Teiser 2007, and on the latter, see Pommaret 1989 and Cuevas 2008.

103. SVF 144.11–145.5. Initially she bestows empowerment to Ab rkong mkhan po Blo bzang rdo rje, Dge tshe mkhan po Dbang chen, and Mgar sprul rin po che in order to extend their lives. This is followed by the longer list of those "defenders of the teachings and beings" whose life she extended in the same year, as given in this paragraph.

104. The term I translate here as "defenders" combines the terms for "army" (*dpung*) and "friend" (*gnyen*), which together denote someone such as a protector or guardian who provides aid, backing, or support (TTC 1633).

105. SVF 145.11–14.

106. I use illocutionary force in J. L. Austin's sense according to his 1962 classic, *How to Do Things with Words*.

107. Samten Karmay suggests that the persecution of Buddhism by Glang dar ma focused on monastic institutions and that nonmonastic tantric movements remained vital during the political fragmentation following the dissolution of the Tibetan empire (1998: 8–12).

108. Don grub rgyal 1997: 439 and 485. *Mgo log rig gnas lo rgyus* also inserts the *bar dar* into its periodization (Pad ma tshe ring 2004, 4: 139–44).

109. Though David Germano does not note the usage of the term *yang dar*, he discusses associations by Tibetans of the Maoist period with the dark age between the early and later propagations (1998: 88–94).

110. Pad ma tshe ring 2004, 4: 144. The Tibetan for these phrases reads: *thub pa'i bstan pa la nyams 'grib chen po* and *bstan pa'i me ro slar yang ljongs 'di nas gso ba*.

111. SVF 145. 10–11. The Tibetan reads: *gangs ljongs bsod nams kyi mkha' la yang dar bstan pa'i nyi gzhon shar ba*.

112. SVF 147.14–148.3. I have emended *yam* to *yams*.

113. See Gayley 2008.

114. This phrase can be found twice in his preface, or "Publisher's Clarification" (*dpe skrun gsal bshad*), in Pad ma 'od gsal mtha' yas 1997: ii.4–5 and iii.1.

115. Makley 2008: 96.

116. The word "faith" (*dad pa*) is prominent in the titles of *rnam thar*. A search for the term in the titles of literary works on www.tbrc.org produces 140 entries, most

of which are titles of *rnam thar*, but they also include historical works, the collected writings of Buddhist masters, and guidebooks to sacred sites. Here is a small sampling of metaphors from the titles of *rnam thar*, which imply the role played by such works: "the chariot of faith" (*dad pa'i shing rta*), "the sun that causes the lotus of faith to bloom" (*dad pa'i pad mo bzhad pa'i nyin byed*), "a supreme ornament of faith" (*dad pa'i rgyan mchog*), "light rays of faith emanating in the ten directions" (*dad pa'i 'od zer phyogs bcur 'phro ba*), and "medicine to heal faith" (*dad pa'i gsos sman*).

117. Personal communications from Lama Chönam of the Light of Berotsana Translation Committee.

118. JG 3.4–6. This comes at the outset of *Jewel Garland*, and a comparable statement can be found at the outset of *Spiraling Vine of Faith*, in which her *rnam thar* is likened to a wondrous string of jewels to be spread as cloud offerings to delight the fortunate without bias (SVF 106.4–5). Additionally, in his preface, Pad ma 'od gsal mtha' yas offers these works for "the viewing pleasure of readers, including researchers of Tibetan culture and history and the populace with great faith in Buddhism" (1997: iii.5–9). Despite this broad claim, there is good reason to suspect that the text is mainly for the consumption of the religious community of Tā re lha mo and Nam sprul rin po che.

3. Inseparable Companions: A Buddhist Courtship and Correspondence

1. This site is located near Xinghai town in Hainan Prefecture, and its name means White Cliff Monkey Fortress. Despite its Rnying ma associations and the use of the mountain as a hermitage by Rnying ma masters and clerics, there is a Dge lugs pa monastery at its base, constructed in 1923. Gyurme Dorje 1999: 593–94.

2. Personal communication from Nam sprul rin po che, May 2007. His first letter in reply contains an extensive praise of this sādhana.

3. In the facsimile edition given to me by Nam sprul rin po che in 2004, their correspondence is divided into two collections within a single volume that serves as an addendum to their treasure corpus. The collections are titled *Adamantine Garland: The Collected Letters by the Lord of Refuge, Namtrul Jigme Phuntsok, to the Supreme Khandro Tāre Lhamo* (*Skyabs rje rin po che nam sprul 'jigs med phun tshogs kyis mkha' 'gro rin po che tā re de vī mchog la phul ba'i zhu 'phrin phyag yig rnams phyogs bsdus rdo rje'i phreng ba*) and *Garland of Lotuses: The Collected Letters by the Mantra-Born One, Khandro Tāre Lhamo, to the Supreme Namtrul Jigme Phuntsok* (*Sngags skyes mkha' 'gro rin po che tā re de vīs nam sprul rin po che 'jigs med phun tshogs mchog la phul ba'i zhu 'phrin phyag yid rnams phyogs bsdus pad ma'i phreng ba*). In these published collections, the letters are arranged chronologically according to author. For this reason, I will list their letters by the number in which they appear in their respective collections, with KTL 5 representing the fifth letter by Tā re lha mo and NJP 9 representing the ninth in Nam sprul rin po che's collection. Complicating matters, Nam sprul rin po che indicated to me that the letters were batched and sent along with gifts and news via a trusted messenger due to the rigors of travel overland on horseback between Snyan lung

and Smar khog during the span of more than a year, in which a large number of letters were exchanged. For this reason, it is only possible to trace the development of their dialogue in broad strokes, rather than letter by letter. Nonetheless, from the dated letters in Tā re lha mo's collection and their content and narrative framing in *Jewel Garland*, I have established a rough chronology, especially with regard to which letters precede and follow their initial meeting in 1979, when Namtrul Rinpoche first journeyed to Smar khog. I count the last four entries in Nam sprul rin po che's collection as addenda, since they are short prophecies that appear to have been added after his final letter welcoming Tā re lha mo to Snyan lung. As a final addendum, there is also a letter at the end of the correspondence as a whole, which Nam sprul rin po che composed on the anniversary of Tā re lha mo's passing on March 26, 2002. This places the publication of their correspondence in its entirety between March 2003 and August 2004, when Nam sprul rin po che kindly shared the facsimile edition with me.

4. I was told that this arduous route took two days of travel at the time, involving crossing one mountain pass, frequently snowy even in the summer, and fording at least one river. There is now a rough dirt road connecting their respective homelands of Pad ma County in Qinghai Province and Gser rta County in Sichuan Province.

5. Personal communication from Nam sprul rin po che, May 2007. This meeting is evident in the letters themselves, and his journey to meet Tā re lha mo is also depicted in JG 41.5–15.

6. This topic proved to be too private for me to probe in interviews with Nam sprul rin po che.

7. Though only eleven of the letters are dated, all from Tā re lha mo, the dates clearly delineate a time frame between the fall of 1978 and late 1979. Her first letter is dated to the hare month of the horse year in 1978, and her final letter is dated to the horse month of the sheep year in 1979. Apart from two letters dated to the horse year, the other nine dated letters fall in the sheep year and line up as follows: dog (KTL 4), Sa ga zla ba (KTL 5 and 10), fifth month (KTL 11), ox (KTL 14), hare (KTL 15 and 22), dragon (KTL 23), and horse (KTL 28). There is no reason to suppose that the letters are not arranged chronologically since the months follow neatly in the same order as the years and months routinely do in Tibetan calendrical systems. Given that two fixed coordinates are provided, namely Sa ga zla ba (fourth month) and the fifth month (given as a numerical value), we can chart the other months fairly confidently as follows: (1) monkey (*spre'u*); (2) bird (*bya*); (3) dog (*khyi*); (4) boar (*phag*); (5) rat (*byi*); (6) ox (*glang*); (7) tiger (*stag*); (8) hare (*yos*); (9) dragon ('*brug*); (10) snake (*sbrul*); (11) horse (*rta*); (12) sheep (*lug*). According to the logic of the months as presented in their correspondence, which appears to be different from the dating systems outlined by Dieter Schuh (1973: 145–46) and Philippe Cornu (1997: 156), the horse month of 1979 would fall on the eleventh month. This would place her final dated letter in late December 1979, suggesting that she traveled to Snyan lung after that, in early 1980. Corroborating my assessment, *Jewel Garland*—in which selections from their correspondence are excerpted—begins the narration of their activities together in 1980.

8. For example, NJP 7: 21.2–3.

9. This image is placed in the ornamental language of poetry (*snyan ngag*) modeled on Indian *kāvya*: "As soon as I heard the queen of drumbeats heralding [your] news, / My mind danced with delight like a peacock displaying its feathers" (*gtam snyan rnga sgra'i rgyal mo thos pa'i mos / bdag yid mdongs mtha' spro bas zlos gar ngoms*, NJP 1: 3.3–4). The "queen of drumbeats" (*rnga sgra'i rgyal mo*) is a kenning that refers to thunder.

10. NJP 1: 6.2–3. The Tibetan reads: *nam zlas bskul ba'i rtsi thog 'bus pa bzhin / las 'phro'i pad ma'i zab gter de ltar ro.*

11. While this shift in policy officially focused on the "four modernizations" (agriculture, industry, technology, and defense), the state also relaxed restrictions on cultural affairs. The effects of liberalization did not reach Tibetan areas immediately, and it was not until the early 1980s that the process of rebuilding and reopening Buddhist monasteries began. Yet a degree of reprieve must have been discernable, since Tā re lha mo and Nam sprul rin po che exchanged images of regeneration that communicate a sense of new possibilities.

12. Inquiry into the role of love in Tibetan revelation has been opened up by Sarah Jacoby in her groundbreaking book, *Love and Liberation: Autobiographical Writings of the Tibetan Buddhist Visionary Sera Khandro* (2014a). I return to this issue later in the chapter.

13. Goldstein 1989: x.

14. On the issues of crafting an epistolary persona, see Ray 2009, which states: "In writing an *epistolario*, the letter writer simultaneously plays the part of author, narrator, and protagonist, choosing which aspect of her experience to present to readers and in what light to do so. . . . What the letter writer chooses to describe, as well as what she chooses to leave out, is central to the construction of her epistolary persona" (216).

15. On the role of sexuality in treasure revelation, see Tulku Thondup 1997: 82–84 and 106–7.

16. On the issue of relative status of author and addressee, see Tibetan letter-writing manuals by the nineteenth-century polymath 'Ju Mi pham and the contemporary scholar Tshe tan zhabs drung (Mi pham rgya mtsho 1984–93, vol. 14: 930 ff. and Tshe tan zhabs drung 2007: 195). Given the geographic proximity of 'Ju Mi pham and the temporal proximity of Tshe tan zhabs drung, writing in the 1950s, these sources best reflect the understandings of letter writing for those in Mgo log and northern Khams prior to the socialist transformations of Tibetan areas in the late 1950s. Farther afield, Hanna Schneider emphasizes the importance of relative rank with respect to epistolary conventions in central Tibet during the seventeenth century (2005). In epistolary literature more generally, according to Janet Altman, the addressee of a letter necessarily influences its style and content as well as how correspondents position themselves in relation to each other over the course of ongoing exchanges (1982: 146 ff.).

17. On the seven parts of a Tibetan letter according to formal epistolary conventions, see Mi pham rgya mtsho 1984–93, vol. 14: 930.4–5 and Tshe tan zhabs drung 2007, vol. 9: 197.4–5. According to these sources, the opening of a formal Tibetan letter should feature a salutation consisting of a praise of the addressee (*gang la skur yul gyi che brjod*) and a deferential statement (*'dud pa dang bcas pa'i zhe sa*).

18. O rgyan mkha' 'gro gling refers to Uḍḍiyāna, said to be the land of Padmasambhava's origin, which is sometimes located in the Swat Valley of present-day Pakistan.

19. NJP 1: 2.1–3.2.

20. Continuing with the structure of a letter according to the sources listed in note 17 above, the middle portion follows after remarks about the recipient's health in the form of a praise or inquiry (khams bde dris ba). It consists of the main purpose of the letter, including one's own news or situation (rang gi gnas tshul) and a petition in context (skabs kyi zhu don, skabs bab dngos don). Hannah Schneider likewise emphasizes the petitionary nature of formal Tibetan letters in her study of seventeenth-century letters in central Tibet (2005).

21. NJP 1: 3.4–4.1. Full translations of select letters are forthcoming.

22. The Tibetan for these phrases reads: zab bcud spel ba and snga 'gyur chu gter spel ba.

23. The Tibetan for these phrases reads: ri dwags mtshan ma and chu gter. In my translation I use the referent of these kennings rather than the kennings themselves, which would be indecipherable to English readers.

24. Leonard van der Kuijp gives the period between 1267 and 1270 as the range for the translation of the Kāvyādarśa by Shang ston lo tsā ba Rdo rje rgyal mtshan and Lakṣmīkara, though, as he notes, Sa skya Paṇ ḍi ta also translated major portions of the text for inclusion in his Mkhas pa rnam la 'jug pa'i sgo, composed between 1220 and 1230 (1995: 395).

25. On the development of free verse in Tibetan literature, see Hartley 2003.

26. According to 'Ju Mi pham and Tshe tan zhabs drung, as above in note 17, the final two elements of a formal Tibetan letter are a virtuous aspiration for the future (slad char dge ba'i smon 'dun) and a conclusion (mjug sdud). The request for a response is what Janet Altman has termed the "epistolary pact" (1982: 89).

27. NJP 1. 6.6–7.1.

28. KTL 1: 76.1–78.1. The Tibetan for the opening and closing of her first letter reads: nam mkha'i snying po'i sprul pa la and pad ma dri med 'od gsal blo gros mtha' yas la phul / de vīs so / gsang rgya. This signature line may be her own, or more likely added by her scribe. Note that while the Sanskrit term devī reflects a part of her name, it also serves to elevate and even divinize her.

29. KTL 2: 78.2–6. These images will be discussed more in the next chapter. The poet 'Brug mo skyid offered an interpretation of this letter as Tā re lha mo's request to Nam sprul rin po che to teach. Personal communication from 'Brug mo skyid, May 2007.

30. See Mkha' 'bum 2005: 97.

31. This contrasts with the odd-syllable poetic meter initially favored by Nam sprul rin po che and also the six-syllable meter common in Lha sa songs (gzhas). An eight-syllable meter can be composed of four dyads (2/2/2/2), an alteration of three-syllable and two-syllable semantic units (3/2/3), or alternatively a single first syllable or monad, followed by two dyads, and a final three-syllable unit (1/2/2/3). Local poets and singers refer to these meters in terms of monads and dyads, rendering the latter as ya cha cha cha ya, where ya represents a single syllable and cha represents a pair. Tā re lha mo's song of marvels follows this format.

32. The term, khu lo, seems to be a local variant of khu byug, which is "the bird who calls out in a melodious voice during spring," namely the cuckoo (TTC: 231).

33. KTL 4: 80.2–5. In my translation, to keep the length of lines somewhat consistent, I have removed a qualifier that may only have served as a meter filler in the original: the Dbus referring to central Tibet before mention of Lha sa and the Jo bo Śākyamuni statue housed in the Jo khang temple there.

34. The Tibetan term for "friend" (*grogs, rogs*) connotes both friendship and amorous liaisons.

35. Sujata 2005: 217–23.

36. The structure here is standard: analogy-analogy-referent (*dpe dpe don*). In the context of Indian poetics, *dpe* translates the Sanskrit *upamā*, meaning "comparison," often but not exclusively a simile. However, in reference to Tibetan folk songs, *dpe* seems to be used more loosely to denote any type of metaphor. I follow Gold 2007 in translating *dpe* as "analogy."

37. I trace the development of epistolary intimacy in their correspondence more closely in "The Love Letters of a Buddhist Tantric Couple: Reflections on Poetic Style and Epistolary Intimacy" (forthcoming in *History of Religions*).

38. Their repertoire of terms of endearment is extensive, including (but not limited to): "vine of the heart" (*snying gi 'khri shing*), "bindu of the heart" (*snying gi thig le*), "mirror of the heart" (*snying gi me long*), "jewel of the heart" (*snying gi nor bu*), "adoring love" (*byams ldan mdza'*), "congenial friend" (*mthun grogs*), "supreme consort" (*grogs mchog*), and "unforgettable companion" (*grogs po brjed med*). These are part of a common repertoire of epithets for lovers; see Tshe tan zhabs drung 2007, vol. 9: 192. Note that I vary the translation of *grogs* to include "friend," "companion," and "consort" in accord with the range of Tibetan usage.

39. The use of Nam sprul rin po che's name as a child, Tshe 'dzin, for his nickname in the correspondence may indicate that they had met in their youth prior to the socialist transformation of Tibetan areas.

40. Called a *gter tsheg*, this mark is composed of two circles stacked on top of each other at the end of each line with a horizontal line between them. Prophetic passages are often also demarcated by symbolic script concluding the prophecy; this unusual script is decipherable only in a visionary process. That said, the line between prophecy and the ordinary speech of a *gter ston* sometimes gets blurred by scribes, and the *gter tsheg* is sometimes added when the content is not strictly speaking a prophecy.

41. KTL 15: 103. 1–2. The Tibetan for these lines of verse reads: *nga mdo med rgan mo bag chags 'thug / spyir dam tshig chags nyams nyes ltung che.*

42. KTL 15: 103.5–6. The Tibetan for these phrases reads: *dpal pad ma'i zhal gzigs lung bstan* and *ma mkha' 'gro'i tha tshig.*

43. KTL 17: 120.2–6.

44. Don grub rgyal refers to this as "ornamentation arranged by number" (*grangs la sbyor ba'i rgyan*) and discusses it within his section of ornamentation unique to Tibetan songs (1997: 532–55).

45. Recall that Janet Gyatso distinguishes between the "studied diffidence" of the first-person voice and the "studied reverence" of the third-person voice in Tibetan biographical literature (1998: 105).

46. JG 45.1–47.6. *Jewel Garland* excerpts a section of KTL 17 to represent Tā re lha mo's speech during their meeting; however, this particular passage is not included.

47. NJP 7: 23.2–24.1. Typically, it is the female consort who heals an older male lama, but Sarah Jacoby offers an important counterexample in which the male lama heals his younger female partner (2014a: 212–22).

48. KTL 15: 103.2 and 104.3 ff.

49. KTL 15: 107.5 and 109.4–5. The Tibetan for the latter reads: *skye sngon mkhar chen dran pa'i bu mor brdzu*.

50. NJP 6: 18.2–3. Recall that Tshe refers to his childhood name, Tshe 'dzin. The Tibetan for this is: *phran gdol spyod smyon pa ban tshe ngas / yid shar cha'i ri mo de dra red.*

51. For a nuanced study of "holy madmen," see DiValerio 2015.

52. KTL 5: 81.6–82.1. The Tibetan for this reads: *'khor 'khor stag mo'i blo sems sprel la 'khor.*

53. For an overview of the dating system according to Tibetan astrology, see Cornu 1997.

54. As an indicator of the visionary content of their respective collections of letters, there are six entries among Nam sprul rin po che's letters marked with *gter tsheg*, the orthographic marker indicating their status as treasures, including four short entries that serve as an addenda to his collection of letters, while there are ten entries interspersed throughout her letters marked as treasures with *gter tsheg* in her collection.

55. This is according to the facsimile edition published prior to 2004, not counting the final addendum, written by Nam sprul rin po che to Tā re lha mo on the one-year anniversary of her passing. In the paperback version, published in 2013, her contributions amount to 68 pages and his to 45.

56. This is similar to medieval European epistles, which Giles Constables has characterized as "self-conscious, quasi-public literary documents, often written with an eye to future collection and publication" (1976: 10). Given its initial secrecy and later publication, the correspondence under consideration here falls somewhere between the public nature of medieval epistles and our contemporary association of letters with intimacy, spontaneity, and privacy.

57. Collections of official or didactic letters in Tibetan literature are too numerous to list here, often occupying a substantial section of one volume in a Buddhist master's collected works. In an example proximate in time and place to this couple, the first volume of the collected works of the Third Rdo grub chen 'Jigs med bstan pa'i nyi ma (1865–1926) contains short works of advice, a number in the form of letters: *Bslab bya'i snying gtam zhim mngar sbrang rtsi'i gong bu* in *Rdo grub chen 'jigs med bstan pa'i nyi ma'i gsung 'bum* (Chengdu: Si khron mi rigs dpe skrun khang, 2003, vol. 1: 315–455). Letters of didactic advice, and Tibetan epistolary literature more generally, are only beginning to be studied, for example by Jared Rhoton in Sakya Pandita Kunga Gyaltshen 2002 and, more recently, in the panel "Tibetan Letters, Buddhist Lives: Epistolary Approaches to the Study of Tibetan Buddhism," American Academy of Religion conference, San Diego, November 22–25, 2014, organized by Christina Kilby.

58. See the appendices in this book for a catalogue of the correspondence, including notes indicating which letters or sections of letters were excerpted for inclusion in *Jewel Garland*.

59. See note 3 in this chapter for a discussion of the facsimile edition of their correspondence.

60. Nam sprul 'jigs med phun tshogs and Mkha' 'gro Tā re lha mo 2013, vol. 12.

61. *Mthong thos don ldan rdo rje'i sgra dbyangs,* ISRC CN-H09-09-326-00/V.J6. I discuss this DVD and other audio-visual materials produced by Snyan lung in the epilogue.

62. NJP 11: 34.3–5. The Tibetan reads: *bod bsil ldan gangs ri'i yul ljongs 'dir / dus skye ba bdun la mnyam du 'dzoms ... de 'u dran yid dga' snying gi grogs?*

63. The whole passage in Nam sprul rin po che's voice can be found in KTL 15: 104.2–107.3.

64. For a short biography of this figure, also known as Hūṃkara, see Dudjom Rinpoche 1991: 475–77. Note that Hūṃ chen ka ra is also counted among the past lives of Bdud 'joms gling pa.

65. According to Douglas Penick, in the Ge sar epic, Me tog lha mdzes serves as the princess of a southern kingdom, who was won in battle as the bride for Ge sar's nephew (1996: 115–22).

66. It is not clear to me whether this is an alternate name for the Prince of 'Jang or Nam sprul rin po che is being identified with another figure during the same period. On the possible referents for the name Thod kar and its variants, see "Tibet Antiqua III: A propos du mot *gcug-lag* et de la religion indigène" (Stein 1985: 123); this work has recently been translated into English by Arthur McKeown.

67. Rdo rje mtsho of the Shel dkar family is counted among the female disciples of Padmasambhava in Tulku Thondup 1996: 92 and Dudjom Rinpoche 1991: 536. Additionally, she appears several times in the *rnam thar* of Ye shes mtsho rgyal by Stag sham nus ldan rdo rje (Padmakara Translation Committee 2002: 165, 180, 182, 208). The treasure corpus of Pad ma gling pa also contains a dialogue between Nam mkha'i snying po and Princess Rdo rje mtsho in his cycle, *Bla ma nor bu rgya mtsho* (Harding 2003a: 99–114).

68. KTL 9: 87.1.

69. For example, KTL 15: 105.1, NJP 5: 15.4, and NJP 20: 51.1; in the first example from Nam sprul rin po che's letters, Me tog lha mdzes is referred to as the "lady of Mon" (*mon za*) and in the second as "lady of Ling" (*gling za*).

70. According to Stein, G.yu lha is the son of Sa tham, who surrenders the kingdom of 'Jang (1959: 44).

71. Contemporary figures from the region for whom this is the case include: Mkhan po 'Jigs med phun tshogs, Nam mkha' dri med, and the Eleventh Drung pa, Chos kyi rgya mtsho, known in the West as Chögyam Trungpa.

72. For example, Se ra mkha' 'gro's short autobiography as excerpted in *Spiraling Vine of Faith* contains several identifications not found in the available sources for Tā re lha mo's life, including Ut pal ma, Ro lang bde rol, and Byang chub sgron (SVF 110.16–111.1). Her extensive autobiography mentions the figure Bkra shis spyi 'dren, also not found among Tā re lha mo's female antecedents; this figure is framed by Se ra mkha' 'gro as a concurrent emanation of Ye shes mtsho rgyal, alongside Shel dkar Rdo rje mtsho and Kālasiddhi (Jacoby 2014a: 80 ff.). Tā re lha mo's identification with Kālasiddhi and Shel dkar Rdo rje mtsho can be found in KTL 15: 105.4 and NJP 11: 34.3.

73. Se ra mkha' 'gro's writings were published by 'Ju skal bzang under the auspices of the Mgo log khul gna' rtsom bya ba'i gzhung las khang as *Zab gsang theg pa mchog gi rnal 'byor ma chen po dbus bza' mkha' 'gro kun bzang bde skyong dbang mo bde ba'i rdo rje'i gsung 'bum legs bshad nor bu'i me long* (Chengdu: Si khron mi rigs dpe skrun khang, 2009).

74. Klu shul mkhan po Dkon mchog sgron me was a highly regarded cleric-scholar from Rdo grub chen Monastery. This third association was added in Tulku Thondup's translation of the *Jewel Lantern of Blessings* into English and also mentioned in his work, *Masters of Meditation and Miracles: The Longchen Nyingthig Lineage of Tibetan Buddhism* (1996: 236).

75. KTL 9, 15, 17, 18, and 29; NJP 3–5, 8, 11, 20 and 24. See the appendices for more information.

76. NJP 8: 25.6–26.4.

77. On this figure, see Jann Ronis, "Bdud 'dul rdo rje (1615–1672) and Rnying ma Adaptations to the Era of the Fifth Dalai Lama," in *Power, Politics, and the Reinvention of Tradition*, ed. Bryan Cuevas and Kurtis Schaeffer (Leiden: Brill, 2006). Bdud 'dul rdo rje is listed in Nam sprul rin po che's past life genealogy in *Jewel Garland* (Pad ma 'od gsal mtha' yas 2003: 5.14), and this figure was also an important antecedent for Bdud 'joms gling pa, one of the great *gter ston* of nineteenth-century Mgo log.

78. Clarifying this point, in *Jewel Lantern of Blessings*, A bu dkar lo adds to Tā re lha mo's past life genealogy a certain Mi 'gyur dpal sgron from Khams, though I have been unable to identify this figure (JLB 9.5). Note that her identification with this figure is not mentioned in *Spiraling Vine of Faith*.

79. As discussed in the epilogue, his identification as Dri med 'od zer was only made public after Tā re lha mo's passing. Although not included in *Jewel Garland* (published in 1997), this identification has been inserted into Nam sprul rin po che's past life genealogy in its reproduction, retitled *Skyabs rje nam sprul rin po che 'jigs med phun tshogs kyi rnam thar dbang chen dgyes pa'i mchod sprin*, in the 2013 paperback version of their treasure corpus. Here Dri med 'od zer appears in his past life genealogy as Pad ma las 'brel 'gro 'dul gsang sngags gling pa (2013, vol. 14: 16.3), and other prophecies are added to this effect.

80. This identification appears in works by A bu dkar lo, a short biography of A phang gter chen published in 2000 and the couple's own abbreviated life story, *Jewel Lantern of Blessings*, published in 2001 and largely derivative of *Jewel Garland*. See JLB 2.12–13 and A bu dkar lo et al. 2000: 213. I discuss this issue in more detail in the epilogue.

81. On the distinction between *jātakas* and *avadānas*, see Ohnuma 2006.

82. Past-life recollections, as found in their correspondence, are normative within Buddhist conceptions of memory. Narratives of the eve of the Buddha's enlightenment include the recollections of his former lives in the first of three watches of the night. Though not a prerequisite to attaining enlightenment, the ability to remember past lives has been considered an extraordinary form of knowledge, included in lists of the six superknowledges (*abhijñā*), three gnoses (*vidyā*), and ten powers (*bala*). See Lopez 1992.

83. Lopez 1992: 24.

84. KTL 7: 83.4–5. The Tibetan reads: *nyin lan brgyar dran pa'i sems gi rten / nga'i yid mthun grogs po sems la shar / skye sngon ma'i ri mo je gsal red / thugs 'dun ma'i brtse*

gdung je che red. The phrase *sems gi rten* (more properly spelled *sems kyi rten*) is discussed below.

85. NJP 6: 17.5–6 and 18: 47.3. The Tibetan for these passages reads: *skye sngon ma'i 'brel tshul sems la shar / yid dga' skyo mchi ma'i char rgyun babs* and *skye sngon ma'i ri mo je gsal red / yid dga' ba'i rtse gdung yang yang dran.*

86. Sa ga zla ba (Skt: Vaiśākha) celebrates the Buddha's enlightenment and parinirvāṇa.

87. KTL 5: 80.5–6. The Tibetan for these phrases reads: *zla gzhon 'dzum zhal ngoms* and *yid mthun dga' ba.*

88. KTL 5: 81. 5–6. The Tibetan for these phrases reads: *dung dung smra ba* and *rtse gdung ba'i sems gi smug pa dwengs.* I take *dwengs* to be either a variant or misspelling of *dwangs pa,* which can mean "to clear away" or "to illuminate."

89. KTL 6: 82.2–83.4. The Tibetan for this phrase, in the opening stanza of the letter, reads: *yid spro sems 'khol ba.*

90. In this letter, Tā re lha mo explicitly states that the treasure is also hidden in the "vast casket of the innermost sanctum of the mind" (*thugs yang gsang tsi ta'i sgrom rgya,* KTL 6: 83.2); note that *tsi ta* is the Tibetan transliteration for the Sanskrit *citta.* This point is relevant to the discussion of sexuality in the revelation process later in this chapter.

91. KTL 6: 83.1 and 3. The Tibetan for these phrases reads: *pad ma'i pha phog bu* and *snyigs ma'i ru 'dzing bzlog pa'i thabs.*

92. In addition to providing the location of a treasure, the *gter byang* also often lists the titles of texts contained in the treasure as well as relics and other sacred objects.

93. KTL 6: 82.4. The Tibetan for this phrase reads: *rdo ri mo bskos bzhin lhang nger dran.*

94. In their attempt to bridge a spatial distance, one could draw a parallel here to devotional songs that "call to the guru from afar" (*bla ma rgyang 'bod*). Thank you to Heather Stoddard for this suggestion.

95. For more about this genre, see Rossi 1992 and Anton-Luca 2002.

96. The original literally reads "heart of the internal cavity" or "heart in the chest" (*khog pa'i snying*), giving the location of the heart in the body. This seems like an unnecessary redundancy, left out in translation. I render *dpral ba'i mig,* literally "the eyes of the forehead," as "the eyes on the face."

97. NJP 9: 26.4–28.6.

98. In a technical sense the same term is used for mindfulness, translating the Sanskrit *smṛti,* in reference to meditation practice. Buddhist notions of memory derive from what Collette Cox calls an "interrelated semantic complex" in which the term *smṛti* in Sanskrit refers to (1) a "mode of attentiveness" as a technique in meditation, often translated as "mindfulness"; and (2) "recollection," including the recollection of past lives (1992: 62 ff.). Tibetan usage of the term, *dran pa,* encompasses this semantic complex and adds to it an affective dimension in its meaning "to miss."

99. Cox 1992: 62 ff.

100. As such, this type of memory has become a frequent trope in pop songs today, sung by urban Tibetan youth who wax nostalgic about the grasslands in songs of remembrance (*dran glu*).

101. NJP 11: 34.1–5. Kālasiddhi is also considered to be another consort of Padmasambhava.

102. As a verbal figure, the phonemic repetition of syllables, or *yamaka* in Sanskrit, is found in ornate poetry and songs, with numerous variations depending on where those syllables fall within the *pāda* or line of poetry and whether the repetition is continuous, with repeated syllables side by side, or discontinuous, for example, when repeated in successive lines as in this passage. See Sujata 2005: 166–80.

103. In Tibetan, the verb comes at the end of a line or sentence and does not require a pronoun. In my translation, I shift the term *dran* for "memory" to a gerund at the front of each line to capture the same sense of repetition, unencumbered by a pronoun.

104. Here Namtrul Rinpoche refers to a "lake treasure" (*mtsho gter*) awaiting the couple at the Gnyan po g.yu rtse mountain range; its revelation is described in chapter 5.

105. NJP 11: 36.2–37.2.

106. For example, about Shel brag, he states: "Recalling the jeweled treasure gate at the white cliff, Sheldrak / This is the sacred place where we two friends made aspirations" (NJP 11: 35.4).

107. NJP 11: 37.1 and KTL 7: 83.4. Another instance is NJP 19: 49.6, discussed below. A related passage in KTL 13: 95.4–5 depicts Nam sprul rin po che as her "support" (*rten*) and "method companion" (*thabs grogs*), as discussed in the next chapter.

108. NJP 19: 49.5–50.3.

109. NJP 19: 49.5.

110. There is no evidence to indicate any influence in the letters of Chinese notions of romantic love and/or fate that would become popularized in the late 1980s as Tibetan pop music began to flourish. See Morcom 2004 regarding how Tibetan pop music, particularly in its early stages, borrowed heavily on models from Taiwan and Hong Kong.

111. The term *las dbang* can be found a series of verses in NJP 19: 49.2–5. In the parallelism of these verses, it is rendered comparable to the term I translate as "worldly legacy" (*srid pa'i bkod thang*). I discuss the deployment of destiny and the terms they use in the correspondence in more detail in chapter 4.

112. According to Stein, "In the Mila Rêpa's songs we find, for the first time, the standard animals of each realm of nature which still characterize folk-songs of the modern period: the white lioness with her turquoise mane among the glaciers, the eagle, 'king of the birds,' on the rocks, the tiger, 'the variegated one', in the forests and the 'golden eye' fish in the lakes" (1972: 260). The garuḍa and vulture may also substitute for the eagle in this schema; see Chang 1999: 1–10 and 38–42.

113. NJP 18: 46.3–6. The passage goes on to praise the guru as the supreme protector, Padmasambhava as the supreme refuge, Rdzogs chen as the supreme dharma, and Tā re lha mo, referred to by the name of her previous lifetime as Bde ba'i rdo rje, as the "supreme companion" (*grogs gcig chog*).

114. What follows is my paraphrase of this passage from NJP 12: 37.5–38.3. To derive "wobble," I emended *yos bzur* to *g.yos bzur*. This appears to be a colloquial expression. My thanks to Mkhan sprul Phun tshogs dge legs for explaining it to me. Stein records "white breast" (*thang dkar*) as an epithet for the eagle (1972: 265), and

here Nam sprul rin po che appears to use a comparable expression, *thang li*, whereby *li* designates an amalgamation of metals used to make cymbals and other musical instruments; it can designate also a color, as in *li ser* (TTC: 2778–80).

115. According to Stein, the sixfold smile (*'dzum drug*) is an indigenously Tibetan metaphor for a tiger or a strong man's body (Stein 1972: 265), though I prefer to translate it as "six stripes" since *'dzum* can also designate a curved pattern and fits well with tiger stripes. Throughout their correspondence, this attribute characterizes a tigress (*stag mo*) rather than a tiger, perhaps in deference to Tā re lha mo, who was born in the tiger year.

116. NJP 13: 39.2–40.4. In order to maintain the even flow of the verse, I leave out one attribute of the gold-eyed fish in this passage, its "white belly" (*lto dkar*). Such embellishments often serve as meter fillers in the Tibetan.

117. NJP 13: 40.3–4. The Tibetan reads: *mi 'gyang bde bar nga dang grogs khyed gnyis 'phrad 'ong*.

118. In this alternate spelling of *rogs 'then*, the second part of the term, which literally means "to pull," refers to singing a song or pulling in a girl (*zhi mo 'then*). Personal communication from Lama Jabb, November 2014.

119. Personal communication from 'Brug mo skyid and Snying po tshe ring, May 2007.

120. Snying po tshe ring at the Gesar Research Institute in Xining suggested that this involuntary separation is usually due to objections by parents or a clan leader (*dpon po*) over the match. Tā re lha mo and Nam sprul rin po che faced several obstacles, including state policy, local gossip, and the reluctance of Tā re lha mo's relatives to see her leave Pad ma County for Snyan lung, to be discussed further in the next chapter.

121. Personal communication from Snying po tshe ring, May 2007.

122. Uray suggests that repetition formulas, even when not contiguous, share certain properties with the duplication of the stem of a word as follows: "Stem duplication is a repetition of a word, and according to its basic functions it denotes the iterated, various, indistinct, multiple or emphatic manifestation of a thing, an idea, a quantity, a property, a circumstance, a property expressed as the basis" (1955: 186).

123. To do so necessitated condensation in two lines; thus "turquoise dragon of the south" becomes "turquoise dragon" and "juniper bush leaves" becomes "juniper branch" in my translation.

124. KTL 25: 139.1–139.4 and 140.1.

125. Personal communication from Snying po tshe ring, May 2007.

126. A similar repetition formula is found in NJP 9: 26.6, where Nam sprul rin po che uses *a bu lo lo wo*, addressing a bee and inviting it to partake of honey. Ringu Tulku glossed this usage as a calling sound.

127. KTL 27: 148.4–148.6. The phrase repeated in each verse is *thabs med*, which literally means "no means." So the passage is saying that the snow lion has no means to assume its awesome standing pose (*'gying*) without the white snowy peak. Except for inside a lake, the fish cannot survive, i.e., it has no means to live (*gnas thabs med*). Completing the parallelism, without Tā re lha mo, Nam sprul rin po che also cannot survive.

128. NJP 14: 41.2–6.

129. It is not clear that any formal marriage ceremony occurred, but the fact of their domestic cohabitation and religious partnership over more than two decades substantiates the importance of mutual commitment in their letters. Tibetan marriages do not necessarily center on a formal ceremony or specific vows and can be as simple as the symbolic and practical integration of the bride into the groom's household followed by a celebration between the two families.

130. The song "Unforgettable," composed by Irving Gordon, was recorded by Nat King Cole in 1951 on an album of the same name, produced by Capitol Records.

131. NJP 7: 20.6–21.3. I have emended *khang ba* to *khang pa* and *gcug* to *gcugs*.

132. See Vaudeville 1962 on the prevailing model of the *parakīyā* as the ideal partner with whom to engage in the tantric rite of sexual union in Indian sources. The ubiquity of this characterization and the univocality of Indian tantric sources on this point have since been challenged in Bernacki 2007.

133. KTL 24: 138.1–3.

134. On this term, see TTC 1212. Other synonyms from *mdza' ba* can be found under *mdza' grogs* (TTC 2335). In this correspondence, they tend to use *brtse gdung* and *brtse grogs* more often, which I translate as "beloved."

135. KTL 24: 138.3. The Tibetan for these phrases reads: *dus rnam pa kun tu 'grogs pa'i grogs* and *skye 'di dang tshe rabs thams cad du*.

136. Giddens 1992: 46.

137. Giddens 1992: 60.

138. KTL 15: 103.5, plus a footnote that adds a missing line from the letter. The Tibetan for these phrases reads: *srid 'khor ba'i las la chags pa* and *nang nyon mongs 'khrul ba*.

139. Here *'khor ba zin* refers to "keeping a home," cognate to "householder" (*'khor ba 'dzin pa*). Thank you to Lama Chönam for clarifying the colloquial expressions in this passage.

140. The eight worldly concerns or more literally "eight [worldly] dharmas" (*chos brgyad*) are gain or loss, pleasure or pain, praise or scorn, fame or censure.

141. KTL 15: 103.3–6.

142. In Tibetan, the verb comes at the end of the sentence. In my translation, I have placed the "I am" and "not" statements at the beginning of each line, as is more natural in English.

143. Don grub rgyal 1997: 490. This Tibetan phrase reads: *dngos yod kyi 'tsho ba'i rmang gzhi*.

144. Jacoby 2014a: 262–63 provides a useful chart of Tibetan terms, drawn from Se ra mkha' 'gro's writings, related to love and lust, broken down into negative, context-dependent, neutral, and positive valences.

145. These topics are treated in chapter 5 of Jacoby 2014a; on the latter point, see especially 294 ff.

146. Jacoby summarizes and provides instances of those prevailing assumptions on 2014a: 253.

147. See Ahearn 2001b on this point in her study of love letters and development narratives in modern Nepal.

148. See Gyatso 1999: 179 and Jacoby 2014a: 92–100.

149. For example, NJP 3 and KTL 8. I discuss these letters and related passages at length in my article, "The Love Letters of a Buddhist Tantric Couple: Reflections on Poetic Style and Epistolary Intimacy" (forthcoming in *History of Religions*).

150. For example, KTL 27 and NJP 25, which I discuss below. On this point, see *Esoteric Instructions* from *The Treasury of Knowledge* in Jamgön Kongtrul 2008: 167–73 and 240–41.

151. See Thondup 1997: 82–84 and 106–7.

152. According to Stein, in the Ge sar epic, A chen refers to a region to the north of Gling along the upper reaches of the Yellow River with A mye rma chen as its tutelary deity. Perhaps due to a historical caravan route through the region, the appellation *gzhung lam* (highway or main road) is used here (Stein 1959: 194–99 and 198–99).

153. Likely *Dbus gtsang*, the term for central Tibet, is characterized as a *dag pa'i zhing* due to its sacred sites and popularity as a pilgrimage destination rather than being literally a "pure land" per se. It is not clear, however, why this would be the destination for a pair of adepts in tantric embrace.

154. This is generally understood to be a ḍākinī abode. That said, at least one Tibetan pilgrim, O rgyan pa, sought out Dhu ma tha la as a geographical location in Uḍḍiyāna, the land in northwest India associated with Padmasambhava (Huber 2008: 103–4).

155. NJP 22: 55.5–56.5. I have emended a scribal error in the last stanza, changing *mdo khal* to *mdo khams*.

156. The Zal mo Range seems to be a general term to refer to the "four rivers and six mountain ranges" (*chu bzhi sgang drug*) of eastern Tibet (Ngawang Zangpo 2001: 87). In contemporary usage, it covers the region from Dpal yul through Gser shul (TTC: 2455). Gser rta and Pad ma are directly east of the Gser shul grasslands.

157. NJP 1: 6.5–6.

158. The image of the hook appears elsewhere in a more romantic key, as where Nam sprul rin po che confesses to Tā re lha mo being caught "by the hook of your loving affection" (*khyed kyis so byams brtse'i lcags kyu yis*, NJP 9: 27.5).

159. In this final section of the chapter, I focus on explicit references to the tantric rite of sexual union; for a fuller discussion of implicit reference to this rite through erotic motifs and innuendo throughout this correspondence, see my "The Love Letters of a Buddhist Tantric Couple: Reflections on Poetic Style and Epistolary Intimacy" (forthcoming in *History of Religions*).

160. KTL 5: 81.6. See Ingalls 1968: 138–46.

161. KTL 10: 88.5. The Tibetan reads: *lus bkrag mdangs rgyas pa ha lo'i drin / sgro gdugs skor ngom pa . . .*

162. NJP 1: 6.5–6.

163. Important exceptions are the full-length biographies of two of Tā re lha mo's predecessors, Ye shes mtsho rgyal and Se ra mkha' 'gro. See Padmakara Translation Committee 2002 and Jacoby 2014a.

164. On the four joys, see Farrow and Menon 2001: 94–98.

165. See Tulku Thondup 1997 for a translation and analysis of *Las 'phro gter brgyud kyi rnam bshad nyung gsal ngo mthar rgya mtsho* by the Third Rdo grub chen 'Jigs med bstan pa'i nyi ma.

166. See Thondup 1997: 106–7. The physical treasure provides a mnemonic cue to help the *gter ston* unlock the treasure sealed in his or her mind during a previous lifetime (Gyatso 1986).

167. Thondup 1997: 107.

168. NJP 3: 9.6. The Tibetan reads: *reg grol phyag rgya'i nye lam a nu'i zab chos.*

169. KTL 27: 145.1–3. My thanks to Lama Chönam of the Light of Berotsana Translation Committee for his help deciphering this verse.

170. Personal communication by Nam sprul rin po che, July 2006.

171. I identify this as the last "actual letter" in his half of the correspondence, since the next four entries are all prophecies and seem to serve as addenda to the collection of his letters.

172. NJP 25: 65.4. The Tibetan reads: *chags chen gyis bde dgas rab bskul.*

173. NJP 25: 65.4–5. The Tibetan reads: *rtsol med kyi gter sgo ngang gis 'byed.*

174. NJP 25: 65.5. The Tibetan reads: *nga chags spyod rol pa'i rdo rje dang / khyod bde stong mchog gi mdza' na mo.*

175. Note that the term *glu gzhas* is a synonym for Amdo love songs (*la gzhas*) according to Pad ma 'bum 1997, yet here the content is far more tantric than a love song would normally be.

176. NJP 25. 60.2–3. The Tibetan for these lines of verse reads: *yab dpa' bo'i bro brdung 'khrabs se 'khrab* and *yum dpa' mos glu len sha ra ra.*

177. NJP 25: 62.4 and 63.4. The Tibetan for these phrases reads: *thabs shes rab mtshon pa'i rdzas chen* and *grogs 'u gnyis 'bral ba med pa'i chang.*

178. In sources such as the *Hevajratantra*, it appears that originally sexual fluids were considered to be potent substances, consumed during the secret *abhiṣeka* of a tantric initiation (Farrow and Menon 2001: 121, 185). While depicted as such in Indian tantric literature, in Tibetan contexts the elixir used in tantric initiations is generally made from blessed pills containing a variety of secret ingredients. For a discussion of the status of sexual fluids and the domestication of tantric initiation, see also Kvaerne 1975, Davidson 2002, and White 2003.

179. See Jacoby 2014a: 193–222.

180. This refers to Zangs mdog dpal ri, the sacred mountain of Padmasambhava's pure land.

181. NJP 25: 62.4–64.2.

182. The Tibetan for these phrases reads: *nyams rtogs yon tan rgyas, rtsa gsum 'khor lnga grol,* and *bde stong ye shes bskyed.* This list at the end of the passage cited above uses different verbs in each line: tasting (*bzhes*), consuming (*gsol*), drinking (*gtung*), partaking (*rol*), and enjoying (*spyod*).

183. NJP 25: 66.4. The Tibetan reads: *las bzang ngan gang 'brel 'gro ba kun.*

184. NJP 25: 66.3–5. The Tibetan for these phrases reads: *'khor ba dong sprugs smon* and *zhing rnga yab dpal rir 'dren nus smon.* On a pure land orientation in Tibetan Buddhism, see Kapstein 2004.

185. NJP 25: 63.2. The Tibetan for the two relevant lines of this passage reads: *mgon pad ma'i thugs bzhed 'grub pa'i chang* and *gter zab rgyas chos la spyod pa'i chang.*

186. NJP 25: 66.6–67.1. The Tibetan reads: *chos sangs rgyas bstan pa'i rgyal mtshan bsgreng / ma 'gro la bde skyid nyi ma shar / dus snyigs ma'i rgud pa'i ru 'dzing zhi.*

187. Tulku Thondup mentions Pad ma dbang gi rgyal po and 'Ja' tshon snying po (1997: 82) as exceptions to this rule as celibate monks. Mkhan po 'Jigs med phun tshogs is another exception (Germano 1998).

188. Even in the rare case of a *gter ston* couple, their revelactions are usually collected separately. For example, Se ra mkha' 'gro and Dri med 'od zer had separate collections of treasures. Her *gter chos* has been preserved in four volumes (Se ra mkha' 'gro 1978), while his collection has thus far not come to light.

4. Emissaries of Padmasambhava: Tibetan Treasures and Healing Trauma

1. KTL 17: 122.1–3. This verse is marked as a prophecy with a *gter tsheg*, the orthographic mark that sets treasure revelations apart from ordinary speech, two circles stacked vertically with a horizontal line between them.

2. The standard term I translate here as "emissary" (*pho nya*) appears in NJP 23: 57.4.

3. The centrality of Padmasambhava to treasure revelation emerged by the twelfth century in the writings and revelations of Myang ral Nyi ma 'od zer, while the language of degenerate times became well developed by the fourteenth century in the prophecies of O rgyan gling pa.

4. Note that versification lends itself to coded language, such that self-censorship during the composition process seems more likely than later editing. Moreover, any sensitive content could have been transmitted orally through their trusted messenger, who remained a close disciple throughout their long teaching career.

5. The "four olds" (Tib.: *rnying pa bzhi*, Ch.: *si jiu*) are old ideas, old culture, old customs, and old habits (*bsam blo rnying pa, rig gnas rnying pa, yul srol rnying pa, goms gshis rnying pa*).

6. As discussed in the introduction, I borrow the term "subaltern pasts" from Chakrabarty 2000, in which it refers to pasts articulated by subordinated minority groups in terms outside the epistemological limits of the discipline of history. Here I invoke the term to refer to the alternative reconstruction of the past in the correspondence of Tā re lha mo and Nam sprul rin po che that characterizes the Maoist period in inverse terms to the official account by the state, what Rubie Watson refers to as the "enforced historical orthodoxies" under state socialism (1994: 2).

7. Chakrabarty 2000: 103.

8. Borrowing the rubric of *tradent* from Talmudic hermeneutics to add nuance to the understanding of Tibetan treasures, Robert Mayer challenges the notion that treasure texts, specifically their esoteric and ritual content, are original or innovative. See his "gTer ston and Tradent: Innovation and Conservation in Tibetan Treasure Literature, *Journal of the International Association of Buddhist Studies* 36–37/1–2 (2013–14 [2015]). On other aspects of innovation in the treasure tradition as listed here, see Gayley 2008.

9. In reference to the Santal Rebellion of 1855, Chakrabarty suggests that the Santal's claim that Thakur spurred them to rebel has to be "anthropologized" before

it can be included in history, meaning "converted into somebody's belief or made into an object of anthropological analysis." The act of writing history thus becomes a colonial act to the extent that minority histories are *epistemologically* not permissible (2000: 105).

10. Ortner 1989: 60–61 and 126–29. In my analysis, I do not follow Ortner's line of reasoning that cultural schemas follow from "central contradictions" in a given culture.

11. This epithet for Padmasambhava, also known as Padmākara, is usually *mtsho skyes bla ma*; here it is *mtsho byung rin po che*. The latter can also refer to Sarasvatī but in context makes more sense as referring to Padmasambhava.

12. NJP 7: 20.3–6.

13. KTL 6: 83.1–4.

14. See J. L. Austin 1962.

15. See Nattier 1991 regarding Buddhist notions of time.

16. PTC Vol. 11: 7.5– 8.3. I have emended *tha* in the first line to *mtha'*.

17. I discuss this trope of decline and revival in more detail in Gayley 2008.

18. Against this pan-Tibetan myth regarding the decline in Buddhism at the end of the imperial period, Samten Karma argues that, while institutional forms of Buddhist monasticism suffered, the end of the Tibetan empire and with it the imperial regulation of Buddhism allowed tantric movements to thrive (1998: 8–12).

19. This work has been translated into English in Douglas and Bays 1978. Janet Gyatso states: "The content of a Treasure text is said to have been formulated specifically to benefit the Tibetans at a particular moment in their history. The Treasure prophecies often describe wars and political upheavals of such moments, their traumas somehow to be alleviated by the new religious practices introduced by the Treasure scripture" (1998: 151).

20. See for example NJP 2: 7.5, NJP 11: 37.4, NJP 25: 67.1, KTL 10: 90.3–4, KTL 15: 99.6, KTL 17: 118:1, and KTL 22: 134.2.

21. Personal communication by Nam sprul rin po che, May 2007. I discuss the term *bstan pa yang dar* in the next chapter.

22. Dung dkar blo bzang 'phrin las (2002: 942–43) lists the five degenerations as: (1) *sems can snyigs ma*: the decline in people's values (*bsam blo*), behavior (*kun spyod*), and wealth (*dpal 'byor*); (2) *nyon mongs snyigs ma*: the fortification of people's desire, hatred, pride, and jealousy; (3) *dus snyigs ma*: continuous plague (*nad yams*), famine (*mu ge*), and warfare (*'thab rtsod*) on earth; (4) *tshe snyigs ma*: shortening of the average lifespan to fifty years; and (5) *lta ba snyigs ma*: a time when many no longer believe in the Three Jewels and reincarnation.

23. Wang 2004: 114. While Ban Wang uses the term "symbolic resources" to describe such resources, Erik Mueggler prefers "cultural resources." In *The Age of Wild Ghosts*, he draws attention to the "concrete practices and poetics" of negotiating and reshaping the collective relationship to recent history and the Chinese state among the Lòlop'ò nationality in Zhizuo as "a community in the aftermath of violence" (2001: 1–21).

24. KTL 22: 134.1–4.

25. These phrases can be found in NJP 2: 7.5 and KTL 17: 118.1, KTL 15: 99.6, and KTL 10: 90.3–4 respectively.

26. Watson 1994: 2 and 6.

27. Brison 1999: 41.

28. Such passages—though often identical in meter to other folk styles—were singled out by the poets and singers I consulted for their distinctive martial tone and references to the warriors and maidens of Ling, war gods such as *dgra bla* and *wer ma*, as well as an indigenous cosmology. While the genre is indicated in some letters, others song styles in the correspondence were identified for me by scholars and singers in Xining and Mgo log based on the meter, language, and mood of the passage. My appreciation to Snying po tshe ring at the Gesar Research Institute at Qinghai Minyuan and Mkha' 'bum at Shefan Daxue for their explanations of song styles during field research in May 2007, and to Lama Chönam of the Light of Berotsana Translation Committee for his help identifying passages in the style of the Ge sar epic and working through other challenging passages. Even though it shares a common meter with A mdo folk songs, Snying po tshe ring emphasized that when performed, the Ge sar epic features a range of melodies according to character and mood.

29. KTL 15: 99.6–100.5. Though *rmong tshig* literally means "foolish words," it is a colloquial phrase connoting the words exchanged between lovers; personal communication from Lama Chönam.

30. This is a reference to the eighteen *rdzong* conquered by Ge sar. My thanks to Brandon Dotson for pointing this out. The term *rdzong* can refer to a district or the fortress that served as its administrative center. Today, the term generally refers to the county level of administration within the prefectures of China.

31. KTL 10: 89.6–90.5.

32. The Tibetan reads: *chos sangs rgyas bstan la 'tshe ba'i dgra / bdud ma rungs glo snying za ba'i glu.*

33. The Nālandā Translation Committee has translated this as the "Warrior Song of Drala" (*Dgra bla'i dpa' glu*). See Nālandā Translation Committee 1997: 401–5.

34. Elsewhere I discuss in more detail performative utterances in this correspondence, based on John Searle's taxonomy of performative statements: "Tibetan Epistolary Revelations: Performative Speech in the Correspondence of a Buddhist Visionary Couple," in *Reading Tibetan Literature,* ed. Kurtis Schaeffer and Andrew Quintman (forthcoming). See John Searle, "A Taxonomy of Illocutionary Acts," in *Language, Mind, and Knowledge,* ed. Keith Gunderson (Minneapolis: University of Minnesota Press, 1975).

35. Humphrey 1994: 23. In coining this term, she modifies James Scott's well-known rubric of "hidden transcripts" (1990). Emphasis in the original.

36. The Tibetan reads: *bod phongs rgud nyam thag gso ba'i phyir / nom bkra shis g.yang zhags 'khyil ba'i glu.*

37. Mkha' 'bum 2005: 97.

38. KTL 2: 78.2–78.6. The term "black headed" (*mgo nag*) is a long-standing epithet for Tibetans and bears no relation to "black hat" (*zhwa nag*), a neologism related to the Maoist period.

39. In this stanza, I have made an amendment to this passage, changing *bya nga tsho'i* to *bya nga tshos.*

40. KTL 2: 78.2–78.6.

41. On standard animals associated with different habitats in Tibetan folk songs, as found in the *mgur* of Mi la ras pa, see Stein 1972: 260. Stein interprets the king of birds (*bya rgyal*) as the eagle, whereas Garma Chang interprets it as the garuḍa (1999: 10, n. 29).

42. It is not readily apparent what the snow lion might symbolize here. 'Brug mo skyid, a poet and professor at Qinghai Minyuan, suggested that the unfurling of the lion's turquoise mane could be interpreted as a call for Nam sprul rin po che to begin teaching the dharma (*chos gsung*). This interpretation is supported by Tā re lha mo's closing greetings: "Ala, how wondrous! Long life! May your teachings spread far and wide. May there be auspiciousness." Personal communication from 'Brug mo skyid, May 2007.

43. If we follow the chronological arrangement of the letters, as discussed in the previous chapter, then the rabbit year would refer to the eighth month of the lunar calendar, placing it in October 1978. For a discussion of the dating of letters in the correspondence, see chapter 3, note 7.

44. Her next letter, KTL 16, makes clear that she plans to formally greet him with her uncles and aunts.

45. KTL 15: 100.5 and 101.3. Once again, the term *rmong tshig* connotes amorous or sentimental speech. It is difficult to imagine precisely the context of this meeting, though one of the next letters (NJP 15) by Nam sprul rin po che makes clear that Tā re lha mo did come to greet him prior to their formal meeting with her relatives.

46. KTL 15: 101.6 ff.

47. This is one of the few passages in their correspondence in which *rten 'brel* is used in a technical sense as *pratītyasamutpāda* or "dependent origination."

48. JG 41.5–15.

49. NJP 15: 43.3–5. Note that *Jewel Garland* places KTL 17 alongside NJP 6 as if in dialogue. However, it makes sense to regard their letters as more closely corresponding in numbering. In the next passages, it is clear that NJP 15 chronicles his journey to visit Tā re lha mo.

50. The name of Ge sar's horse, whose speed surpassed all in the famous race by which he regained his throne, has a number of variants: Rkyang bu, Rkyang byung, Rkyang chung kha dkar, Rkyang rgod pher po, etc. (Stein 1959: 538ff). Perhaps here Nam sprul rin po che imagines his horse as comparable in strength to that of Ge sar's horse.

51. NJP 15: 44.1–2. The Tibetan reads: *sa rdo smrar gnyis de kha thag nye / lho 'dzam gling bskor dgos byung na yang / lus ngal dub byung yang 'gyod pa med.*

52. KTL 10: 91.6–92.1. The Tibetan reads: *chos sangs rgyas bstan pa mi nub phyir / srog brdos nas gzhan don khur khyer gyis / thugs bskyed kyi go cha brtsan po bgos.* In my translation, I have interpreted *srog brdos* as *srog bsdos*, meaning "at risk of one's life."

53. NJP 15: 43.5–44.1. The last line is a colloquial expression for joking, per Ringu Tulku.

54. Sujata 2005: 306.

55. Personal communication by 'Jam dbyangs nyi ma, May 2006.

56. KTL 15: 101.1–3.

57. Because Tā re lha mo left Pad ma for Gser rta across province borders, she could not hold the official title of *dgon bdag* for her father's monastery as registered with the government; this title is held by her kinsman, 'Jam dbyangs nyi ma.

58. Buddhaghosa 1991: 553 ff. In the *Abhidharmakośa*, Vasubandhu offers two different possible etymologies for the term denoting "having attained appearance" or "arising together, by reason of such and such a coming together of causes" (De La Vallée Poussin 1988: 413–15). In discussing its Pali equivalent, in the *Visuddhimagga*, Buddhaghosa insists on the latter interpretation, because he deems that "co-arising" is crucial to the definition. In his words, "it is a co-arising . . . in combination with conditions, not regardless of them" (1991: 529).

59. In its translation into Tibetan, *pratītyasamutpāda* (*rten cing 'brel bar 'byung ba*) denotes "arising" (*'byung ba*) of results in "dependence" (*rten*) upon causes and in "connection" (*'brel ba*) with multiple conditions. See TTC: 1073.

60. Gyatso 1998: 179.

61. This translation is borrowed from the Nālandā Translation Committee. In the context of the correspondence, I translate *rten 'brel* as "coincidence" to highlight the sense of contingency apparent in its usage by Tā re lha mo and Nam sprul rin po che. As the combination of "co" (with) and "incidence" (occurrence), etymologically "coincidence" conveys that multiple factors must converge to give rise to present experience. And because of its associations in English with luck, "coincidence" captures well the colloquial Tibetan sense of felicity when circumstances come together to produce good fortune. When conversing about causes and conditions, the couple did so in order to assess whether or not circumstances were favorable to their endeavor of treasure revelation. In my choice of a translation, I also sought a succinct term in order to mirror the compactness of Tibetan verse as much as possible. In addition to being cumbersome, "dependent origination" would be slightly misleading in this context, since for the most part Tā re lha mo and Nam sprul rin po che are not engaged in a technical or scholastic discussion of causation.

62. TTC: 1075. The Tibetan reads: *snga ltas sam 'byung 'gyur gyi rtags mtshan*. The other definitions are *rten cing 'brel bar 'byung ba* as above in note 59, the twelve nidānas, and a celebration.

63. Tulku Thondup 1997: 243, n. 156.

64. See for example Gyatso 1998: 177–81. With regard to revelations by the Bhutanese *gter ston* Pad ma gling pa, Michael Aris makes the point that "unless the auspices were exactly as stipulated in the prophecy foretelling each discovery, all kinds of injuries would befall those involved in the quest" (1988: 44). Thereafter Aris provides examples of such injuries and illnesses incurred by Pad ma gling pa and his followers during the treasure quest.

65. I use "click" as a homophonic translation of the Tibetan *'grigs* as well as "fall into place." The term *'grig pa* means "suitable" in the sense of events unfolding in an appropriate manner (TTC: 511).

66. NJP 15: 43.1–2. The Tibetan reads: *yid smon pa 'grub pa'i rten 'brel 'grigs*.

67. KTL 17: 116.3. The Tibetan reads: *thabs mang po'i rten 'brel legs na yang / 'phral mu stegs gdug pa'i 'tshe ba 'byung*.

68. NJP 2: 7.5–6. The Tibetan reads: *ring min rnyed pa'i rten 'brel 'grigs*.

69. KTL 11: 93.1. The Tibetan reads: *des 'phral rkyen zhi nas bde legs nges*.

70. In this context, *rgyu rkyen* refers to the material arrangements for a *tshogs*. My thanks to Lama Chönam for this clarification.

71. KTL 1: 77.1–78.1.

72. This well-known pilgrimage site is identified in chapter 3, note 1.

73. The Tibetan for this is *rten 'brel snying po*, abbreviated here as *rten snying*. It refers to a well-known formula explaining causation, frequently used in tantric ritual: *Oṃ ye dharmā hetu prabhavā hetuṃ teṣām tatāgato hyavadat teṣām ca yo nirodha evaṃ vādī mahāśramaṇaḥ svāhā*. An old Pali source for this classic Buddhist formula would be Mahāvagga 1.23.

74. NJP 3: 10.3–4 features the reference to the recitation of this mantra and its benefits.

75. NJP 3: 10.5. The Tibetan reads: *byas na las smon rten 'brel gtad rgya'i mthu sad*.

76. NJP 3: 10.5–6. The Tibetan reads: *shar phyogs g.yu mtsho'i dus su rin chen sgrom rgyar / zab bcud bde stong dga' bzhi'i gsang lam zhes bya / dus su bab tshe ma dang mkha' 'gro'i lung ston*.

77. This sampling of their ritual prescriptions is drawn from NJP 11, KTL 11, and KTL 17.

78. KTL 22: 134.4–135.2.

79. KTL 22: 135.2. The Tibetan reads: *'phral rkyen de nges par zhi snyam pa byung*.

80. KTL 9: 87.2. The Tibetan reads: *bsod nams rten du 'dzoms pa'i skal ba mchis*.

81. For example, when praising the Ye shes mtsho rgyal sādhana that Tā re lha mo sent with her first letter, Nam sprul rin po che refers to it as "the profound secret treasure, the nectar of mind and the inheritance / from the only father and guru, the exalted Lotus-Born One" (NJP 1: 5.4–5). The Tibetan reads: *pha cig rje btsun mtsho skyes bla ma yi / pha phog thugs bcud gsang ba zab mo'i gter*.

82. Etymologically, it suggests an array of some sort. It is a rather curious term that combines the verb "to array" (*bkod pa*) with the noun meaning "plain" (*thang*) or flat expanse of some sort.

83. KTL 17: 117.2. Note that the term I translate as "deeds" (*las*) is the same word for karma, which literally means "action" and refers to intentional action in a Buddhist context that bears fruit in future consequences. The Tibetan reads: *tshe sngon ma'i las gi bkod thang dran*.

84. KTL 13: 95.4–5. The Tibetan reads: *rten thabs grogs so pad ma'i bkod thang red*. The *so* here is a meter filler. In the same letter, she describes rain as the "worldly legacy" (*srid pa'i bkod thang*) of a cloud, and the propensity of a bee to circle a lotus flower as its "legacy from the past" (*sngon las bskos thang*), using a cognate term. See KTL 13: 95.1–2 and 95.6.

85. KTL 13: 96.5–6. The reference to flowers here likely refers to the act of tossing a flower onto a maṇḍala in order to indicate one's tutelary deity (*yi dam*) during a tantric initiation.

86. The power of "words of truth" (Skt.: *satyavacana*; Tib.: *bden tshig*)—"that truth has a power which a person with the right qualifications can invoke"—is a long-standing trope in Indian literature that Tibetans inherited. See Brown 1972.

87. Thondup 1997.

88. NJP 3: 9.4–10.2. Note that I break the fourth line in the second stanza into two lines in my translation.

89. NJP 3: 9.6. This is a single line of verse in the original. The Tibetan reads: *reg grol phyag rgya'i nye lam a nu'i zab chos*.

90. NJP 3: 10.2. The Tibetan for this phrase reads: *bka' mchid mi 'gyur rdo rje'i phreng ba*.

91. NJP 5: 16.2–3.

92. KTL 17: 117.3–4. The Tibetan phrases are: *'bral ba med pa'i mtshe ma* and *dam tshig gcig pa'i spun zla*.

93. NJP 8: 25.6–26.1. The context for this image is a short letter that references their past lives as Bdud 'dul rdo rje and Mi 'gyur dpal sgron (but not the famous daughter of Gter bdag gling pa). See brief discussion of this past life identification in the previous chapter.

94. KTL 15: 106.6–107.2.

95. NJP 2: 7.5–6.

96. Victoria Sujata provides an overview of interjections, particular to *mgur*, and indicates different views on their meanings (2005: 228–45). "E ma!" also conveys a sense of wonder (TTC: 3141).

97. We can only judge the pacing of the letters by those composed by Tā re lha mo, since her scribe dated a total of eleven letters. According to the dating discussed in note 7 of chapter 3, their exchange started slowly over the fall and winter of 1978, with several months transpiring between each letter she sent. The affection picks up in the spring, once the snow melts on the mountain passes and travel becomes easier. From October 1978 to May 1979, Tā re lha mo sent four letters. Then in Sagadawa, the fourth month of the Tibetan calendar, which generally falls in May or June, she sent six letters. These could have been sent in two batches, since two letters are dated for that period, but nonetheless the increase in output is significant. Then in the fifth and sixth months of the lunar calendar, which occur during the summer, she sent another four letters. Then in a single month, when Nam sprul rin po che visited Smar khog, they exchanged eight to eleven letters, depending on how you count them. This is the hare month, spanning September and October in 1979. There are five letters in the next month, the dragon, which in the system used in the letters would be the ninth month, spanning October and November that year. What appears to be the last actual letter, with a date and formal opening and closing, is dated to the horse month or eleventh month, which spans December and January. According to the chart in Cornu 1997, the eighth day would fall on December 28th, 1979. Thus, their correspondence took place over approximately fourteen months.

98. NJP 17: 45.3. The Tibetan reads: *da mi ring 'gro ba'i dus babs*.

99. This passage supports a date for her arrival in Snyan lung in 1980 rather than late 1979, the last date available in the correspondence. When she refers to next year, Tā re lha mo could be referring to the secular calendar of the Chinese state or, more likely, the Tibetan new year (*lo gsar*), which according to the lunar calendar falls in February or March. In 1980, the Tibetan new year was February 17 according to Cornu 1997.

100. KTL 18: 124.3–5.

101. This type of onomatopoeia, according to R. A. Stein, derives from an archaic style that survived to the present in the Ge sar epic, and it is not restricted to representing sounds by likeness but utilizes standard associations by convention. Stein

notes that *kyu ru ru* is the sound of laughter, songs, or the warble of a bird and lists *tha ra ra* for "clouds" of warriors assembling (1972: 258), whereas Tāre Lhamo uses *tha la la* for actual clouds gathering and the resulting rains. The effect is rousing. This is no lament; it is an appeal and further enticement.

102. This is the poetic figure of contiguous yamaka, similar to NJP 19 discussed in the previous chapter. On Daṇḍin's presentation of this type of yamaka, see Eppling 1989: 200–4. Examples of its application in *mgur* can be found in Sujata 2005: 166 ff.

103. NJP 24: 58.3–4.

104. KTL 25: 139.3. The Tibetan reads: *smin smin nga smin*. A translation of this delightful passage can be found in chapter 3.

105. NJP 25: 59.6–60.2.

106. This is a case of discontiguous phonemic repetition, similar to NJP 11 discussed in the previous chapter. On Daṇḍin's presentation of this type of yamaka, see Eppling 1989: 204–6. Though in my translation "today" comes at the end of each line, in the Tibetan it is syllables six and seven in an eight-syllable meter.

107. What I translate here as "demonic forces" is literally given in the song as the four māras (*bdud bzhi*). Despite the usual association of the four māras with internal demons, given their evocations throughout the correspondence of demonic forces obstructing them, this line seems to refer to external conditions, finally surmounted.

108. NJP 25: 66.5–67.2.

5. A Tantric Couple: The Hagiography of Cultural Revitalization

1. See the appendices with catalogues of the correspondence between Tā re lha mo and Nam sprul rin po che. These excerpted letters, and where they are found in *Jewel Garland*, are clearly marked.

2. The *gser 'phreng* collections, as discussed in Quintman 2014, provides an example of biographical compilations of religious lineages in the Bka' brgyud tradition, whereas genealogies in Pad ma 'od gsal mtha' yas 2000 and 2003 of the Bdud 'joms line represent a more local flavor in which family and religious lineage descent overlap.

3. For example, the *rnam thar* of Bde chen chos kyi dbang mo includes scenes of her teachings and revelations with Gsang sngags gling pa in which they are described as *gter chen yab yum* (Rossi 2008). In addition, in the interwoven auto /biographical corpus of Se ra mkha' 'gro and Dri med 'od zer, the destined consorts are depicted interacting on numerous occasions even as they spent much of their lives apart (see Jacoby 2014a).

4. JG 47.14–17. The Tibetan reads: *de nas bzung bstan 'gro'i dpung gnyen skyabs rje yab yum zung gdan thog gcig tu 'dzoms nas snyigs dus kyi rgud pa mtha' dag gso ba'i las smon rten 'brel mnyam du sad.*

5. For example, JG 68.9 and 100.8. As mentioned in chapter 2, this language can also be found in the preface to their *rnam thar*; see Pad ma 'od gsal mtha' yas 1997: ii.4–5 and iii.1.

6. JG 68.4–10. This phrase comes from the following line in Tibetan: *'dzam gling sa bcud gso phyir gnas chen rnams su gter bum brgya phrag du ma sbas.*

7. JLB 25.6–8.

8. Germano 1998: 72.

9. For example, see Gyatso 1989, Mumford 1989, Macdonald 1991, Huber 1994 and 1999.

10. Gyatso 1989.

11. Huber 1999: 26 ff.

12. Galtung 1995 has used the terms "anomy" and "atomy" (or in his spelling, "anomie" and "atomie"), to describe the social costs in the process of modernization. I am here extending his usage to describe collective trauma.

13. Makley 2007: 29–75.

14. Including the brief frame given to the letters by Pad ma 'od gsal mtha' yas, the excerpts of her letters introducing this section extends from JG 27.12 to 34.10. If we included the final excerpt from her letters, which closes this section (JG 45.1–47.6), then excerpts from her letters take up nearly ten pages of *Jewel Garland*.

15. In *Jewel Garland*, this figure is identified as the "great lord of siddhas" (*grub pa'i dbang phyug chen po*) and a relative of the Fourth Rdo grub chen incarnation, Rig 'dzin 'ja' lus rdo rje, who was one of Tā re lha mo's main teachers. This is likely not the same person as Pad ma tshe dbang, whose prophecy is included later in *Jewel Garland* and discussed in note 19 below, though his name is sometime abbreviated to Rgyal sras Pad lo (A bu dkar lo et al. 2000: 246–49).

16. JG 35.17 and 36.1.

17. JG 36.16–37.2.

18. KTL 13: 95.4–5.

19. According to the *Mgo log sman rtsis rig pa'i lo rgyus*, Pad ma tshe dbang was the son of Mgar ra rgyal sras Pad ma rnam rgyal and his consort Gsa' [Gsal?] sgron (A bu dkar lo et al 2000: 246–49). In this source, he is stated to be the mind incarnation (*thugs kyi sprul sku*) of Mgar klong Pad ma bdud 'dul dbang phyug gling pa, his grandfather and a local gter ston of renown based at Bag nag dgon in Pad ma County.

20. JG 40.11–13.

21. JG 40.17. The Tibetan for this reads: *a bhya tā re thabs shes zung.* I am reading *a bhya* as shorthand for *abhaya.*

22. The full prophecy can be found in JG 40.13–41.3. This phrase reads in Tibetan: *gter gsar rnying gi bstan pa phyogs bcur spel.*

23. When I tried to inquire about the circumstances of his new name, the topic appeared to be taboo.

24. JG 34.11–35.3. This vision is dated to the sixth month of the earth horse year (1978).

25. JG 35.12–14. The Tibetan for this reads: *de phyis su mtsho rgyal dngos kyi sprul ba mkha' 'gro tā re de vī dang mnyam 'dzoms byung ba'i rtags mtshan yin.* As previously mentioned, Devī means "goddess" in Sanskrit and is translated by the Tibetan term *lha mo* as in the second part of Tā re lha mo's name. The whole episode, vision, and gloss can be found in JG 35.3–14.

26. JG 56.1–10.

27. JG 17.13–17.

28. JG 71.3–77.17.

29. JG 49.11–15.

30. Personal communication from Bya bral chos dbyings in May 2006 in reference to a cure the Tā re lha mo effected for his mother. Bya bral chos dbyings, who is better known locally as A khu Chos dbyings, shares a past life identification with Tā re lha mo; both are considered emanations of Khra dge slong Tshul khrims dar rgyas.

31. JG 59.2–7.

32. Shin ho may be a phoneticization of Xinghai County in Hainan Prefecture of Qinghai Province. When I traveled to Brag dkar spral rdzong in 1997, the county seat was several hours by car on a rough dirt road through a steep gorge and river basin. No doubt, a decade earlier, it was perilous to drive this route in the rain.

33. JG 66.9–70.3.

34. Recall the miracle tale recounted in chapter 2, based on oral accounts from her homeland, of Tā re lha mo preventing a hailstorm from EGT 9.35–41.

35. JG 56.10–15. Pad ma gtum po also confirmed them as emanations of Nam mkha'i snying po and Ye shes mtsho rgyal.

36. JG 51.8–16.

37. JG 53.2–5.

38. JG 51.17–52.4.

39. The ritual of "averting the call of the ḍākinīs" (*mkha' 'gro'i sun bzlog*) is performed for someone extremely ill or on the brink of death JG 53.12–54.8.

40. JG 81.6–7. The full account from which this is drawn can be found on JG 80.17–82.9. The Gesar performance can be found in their treasure corpus *Gling seng chen nor bu dgra 'dul dang 'jang g.yu lha'i rtogs brjod dpa' bo'i gad rgyang las a khyung ke ru'i rgyal khab chos la bkod tshul gyi rnam thar bsdus pa ngo mtshar lha yi rol mo* in PTC vol. 12: 1–91, also found in the newly published paperback addition of their treasure corpus (2013, vol. 9: 1–110).

41. JG 81.10–12.

42. JG 54.12–13. The Tibetan reads: *thugs brtse ba chen pos rjes su bzungs te smin grol gyi chos bka' du ma gnang*. In *Jewel Garland* as well as in *Spiraling Vine of Faith*, Mkhan po 'Jigs med phun tshogs is referred to variously as Mkhan chen dam pa, Mkhan rin po che, Mkhan yid bzhin nor bu, and Mkhan chen nyid as well as by his full name, Mkhan chen 'Jigs med phun tshogs 'byung gnas.

43. JG 48.15–49.10 and 62.1–7. The first passage is translated below.

44. JG 52.15–53.2, JG 59.7–14, and 59.14–17 respectively.

45. JG 70.10–14. Mdo bla Chos kyi nyi ma also happens to be the father of the Bdud 'joms yang srid whom Tā re lha mo identified in Golok, born that same year.

46. As previously mentioned in the introduction, his name is Sangs rgyas pad ma bzhad pa. See http://www.nyingma.com/artman/publish/dudjom_yangsis.shtml.

47. Confirming the centrality of these three sets of teachings in the couple's teaching and transmission stream, in 2007, when Nam sprul rin po che transmitted the entirety of their treasure corpus, he also transmitted the teachings of A phang gter chen and Bdud 'joms rin po che.

48. JG 48.15–49:10.

49. JG 58.3–6. Glosses are included in the original; I have separated them out in my translation and discussion.

50. JG 54.13–55.2. Dbang chen nyi ma was Tā re lha mo's elder brother and the natural successor to his father's treasure corpus. Given that he did not survive the early decades of the Chinese occupation, Mkhan po 'Jigs med phun tshogs reinterprets the prophecy to refer to Nam sprul rin po che.

51. This is quite a different image from the one that Tā re lha mo offered in her fifth letter, mentioned in chapter 3, where the tigress circles the monkey in the sport of attraction.

52. JG 58.8–58.12.

53. I confirmed this with the Sakya Trizin in a visit to Dehradun in April 2007. He told me that although he never met Tā re lha mo, they communicated by mail and phone and discussed trying to meet on several occasions in either Singapore or Taiwan.

54. These events are chronicled in JG 62.1–8, JG 64.16–65.14, and JG 69.7–13. During the Kālacakra initiation, Mkhan po 'Jigs med phun tshogs also privately gave them transmissions for one of Las rab gling pa's treasures.

55. JG 69.9–11.

56. JG 56.1–10.

57. JG 62.9–13. The Tibetan reads: *sngon 'jam dbyangs mkhyen brtse dbang pos mchog gyur bde chen gling pa gter ston 'khrul med du mnga' gsol ba bzhin ngas kyang khyed yab yum o rgyan pad ma'i rgyal tshab 'khrul med du mnga' gsol ba yin / phyin chad gter chos mang po 'bri dgo.*

58. JG 62.16–17. The Tibetan reads: *rang cag tshe rabs mang por 'bral ba med / khyod gnyis kyis gzhan la dbang khrid sogs gang mang gnang dgos.*

59. JG 65.15–17. The Tibetan reads: *da ni khyed zung mtsho sngon po dang / brag dkar sprel 'dzong / rma chen gangs dkar sogs su byon dang dgos pa rgya chen yod.*

60. Personal communication from Tulku Thondup, August 2004.

61. JG 48.3. The Tibetan reads: *gangs ljongs bstan 'dzin yongs kyi zhabs pad yun du brtan phyir.* The full account of this revelation can be found in JG 48.1–15.

62. "Treasure casket" (*gter sgrom*) is a standard term for the container of treasures, but the treasures displayed by Nam sprul rin po che on my first visit to Snyan lung dgon in 2004 were mostly stones of different sizes with various markings.

63. SVF 141.11–145.5.

64. The account of their second joint revelation in this paragraph comes from JG 50.5–11. The Tibetan for this phrase reads: *slob dpon pad ma'i phyag tham can.*

65. JG 50.8–9. The Tibetan reads: *tshogs 'khor gyi grangs ma 'khyol ba sogs yul dus kyi rten 'brel 'ga' zhig.*

66. JG 50.11–14. The Tibetan reads: *dgun khar yang sa la drod 'bar te smug sprin lang long du 'khrigs shing me tog gi char babs / mtsho mthar me tog sna tshogs gsar du bzhad pa sogs bkra shis pa'i dge mtshan mang po byung.*

67. JG 48.10–15.

68. JG 95.3–4. The Tibetan reads: *grub pa'i rtags mtshan sna tshogs kyis rtog ge ba kha cig kyang dad pa'i lam la bkod.*

69. The three major clan divisions in Golok that trace their origins to Gnyan po g.yu rtse are: A skyong 'bum in Gcig sgril, Dga' bde, and Rma chen; Dbang chen 'bum in Dar lag; and Pad ma 'bum in Pad ma. On the origins of the Golok clans, see Don grub dbang rgyal and Nor sde, *Mgo log lo rgyus deb ther* (1992: 115–32), Rock 1956:

123–29, and the first chapter of the *Mdo mkhyen brtse ye shes rdo rje'i rnam thar* (Sichuan: Mi rigs dpe skrun khang, 1997): 3–24. On the the ancestral relations between Drong ri and the Wa shul (alt. Dbal shul) clan, see Jacoby 133 ff.

70. Several *gnas yig* for this site can be found in *Gnas mchog bkra shis sgo mang gi gnas yig phyogs bsdus rin chen 'phreng ba* (O rgyan 'phrin las bzang po, n.d.), including one attributed to Nam sprul Tā re lha mo zung, composed by Tā re lha mo based on a brda yig revealed by Nam sprul rin po che (47–54).

71. JG 60.6–10.

72. Given the publication of *Jewel Lantern of Blessing* in 2001, it is unclear whether the thirteenth volume could refer to an earlier version of their collected correspondence. The facsimile edition that Nam sprul rin po che gave me in 2014 included a final letter that he wrote to Tā re lha mo on the one-year anniversary of her passing, so its publication date would have been c. 2003–4. This letter is discussed at length in the epilogue.

73. A bu dkar lo 2001: 23.12–24.6. On the typology of treasures, see Doctor 2005.

74. Personal communication by Nam sprul rin po che, July 2006.

75. JG 61.13–16.

76. Orgyen Tobgyal 1988: 21.

77. Personal communication from Pad ma 'od gsal mtha' yas, June 2006.

78. JG 64.16–65.14.

79. JG 65.9–14. *Jewel Garland* records other shared visions during their visit to Wutai Shan: at a stūpa called Rgya nag shes ngan, a Chinese girl dressed in red appeared to be an apparition of the Chinese princess Kong jo, and at Yan gro si (Ch: Yuanzhaosi), the first temple of the Dge lugs sect in China, Sarasvatī sang to them in the guise of a cuckoo bird. Rituals dedicated to Sarasvatī (Tib.: *Dbyangs can lha mo*) can be found in Vol. 6 (Cha): 123–196 of their treasure corpus.

80. JG 65.17–66.8.

81. Their treasure corpus is predominantly ritual in content, organized by deity and topic rather than by treasure cycle.

82. JG 47.10–14. On the various forms of Vajrayoginī, see English 2002.

83. JG 67.17–68.4.

84. JG 67.17–68.4 and 96.15–17.

85. JG 85.6–96.12.

86. Personal communication from Nam sprul rin po che, June 2006.

87. The initial extraction of this treasure occurs in JG 89.5–8, and the occasion on which they set it down is depicted in JG 91.14–17.

88. JG 91.12–14.

89. JG 87.14–88.4.

90. JG 86.13–15. The Tibetan for this phrase reads: *mdo khams sogs yul gru du ma nas dad ldan gyi mjal skor ba stong phrag mang po*. The text title is *O rgyan chen po'i sgrub pa thig le gsang rdzogs*.

91. KTL 14: 97.2–99.2.

92. JG 91.4–10.

93. These are listed in JG 101: 3–8, reiterated in JLB 24.6–13.

94. See Germano 1998: 72.

5. A TANTRIC COUPLE

95. JG 50.15–17. The Tibetan for this phrase reads: *a phang gter chen o rgyan 'phrin las gling pa'i zab gter yongs kyi smin grol gdams pa'i man ngag rnams phyogs bcu kun tu spel ba'i rten 'brel phun sum tshogs . . .*

96. A pang O rgyan mkha' spyod gling pa is mentioned as the author of several *gnas yig* for Bkra shis sgo mang (O rgyan 'phrin las bzang po, n.d. 2 and 26–40). It is possible that this is another name for A phang gter chen.

97. JG 60.11–61.7.

98. Don grub dbang rgyal and Nor sde 1992: 145–221.

99. See *Khams phyogs dkar mdzes khul gyi dgon sde so so'i lo rgyus gsal bar bshad pa thub bstan gsal ba'i me long* (Krung go'i bod kyi shes rig zhib 'jug lte gnas kyi chos lugs lo rgyus zhib 'jug 1995, 2: 283–378).

100. Personal communication from 'Jam dbyangs nyi ma, May 2006.

101. On the emergence of the ritual of *bde chen zhing sgrub*, see Kapstein 2004: 32 ff.

102. JG 60.15–17. For a discussion of these vows, see Jamgön Kongtrul 1998: 79–159 and Sakya Pandita 2002: 41–80.

103. JG 60.17–61.4.

104. Personal communication from Tulku Thondup, autumn 2004.

105. See my "Reimagining Buddhist Ethics on the Tibetan Plateau" (2013).

106. JG 61.7–12.

107. JG 100.15–17. This is a prophecy attributed to Stag sham [nus ldan] rdo rje regarding a "regent of Padma" (*pad ma'i rgyal tshab*), who is a "fearless" (*'jigs med*) protector of beings and meets one named Tā re. The Tibetan reads: *zab gter nam mkha' mdzod kyi sgo 'phar 'byed / 'brel tshad rnga yab dpal rir 'dren par 'gyur.*

108. Personal communication from Nam sprul rin po che, May 2007. The transcription for this statement is: *phyogs so so nas yong pa'i bla ma tshos sa de ru chos zhu ru yong dus chos 'brel chang pa red.*

109. The technical term is "vajra sibling" or *rdo rje'i mched lcam*. On the various typologies of "siblings," see Jamgön Kongtrul 1998: 280–81 and 481 notes 174–75.

110. JG 61.7–61.12.

111. Liturgical texts dedicated to Thugs chen pad dkar can be found in Vol. 4 (Nga) of the treasure corpus of A phang gter chen, titled *Rgyal dbang pad ma'i rgyal tshab o rgyan phrin las gling pa'i zab gter nor bu'i phreng ba.*

112. JG 58.12–59.1.

113. Personal communication by Sprul sku Lhag bsam rnam dag, June 2014.

114. JG 63.9–64.5.

115. These monasteries will be listed later in this chapter.

116. JG 64.9–15.

117. JG 67.3–7.

118. JG 67.7–9. The Tibetan for this phrase reads: *bla grwa yongs la smin grol gyi chos bka' du ma bstsal.*

119. JG 67.11–16.

120. JG 68.10–13.

121. JG 68.16–69.6.

122. JG 69.13–17.

123. JG 69.17–70.5.

124. JG 70.5–9. The Tibetan for these phrases reads: *bla grwa yongs la smin grol gyi chos bka', mang tshogs yongs la chos 'brel gsungs,* and *ser skya yongs la smin grol gyi chos bka' ci rigs bstsal.* I understand *chos 'brel gsungs* to mean *chos 'brel su gsungs,* in accordance with its appearance elsewhere in *Jewel Garland* (i.e., 61.11).

125. JG 78.16–79.11.

126. JG 80.6–13.

127. Eventually, Rig 'dzin Nyi ma moved from Snyan lung, or Snyan lung theg chen chos skor gling in its full name, and established a hermitage nearby, leaving the monastery in charge of Tā re lha mo and Nam sprul rin po che.

128. *Snyan lung dgon gyi lo rgyus* (hereafter HON): 341.7–14. The passage continues to describe the various buildings that were constructed and sacra that were installed, as discussed below.

129. Personal communication from Nam sprul rin po che, May 2007. His clan is the Rus gsar ma (alt. Bu chung Ru gsar ma), with three to four hundred families scattered throughout the valleys in and around Snyan lung.

130. Personal communication from Tulku Thondup.

131. *Snyan lung dgon gyi lo rgyus* lists the structures and sacra at Snyan lung prior to 1958 as follows: two temples, a main assembly hall, approximately thirty monk's quarters, a collection of scriptures totaling more than five hundred volumes, including the *Bka' 'gyur* and *Bstan 'gyur, Rnying ma rgyud 'bum, Mdzod bdun, Snying thig ya bzhi,* as well as statues, scroll paintings, musical instruments, silk banners, and parasols (HON 340.25–341.3). Also mentioned are a *bshad grwa* and *sgrub grwa* established by Gzhu chen Vai ro mi 'gyur ye shes rdo rje and Gzhu chen sprul sku Kun bzang nyi ma (HON 340.8–10).

132. HON 341.14–20.

133. The dating of the annual event and approximate numbers in attendance come from an interview with Sprul sku Lhag bsam in June 2014.

134. This footage can be found on a set of two VCDs (video CDs) titled *Snyan mo lung gyi sgra dbyangs,* which was produced by Snyan lung dgon after March 2002, since it shows the consecration of Tā re lha mo's sku gdung, and prior to August 2004, when I received a copy from Nam sprul rin po che.

135. This list comes from *Snyan mo lung gyi sgra dbyangs,* where the names of these structures are given as: Slob grwa ma rig mun sel gling, Sgrub grwa gsang sngags smin grol gling, Sgom grwa dgongs pa rang shar gling, Rdor sems sgrub grwa mnyam 'chad rang grol gling, Bshad grwa thos bsam nor bu'i gling, Rin po che yab yum la gzim khang rigs 'dzin dga' tshal, Bde mchog dga' tsal, Zab don a ti rdo'i lha khang, Gzhi 'od bsil khang, Gu ru'i lha khang mthong ba don ldan, and Sgom khang kun bzang 'od zer gling.

136. HON 339: 1–16 and JG 8.10–9.6.

137. HON 339.21–22. The Tibetan reads: *rgyal ba kaḥ thog pa'i ring lugs dri ma med pa'i bshad sgrub kyi rgyun bskyang ba'i srol bzang da lta'i bar gnas so.*

138. Personal communication from Dge legs nyi ma and some of the retreatants, June 2006.

139. Personal communication from Nam sprul rin po che, July 2006.

140. HON 339.22–340.1.

141. Personal communication from Nam sprul rin po che, May 2007.

142. Kolas and Thowsen 2005: 52.

143. Don grub dbang rgyal and Nor sde 1992: 154–55.

144. Personal communication from 'Jam dbyangs nyi ma, May 2006.

145. Personal communication from Nam sprul rin po che, September 2005.

146. JLB 26.4–8.

147. 'Os za dgon, possibly conflated with A bzod in Gcig sgril discussed below.

148. The information in this paragraph comes from an interview with Yon tan dpal bzang in July 2007.

149. Thus, his full name is A phang sprul sku O rgyan tshe dbang grags pa, alias 'Jigs med dbang drag rdo rje, but locally he is known by the nickname, Sprul sku Tshe bo. The information in this paragraph comes from an interview with 'Jigs med dbang drag rdo rje in May 2006.

150. See chapter 1, note 36 for a list of the names and locations for these six temples. The description in this paragraph is based on my own observation of the site and other state-recognized Gesar temples during May 2006.

151. JG 68.7–9 and HON 341.22–27.

152. Personal communication from Nor sde, May 2006.

153. Makley 2008: 96.

154. JG 91.7–10.

Epilogue: The Legacy of a Tantric Couple

1. The newest version of her life story by Rig 'dzin dar rgyas, as yet unpublished, focuses on her youth and therefore also does not include an account of Tā re lha mo's final years.

2. The content of this section precedes the narration of her final years and death by Nam sprul rin po che during a marathon interview in July 2006.

3. The transcription for Nam sprul rin po che's statement is: *dgu bcu go lnga / de nas de tshun chod kyi gsar ba zig cig cang yod rgyu ma red / dgon par song na sngon chad rnam thar gong ma yi rnam thar / de las sngon gyi rnam thar nang dgon pa tsho'i nang la song ba / de ring yang dbang bskur yod rgyu red chos bshad yod rgyu red / de 'dra yod rgyu red.*

4. The transcription for this statement is: *da dgon pa gcig gi nang dper na thengs gcig la thengs mang po song ba bris na / yang lo re nang yang der song ba bris ba phan pa yod ni e red bo.*

5. The transcription for this statement is: *lo cha shas kyi 'phror 'gro ba las lo re rer 'gro gi yod ni ma red / mang che ba de dus rgyun 'di nas bsdad 'dug ni red / 'dir dus rgyun da dgon pa brgya phrag mang po de nas khong tsho bla sprul cha ga dang de nas tshur la yong na / de nas mkha' 'gros dbang bskur de dus rgyun du nga tshos nyi ma gcig la mtshams la 'dug dus min pa nyi ma gcig ga khom pa yang dag yod ni ma red / khong tsho yang mang po thon yang mang po thon nas dbang bskur zer ni red.*

6. Janet Gyatso 1997 discusses the use of diaries and calendars in the composition of Tibetan autobiographies, and here it appears that contemporary paperback astrological charts served as a locus for taking notes. The booklets contain astrological

charts for each week and indicate auspicious days in general terms and as they relate to specific birth years. Such calendars are routinely used to discern auspicious days for public events such as rituals as well as to decide when to pursue certain types of personal endeavors, such as inaugurating travel or business.

7. Personal communication from Pad ma 'od gsal mtha' yas, June 2006.

8. The content for his narration of Tā re lha mo's final years and death by Nam sprul rin po che in this section derives from an interview in July 2006.

9. This detail is mentioned in JLB 18.18–19, where it specifies that they remained in retreat for six to seven months each year.

10. Mkhan po Chos skyabs was a revered elder and cleric-scholar in the region of Gser rta.

11. Personal communication from Nam sprul rin po che, July 2006. The transcription for this phrase is: *dgon pa cha ga song zig yang 'dra 'dra red.*

12. Personal communication from Nam sprul rin po che, July 2006. The transcription for this statement is: *mkha' 'gro khong yun ring bor sku mi bzhugs pa'i rmi lam.*

13. Personal communication from Tulku Thondup. My thanks to Yang ga for providing the English equivalent for *bad kan gre thog.*

14. The description and quotations in this paragraph and the next come from a two-page document that provides a brief account of Tā re lha mo's passing and includes her final remarks to a gathering of disciples. For this reason, I will refer to this document as her "last testament" (*bka' chems*), as it has no title, though the final line refers to it as a "Brief Account of Khandro's Departure" (2.23–24, *mkha' 'gro gshegs pa'i lo rgyus mdor bsdus,* hereafter abbreviated KD). It consists of a computer printout that Nam sprul rin po che gave me in August 2004.

15. KD 2.8–9. The Tibetan for this reads: *bla ma gtan grogs mchog sprul rin po che'i ci gsung bsgrub te sgo gsum gyi zhabs zhu ci nus.*

16. KD 2.11–14. The Tibetan reads: *nga ni gtan grogs rin po che dang byang chub bar du skad cig tsam yang mi 'bral bar bstan 'gro'i don kun 'bad med 'byung bar ngas rtsa gsum srung ma dang a nyo rin po che (a phaṃ gter chen) la yang skyabs bcol dang smon lam dam bca' yin zhes sogs gsungs.*

17. Her last testament reads that she passed away in the "elephant resting posture" (KD 2.15–16, *glang chen nyal stabs*), possibly a variation on Śākyamuni's lion resting posture (Skt.: *siṃhāsana*; Tib.: *seng ge nyal stabs*) in which he reportedly entered parinirvāṇa.

18. KD 2.17–18. The Tibetan reads: *de tshe khyim nang du dri bzang dang phyi nang kun du 'ja' sprin kha dog sna tshogs pa yang shar.*

19. KD 2.20–21. In understanding the second miraculous sign to be vulture feathers, I have emended *bya rgod gyi thul* to *bya rgod kyi thu.*

20. KD 2.22–23.

21. NJP 30: 181.1–188.4.

22. NJP 30: 181.1–2. This is printed in smaller letters, suggesting that it serves as the prelude providing the time and place of the letter's composition.

23. NJP 30: 181.5–6. The Tibetan reads: *mtsho rgyal mi mo'i zol 'chang gtan gyi grogs / sngags skyes mtshan ldan tā re mkha' 'gro dang / bde stong thabs shes zung 'jug grogs bgyis nas . . .*

24. NJP 30: 182.4–183.1.

25. The verse literally says *gzim chung*, and I take this to refer to their small retreat hut above their residence, Gzim khang rigs 'dzin dga' tshal. See chapter 5, note 135.

26. This passage can be found in Padmakara Translation Group 1999: 137–46 and, more briefly, in Jacoby 2014a: 312.

27. Jacoby emphasizes that Se ra mkha' 'gro drew on this well-known version of of Ye shes mtsho rgyal's life as a literary model for her own visionary exchange with Dri med 'od zer after his passing, found at the end of his biography (2014a: 306–15).

28. I have emended *'khrul* to *'khril* to render the phrase describing her dance as: *mnyen lcug 'khril ldem*.

29. NJP 30: 184.1–185.1.

30. NJP 30: 185.1–187.6. Note that Nam sprul rin po che uses the highly honorific epithet for a Buddhist teacher, "Wish-Fulfilling Jewel" (*yid bzhin nor bu*), to refer to both of them.

31. His description of the vision's dissolution and its effects spans NJP 30: 187.6–188.4, marking the conclusion of their collected correspondence.

32. The recording and lyrics were given to me by one of the female singers, who I know only as Sgrol ma. This song does not appear on any of the tapes or VCDs for sale at Snyan lung to which I had access, though it was played during the *chos tshogs* in 2006. A music video of the song, rendered in Chinese by the same group of female singers, is available on the home page of the Chinese website for Snyan lung dgon (Ch.: Nianlong si): http://www.nianlongsi.com/index_zh.php (accessed January 18, 2016). The Tibetan for these lyrics reads: *'jigs med phun tshogs rin po che / mkha' 'gro tā re lha mo lags / khyed zung ni nyi ma dang zla ba bzhin / kun khyab du 'od snang 'bar 'dug / a rin po che / khyed ni nga tsho'i sems gting gi glu / khyed ni 'gro ba yi skyabs mgon*.

33. Snyan mo lung gyi sgra dbyangs, a set of two VCDs, must have been produced after March 2002, since it shows the consecration of Tā re lha mo's reliquary (*sku gdung*), and prior to August 2004, when I received a copy from Nam sprul rin po che. It has no ISRC number.

34. A bu dkar lo 2001. The Chinese title is *Nianlong shangshi fumu renboqie lüezhuan*, which roughly translates as *A Brief Biography of the Precious Nyenlung Teaching Couple*. *Jewel Lantern of Blessings* also appears in a small volume in translation into Chinese and English, though there is no publication information for either. In the last five years, Snyan lung dgon has also published their life stories and teachings in Chinese in two volumes. These are: *Yanjiao huibian: Erli renyun moni baoman*, or roughly *A Collection of Oral Instructions: The Precious Garland of Jewels Spontaneously [Giving Rise to] the Two Benefits*, a collection of oral instructions attributed to the couple that includes teachings by Nam sprul rin po che after Tā re lha mo passed away; and *Nianlong shangshi fumu guangzhuan: Wugou moni baoman*, or roughly *The Extensive Biographies of the Nyenlung Teaching Couple: A Precious Garland of Jewels*. The latter is a rendering of their life stories that has been rearranged to separate the individual accounts of their early lives from the joint narration of their activities together later in life. This second volume, published in 2009, also includes teachings attributed to the couple. My appreciation to Shes rab dbang mo for her help rendering the transliteration and translations of these titles.

35. For a discussion of monastery-produced VCDs, see my "T-Pop and the Lama: Buddhist 'Rites out of Place' in Tibetan Monastery-Produced VCDs," in *Religion and Modernity in the Himalaya* (New York: Routledge, 2016). VCD technology has gradually given way to DVDs in recent years.

36. *Mdzad bsdus mthong tshad rang grol* is a set of four VCDs (no ISRC number) chronicling Nam sprul rin po che's solo pilgrimage in 2004. With vocals by his son, Sprul sku Lhag bsam rnam dag, and the singer Dar mtsho from Gser rta set to *rdung len* melodies and instrumentation, it has had two separate production runs, the latter with slightly better production quality.

37. *Mthong thos don ldan rdo rje'i sgra dbyangs*, ISRC CN-H09–09–326–00/V.J6. This set of two DVDs includes footage from the 2007 transmission by Nam sprul rin po che of the couple's treasure corpus alongside those of A phang gter chen and Bdud 'joms rin po che. Overall, its production value is much higher and features a variety of well-known singers, such as Sher brtan, Rig dga', Sgron pe, Mgon po don grub, and Lha skyid, and includes songs by Lhag bsam rnam dag, who is referred to as Gzhi sprul rin po che Lhag bsam rnam dag, and Dar mtsho, who also provided the vocals for the previous VCD compilation.

38. In this paragraph, I am following the chronology presented in *Mdzad bsdus mthong tshad rang grol*, which suggests that Nam sprul rin po che visited the monasteries in Pad ma on his return trip—with the exception of Bkra shis sgo mang, with which his trip began, and Shugs 'byung, which he visited earlier in the summer.

39. When the laity practiced alone, the liturgy was usually *Rdo rje'i tshig bdun gyi zab sgrub dpal be'u'i rgya can*, a prayer book produced by Snyan lung dgon with no publication information.

40. The main events for the ten-day program from June 14–23, 2006 were as follows: *Bsam pa lhun 'grub ma* (6/14), *Tshig bdun gsol 'debs kyi dbang* and *Zab lam chos drug gi lung* (6/15), *Sems khrid man ngag* (6/16), *Rig pa'i rtsal dbang* (6/17), *Chos 'khor* and *Khrom dbang* of *Sangs rgyas stong 'brel tshad don ldan* (6/18), *Bsam pa lhun 'grub ma* (6/19), *Bdud 'joms rin po che'i gsung chos nas rab gnas* (6/20), *Pad ma 'od 'bar gyi tshogs* (6/21), *Rdo rje sems dpa' bsang ba dri med* (6/22), *A phang gter chen gyi thugs rje chen po* and *Mkha' 'gro ye shes mtsho rgyal gyi tshogs* (6/23). As mentioned, some of these events were restricted to particular segments of participants.

41. These estimates were articulated by his son, Sprul sku Lhag bsam, in June 2014. There is also a website in Chinese dedicated to Snyan lung dgon: www.nianlongsi.com.

42. Dongbei contains the northeast provinces of China, formerly Manchuria, and the two centers there are in Dashiqiao and Panjin. Personal communication from Sprul sku Lhag bsam, June 2014. My thanks to Pad ma 'tsho for her help with this interview and transcribing the names of Chinese cities.

43. The new assembly hall, completed in 2007, has a larger throne that could, in theory, seat two. It features a photograph of Tā re lha mo and Nam sprul rin po che when not in use.

44. Buddhist Studies scholars have attempted to resolve this seeming paradox in different ways; see Gombrich 1966, Tambiah 1984, Strong 1989, Eckell 1992, Kinnard 1999, and Swearer 2004.

45. Personal communication from Dge legs nyi ma, June 2006.

46. This was true while Nam sprul rin po che was still alive. Now that he has passed away, Kun bzang sgrol ma has assumed the seat by his bed where Tā re lha mo used to sit, presiding over his room as a shrine. Nonetheless, the picture over the bed depicts Nam sprul rin po che with Tā re lha mo by his side.

47. Written statement by Nam sprul rin po che in my notebook in August 2004. The Tibetan reads: *Nga rang ni dri med gi yang sprul dang a pang gter ston kyi phrin las kyi sprul pa yin zer bas gter chos ni nged gnyis kyis bri dgos pa dang dbang lung ni nged gnyis kyis spel ba red.*

48. JLB 1.12–2.13. *Snyan mo lung gyi sgra dbyang* (VCD 1 of 2) 12: 50–53. This identification has also been inserted into the *rnam thar* of Nam sprul rin po che in its reproduction in volume 14 of the 2013 paperback version of their treasure corpus (2013, vol. 14: 16.3 ff.), retitled *Skyabs rje nam sprul rin po che 'jigs med phun tshogs kyi rnam thar dbang chen dgyes pa'i mchod sprin.*

49. For example, when I asked Pad ma theg mchog rgyal mtshan, the great-grandson of Bdud 'joms gling pa and great-nephew of Dri med 'od zer, to name the incarnations of Dri med 'od zer, he listed the following: 'Phrin las nor bu (son of Bdud 'joms rin po che 'Jigs bral ye shes rdo rje), Shes rab thog med (son of Rdzong gter Kun bzang nyi ma), Sprul sku Bkra po (son of Lha chen stobs rgyal), and Se ra yangs sprul (alias Rig 'dzin Gsang sngags gling pa). Personal communication, August 2004.

50. JLB 2.12–13. *Mgo log sman rtsis rig pa'i lo rgyus* lists Nam sprul rin po che as the "activity emanation" (*'phrin las kyi sprul sku*) of A phang gter chen (A bu dkar lo et al 2000: 213); the other emanations of A phang gter chen according to this source are given in chapter 1, note 49. This identification is obliquely referenced in *Jewel Garland* using the Sanskrit, Dharmadhātu Vajra, which translates Chos dbyings rdo rje. By contrast, in *Jewel Lantern of Blessings*, Nam sprul rin po che is presented more prominently as the joint emanation (*sprul pa zung du 'jug*) of the previous Nam mkha'i snying po at Zhu chen Monastery and A phang gter chen.

51. Nam sprul Rin po che made this announcement during the 2006 *chos tshogs* at Snyan lung dgon. Tā re lha mo's son was Dbang phyug rdo rje (alt. Dbang grags rdo rje).

52. Personal communication from Sprul sku Lhag bsam, June 2014. This paragraph is also supplemented by information from a conversation with him in June 2006.

53. Personal communication from Dge legs nyi ma, June 2014. The next two paragraphs are based on the same interview. Nam sprul rin po che had mentioned liver problems as far back as June 2006, when I asked about his recurrent bouts of illness.

54. I first heard about this identification from Rig 'dzin dar rgyas in May 2011, but was asked to keep it secret until confirmed. The identification is now official, and during my last visit to Gser rta in June 2014, both Rig 'dzin dar rgyas and Sprul sku Lhag bsam gave me permission to include it in this book. Rig 'dzin dar rgyas referred to her as Kun dga' dpal ldan. Here I am using her full name: Rje btsun Kun dga' 'phrin las dpal ster.

55. When I had a brief interview with the Sakya Trizin in Boulder, Colorado, in April 2015, he acknowledged the visits by Mkhan po Rig 'dzin dar rgyas and Sprul sku Lhag bsam to Dehradun but would neither confirm nor deny the recognition.

56. As their names were written down by Sprul sku Lhag bsam in June 2014, his son is Dri med dbang phyug, and his six daughters are Dbyangs can sgrol ma, Thang stong lha mo, Kar dbang sgrol ma, Rig 'dzin sgrol ma, Rat na mtsho, and Lha bab sgrol ma.

Appendix A

1. NJP 3: 8.1–12.3 in JG 37.7–40.7. Missing are three lines in the middle (10.2) and the signature line (12.4).

2. NJP 5: 13.6–17.5 is excerpted in JG 41.15–44.8.

3. NJP 6: 17.5-18.3 is excerpted in JG 44.8-17.

4. The two versions make the break between NJP 14 and NJP 15 at different points. The facsimile edition breaks prior to a short prose interlude on 41.6–42.2, whereas the paperback version includes a space after the prose interlude on 26.1–4, but does not indicate a break into a new letter. I have decided to follow the facsimile edition, given the change in style signaled by the prose interlude, ending a series of three letters using folksy images of animals and their habitats in the lead up to Nam sprul rin po che's journey to Smar khog.

5. Here again the paperback version leaves a space between passages but does not indicate a letter break. Since the content and style shifts radically, I follow the facsimile edition in considering this a break between letters.

6. It is not clear here if Nam sprul rin po che is laying claim to a past life as Rig 'dzin 'Ja lus rdo rje or whether he is more euphemistically referring to the "vajra rainbow body" in union (*zung 'jug*) with a female partner of good quality (*rigs ldan mi mo*). Rig 'dzin 'Ja' lus rdo rje was one of the Fourth Rdo grub chen incarnations, who served as Tā re lha mo's teacher. Since he passed away after being imprisoned in 1958, it is more likely that Nam sprul rin po che refers to one of the names of Mdo mkhyen brtse ye shes rdo rje, if he is indeed claiming a past life association here. There is also a reference to Bde chen nam kha'i rdo rje, which may refer to the nineteenth-century *gter ston*, Bde chen zil gnon nam mkha' rdo rje.

7. This letter, which I classify as an addendum along with the other three entries that follow, features *gter tshegs* in the paperback version but not in the facsimile edition. This is true of the other three entries, except for one such mark at the end of NJP 28 in the facsimile edition.

8. This letter only exists in the facsimile edition.

Appendix B

1. KTL 1: 76.1–78.1 is excerpted in JG 27.16–28.13.

2. KTL 3: 78.6–79.2 is excerpted in JG 28.14–17.

3. KTL 6: 82.3–83.4 is excerpted in JG 28.17–29.14.

4. KTL 9: 86.4–87.2 is excerpted in JG 29.14–30.6.

5. KTL 11: 93.2–3 is excerpted in JG 30.6–10.

6. KTL 12: 93.5–94.4 is excerpted in JG 30.10–31.3.

7. KTL 13: 96.5–6 is excerpted in JG 31.4–7.

8. This letter has several sections marked orthographically in the facsimile edition but not as breaks between letters. These are marked as separate letters in the paperback version. Here I follow the facsimile edition, given that the section breaks in the paperback version span her vision of a *wer ma*, despite the otherwise diverse content of the letter.

9. KTL 17: 116.1–6 excerpted in JG 31.7–17, KTL 17: 117.1–3 excerpted in JG 31.17–32.4, KTL 17: 118.1–5 excerpted in JG 32.5–14, KTL 17: 122.1–3 excerpted in JG 32.14–33.1, and KTL 17: 112.4–115.4 excerpted in JG 45.1–47.6.

10. The genre tag comes toward the end of KTL 18 on 126.4 to characterize all that has come before. After that, the *gter tshegs* are no longer used, signaling a shift into ordinary speech.

11. KTL 23: 136.6–137.2 is excerpted in JG 33.1–4.

12. According to the logic outlined in chapter 3, note 7 and the chart in Cornu 1997, this letter would be dated to the end of December 1979.

13. This letter contains numerous orthographic markings in the facsimile edition and paperback version that ordinarily indicate a break in the letter. However, I interpret this as a single letter because it is framed as an exchange between Tar po and Tshe bo, composed by Tā re lha mo herself. Moreover, the letter has a clear beginning and end, being dated at the beginning and with a colophon at the end.

14. Due to changes I made on the numbering of letters when this book was already in press, these passages span three letters: KTL 27: 145.5–6 excerpted in JG 33: 4–6, KTL 29: 161.6–162.6 excerpted in JG 33.7–34.3, and KTL 31: 168.3–5 excerpted in JG 34.3–7.

15. This is not marked as a distinct letter in the facsimile edition, but given that it follows the colophon from the previous letter, it logically it serves as a new entry. It is marked as a letter break in the paperback version.

16. In the paperback version, the last part of this letter is marked with tertsek, but it is not in the facsimile edition.

17. I have gone back and forth on whether to consider these final ten entries to be a long string of addenda or another duet following from KTL 27. If the latter is the case, they are less obviously coded as a duet, with the sections once again marked as separate letters. Yet, as evidence of a duet, the final entry clearly has another voice calling out to her as Tar po lo, and two entries before that begins with Tar po much like in KTL 27. Meanwhile, as further evidence, the gender changes in the first line of the final two entries from *gtan grogs bzang po* to *gtan gyi grogs bzang ma*, addressing a male friend or lover in the first case and a female one in the second case.

Glossary of Tibetan Names

Abu Karlo	A bu dkar lo
Abzö Gompa	A bzod dgon pa
Achung	A chung
Adrön	A sgron
Adzom Chögar	A 'dzom chos sgar
Adzom Drukpa	A 'dzom 'brug pa
Akong Khenpo Lozang Dorje	Ab rkong mkhan po Blo bzang rdo rje
Akyong Bum	A skyong 'bum
Alogowa	A blo 'go ba
Amdo	A mdo
Amnye Machen	A myes (alt. mye) rma chen
Apang	A phang (alt. A pang, A paṃ)
Apang Orgyan Kachö Lingpa	A pang O rgyan mkha' spyod gling pa
Apang Terchen Orgyan Trinle Lingpa	A phang gter chen O rgyan 'phrin las gling pa, alias Dpa' bo Chos dbyings rdo rje
Atsara Sale	A tsa ra sa le
Banak Gompa	Ban nag dgon pa
Barkam	'Bar khams
Bathang	'Ba' thang
Bodong Chogle Namgyal	Bo dong Phyogs las rnam rgyal

Bökyi Yumo Lung	'Bos kyi yu mo lung
Bön	Bon
Böpa	'Bos spa
Bumlung	'Bum lung
Chabdrol	Skyabs grol
Chagri Gompa	Lcags ri dgon pa
Chatral Sangye Dorje	Bya bral sangs rgyas rdo rje
Chimpu	Mchims phu
Chokgyur Dechen Lingpa	Mchog gyur bde chen gling pa
Chokgyur Nupban Namkhai Nyingpo	Mchog gyur gnubs ban Nam mkha'i snying po
Choktrul Sherab Thokme	Mchog sprul Shes rab thogs med
Chökyi Drönma	Chos kyi sgron ma
Ḍākki Tāre Dechen Gyalmo	Ḍāk ki Tā re bde chen rgyal mo, alias Mkha 'gro Tā re lha mo
Damtsik Drolma	Dam tshig sgrol ma
Darlag	Dar lag
Dartsang	Brda tshang
Dartsedo	Dar rtse mdo
Dechen Chokyi Wangmo	Bde chen chos kyi dbang mo
Dechen Namkhai Dorje	Bde chen nam mkha'i rdo rje
Dege	Bde dge
Dewe Dorje	Bde ba'i rdo rje, alias Se ra mkha' 'gro
Dilgo Khyentse	Dil mgo mkhyen brtse
Do Dasal Wangmo	Mdo Zla gsal dbang mo
Do Kham	Mdo khams
Do Khyentse Yeshe Dorje	Mdo mkhyen brtse Ye shes rdo rje
Do Rinpoche Khamsum Zilnön Gyepa Dorje	Mdo rin po che Khams gsum zil gnon dgyes pa rdo rje
Do River	Rdo chu
Dodrupchen	Rdo grub chen
Dodrupchen Gompa	Rdo grub chen dgon pa
Dodrupchen Jigme Tenpe Nyima	Rdo grub chen 'Jigs med bstan pa'i nyi ma
Dodrupchen Jigme Trinle Özer	Rdo grub chen 'Jigs med 'phrin las 'od zer

Dogama	Mdo 'gab ma
Dogongma	Mdo gong ma
Dola Chökyi Nyima	Mdo bla Chos kyi nyi ma
Doli Nyima	Mdo li nyi ma
Dondrup Gyal	Don grub rgyal
Dong Dzong Gompa	Gdong rdzong dgon pa
Do-ngag Tenpe Nyima	Mdo sngags Bstan pa'i nyi ma
Dorje Dradul	Rdo rje dgra 'dul
Dorje Phagmo	Rdo rje phag mo
Dorje Rachigma	Rdo rje rwa gcig ma
Drakar Tredzong	Brag dkar sprel rdzong
Drakar Gompa	Brag dkar dgon pa (in Pad ma)
Drakor Gompa	Bkra skor dgon pa (in 'Dzam thang)
Drango	Brag 'go
Drasar	Sbra gsar
Drime Kunden	Dri med kun ldan
Drime Özer	Dri med 'od zer, alias Pad ma las 'brel
Drongri	'Brong ri (alt. 'Brong ri smug po)
Dröphug Khandrö Duling	'Bros phug mkha' 'gro'i 'du gling
Dudjom Lingpa	Bdud 'joms gling pa
Dudjom Rinpoche Jigdral Yeshe Dorje	Bdud 'joms rin po che 'Jigs bral ye shes rdo rje
Dudul Dorje	Bdud 'dul rdo rje
Dudul Rolpatsal	Bdud 'dul rol ba rtsal
Dumda	Dhu mda'
Dungkar Monastery	Dung dkar dgon pa
Dzamthang	'Dzam thang
Dzogchen Monastery	Rdzogs chen dgon
Dzongter Kunzang Nyima	Rdzong gter Kun bzang nyi ma
Gabde County	Dga' bde rdzong
Ganden Phodrang	Dga' ldan pho brang
Gangpa Monastery	Gangs pa dgon (alt. Gang spa dgon)
Gangri Thökar	Gangs ri thod dkar
Garra Gyalse	Mgar ra rgyal sras, alias Pad ma tshe dbang
Garra Tertön	Mgar ra gter ston

Gartrul Rinpoche	Mgar sprul rin po che
Gelek Nyima	Dge legs nyi ma
Geluk	Dge lugs
Gesar	Ge sar
Getse Khenpo Wangchen	Dge rtse (alt. tshe) Mkhan po Dbang chen
Getse Gompa	Dge rtse dgon pa
Golok	Mgo log
Gyalrong	Rgyal rong
Gyalrong Drak	Rgyal rong brag
Gyatrul Rinpoche	Rgyal sprul rin po che
Gyurme Dorje	'Gyur med rdo rje
Gyurme Gyatso	'Gyur med rgya mtsho
Hor	Hor
Hūṃchenkara	Hūṃ chen ka ra
Jamda Gompa	Lcam mda' dgon pa
Jamgön Kongtrul	'Jam mgon kong sprul
Jamyang Khyentse Wangpo	'Jam dbyangs mkhyen brtse'i dbang po
Jamyang Nyima	'Jam dbyangs nyi ma
Janak Shengan	Rgya nag shes ngan
Jang Yulha	'Jang yul lha, alias G.yu lha thog 'gyur
Jetsun Kunga Trinley Palter	Rje btsun Kun dga' 'phrin las dpal ster
Jetsun Mingyur Paldrön	Rje btsun Mi 'gyur dpal sgron
Jigdril County	Gcig sgril rdzong
Jigme Lingpa	'Jigs med gling pa
Jigme Wangdrak Dorje	'Jigs med dbang drag rdo rje
Jokhang	Jo khang
Jomo Menmo	Jo mo smon mo
Jonang	Jo nang
Jowo Śākyamuni	Jo bo Śākyamuni
Ju Kalzang	'Ju skal bzang
Kachö Wangmo	Mkha' spyod dbang mo
Kagyu	Bka' brgyud
Kandze	Dkar mdzes
Karma Chagme	Kar ma chags med
Katok	Kaḥ thog
Kham	Khams

Khandro Chöchan	Mkha' 'gro Chos spyan
Khandro Tāre Lhamo	Mkha' 'gro Tā re lha mo
Khandro Rinpoche	Mkha' 'gro rin po che
Khenpo Chökyab	Mkhan po Chos skyabs
Khenpo Chöthun	Mkhan po Chos mthun
Khenpo Jigme Phuntsok	Mkhan po 'Jigs med phun tshogs
Khenpo Munsel	Mkhan po Mun sel
Khenpo Rigdzin Dargye	Mkhan po Rig 'dzin dar rgyas
Khenpo Tsultrim Lodrö	Mkhan po Tshul khrims blo gros
Khen Rinpoche Jigme Senge	Mkhan rin po che 'Jigs med seng ge
Kongjo	Kong jo
Kumbum	Sku 'bum
Kunga Bumpa	Kun dga' 'bum pa
Kunga Palden	Kun dga' dpal ldan
Kunzang Chökyi Drolma	Kun bzang chos kyi sgrol (alt. sgron) ma
Kunzang Dekyong Chönyi Wangmo	Kun bzang bde skyongs chos nyid dbang mo, alias Se ra mkha' 'gro
Kusum Lingpa	Sku gsum gling pa, alias Pad ma gtum po
Labrang Tashi Khyil	Bla brang bkra shis 'khyil
Lake Kokonor	Mtsho sngon po
Laksam Namdak	Lhag bsam rnam dag
Lama Rigdzin Nyima	Bla ma Rig 'dzin nyi ma
Lama Sang-ngak	Bla ma Gsang sngags
Langdarma	Glang dar ma
Larung Buddhist Academy of the Five Sciences	Bla rung dgon rig lnga'i nang bstan slob grwa
Lerab Lingpa	Las rab gling pa
Lhacam Chökyi Drolma	Lha lcam Chos kyi sgrol ma
Lhalung Drakar	Lha lung brag dkar
Lingtrul Rinpoche	Gling sprul rin po che
Lingtsang	Gling tshang
Lochen Dharmaśrī	Lo chen dhar ma śrī
Longchen Rabjam	Klong chen rab 'byams, alias Klong chen pa Dri med 'od zer

Longchenpa Drime Özer	Klong chen pa Dri med 'od zer
Longsal Nyingpo	Klong gsal snying po
Lunghop	Lung hob, alias Ri zab
Lungkhar Khandroma	Lung dkar mkha' 'gro ma
Lushul Khenpo Könchok Drönme	Klu shul mkhan po Dkon mchog sgron me
Ma River	Rma chu
Machen County	Rma chen rdzong
Machig Labdrön	Ma cig lab sgron (alt. Ma gcig lab sgron)
Machig Zhiwatso	Ma cig Zhi ba mtsho
Magyal Pomra	Rma rgyal sbom (alt. spom) ra
Maṇi Lochen Rigdzin Chönyi Zangmo	Ma ṇi lo chen Rig 'dzin Chos nyid bzang mo
Mar River	Smar chu
Markhok	Smar khog
Matö County	Rma stod rdzong
Mayum Tenma	Ma yum brtan ma
Metok Drön	Me tog sgron
Metok Lhadze	Me tog lha mdzes
Milarepa	Mi la ras pa
Mindrolling	Smin grol gling
Mingyur Dorje	Mi 'gyur rdo rje, alias Sprul sku Mi lo and Pad ma 'od gsal snying po
Mingyur Paldrön	Mi 'gyur dpal sgron
Minthang	Smin thang
Minyak	Mi nyag
Mön	Mon
Munchen Thökar	Mun chen thod kar
Namkhai Nyingpo	Nam mkha'i snying po
Namtrul Jigme Phuntsok	Nam sprul 'Jigs med phun tshogs, alias Nam sprul rin po che
Namtrul Rinpoche	Nam sprul rin po che
Natsok Rangdrol	Sna tshogs rang grol
Ne'u Chung	Ne'u chung
Ngakmang Research Institute	Sngag mang zhib 'jug
Ngawa	Rnga ba
Ngayab Palri	Rnga yab dpal ri

Ngöntso	Sngon mtsho
Norde	Nor sde
Nyenchen Thangla	Gnyan chen thang lha
Nyenlung Monastery	Snyan lung dgon pa
Nyenpo Yutse	Gnyan po g.yu rtse
Nyingma	Rnying ma
Orgyan Chökyi	O rgyan chos skyid
Orgyan Jigme Namkha Lingpa	O rgyan 'jigs med Nam mkha' gling pa, alias Nam sprul rin po che
Orgyan Khandro Ling	O rgyan mkha' 'gro gling
Orgyan Namkha Dorje	O rgyan nam mkha' rdo rje
Padma Bum	Pad ma 'bum
Padma County	Pad ma rdzong
Pal Lhundrup Thubten Chökor Ling	Dpal lhun grub thub bstan chos 'khor gling
Palden Gyatso	Dpal ldan rgya mtsho
Palkyi Lodrö	Dpal gyi blo gros
Palri Monastery	Dpal ri dgon
Paṇchen Lama	Paṇ chen bla ma
Patrul Rinpoche	Dpal sprul rin po che
Pawo Chöying Dorje	Dpa' bo Chos dbying rdo rje, alias A phang gter chen O rgyan 'phrin las gling pa
Payul	Dpal yul
Payul Karma Chagme	Dpal yul Karma Chags med
Payul Tarthang	Dpal yul Dar thang
Pema Drime Lodrö	Pad ma dri med blo gros, alias Nam sprul rin po che
Pema Drime Ösal Lodrö Thaye	Pad ma dri med 'od gsal blo gros mtha' yas, alias Nam sprul rin po che
Pema Lingpa	Pad ma gling pa
Pema Ösal Nyingpo	Pad ma 'od gsal snying po, alias Sprul sku Mi lo and Mi 'gyur rdo rje
Pema Ösal Thaye	Pad ma 'od gsal mtha' yas
Pema Thegchok Gyaltsen	Pad ma theg mchog rgyal mtshan
Pema Tsewang	Pad ma tshe dbang, alias Mgar ra rgyal sras

Pema Tumpo	Pad ma gtum po, alias Sku gsum gling pa
Pemasal	Pad ma gsal
Phosatin	Pho sa tin
Pongyu	Spong yul (alt. Spang yus)
Ragya Gompa	Rwa rgya dgon pa
Raktram Monastery	Rags bkram dgon pa
Rasa Tsuklakhang	Ra sa gtsug lag khang
Rebkong	Reb kong
Rigdzin Dudul Dorje	Rig 'dzin Bdud 'dul rdo rje
Rigdzin Gödem	Rig 'dzin Rgod ldem
Rigdzin Jalu Dorje	Rig 'dzin 'Ja' lus rdo rje, alias Sprul sku Rig lo
Rigdzin Longsal Nyingpo	Rig 'dzin Long gsal snying po
Rigdzin Nyima	Rig 'dzin nyi ma
Rigdzin Sang-ngak Lingpa	Rig 'dzin Gsang sngags gling pa, alias Se ra yang sprul
Rusarma	Rus gsar ma (alt: Ru gsar ma)
Rizab	Ri zab, alias Lung hob
Rongpo Monastery	Rong po dgon pa
Sagadawa	Sa ga zla ba
Sakya Trizin	Sa skya khri 'dzin
Samye	Bsam yas
Samye Chimpu	Bsam yas chims phu
Sang-ngag Lingpa	Gsang sngags gling pa
Ser River	Gser chu
Ser Valley	Gser thang
Sera Khandro	Se ra mkha' 'gro, alias Bde ba'i rdo rje and Kun bzang bde skyongs chos nyid dbang mo
Sera Yangtrul Tsultrim Gyatso	Se ra yang sprul Tshul khrims rgya mtsho, alias Rig 'dzin Gsang sngags gling pa
Serkhar	Gser mkhar (alt. Sras mkhar)
Sershul	Gser shul
Serta	Gser rta (alt. Gser thang, Gser thar)
Shabkar Tsokdruk Rangdrol	Zhabs dkar Tshogs drug rang grol

Shedrup Tenpe Nyima	Bshad sgrub bstan pa'i nyi ma
Sheldrak	Shel brag
Shelkar Dorje Tso	Shel dkar rdo rje mtsho
Sherab Togme	Shes rab thogs med
Shimtso	Bye'u mtsho
Sholung Gomkhang	Sho lung sgom khang
Shugsep Nunnery	Shug gseb dgon pa
Shukjung Lama Tsedzi	Shugs 'byung bla ma tshe rdzi
Shukjung Monastery	Shugs 'byung dgon pa
Shukjung Pema Bumdzong	Shugs 'byung Pad ma 'bum rdzong
Silethang	Si le thang
Sönam Detsun	Bsod nams lde'u btsun
Sönam Paldren	Bsod nams dpal 'dren
Songtsen Gampo	Srong bstan sgam po
Soru Village	Sog ru shang (alt. Sog ru ma)
Soza Dröpo	Sog bza' 'Bros po
Taklung Gompa	Stag lung dgon pa
Takmo Yangdzong	Stag mo yang rdzong
Taksham Nuden Dorje	Stag sham nus ldan rdo rje
Takthog Monastery	Stag thog dgon pa
Taktse Monastery	Stag rtse dgon pa
Tarpo	Tar po
Tashi Lhatang Norbu Festival	Bkra shis lha thang nor bu'i dga' tshal
Tashi Gomang	Bkra shis sgo mang
Tashi Tobgyal	Bkra shis stobs rgyal
Tawu	Rta'u
Tenzang	Rten bzang
Terdak Lingpa	Gter bdag gling pa
Tertön Chögar	Gter ston chos sgar
Thangtong Gyalpo	Thang stong rgyal po
Tharwa	Thar ba
Thopa	Tho pa (alt. Thos pa)
Thubten Chödar	Thub bstan chos dar
Thubten Chökyi Nyima	Thub bstan chos kyi nyi ma
Thubten Trinle Palzangpo	Thub bstan 'phrin las dpal bzang po
Tidro	Ti sgro
Tongkyab Gompa	Stong skyabs dgon pa

Tra Gelong Tsultrim Dargye (alt. Lodrö)	Khra dge slong Tshul khrims dar rgyas (alt. blo gros)
Trachugmo Pass	Khra phyug mo'i la kha
Trisong Detsen	Khri srong de'u bstan
Tsangnyön Heruka	Gtsang smyon he ru ka
Tsebo (from Tsedzin)	Tshe po (from Tshe 'dzin), alias Nam sprul rin po che
Tsekhok County	Rtse khog rdzong
Tseringma	Tshe ring ma
Tseten Zhabdrung	Tshe tan zhabs drung
Tsogyal Latso	Mtsho rgyal bla mtsho
Tsopu Dorlo	Mtsho phu rdor lo
Tsimda Gompa	Rtsis mda' dgon pa
Tsurphu	Tshur phu
Tulku Milo	Sprul sku Mi lo, alias Mi 'gyur rdo rje
Tulku Riglo	Sprul sku Rig lo, alias Rig 'dzin 'Ja' lus rdo rje
Tulku Thondup	Sprul sku Don grub
Tulku Wulo	Sprul sku Bu lo
Tulku Yuba	Sprul sku G.yu ba
U	Dbus
Utsa Gompa	Sbu tsha (alt. Bu rtsa) dgon pa
Utsal Serkhang	Dbu tshal gser khang
Utsang	Dbus gtsang
Uza Khandro	Dbus bza' mka' 'gro, alias Se ra mkha' 'gro
Wangchen Nyima	Dbang chen nyi ma, alias Sgrib bral rig pa'i rdo rje
Wangda Monastery	Dbang mda' dgon pa
Washul	Wa shul (alt. Dbal shul)
Woeser	'Od zer
Yandrosi	Yan dro si
Yangdzong	Yang rdzong
Yarlung	Yar lung
Yarlung Pemakö	Yar lung Pad ma bkod
Yeshe Tsogyal	Ye shes mtsho rgyal
Yonten Palzang	Yon tan dpal bzang

Yulha Thogyur	G.yu lha thog 'gyur, alias 'Jang yul lha
Yuyi Thortsug	G.yu yi thor gtsug
Zalmo	Zal mo
Zangkyong	Bzang skyong
Zangtok Palri	Zangs mdog dpal ri
Zhuchen Kunzang Nyima	Gzhu chen Kun bzang nyi ma
Zhuchen Monastery	Gzhu chen (alt. Gzhi chen) dgon pa
Zhuchen Namtrul Jigme Ösal Dorje	Gzhu chen nam sprul 'Jigs med 'od gsal rdo rje
Zhuchen Pande Chökyi Nyima	Gzhu chen Phan bde chos kyi nyi ma

Bibliography

A bu dkar lo. *Gter ston grub pa'i dbang phyug gzhi chen nam sprul dang mkha' 'gro tā re bde chen lha mo zung gi mdzad rnam nyer bsdus byin rlabs nor bu'i sgron me.* Xining: Mtsho sngon nang bstan rtsom sgrig khang, 2001.

——. *Gter ston grub pa'i dbang phyug o rgyan sku gsum gling pa'i rnam thar mdo tsam brjod pa ma tshogs rig 'dzin bzhad pa'i rang gdangs.* Zhang kang then mā dpe skrun khang, 2003.

A bu dkar lo, Dung gces, and Gsang bdag tshe ring. *Mgo log sman rtsis rig pa'i lo rgyus ngo mtshar nor bu'i rlabs phreng.* Xining: Qinghai Minorities Publishing House, 2000.

Abelard, Peter. *The Letters of Abelard and Heloise.* Trans. Betty Radice. London: Penguin, 2003.

Abu-Lughod, Lila. "The Romance of Resistance: Tracing Transformations of Power Through Bedouin Women." *American Ethnologist* 17, no. 1 (1990): 41–55.

——. *Writing Women's Worlds.* Berkeley: University of California Press, 1993.

Ahearn, Laura. "Language and Agency." *Annual Review of Anthropology* 30 (2001a): 109–37.

——. *Invitations to Love: Literacy, Love Letters, and Social Change in Nepal.* Ann Arbor: University of Michigan Press, 2001b.

Alak Tsayu Tenzin Palbar. "The Tragedy of My Homeland." Unpublished manuscript, 1997.

Alexander, Jeffrey. "Toward a Theory of Cultural Trauma." In *Cultural Trauma and Collective Identity*, ed. Jeffrey Alexander, Ron Eyerman, Bernhard Giesen, Neil Smelser, and Piotr Sztompka. Berkeley: University of California Press, 2004.

Allione, Tsultrim. *Women of Wisdom.* Boston: Routledge & Kegan Paul, 1984.

Almond, Philip. *The British Discovery of Buddhism.* Cambridge: Cambridge University Press, 1998.

Altman, Janet. *Epistolarity: Approaches to a Form.* Columbus: Ohio State University Press, 1982.

Ames, Roger with Wimal Dissanayake and Thomas Kasulis, eds. *Self as Person in Asian Theory and Practice*. Albany: State University of New York Press, 1994.

Anton-Luca, Alexandru. *"Glu and La ye in A mdo: An Introduction to Contemporary Tibetan Folk Songs."* In *Amdo Tibetans in Transition: Society and Culture in the Post-Mao Era*, ed. Toni Huber. Leiden: Brill, 2002.

A phang gter chen O rgyan phrin las gling pa. *Rgyal dbang pad ma'i rgyal tshab o rgyan phrin las gling pa'i zab gter nor bu'i phreng ba*. Gser rta: Snyan lung dgon, n.d.

Aris, Michael. *Hidden Treasures and Secret Lives: A Study of Pemalingpa, 1450–1521, and the Sixth Dalai Lama, 1683–1706*. Delhi: Motilal Banarsidass, 1988.

Atkinson, Clarissa, Constance Buchanan, and Margaret Miles. *Immaculate and Powerful: The Female in Sacred Image and Reality*. Boston: Beacon, 1985.

Austin, J. L. *How to Do Things with Words*. Oxford: Clarendon Press, 1962.

Aziz, Barbara. "Moving Towards a Sociology of Tibet." In *Feminine Ground: Essays on Women in Tibet*, ed. Janice Willis. Ithaca, NY: Snow Lion, 1989.

Baranovitch, Nimrod. "Between Alterity and Identity: New Voices of Minority People in China." *Modern China* 27, no. 3 (2001): 359–401.

Barnett, Robert and Shirin Akiner, eds. *Resistance and Reform in Tibet*. Bloomington: Indiana University Press, 1994.

Barnett, Robert and Ronald Schwartz, eds. *Tibetan Modernities: Notes from the Field on Social and Cultural Change*. Leiden: Brill, 2008.

Barnouin, Barbara and Yu Changgen. *Ten Years of Turbulence: The Chinese Cultural Revolution*. London: Kegan Paul, 1992.

Batt, Herbert, trans. and ed. *Tales of Tibet: Sky Burials, Prayer Wheels, and Wind Horses*. Lanham, MD: Rowman & Littlefield, 2001.

Batt, Herbert and Tsering Shakya, eds. *Song of the Snow Lion*. Manoa 12, no. 2 (2000): 28–40.

Benjamin, Walter. *Illuminations*. Trans. Harry Zohn. New York: Schocken, 1969.

Berger, Peter. *The Sacred Canopy: Elements of a Sociological Theory of Religion*. New York: Anchor, 1990.

Bessenger, Suzanne. "Echoes of Enlightenment: The Life and Legacy of Sonam Peldren." Ph.D. diss., University of Virginia, 2010.

Beyer, Stephen. *The Cult of Tārā: Magic and Ritual in Tibet*. Berkeley: University of California Press, 1978.

Biernacki, Loriliai. *Renowned Goddess of Desire: Women, Sex, and Speech in Tantra*. Oxford University Press, 2007.

Bla rung ar ya tā re'i dpe tshogs rtsom sgrig khang, ed. *'Phags bod kyi skyes chen ma dag gi rnam par thar ba pad ma dkar po'i phreng ba*. Lha sa: Bod ljongs bod yig dpe rnying dpe skrun khang, 2013.

Blondeau, Anne-Marie. "Analysis of the Biographies of Padmasambhava According to Tibetan Tradition." In *Tibetan Studies in Honour of Hugh Richardson*, ed. Michael Aris and Aung San Suu Kyi. Warminster: Aris & Phillips, 1980.

Bodhi, Bhikku. *The Connected Discourses of the Buddha: A Translation of the Samyutta Nikaya*. Boston: Wisdom, 2002.

Bourdieu, Pierre. *Outline of a Theory of Practice*. Cambridge: Cambridge University Press, 1977.

Brison, Susan. "Trauma Narratives and the Remaking of the Self." In *Acts of Memory*, ed. Mieke Bal, Jonathan Crewe, and Leo Spitzer. (Hanover, NH: University Press of New England, 1999.

Brown, W. Norman. "Duty as Truth in Ancient India." *Proceedings of the American Philosophical Society* 116, no. 3 (1972): 252–68.

Buddhaghosa, Bhadantācariya. *The Path of Purification (Visuddhimagga)*. Trans. Bhikkhu Ñāṇamoli. Onalaska, WA: Pariyatti Publishing, 1991.

Burlinghame, Eugene. *Buddhist Legends*. Cambridge, MA: Harvard University Press, 1921.

Cabezón, José and Roger Jackson, eds. *Tibetan Literature: Studies in Genre*. Ithaca, NY: Snow Lion, 1996.

Campbell, June. *Traveller in Space: In Search of Female Identity in Tibetan Buddhism*. New York: George Braziller, 1996.

Carrasco, Pedro. *Land and Polity in Tibet*. Seattle and London: University of Washington Press, 1959.

Caruth, Cathy, ed. *Trauma: Explorations in Memory*. Baltimore: Johns Hopkins University Press, 1995.

——. *Unclaimed Experience: Trauma, Narrative, and History*. Baltimore: Johns Hopkins University Press, 1996.

Chakrabarty, Dipesh. *Provincializing Europe: Postcolonial Thought and Historical Difference*. Princeton: Princeton University Press, 2000.

Chang, Garma. *The Hundred Thousand Songs of Milarepa*. Boston: Shambhala, 1999.

Cherewatuk, Karen and Ulrike Wiethaus, eds. *Dear Sister: Medieval Women and the Epistolary Genre*. Philadelphia: University of Pennsylvania Press, 1993.

Chong, Woei Lien. *China's Great Proletarian Cultural Revolution: Master Narratives and Post-Mao Counternarratives*. Lanham, MD: Rowman & Littlefield, 2002.

Chos kyi dbang phyug, Guru. "Gter 'byung chen mo." In *The Autobiography and Instructions of Gu-ru Chos-kyi-dbaṅ-phyug*. Paro, Bhutan: Ugyen Tempai Gyaltsen, 1979, 2: 75–193.

Choy, Howard. *Remapping the Past: Fictions of History in Deng's China, 1979–1997*. Leiden: Brill, 2008.

Clarke, Graham. "Aspects of Social Organisation of Tibetan Pastoral Communities." In *Tibetan Studies, Proceedings of the 5th Seminar of the International Association for Tibetan Studies, Narita 1989*, ed. Ihara Shōren and Yamaguchi Zuihō. Tokyo: Naritasan Shinshoji, 1992.

Coakley, John. *Women, Men, and Spiritual Power: Female Saints and Their Male Collaborators*. New York: Columbia University Press, 2006.

Constable, Giles. *Letters and Letter-Collections*. Typologie des Sources du Moyen Âge Occidental, Fascicle 17. Turnhout, Belgique: Éditions Brepols, 1976.

Conze, Edward. *Thirty Years of Buddhist Studies: Selected Essays*. Columbia: University of South Carolina Press, 1968.

——. *The Perfection of Wisdom in Eight Thousand Lines and Its Verse Summary*. Bolinas, CA: Four Seasons Foundation, 1973.

——. *The Large Sutra on Perfect Wisdom, with the Divisions of the Abhisamayālaṅkāra*. Berkeley: University of California Press, 1975.

Coon, Lynda. *Sacred Fictions: Holy Women and Hagiography in Late Antiquity*. Philadelphia: University of Pennsylvania Press, 1997.

Cornu, Philippe. *Tibetan Astrology.* Boston: Shambhala, 1997.

Cowell, E. B., ed. *The Jātaka or Stories of the Buddha's Former Births.* Vols. 1–6. Cambridge: University Press, 1895–1907.

Cox, Collette. "Mindfulness and Memory: The Scope of Smṛti from Early Buddhism to the Sarvāstivādin Abhidharma." In *In the Mirror of Memory: Reflections on Mindfulness and Remembrance in Indian and Tibetan Buddhism,* ed. Janet Gyatso. Ithaca: State University of New York Press, 1992.

Cuevas, Bryan. *The Hidden History of the Tibetan Book of the Dead.* Oxford: Oxford University Press, 2003.

——. *Travels in the Netherworld: Buddhist Popular Narratives of Death and the Afterlife in Tibet.* Oxford: Oxford University Press, 2008.

Das, Veena and Arthur Kleinman. Introduction to *Remaking a World: Violence, Social Suffering and Recovery,* ed. Veena Das, Arthur Kleinman, Margaret Lock, et al. Berkeley: University of California Press, 2001.

Davidson, Ronald. *Indian Esoteric Buddhism.* New York: Columbia University Press, 2002.

——. *Tibetan Renaissance: Tantric Buddhism in the Rebirth of Tibetan Culture.* New York: Columbia University Press, 2005.

Davidson, Ronald and Steven Goodman. *Tibetan Buddhism: Reason and Revelation.* Albany: State University of New York Press, 1992.

de Certeau, Michel. *The Practice of Everyday Life.* Berkeley: University of California Press, 1984.

de La Vallée Poussin, Louis. *Abhidharmakośabhāṣyam.* English translation by Leo Pruden. Berkeley: Asian Humanities Press, 1988.

deVries, Marten. "Trauma in Cultural Perspective." In *Traumatic Stress: The Effects of Overwhelming Experience on Mind, Body, and Society,* ed. Bessel van der Kolk with Alexander McFarlane and Lars Weisaeth. New York: The Guildford Press, 1996.

Diemberger, Hildegard. *When a Woman Becomes a Religious Dynasty: The Samding Dorje Phagmo of Tibet.* New York: Columbia University Press, 2007.

Dietz, Siglinde. "Die buddhistische Briefliteratur Indiens. Nach dem tibetischen Tanjur herausgegeben, übersetzt und erläutert." *Asiatische Forschungen* 84. Wiesbaden: Otto Harrassowitz, 1984.

Dissanayake, Wimal, ed. *Narratives of Agency: Self-Making in China, India, and Japan.* Minneapolis: University of Minnesota Press, 1996.

Dittmer, Lowell. "Learning from Trauma: The Cultural Revolution in Post-Mao Politics." In *New Perspectives on the Cultural Revolution,* ed. William A. Joseph et al. Cambridge, MA: Harvard University Press, 1991.

DiValerio, David. *The Holy Madmen of Tibet.* Oxford: Oxford University Press, 2015.

Doctor, Andreas. *Tibetan Treasure Literature: Revelation, Tradition, and Accomplishment in Visionary Buddhism.* Ithaca, NY: Snow Lion, 2005.

Don grub dbang rgyal and Nor sde. *Yul mgo log gi lo rgyus deb ther pad ma dkar po'i chun po* (abbreviated as *Mgo log lo rgyus deb ther*). Xining: Mtsho sngon mi rigs dpe skrun khang, 1992.

Don grub rgyal. *Bod kyi mgur glu byung 'phel gyi lo rgyus dang khyad chos bsdus par ston pa rig pa'i khye'u rnam par rtsen pa'i skyed tshal.* Beijing: Mi rigs dpe skrun khang, 1997.

Douglas, Kenneth and Gwendolyn Bays. *The Life and Liberation of Padmasambhava.* Emeryville, CA: Dharma Publishing, 1978.

Dowman, Keith. *Sky Dancer: The Secret Life and Songs of the Lady Yeshe Tsogyal*. Ithaca, NY: Snow Lion, 1996.

Duara, Prasenjit. *Rescuing History from the Nation: Questioning Narratives of Modern China*. Chicago: University of Chicago Press, 1995.

Dudjom Rinpoche Jikdrel Yeshe Dorje. *The Nyingma Schools of Tibetan Buddhism: Its Fundamentals and History*. Trans. and ed. Gyurme Dorje and Matthew Kapstein. Boston: Wisdom, 1991.

Duncan, Marion. *Love Songs and Proverbs of Tibet*. London: Mitre Press, 1961.

Dung dkar Blo bzang 'phrin las. *Dung dkar tshig mdzod chen mo*. Beijing: Krung go'i bod rig pa dpe skrun khang, 2002.

Earl, Rebecca. *Epistolary Selves: Letters and Letter-Writers, 1600–1945*. Aldershot: Ashgate, 2009.

Eckell, David. *To See the Buddha: A Philosopher's Quest for the Meaning of Emptiness*. San Francisco: HarperCollins, 1992.

Edou, Jérôme. *Machig Labdrön and the Foundations of Chöd*. Ithaca, NY: Snow Lion, 1995.

Ekvall, Robert. *Fields on the Hoof*. Prospect Heights: Waveland, 1968.

——. *The Lama Knows*. Novato, CA: Chandler and Sharp, 1981.

Eliade, Mircea. *The Myth of the Eternal Return*. Trans. Willard Trask. New York: Pantheon, 1954.

English, Elizabeth. *Vajrayoginī: Her Visualizations, Rituals, and Forms*. Boston: Wisdom, 2002.

Eppling, John Frederick. "The Calculus of Creative Expression: The Central Chapter of Daṇḍin's Kāvyādarśa." Ph.D. diss., University of Wisconsin, Madison, 1989.

Erikson, Kai. "Notes on Trauma and Community." In *Trauma: Explorations in Memory*, ed. Cathy Caruth. Baltimore: Johns Hopkins University Press, 1995.

Farrow, G. W. and I. Menon. *The Concealed Essence of the Hevajra Tantra*. Delhi: Motilal Banarsidass, 2001.

Foucault, Michel. *Power/Knowledge: Selected Interviews and Other Writings 1972–1977*. Trans. and ed. Colin Gordon. New York: Pantheon, 1980.

Fronsdale, Gil. *The Dhammapada*. Boston: Shambhala, 2006.

Galtung, Johan. "Anomie/Atomie: On the Impact of Secularization/Modernization on Moral Cohesion and Social Tissue." *International Journal of Sociology and Social Policy* 15, nos. 8–10 (1995): 121–47.

Gayley, Holly. Introduction. In Sarah Harding, *The Life and Revelations of Pema Lingpa*. Boulder, CO: Snow Lion, 2003a.

——. "Ontology of the Past and Its Materialization in Tibetan Treasures." In *The Invention of Sacred Tradition*, ed. Olav Hammer and James Lewis. Cambridge: Cambridge University Press, 2008.

——. "The Ethics of Cultural Survival: A Buddhist Vision of Progress in Mkhan po 'Jig phun's *Heart Advice to Tibetans of the 21st Century*." In *Mapping the Modern in Tibet*, ed. Gray Tuttle. Sankt Augustin, Germany: International Institute for Tibetan and Buddhist Studies, 2011.

——. "Reimagining Buddhist Ethics on the Tibetan Plateau." *Journal of Buddhist Ethics* 20 (2013): 247–86. http://blogs.dickinson.edu/buddhistethics/files/2013/08/Gayley-Reimagining.pdf.

——. "T-Pop and the Lama: Buddhist 'Rites out of Place' on Tibetan Monastery-Produced VCDs." In *Religion and Modernity in the Himalaya,* ed. Megan Sijapati and Jessica Birkenholtz. New York: Routledge, 2016.

Geary, Patrick. *Furta Sacra: Thefts of Relics in the Central Middle Ages.* Princeton: Princeton University Press, 1978.

——. "Saints, Scholars and Society: The Elusive Goal." In *Saints: Studies in Hagiography,* ed. Sandro Sticca. Binghamton, NY: Medieval & Renaissance Texts & Studies, 1996.

Geertz, Clifford. "Religion as a Cultural System." In *The Interpretation of Cultures.* New York: Basic Books, 1973.

Gellner, David. *Monk, Householder, and Tantric Priest: Newar Buddhism and Its Hierarchy of Ritual.* Cambridge: Cambridge University Press, 1992.

——. *The Anthropology of Buddhism and Hinduism.* Oxford: Oxford University Press, 2001.

George, Christopher, trans. *The Caṇḍamahāroṣaṇa Tantra.* New Haven: American Oriental Society, 1974.

Germano, David. "Re-membering the Dismembered Body of Tibet." In *Buddhism in Contemporary Tibet: Religious Revival and Cultural Identity,* ed. Melvyn Goldstein and Matthew Kapstein. Berkeley: University of California Press, 1998.

Giddens, Anthony. *Central Problems in Social Theory: Action, Structure, and Contradiction in Social Analysis.* Berkeley: University of California Press, 1979.

——. *The Transformation of Intimacy: Sexuality, Love, and Eroticism in Modern Societies.* Stanford: Stanford University Press, 1992.

Gladney, Dru. *Dislocating China: Reflections on Muslims, Minorities, and Other Subaltern Subjects.* London: Hurst, 2004.

Goffman, Erving. *Frame Analysis: An Essay on the Organization of Experience.* Boston: Northeastern University Press, 1974.

Gold, Jonathan. *The Dharma's Gatekeepers: Sakya Paṇḍita on Buddhist Scholarship in Tibet.* Albany: State University of New York Press, 2007.

Goldsmith, Elizabeth, ed. *Writing the Female Voice: Essays on Epistolary Literature.* Boston: Northeastern University Press, 1989.

Goldstein, Melvyn. *Dictionary of Modern Tibetan.* Kathmandu: Ratna Pustak Bhandar, 1983.

——. "Change, Conflict, and Continuity Among a Community of Nomadic Pastoralists: A Case Study from Western Tibet, 1950–1990." In *Resistance and Reform in Tibet,* ed. Robert Barnett and Shini Akiner. Bloomington: Indiana University Press, 1994.

——. *Nomads of Golok: a Report,* 1996. http://www.case.edu/affil/tibet/tibetanNomads/golok.htm.

——. *The Snow Lion and the Dragon: China, Tibet, and the Dalai Lama.* Berkeley: University of California Press, 1999.

——. *On the Cultural Revolution in Tibet: The Nyemo Incident of 1969.* Berkeley: University of California Press, 2009.

Goldstein, Melvyn and Matthew Kapstein, eds. *Buddhism in Contemporary Tibet: Religious Revival and Cultural Identity.* Berkeley: University of California Press, 1998.

Gombrich, Richard. "The Consecration of a Buddha Image." *Journal of Asian Studies* 26, no. 1 (1966): 23–36.

Gross, Rita. "Yeshe Tsogyel: Enlightened Consort, Great Teacher, Female Role Model." In *Feminine Ground: Essays on Women in Tibet*, ed. Janice Willis. Ithaca, NY: Snow Lion, 1989.

——. *Buddhism After Patriarchy: A Feminist History, Analysis, and Reconstruction of Buddhism*. Albany: State University of New York Press, 1993.

Gser tshang Phun tshogs bkra shis. *Gangs ri'i pang gi lang tsho'i rol mo*. Beijing: China Tibetology Publishing House, 2003.

Guenther, Herbert. *Ecstatic Spontaneity: Saraha's Three Cycles of Dohā*. Berkeley: Asian Humanities Press, 1993.

Guha, Ranajit. "On Some Aspects of the Historiography of Colonial India." In *Subaltern Studies I: Writings on South Asian History and Society*, ed. Ranajit Guha. Oxford: Oxford University Press, 1982.

Gyatso, Janet. "Signs, Memory and History: A Tantric Buddhist Theory of Scriptural Transmission." *Journal of the International Association of Buddhist Studies* 9, no. 2 (1986): 7–35.

——. "Down with the Demoness: Reflections on a Feminine Ground in Tibet." In *Feminine Ground: Essays on Women in Tibet*, ed. Janice Willis. Ithaca, NY: Snow Lion, 1989.

——. "Genre, Authorship, and Transmission in Visionary Buddhism: The Literary Traditions of Thang-stong rGyal-po." In *Tibetan Buddhism: Reason and Revelation*, ed. Ronald Davidson and Steven Goodman. Albany: State University of New York Press, 1992.

——. "The Logic of Legitimation in the Tibetan Treasure Tradition." *History of Religions* 33, no. 1 (1993): 97–134.

——. "Drawn from the Tibetan Treasury: The gTer ma Literature." In *Tibetan Literature: Studies in Genre*, ed. José Cabezón and Roger Jackson. Ithaca, NY: Snow Lion, 1996.

——. "Counting Crows' Teeth: Tibetans and Their Diary-Writing Practices." In *Les Habitants du Toit du Monde*, ed. Samten Karmay and Philippe Sagant. Nanterre: Société d'ethnologie, 1997.

——. *Apparitions of the Self: The Secret Autobiographies of a Tibetan Visionary*. Princeton: Princeton University Press, 1998.

——. "A Partial Genealogy of the Lifestory of Ye shes mtsho rgyal." *Journal of the International Association of Tibetan Studies* 2 (August 2006): 1–27. http://www.thlib.org?tid=T2719.

——. "The Relic Text as Prophecy: The Semantic Drift of *Byang-bu* and Its Appropriation in the Treasure Tradition." In *Commemorative Volume for Rai Bahadur T.D. Densapa*, ed. Tashi Tsering. Special issue of *Tibet Journal*, forthcoming.

Gyatso, Janet and Hanna Havnevik, eds. *Women in Tibet: Past and Present*. New York: Columbia University Press, 2006.

Gyurme Dorje. *Tibet Handbook*. Chicago: Passport Books, 1999.

Hall, Amelia. "Revelations of a Modern Mystic: The Life and Legacy of Kun bzang bde chen gling pa 1928–2006." Ph.D. diss., Oxford University, 2012.

Hanna, Span. "Vast as the Sky: The Terma Tradition in Modern Tibet." In *Tantra and Popular Religion in Tibet*, ed. Geoffrey Samuel, Hamish Gregor, and Elisabeth Stutchbury. New Delhi: International Academy of Indian Culture and Aditya Prakashan, 1994.

Harding, Sarah. *Creation and Completion: Essential Points of Tantric Meditation.* Boston: Wisdom, 1996.

——. *The Life and Revelations of Pema Lingpa.* Boulder, CO: Snow Lion, 2003a.

——. *Machik's Complete Explanation: Clarifying the Meaning of Chöd.* Ithaca, NY: Snow Lion, 2003b.

——. *Niguma: Lady of Illusion.* Boston: Snow Lion, 2011.

Harrell, Stevan. Introduction. In *Cultural Encounters on China's Ethnic Frontiers,* ed. Stevan Harrell. Seattle: University of Washington Press, 1995.

Harris, Claire. *In the Image of Tibet: Tibetan Painting After 1959.* London: Reaktion, 2000.

Harrison, Paul. "Who Gets to Ride in the Great Vehicle? Self-Image and Identity Among the Followers of Early Mahāyāna." *Journal of the International Association of Buddhist Studies* 10, no. 1 (1987): 67–89.

Hartley, Lauran. "'Inventing Modernity' in A mdo: Views on the Role of Traditional Tibetan Culture in a Developing Society." In *Amdo Tibetans in Transition: Society and Culture in the Post-Mao Era,* ed. Toni Huber. Leiden: Brill, 2002.

——. "Contextually Speaking: Tibetan Literary Discourse and Social Change in the People's Republic of China (1980–2000)." Ph.D. diss., Indiana University, 2003.

Hartley, Lauran and Patricia Schiaffini-Vedani, eds. *Modern Tibetan Literature and Social Change.* Durham: Duke University Press, 2008.

Havnevik, Hanna. "The Life of Jetsun Lochen Rinpoche as Told in Her Autobiography." Ph.D. diss., University of Oslo, 1999.

Hawley, John Stratton. *Saints and Virtues.* Berkeley: University of California Press, 1987.

Hermann, Judith. *Trauma and Recovery: The Aftermath of Violence—from Domestic Abuse to Political Terror.* New York: Basic Books, 1997.

Herrmann-Pfandt, Adelheid. *Ḍākinīs: Zur Stellung und Symbolik des Weiblichen im tantrischen Buddhismus.* Bonn: Indica et Tibetica Verlag, 1990.

Holmes-Tagchungdarpa, Amy. *The Social Life of Tibetan Biography: Textuality, Community, and Authority in the Lineage of Tokden Shakya Shri.* Lanham, MD: Lexington Books, 2014.

Horlemann, Bianca. "Modernization Efforts in Mgo log: A Chronicle, 1970–2000." In *Amdo Tibetans in Transition: Society and Culture in the Post-Mao Era,* ed. Toni Huber. Leiden: Brill, 2002.

Hortsang Jigme. *Under the Blue Sky: An Invisible Small Corner of the World.* Trans. Lobsang Dawa and Gussje de Schot. Dharamsala, India: Privately published, 1998.

——. "Tibetan Literature in the Diaspora." In *Modern Tibetan Literature and Social Change,* ed. Lauran Hartley and Patricia Schiaffini-Vedani. Durham: Duke University Press, 2008.

Huber, Toni. "Putting the *gnas* Back Into *gnas-skor*: Rethinking Tibetan Buddhist Pilgrimage Practice." *Tibet Journal* 19, no. 2 (1994): 23–60.

——. *The Cult of Pure Crystal Mountain: Popular Pilgrimage and Visionary Landscape in Southeast Tibet.* New York: Oxford University Press, 1999.

——. *The Holy Land Reborn: Pilgrimage and the Tibetan Reinvention of Buddhist India.* Chicago: University of Chicago Press, 2008.

Humphfrey, Caroline. "Remembering an 'Enemy': The Bogd Khaan in Twentieth-Century Mongolia." In *Memory, History, and Opposition Under State Socialism,* ed. Rubie Watson. Sante Fe, NM: School of American Research Press,1994.

Ingalls, Daniel. *Sanskrit Poetry from Vidyākara's "Treasury."* Cambridge, MA: Harvard University Press, 1968.

Iser, Wolfgang. *The Act of Reading: A Theory of Aesthetic Response.* Baltimore, MD: Johns Hopkins University Press, 1980.

Jackson, Michael. *The Politics of Storytelling: Violence, Transgression and Intersubjectivity.* Copenhagen: Museum Tusculanam Press, 2002.

Jackson, Roger. "'Poetry' in Tibet: *Glu, mGur, sNyan ngag,* and 'Songs of Experience.'" In *Tibetan Literature: Studies in Genre,* ed. José Cabezón and Roger Jackson. Ithaca, NY: Snow Lion, 1996.

——. *Tantric Treasures: Three Collections of Mystical Verse from Buddhist India.* Oxford: Oxford University Press, 2004.

Jacoby, Sarah. "'This Inferior Female Body:' Reflections on Life as a Treasure Revealer Through the Autobiographical Eyes of Se ra mkha' 'ro (Bde ba'i rdo rje, 1892–1940)." *Journal of the International Association of Buddhist Studies* 32, nos. 1–2 (2009/2010): 115–50.

——. *Love and Liberation: Autobiographical Writings of the Tibetan Buddhist Visionary Sera Khandro.* New York: Columbia University Press, 2014a.

——. "The Excellent Path of Devotion: An Annotated Translation of Sera Khandro's Short Autobiography." In *Himalayan Passages: Tibetan and Newar Studies in Honor of Hubert Decleer.* Boston: Wisdom, 2014b.

——. "Relational Autonomy in the Life of a Contemporary Tibetan *Ḍākinī.*" *Revue d'Etudes Tibétaines* 34 (December 2015): 79–113.

'Jam dbyangs nyi ma. *Rtsis mda' dgon pa'i lo rgyus mdor bsdus.* Unpublished facsimile in 10 pages; received from author, the acting head of Rtsis mda' dgon, in 2006.

'Jam mgon kong sprul Blo gros mtha' yas. *Zab mo'i gter dang gter ston grub thob ji ltar byon pa'i lo rgyus mdor bsdus bkod pa rin chen vaiḍūrya'i 'phreng ba (Gter ston brgya rtsa'i rnam thar).* In *Rin chen gter mdzod.* New Delhi: Shechen Publications, 2007–8, 1: 341–765.

Jamgön Kongtrul Lodrö Tayé. *Buddhist Ethics.* Trans. and ed. the International Translation Committee founded by the V.V. Kalu Rinpoché. Ithaca, NY: Snow Lion, 1998.

——. *Esoteric Instructions: A Detailed Presentation of the Process of Meditation in the Vajrayāna.* Trans. Sarah Harding. Ithaca, NY: Snow Lion, 2007.

Jigme Lingpa. *Deity, Mantra and Wisdom: Development Stage in Tibetan Buddhist Tantra.* Ithaca, NY: Snow Lion, 2007.

Johnson, Sandy. *The Book of Tibetan Elders: Life Stories and Wisdom from the Great Spiritual Masters of Tibet.* New York: Riverhead, 1996.

'Ju skal bzang, ed. *Khra dge slong Tshul khrims dar rgyas kyi gsung rtsom gces bsgrigs.* Xining: Mtsho sngon mi rigs dpe skrun khang, 2000.

Kālidāsa. *The Loom of Time: A Selection of His Plays and Poems.* Trans. and introduced by Chandra Rajan. New Delhi: Penguin, 1989.

——. *Messenger Poems.* Trans. Sir James Mallinson. New York: New York University Press, 2006.

Kapstein, Matthew. "The Purificatory Gem and Its Cleansing: A Late Tibetan Polemical Discussion of Apocryphal Texts." *History of Religions* 28, no. 3 (1989): 217–44.

——. "Remarks on the *Maṇi bka'-'bum* and the Cult of Avalokiteśvara in Tibet." In *Tibetan Buddhism: Reason and Revelation,* ed. Steven Goodman and Ronald Davidson. Albany: State University of New York Press, 1992.

——. "The Royal Way of Supreme Compassion." In *Tibetan Religions in Practice*, ed. Donald Lopez. Princeton: Princeton University Press, 1997.

——. *The Tibetan Assimilation of Buddhism: Conversion, Contestation, and Memory.* Oxford: Oxford University Press, 2000.

——. "The Indian Literary Identity in Tibet." In *Literary Cultures in History: Reconstructions from South Asia*, ed. Sheldon Pollock. Berkeley: University of California Press, 2003.

——. "Pure Land Buddhism in Tibet? From Sukhāvatī to the Field of Great Bliss." In *Approaching the Land of Bliss: Religious Praxis in the Cult of Amitābha*, ed. Richard Payne and Kenneth Tanaka. Honolulu: University of Hawaii Press, 2004.

Karma Lekshe Tsomo, ed. *Eminent Buddhist Women.* Albany: State University of New York Press, 2014.

Karmay, Samten. *The Treasury of Good Sayings: A Tibetan History of Bon.* Oxford: Oxford University Press, 1972.

——. *The Great Perfection (rDzogs chen): A Philosophical and Meditative Teaching in Tibetan Buddhism.* Leiden: Brill, 1988.

——. *The Arrow and the Spindle: Studies in History, Myths, Rituals, and Beliefs in Tibet.* Kathmandu: Mandala Book Point, 1998.

Keyes, Charles and E. Valentine Daniel, eds. *Karma: An Anthropological Inquiry.* Berkeley: University of California Press, 1983.

Khoroche, Peter. *Towards a New Edition of Ārya Śūra's Jātakamālā* (Indica et Tibetica 12). Bonn: Indica et Tibetica Verlag, 1987.

——. *Once the Buddha Was a Monkey: Ārya Śūra's Jātakamālā.* Chicago: University of Chicago Press, 1989.

Kieckhefer, Richard and George Bond, eds. *Sainthood: Its Manifestation in World Religions.* Berkeley: University of California Press, 1988.

Kimura, Takayasu, ed. *Pañcaviṃśatisāhasrikā Prajñāpāramitā.* Tokyo: Sankibo Busshorin, 1990.

Kinnard, Jacob. *Imagining Wisdom: Seeing and Knowing in the Art of Indian Buddhism.* London: Curzon, 1999.

Klein, Anne. "Primordial Purity and Everyday Life: Exalted Female Symbols and Women in Tibet." In *Immaculate and Powerful: The Female in Sacred Image and Reality*, ed. Clarissa Atkinson, Constance Buchanan, and Margaret Miles. Boston: Beacon, 1985.

Knauft, Bruce. Introduction. In *Critically Modern: Alternatives, Alterities, Anthropologies*, ed. Bruce Knauft. Bloomington: Indiana University Press, 2002.

Knight, Sabina. *The Heart of Time: Moral Agency in Twentieth-Century Chinese Fiction.* Cambridge, MA: Harvard University Press, 2006.

Kolas, Ashild and Monika Thowsen. *On the Margins of Tibet: Cultural Survival on the Sino-Tibetan Frontier.* Seattle: University of Washington Press, 2005.

Krang dbyi sun, ed. *Bod rgya tshig mdzod chen mo* (abbreviated TTC). Beijing: Mi rigs dpe skrun khang, 1998.

Krung go'i bod rig pa zhib 'jug lte gnas kyi chos lugs lo rgyus zhib 'jug so'o, Krung go bod brgyud nang bstan mtho rim slob gling, Zi khron zhing chen dkar mdzes khul chos lugs cud, and Dkar mdzes khul yig bsgyur cud. *Khams phyogs dkar mdzes khul gyi dgon sde so so'i lo rgyus gsal bar bshad pa thub bstan gsal ba'i me long.* Beijing: Krung go'i bod kyi shes rig dpe skrun khang, 1995.

Kunsang, Erik Pema. *The Lotus Born: The Life Story of Padmasambhava.* Boston: Shambhala, 1999.

Kvaerne, Per. "On the Concept of *Sahaja* in Indian Buddhist Tantric Literature." *Temenos* XI (1975): 88–135.

Kyabje Kangyur Rinpoche. *Nagarjuna's Letter to a Friend.* Trans. the Padmakara Translation Group. Ithaca, NY: Snow Lion, 2006.

LaFleur, William. "Biography." In *The Encyclopedia of Religion,* ed. Mircea Eliade. New York: Collier Macmillan, 2 (1987): 220–24.

Li, Wei and Dennis Tao Yang. "The Great Leap Forward: Anatomy of a Central Planning Disaster." *Journal of Political Economy* 113, no. 4 (2005): 840–77.

Link, Perry. *The Uses of Literature: Life in the Socialist Chinese Literary System.* Princeton: Princeton University Press, 2000.

Lopez, Donald. "Memories of the Buddha." In *In the Mirror of Memory: Reflections on Mindfulness and Remembrance in Indian and Tibetan Buddhism,* ed. Janet Gyatso. Ithaca, NY: State University of New York Press, 1992.

——. *Prisoners of Shangri-la: Tibetan Buddhism and the West.* Chicago: University of Chicago Press, 1999.

Lu Xinhua et al. *The Wounded: New Stories of the Cultural Revolution, 77–78.* Hong Kong: Joint Publishing Co., 1979.

Macdonald, A. W. "Hindu-isation, Buddha-isation, Then Lama-isation or: What Happened at La-phyi?" In *Indo-Tibetan Studies,* ed. Tadeusz Skorupski. Tring, UK: The Institute of Buddhist Studies, 1990.

Makley, Charlene. "'Speaking Bitterness': Autobiography, History, and Mnemonic Politics on the Sino-Tibetan Frontier." *Comparative Studies in Society and History* 47, no. 1 (2005): 40–78.

——. *The Violence of Liberation: Gender and Tibetan Buddhist Revival in Post-Mao China.* Berkeley: University of California Press, 2007.

Martin, Dan. "For Love or Religion? Another Look at a 'Love Song' by the Sixth Dalai Lama." *Zeitschrift der Deutschen Morgenländischen Gessellschaft* 138, no. 2 (1988): 349–63.

——. *Unearthing Bon Treasures: Life and Contested Legacy of a Tibetan Scripture Revealer.* Leiden: Brill, 2001.

Mayer, Robert. "gTer ston and Tradent: Innovation and Conservation in Tibetan Treasure Literature." *Journal of the Association of Buddhist Studies* 36–37, nos. 1–2 (2013–14 [2015]): 227–42.

McDermott, James. "Is There Group Karma in Theravāda Buddhism?" *Numen* 23, no. 1 (1976): 67–80.

McGranahan, Carole. *Arrested Histories: Tibet, the CIA, and Memories of a Forgotten War.* Durham,: Duke University Press, 2010.

McMillin, Laurie. *English in Tibet, Tibet in English: Self-Presentation in Tibet and the Diaspora.* New York: Palgrave, 2001.

Merwin, W. S. and J. Moussaieff Masson. *The Peacock's Egg: Love Poems from Ancient India.* San Francisco: North Point Press, 1981.

Meuggler, Erik. *The Age of Wild Ghosts: Memory, Violence, and Place in Southwest China.* Berkeley: University of California Press, 2001.

Mi pham rgya mtsho. *Yig bskur gyi rnam bzhag mdo tsam brjod pa me tog nor bu'i phreng ba.* In *The Expanded Redaction of the Complete Works of 'Ju Mi-pham Series.* Paro, Bhutan: Lama Ngodrup and Sherab Drimey, 1984–93, vol. 14 (Ca): 929–39.

Miller, Barbara Stoler. *Love Songs of the Dark Lord: Jayadeva's Gītagovinda.* New York: Columbia University Press, 1997.

Mdo mkhyen brtse Ye shes rdo rje. *Mdo mkhyen brtse ye shes rdo rje'i rnam thar* (alt. *Rig 'dzin 'jigs med gling pa'i yang srid sngags 'chang 'ja' lus rdo rje'i rnam thar mkha' 'gro'i zhal lung*). Chengdu: Si khron mi rigs dpe skrun khang, 1997.

Mkha' 'bum. "Bod kyi dmangs khrod glu gzhas skor gyi dpyad pa thar thor." *Mang tshogs sgyu rtsal* 88, no. 1 (2005): 79–92.

Mkha' 'gro Tā re lha mo. *Sngags skyes mkha' 'gro rin po che tā re de vīs nam sprul rin po che 'jigs med phun tshogs mchog la phul ba'i zhu 'phrin phyag yid rnams phyogs bsdus pad ma'i phreng ba.* Gser rta: Snyan lung dgon, c. 2003.

Monson, Christina, trans. *The Excellent Path of Devotion: An Abridged Story of a Mendicant's Experiences in Response to Questions by Vajra Kin.* Boulder, CO: Kama Terma Publications, 2013.

Mooney, Catherine, ed. *Gendered Voices: Medieval Saints and Their Interpreters.* Philadelphia: University Pennsylvania Press, 1999.

Morcom, Anna. *Unity and Discord: Music and Politics in Contemporary Tibet.* London: Tibet Information Network, 2004.

Mumford, Stan Royal. *Himalayan Dialogue: Tibetan Lamas and Gurung Shamans in Nepal.* Madison: University of Wisconsin Press, 1989.

Nālandā Translation Committee. "A Smoke Purification Song." In *Religions of Tibet in Practice,* ed. Donald Lopez. Princeton: Princeton University Press, 1997.

Nam sprul 'Jigs med phun tshogs. *Skyabs rje rin po che nam sprul 'jigs med phun tshogs kyis mkha' 'gro rin po che tā re de vī mchog la phul ba'i zhu 'phrin phyag yig rnams phyogs bsdus rdo rje'i phreng ba.* Gser rta: Snyan lung dgon, c. 2003.

——. *Mkha' 'gro sku gshegs pa'i lo rgyus mdor bsdus.* Unpublished account of Tā re lha mo's last testament and death, received from author at Snyan lung dgon in 2004.

Nam sprul 'Jigs med phun tshogs and Mkha' 'gro Tā re lha mo. *O rgyan 'jigs med nam mkha' gling pa dang ḍāk ki tā re bde chen rgyal mo rnam gnyis kyi zab gter chos.* Facsimile edition in 12 volumes. Gser rta: Snyan lung dgon, n.d.

——. *Khyab bdag gter chen bla ma 'ja' lus pa dpal mnyam med nam mkha' gling pa rin po che dang mkha' 'gro rin po che tā re lha mo zung gi zab gter nam mkha' mdzod gyi chos sde.* Chengdu: Si khron mi rigs dpe skrun khang, 2013.

Nandy, Ashis. *The Intimate Enemy: Loss and Recovery of Self Under Colonialism.* Oxford: Oxford University Press, 1988.

Nattier, Jan. *Once Upon a Future Time: Studies in a Buddhist Prophecy of Decline.* Berkeley: University of California Press, 1991.

Naughton, Barry. "The Chinese Economy, Fifty Years Into the Transition." In *China Briefing 2000: The Continuing Transformation,* ed. Tyrene White. New York: Asia Society, 2001.

Ngawang Zangpo. *Sacred Ground: Jamgon Kongtrul on Pilgrimage and Sacred Geography.* Ithaca, NY: Snow Lion, 2001.

Ohnuma, Reiko. *Head, Eyes, Flesh and Blood: Giving Away the Body in Indian Buddhist Literature.* New York: Columbia University Press, 2007.

O rgyan 'phrin las bzang po. *Gnas mchog bkra shis sgo mang gi gnas yig phyogs bsdus rin chen 'phreng ba.* Pad ma County, Qinghai Province: Snga 'gyur rnying ma dpal yul Bkra shis sgo mang thub bstan chos 'khor gling, n.d.

Orgyen Tobgyal. *The Life of Chokgyur Lingpa.* Trans. Tulku Jigmey and Erik Pema Kunsang. Kathmandu: Rangjung Yeshe Publications, 1988.

Ortner, Sherry. *High Religion: A Cultural and Political History of Sherpa Buddhism.* Princeton: Princeton University Press, 1989.

——. *Making Gender: The Politics and Erotics of Culture.* Boston: Beacon, 1996.

Pad ma 'bum. "Tun hong yig rnying gi mgur la dpyod pa'i sngon 'gro." In *Tibetan Studies: Proceedings of the 7th Seminary of the International Association for Tibetan Studies, Graz 1995,* ed. Helmut Krasser. Wien: Verlag der Österreichischen Akademie der Wissenschaften, 1997.

——. *Six Stars with a Crooked Neck: Tibetan Memoirs of the Cultural Revolution.* Trans. Lauran R. Hartley. Dharamsala, India: Bod kyi dus bab, 2001.

Pad ma 'od gsal mtha' yas. *Skyabs rje nam sprul rin po che 'jigs med phun tshogs dang mkha' 'gro tā re lha mo mchog gi rnam thar rig 'dzin mkha' 'gro dgyes pa'i mchod sprin.* Chengdu: Si khron mi rigs dpe skrun khang, 1997.

——. *Sprul ba'i gter ston chen po rig 'dzin nus ldan rdo rje'i rnam thar bsdus pa dngos grub snye ma.* In *Gter chen bdud 'joms yab sras kyi rnam thar.* Ed. Pad ma theg mchog rgyal mtshan. Chengdu: Si khron mi rigs dpe skrun khang, 2000.

——. *Yab mes rigs 'dzin brgyud pa'i byung ba mdor bsdus tsam brjod pa.* In *Deb chung a ru ra'i dga' tshal.* Chengdu: Si khron mi rigs dpe skrun khang, 2003.

Pad ma tshe ring. *Mgo log rig gnas lo rgyus.* Tawu, Qinghai: Srid gros mgo log khul u slob sbyong lo rgyus dang tshan slob rig 'phrod u yon lhan khang, 2004.

Padmakara Translation Group. *The Words of My Perfect Teacher.* San Francisco: HarperCollins, 1994.

——. *Lady of the Lotus-Born: The Life and Enlightenment of Yeshe Tsogyal.* Boston: Shambhala, 2002.

Palden Gyatso. *The Autobiography of a Tibetan Monk.* Trans. Tsering Shakya. New York: Grove Press, 1997.

Patt, David. *Strange Liberation: Tibetan Lives in Chinese Hands.* Ithaca, NY: Snow Lion, 1992.

Paul, Diana. *Women in Buddhism.* Berkeley: University of California Press, 1985.

Penick, Douglas. *The Warrior Song of King Gesar.* Boston: Wisdom, 1996.

Pirie, Fernanda. "Feuding Mediation and the Negotiation of Authority Among the Nomads of Eastern Tibet." Working Paper No. 72. Halle/Saale: Max Planck Institute for Social Anthropology, 2005.

Pommaret, Françoise. *Les revenants de l'au-delà dans le monde tibétain: Sources littéraires et tradition vivante.* Paris: Éditions du Centre national de la recherche scientifique, 1989.

Powers, John. *History as Propaganda: Tibetan Exiles versus the People's Republic of China.* Oxford: Oxford University Press, 2004.

Quintman, Andrew. *The Yogin and the Madman: Reading the Biographical Corpus of Tibet's Great Saint Milarepa.* New York: Columbia University Press, 2014.

Ray, Meredith. *Writing Gender in Women's Letter Collections of the Italian Renaissance.* Toronto: University of Toronto Press, 2009.

Ray, Reginald. "Accomplished Women in Tantric Buddhism of Medieval India and Tibet." In *Unspoken Worlds: Women's Religious Lives in Non-Western Cultures,* ed. Nancy Falk and Rita Gross. San Francisco: Harper and Row, 1980.

Reed, Barbara. "The Gender Symbolism of Kuan-yin Bodhisattva." In *Buddhism, Sexuality, and Gender,* ed. José Cabezón. Albany: State University of New York Press, 1992.

Reynolds, Frank and Donald Capps, eds. *The Biographical Process: Studies in the History and Psychology of Religion.* The Hague: Mouton, 1976.

Rig 'dzin dar rgyas. Untitled and unpublished manuscript that begins *De yang rje btsun sgrol ma ljang mo'i thugs kyi rnam sprul,* received from the author in Gser rta in 2014.

Roberts, Peter. *The Biographies of Rechungpa: The Evolution of a Tibetan Hagiography.* London: Routledge, 2007.

Robben, Antonius Robben and Macelo Suarez-Orozco, ed. *Cultures Under Siege: Collective Violence and Trauma.* Cambridge: Cambridge University Press, 2000.

Robin, Françoise. "'Oracles and Demons' in Tibetan Literature Today: Representations of Religion in Tibetan-Medium Fiction." In *Modern Tibetan Literature and Social Change,* ed. Lauran Hartley and Patricia Schiaffini-Vedani. Durham: Duke University Press, 2008.

Robinson, James. *Buddha's Lions: The Lives of the Eighty-Four Siddhas.* Berkeley: Dharma Publishing, 1979.

Rock, J. F. *The Amnye Machen Range and Adjacent Regions: a Monographic Study.* Roma: Instituto Italiano per il Medio ed Estremo Oriente, 1956.

Ronis, Jann. "Bdud 'dul rdo rje (1615–1672) and Rnying ma Adaptations to the Era of the Fifth Dalai Lama." In *Power, Politics, and the Reinvention of Tradition: Tibet in the Seventeenth and Eighteenth Centuries,* ed. Byran Cuevas and Kurtis Schaeffer. Leiden: Brill, 2006.

Rossi, Donatella. "Some Notes on the Tibetan Amdo Love Songs." In *Tibetan Studies: Proceedings of the 5th Seminar of the International Association for Tibetan Studies, Narita, 1989,* ed. Shōren Ihara and Zuihō Yamaguchi. Tokyo: Naritasan Shinshoji, 1992.

——. "Mkha' 'gro dbang mo'i rnam thar, The Biography of the Gter ston ma Bde chen chos kyi dbang mo (1868–1927?)." *Revue d'Etudes Tibétaines* 15 (2008): 371–78.

Said, Edward. *Orientalism.* New York: Vintage, 1979.

Sakya Pandita Kunga Gyaltshen. *A Clear Differentiation of the Three Codes: Essential Differentiations Among the Individual Liberation, Great Vehicle, and Tantric Systems.* Trans. Jared Rhoton. Ithaca, NY: State University of New York Press, 2002.

Salgado, Nirmala. *Buddhist Nuns and Gendered Practice: In Search of the Female Renunciant.* Oxford: Oxford University Press, 2013.

Samuel, Geoffrey. *Civilized Shamans: Buddhism in Tibetan Societies.* Washington: Smithsonian Institution Press, 1993.

Samuel, Geoffrey with Hamish Gregor and Elisabeth Stutchbury, eds. *Tantra and Popular Religion in Tibet.* New Delhi: International Academy of Indian Culture and Aditya Prakashan, 1994.

Sangren, P. Steven. "Female Gender in Chinese Religious Symbols: Kuan Yin, Ma Tsu, and the 'Eternal Mother.'" *Signs: Journal of Women in Culture and Society* 9, no. 1 (1983): 4–25.

Sangye Khandro and Lama Chonam, trans. *The Lives and Liberation of Princess Mandarava: The Indian Consort of Padmasambhava*. Boston: Wisdom, 1998.

Schaeffer, Kay and Sidone Smith. *Human Rights and Narrated Lives: The Ethics of Recognition*. New York: Palgrave Macmillan, 2004.

Schaeffer, Kurtis. *Himalayan Hermitess: The Life of a Tibetan Buddhist Nun*. Oxford: Oxford University Press, 2004.

——. "Tibetan Biography: Growth and Criticism." In *Edition, éditions: l'écrit au Tibet, évolution et devenir*, ed. Anne Chayet, Cristina Scherrer-Schaub, Françoise Robin, and Jean-Luc Achard. Munich: Indus Verlag, 2010.

Schein, Louisa. "Gender and Internal Orientalism in China." *Modern China* 23, no. 1 (1997): 69–98.

——. *Minority Rules: The Miao and the Feminine in China's Cultural Politics*. Durham: Duke University Press, 2000.

Schiaffini-Vedani, Patricia. "The 'Condor' Flies over Tibet: Zhaxi Dawa and the Significance of Tibetan Magical Realism." In *Modern Tibetan Literature and Social Change*, ed. Lauran Hartley and Patricia Schiaffini-Vedani. Durham: Duke University Press, 2008.

Schneider, Hannah. "Tibetan Epistolary Style." In *The Dalai Lamas: A Visual History*, ed. Martin Brauen, 258–61. Chicago: Serindia, 2005.

Schneider, Nicola. "Self-Representation and Stories Told: the Life and Vicissitudes of Khandro Choechen." *Revue d'Etudes Tibétaines* 34 (December 2015): 171–88.

Schober, Juliane. *Sacred Biography in the Buddhist Traditions of South and Southeast Asia*. Honolulu: University of Hawai'i Press, 1997.

Schuh, Dieter. *Untersuchungen zur Geschichte der tibetischen Kalenderrechnung*. Wiesbaden: F. Steiner, 1973.

Scott, James. *Domination and the Arts of Resistance: Hidden Transcripts*. New Haven: Yale University Press, 1990.

Se ra mkha' 'gro Bde ba'i rdo rje. *Ku su lu'i nyams byung gi gnas tshul mdor bsdus rdo rje'i spun gyis dris lan mos pa'i lam bzang*. In *The Collected Revelations (gter chos) of Se ra mkha' 'gro Bde chen rdo rje*. Kalimpong, India: Dupjung Lama, 1978, 4: 103–29.

Shapiro, Judith Rae. *Mao's War Against Nature: Politics and the Environment in Revolutionary China*. Cambridge: Cambridge University Press, 2001.

Shaw, Miranda. *Passionate Enlightenment: Women in Tantric Buddhism*. Princeton: Princeton University Press, 1994.

Shils, Edward. *Center and Periphery: Essays in Macrosociology*. Chicago: University of Chicago Press, 1975.

Siegel, Lee. *Sacred and Profane Dimensions of Love in Indian Traditions as Exemplified by the Gītagovinda of Jayadeva*. Delhi: Oxford University Press, 1978.

Simmer-Brown, Judith. *Dakini's Warm Breath: The Feminine Principle in Tibetan Buddhism*. Boston: Shambhala, 2001.

Siu, Helen and Zelda Stern, eds. *Mao's Harvest: Voices from China's New Generation*. Oxford: Oxford University Press, 1983.

Skal bzang ye shes and Sri gcod rdo rje. *Rdo grub chen dgon gsang chen dngos grub dpal 'bar gling.* Pad ma: Rdo grub chen dgon, c. 2005.

Smelser, Neil. "Psychological Trauma and Cultural Trauma." In *Cultural Trauma and Collective Identity*, ed. Jeffrey Alexander, Ron Eyerman, Bernhard Giesen, Neil Smelser, and Piotr Sztompka. Berkeley: University of California Press, 2004.

Smith, Gene. *Among Tibetan Texts: History amd Literature of the Himalayan Plateau.* Boston: Wisdom, 2001.

Smith, Warren W. "The Nationalities Policy of the Chinese Communist Party and the Socialist Transformation of Tibet." In *Resistance and Reform in Tibet*, ed. Robert Barnett and Shirin Akiner. Bloomington: Indiana University Press, 1994.

Sørensen, Per. *Divinity Secularized: An Inquiry into the Nature and Form of the Songs Ascribed to the Sixth Dalai Lama.* Wien: Arbeitskreis für Tibetische und Buddhistische Studien, 1990.

Stag sham Nus ldan rdo rje. *Bod kyi jo mo ye shes mtsho rgyal gyi mdzad tshul rnam par thar pa gab pa mngon byung rgyud mngas dri za'i glu phreng.* Kalimpong: Bdud 'joms rin po che, 1972.

Stein, R. A. *L'épopée tibétaine de Gesar dans sa version lamaïque de Ling.* Paris: Presses Universitaires de France, 1956.

——. *Recherches sur l'épopée et le barde au Tibet.* Paris: Presses Universitaires de France, 1959.

——. *Tibetan Civilization.* Trans. J. E. Stapleton Driver. Stanford: Stanford University Press, 1972.

——. "Tibetica Antiqua III: A propos du mot *gcug-lag* et de la religion indigène." *Bulletin de l'École Française d'Extrême Orient* 74, no. 1 (1985): 83–133.

——. *Rolf Stein's Tibet Antiqua with Additional Materials.* Trans. Arthur McKeown. Leiden: Brill, 2010.

Strong, John. "Relics." In *The Encyclopedia of Religion*, ed. Mircea Eliade. New York: Collier Macmillan, 1987, 11: 275–82.

——. "Buddha Bhakti and the Absence of the Blessed One." In *Colloque Étienne Lamotte in Brussels and Liège, Belgium.* Louvain: Université Catholique de Louvain, 1989.

Sujata, Victoria. *Tibetan Songs of Realization: Echoes from a Seventeenth-Century Scholar and Siddha in Amdo.* Leiden: Brill, 2005.

Sunim, Hae-ju. "Can Women Achieve Enlightenment?" In *Buddhist Women Across Cultures*, ed. Karma Lekshe Tsomo. Boston: Wisdom, 1999.

Swearer, Donald. *Becoming the Buddha: The Ritual of Image Consecration in Northern Thailand.* Princeton: Princeton University Press, 2004.

Tambiah, Stanley. *The Buddhist Saints of the Forest and the Cult of Amulets.* Cambridge: Cambridge University Press, 1984.

Teiser, Stephen. *Reinventing the Wheel: Paintings of Rebirth in Medieval Buddhist Temples.* Seattle: University of Washington Press, 2007.

Templeman, David. *Tāranātha's Life of Kṛṣṇācārya/Kāṇha.* Dharamsala, India: Library of Tibetan Works and Archives, 1989.

——. "Dohā, Vajragīti and Caryā Songs." In *Tantra and Popular Religion in Tibet*, ed. Geoffrey Samuel with Hamish Gregor and Elisabeth Stutchbury, New Delhi: International Academy of Indian Culture and Aditya Prakashan, 1994.

Terrone, Antonio. "Householders and Monks: A Study of Treasure Revealers and Their Role in Religious Revival in Eastern Tibet." In *Buddhism Beyond the Monastery: Tantric Practices and Their Performers in Tibet and the Himalayas*, ed. Sarah Jacoby and Antonio Terrone. Leiden: Brill, 2008.

——. "'Anything Can Be an Appropriate Treasure Teaching!' Authentic Treasure Revealers and the Moral Implications of Noncelibate Tantric Practice." In *Tibetan Studies: An Anthology*, rd. Peter Schwieger and Saadet Arslan. Halle: International Institute for Tibetan and Buddhist Studies, 2010a.

——. "Cyberspace Revelations: Tibetan Treasures, Information Technology, and the Transnational Imagined Reader." In *Edition, éditions: l'écrit au Tibet, évolution et devenir*, ed. Anne Chayet, Cristina Scherrer-Schaub, Françoise Robin, and Jean-Luc Achard. Munich: Indus Verlag, 2010b.

——. *Hidden Teachings of Tibet*. Boston: Wisdom, 1997.

Thub bstan chos dar. *Mdo zla gsal dbang mo'i rnam thar*. In *Mdo mkhyen brtse ye shes rdo rje'i gdung rgyud rim byon gyi rnam thar*. Mi nyag: Krung go'i bod rig pa dpe skrun khang, 2008.

Tibet Information Network. *A Poisoned Arrow: The Secret Report of the 10th Panchen Lama*. London: Tibet Information Network, 1997.

Tsering Shakya. *The Dragon in the Land of Snows: A History of Modern Tibet Since 1947*. New York: Columbia University Press, 1999.

——. "The Waterfall and Fragrant Flowers: The Development of Tibetan Literature Since 1950." *Manoa* 12, no. 2 (2000): 28–40.

——. "Language, Literature, and Representation in Tibet." Foreword to Herbert Batt, trans. and ed., *Tales of Tibet: Sky Burials, Prayer Wheels, and Wind Horses*. Lanham, MD: Rowman & Littlefield, 2001.

——. "The Development of Modern Tibetan Literature in the People's Republic of China in the 1980s." In *Modern Tibetan Literature and Social Change*, ed. Lauran Hartley and Patricia Schiaffini-Vedani. Durham: Duke University Press, 2008.

Tshe tan zhabs drung. *Snyan ngag me long gi spyi don sdeb legs rig pa'i char go*. Lanzhou: Kan su'u mi rigs dpe skrun khang, 1981.

——. *'Phrin yig spel tshul lhag bsam pad mo 'dzum pa'i nyin byed*. In *Tshe tan zhabs drung rje btsun 'jigs med rigs pa'i blo gros mchog gi gsung 'bum*. Dan tig: Mthu ba dgon, 2007, 9: 187–216.

Tshul khrims blo gros. *Snyigs dus bstan pa'i gsal byed gcig bu chos rje dam pa yid bzhin nor bu 'jigs med phun tshogs 'byung gnas dpal bzang po'i rnam thar bsdus pa dad pa'i gsos sman*. In *Chos rje dam pa yid bzhin nor bu 'jigs med phun tshogs 'byung gnas dpal bzang po'i gsung 'bum*. Hong Kong: Xianggang xinzhi chubanshe, 2002, 3: 364–418.

Tubten Khétsun. *Memories of Life in Lhasa Under Chinese Rule*. Trans. Matthew Akester. New York: Columbia University Press, 2008.

Tulku, Thondup. *Masters of Meditation and Miracles: The Longchen Nyingthik Lineage of Tibetan Buddhism*. Boston: Shambhala, 1996.

Tulku Thondup and Matthew Kapstein. "Tibetan Poetry." In *The New Princeton Encyclopedia of Poetry and Poetics*. Princeton: Princeton University Press, 1993.

Tuttle, Gray. *Tibetan Buddhists in the Making of Modern China*. New York: Columbia University Press, 2005.

——, ed. *Mapping the Modern in Tibet*. Sankt Augustin, Germany: International Institute for Tibetan and Buddhist Studies, 2011.

Uray, Géza. "Duplication, Germination and Triplication in Tibetan." *Acta Orientalia Academiae Scientiarum Hungaricae* 4, no. 1–3 (1954): 177–44.

van der Kolk, Bessel. "Trauma and Memory." In *Traumatic Stress: The Effects of Overwhelming Experience on Mind, Body, and Society*, ed. Bessel van der Kolk with Alexander McFarlane and Lars Weisaeth. New York: The Guildford Press, 1996.

van der Kolk, Bessel with Alexander McFarlane and Lars Weisaeth, eds. *Traumatic Stress: The Effects of Overwhelming Experience on Mind, Body, and Society*. New York: The Guildford Press, 1996.

van der Kuijp, Leonard. "On the Interpretation of *Kāvyādarśa* II: 271." *Studien zur Indologie und Iranistik* 8, no. 9 (1982): 69–76.

——. Review of *Snyan-ngag me-long-gi spyi don sdeb-legs rig-pa'i char-go* by Tshe tan Zhabs-drung 'Jigs-med rig-pa'i blo-gros. *Indo-Iranian Journal* 28, no. 3 (1985): 212–14.

——. "Sa-skya Paṇḍita Kun-dga' rgyal mtshan on the Typology of Literary Genres." *Studien zur Indologie und Iranistik* 11, no. 12 (1986): 41–52.

——. "Tibetan Belles-Lettres: The Influence of Daṇḍin and Kṣemendra." In *Tibetan Literature: Studies in Genre*, ed. José Cabezón and Roger Jackson. Ithaca, NY: Snow Lion, 1996.

Vargas-O'Brian, Ivette. "The Life of Dge slong ma Dpal mo: The Experience of a Leper, Founder of a Fasting Ritual, a Transmitter of Buddhist Teachings on Suffering and Renunciation in Tibetan Religious History." *Journal of the International Association of Buddhist Studies* 24, no. 2 (2001): 157–85.

Vaudeville, Charlotte. "Evolution of Love-Symbolism in Bhagavatism." *Journal of the American Oriental Society* 82 (1962): 31–40.

Viser, Irene. "Decolonizing Trauma Theory: Retrospect and Prospects." *Humanities* 4 (2015): 250–65.

Wallis, Glenn. 2004. *The Dhammapada: Verses on the Way*. New York: Modern Library.

Wang Ban. *Illuminations from the Past: Trauma, Memory, and History in Modern China*. Stanford: Standford University Press, 2004.

Wang, David Der-wei. *The Monster That Is History: History, Violence, and Fictional Writing in Twentieth-Century China*. Berkeley: University of California Press, 2004.

Wangdu, Pasang and Hildegard Diemberger. *dBa' bzhed: The Royal Narrative Concerning the Bringing of the Buddha's Doctrine to Tibet*. Wien: Verlag der Österreichischen Akademie der Wissenschaften, 2000.

Warder, A. K. *Indian Kāvya Literature*. 6 vols. Delhi: Motilal Banarsidass, 1972.

Watson, Rubie, ed. *Memory, History, and Opposition Under State Socialism*. Sante Fe, NM: School of American Research Press, 1994.

Wayman, Alex. *The Buddhist Tantras: Light on Indo-Tibetan Esotericism*. Delhi: Motilal Banarsidass, 1996.

Weber, Max. *The Religion of India: The Sociology of Hinduism and Buddhism*. Trans. and ed. Hans Gerth and Don Martindale. Glencoe, IL: Free Press, 1958.

——. *Economy and Society*. Berkeley: University of California Press, 1978.

White, David Gordon. *The Alchemical Body*. Chicago: University of Chicago Press, 1996.

——. *Kiss of the Yogini*. Chicago: University of Chicago Press, 2003.

Williams, Paul. *Songs of Love, Poems of Sadness: The Erotic Verse of the Sixth Dalai Lama*. London: I. B. Tauris, 2004.

Willis, Janice, ed. *Feminine Ground: Essays on Women in Tibet*. Ithaca, NY: Snow Lion, 1989.

——. "Tibetan Buddhist Women Practitioners, Past and Present: A Garland to Delight Those Wishing Inspiration." In *Buddhist Women Across Cultures: Realizations*, ed. Karma Lekshe Tsomo. Albany: State University of New York Press, 1999.

Wilson, Liz. *Charming Cadavers: Horrific Figurations of the Feminine in Indian Buddhist Hagiographic Literature*. Chicago: University of Chicago Press, 1996.

Willson, Martin. *In Praise of Tara: Songs to the Saviouress*. Boston: Wisdom, 1986.

Yan, Jiaqui and Gao Gao. *Turbulent Decade: A History of the Cultural Revolution*. Trans. and ed. D.W.Y. Kwok. Honolulu: University of Hawai'i Press, 1996.

Yang, Dennis Tao. "China's Agricultural Crisis and Famine of 1959–1961: A Survey and Comparison to Soviet Famines." *Comparative Economic Studies* 50 (2008): 1–29.

Young, James. *Writing and Rewriting the Holocaust: Narrative and Consequences of Interpretation*. Bloomington: Indiana University Press, 1988.

Yü, Dan Smyer. *The Spread of Tibetan Buddhism in China: Charisma, Money, Enlightenment*. New York: Routledge, 2014.

Index

Abu Karlo, 9, 97, 210, 216, 230–31, 233, 249, 274, 293n39, 323n78
Abzö Monastery, 250–51
Adamantine Songs, Meaningful to Hear and Behold (DVD set), 269, 272, 347n37
Adzom Drukpa, 49, 301n51
agency, 5, 21, 23, 24, 26; and Buddhism/karma, 17–19, 23–24, 85–87, 171, 255; and cultural schemas, 173; defined, 17–18; deflection to a divine source, 35–36, 54–61, 73–74, 108; deflection to Padmasambhava, 172 (*see also* Padmasambhava: Tāre Lhamo and Namtrul Rinpoche as emissaries of); and gender, 7, 35–37; and hagiography, 21; and *Jewel Garland*, 57–59, 209–10, 255; and letters of Tāre Lhamo and Namtrul Rinpoche, 114, 119, 155, 164–66, 168, 172–73, 186–87; and miracle tales, 75–76; and namthar, 20, 37; and past lives, 35–36; and prophecy, 110, 171; and rhetoric of destiny, 67, 172, 192; and Sera Khandro, 64–67; and *Spiraling Vine of Faith*, 46, 54–63, 90–94, 108; and subaltern pasts, 170–76; and Tāre Lhamo, 35–37, 54–63, 69,

75–76, 90–94, 100, 108; and tantric partnership of Tāre Lhamo and Namtrul Rinpoche, 26, 119, 155, 164–66, 168, 209–10, 220, 238; and tertöns, 172; and Yeshe Tsogyal, 61–64
Ahearn, Laura, 17
Akong Khenpo Lozang Dorje, 109
Alogowa (attendant of Tra Gelong), 68
Altman, Janet, 281n16, 319n26
Amnye Machen (sacred mountain range), 232, 243, 251–52
animals: ethical treatment of, 239; ransoming the lives of, 45, 244, 261
Apang Terchen, 38, 237–38, 248, 298nn14,16; biography of, 274; children recognized as reincarnations of local religious figures, 49; emanations of, 49, 225, 250, 301n49; founding of Tsimda Monastery, 8, 48, 237; images of, 39; initiation for treasure corpus bestowed on Tāre Lhamo and Namtrul Rinpoche, 222–24; Namtrul Rinpoche as activity emanation of, 8–9, 49, 135, 274, 301n49, 348n50; other names, 290n9; prophecies

connectivity, 234–36, 252–53; dharma connections, 210–11, 237, 239–41, 243–44; and healing of cultural trauma, 210–13; Namtrul Rinpoche on, 240; place connections, 210–13, 233–36; and relational conception of identity, 35, 36; and treasure revelation, 155

consort, 320n38; often elided in Tibetan sources, 7, 23; sociological dimensions of, 50, 56; Tāre Lhamo cast in the role of, 9, 128, 213–17; and tantric practice, 154, 159–60. *See also* tantric practices; *yab yum* partnership

Constable, Giles, 321n56

Cultural Revolution, 81–82; impact on religious communities, 3–4, 42, 170, 245, 250; and scar literature, 83, 87, 107, 179; and "search for roots" movement, 179; Tāre Lhamo's son lost during, 78; as trauma, 77

cultural schemas, 173

ḍākinīs, 292n29; centrality in stories of female religious figures, 54–55, 65–67; and death of Tāre Lhamo, 261; and female agency, 23, 35–36; Namtrul Rinpoche as beneficiary of the ḍākinīs, 94–96; oath of ḍākinīs as a cultural resource, 154, 171, 200–201; ritual to avert the call of, 219–20, 261, 339n39; Tāre Lhamo as ḍākinī-in-action, 35–36, 54, 56, 65–66, 73–75, 88, 103, 128, 254. See also *khandroma*

Damtsik Drolma, 33, 35, 301n55

Dartsang, 38, 40

Das, Veena, 77

Dechen Chökyi Wangmo, 209, 337n3

degeneration: "five degenerations," 179, 331n22; healing the damage of degenerate times, 5, 12, 26, 175–82, 210–11, 253, 255, 331n19

Deng Xiaoping, 6, 83, 118

destiny, 143–44, 172, 175, 197–201. *See also* collective trauma; karma

dharma connections, 210–11, 237, 239–41, 243–44

Diemberger, Hildegard, 303n80

Do Dasal Wangmo, 97–98, 105

Dodrupchen, Third (Jigme Tenpe Nyima), 160; incarnations of, 298n17

Dodrupchen Monastery, 41, 69

Do Khyentse Yeshe Dorje, 49, 97

Dola Chökyi Nyima, 222; as father of Dudjom Rinpoche incarnation, 292n31

Doli Nyima, 42, 299nn26,28

Do-ngag Tenpe Nyima, 102–3

Dong Dzong Monastery, 243

Do Rinpoche. *See* Khamsum Zilnön Gyepa Dorje

Dorje Phagmo. *See* Vajravārāhī

Dorje Rachigma (protector), 105–6

Drakar Tredzong (pilgrimage site), 116, 141, 194, 218, 232–33, 316n1

Drakor Monastery, 242, 249–50

Drasar Monastery, 250

Drime Özer, 60, 135, 154, 264; emanations of, 348n49; Namtrul Rinpoche as an emanation of, 9, 274, 323n79

Drongri (sacred mountain), 38, 226–29, 232, 234; images of, 2, 226

Drukmo Kyi, 188

drupthob, 56–57

Dudjom Lingpa, 40, 47, 274; reincarnations of, 49

Dudjom Rinpoche (Jigdral Yeshe Dorje), 8, 33, 66, 222; enthronement of Apang Terchen's reincarnation, 250; prophecies by, 49–50; Tāre Lhamo's recognition of his reincarnation, 8, 292n31; visit of his reincarnation to Nyenlung Monastery, 260, 268

Dudul Dorje. *See* Rigdzin Dudul Dorje

Dumda Monastery, 244

Khandro Chöchan, 62, 292n30, 307n109
khandroma, 8, 36, 43, 56–57. See also
    ḍākinīs; Tāre Lhamo: as khandroma
Khandro Rinpoche, 98–99
Khenpo Chökyab, 260
Khenpo Chöthun, 109
Khenpo Jigme Phuntsok, 96–97,
    99, 105, 106, 109, 239, 262, 270,
    313n79, 315n100, 322n71, 330n186;
    as founder of Larung Buddhist
    Academy, 298n3; images of, 224;
    pilgrimage to Wutai Shan, 45, 232;
    role in revitalizing Buddhism, 43,
    211; teachings and authorizations to
    Tāre Lhamo and Namtrul Rinpoche,
    221–26
Khenpo Munsel, 43, 99, 109
Khenpo Rigdzin Dargye. *See* Rigdzin
    Dargye
Kleinman, Arthur, 77
knife healing, 217
Kolas, Ashild, 16, 248
Kunga Bumpa, 62, 307n109
Kunzang Drolma, 274
Kusum Lingpa (Pema Tumpo), 96–97,
    99, 219, 222

Lafleur, William, 53
Lake Kokonor, 141, 232, 236, 268
Lakṣmīṅkarā, 59, 305n97
Lerab Lingpa, 222
letters of Tāre Lhamo and Namtrul
    Rinpoche, 1, 25, 29, 43, 116–207,
    316–17nn3,7, 336n97; and agency,
    114, 119, 155, 164–66, 168, 172–73,
    186–87; authorial voices, 119, 126–31,
    182, 186; catalogue of, 279–86; and
    contingency and coincidence, 191–
    97, 334n61; contrast to *Jewel Garland*,
    206; contrast to *Spiraling Vine of Faith*,
    118; and cultural constraints on
    first-person expression, 119, 126–30;
    expressions of affection, 4, 25, 119,
    120, 136–43, 320n38; final letter to
    Tāre Lhamo on the anniversary
    of her death, 262–67, 341n72; and

framing of Maoist period, 176–82,
    185–96; and gender, 119–20; and
    healing/revitalization of Buddhism,
    4–5, 20, 117–18, 120, 167–70, 176–82,
    184, 205; heroic and optimistic tenor
    of, 20, 118, 168, 182–86; hierarchies
    in gestures of praise and deference,
    128–29; and historical contingencies
    and challenges of the late 1970s,
    25–26, 169–70, 186–91; humor in,
    190–91; images of fertility and
    regeneration, 117, 138, 156; initiation
    of courtship and correspondence, 4,
    12, 44, 116, 123–24, 130; and legacy
    of the past, 197–201; literary styles
    used in, 25, 119–25, 142–43, 145–49,
    157, 169, 176, 182–87, 198–99, 203–4,
    319n31, 325n102, 332n28; (*see also*
    folk song style in letters of Tāre
    Lhamo and Namtrul Rinpoche) and
    love not motivated by personal
    need or desire, 150–55; modes of
    address, 119, 121–22, 125, 142, 148,
    318n16, 320n38; nicknames and
    terms of endearment, 125, 320n38;
    and obstacles to their union, 166,
    170, 186–87, 326n119; omission
    of details about conditions under
    Chinese occupation, 168; overview
    of contents and themes, 4, 120;
    and Padmasambhava, 175; and
    pairings in the natural landscape
    120–21, 143–50, 326n126; past-
    life recollections, 4, 25, 36, 125,
    131–33, 193, 323n82; pledges of
    steadfastness/fidelity, 149–51;
    prophetic passages, 25, 29, 36,
    116, 137, 167, 320n40; publication
    of, 130–31, 291n24, 316n3; and
    relational conception of identity,
    35, 36, 119; and rhetoric of destiny,
    191–201; ritual prescriptions,
    194–97; selections performed as
    devotional songs, 131; and sexuality,
    4, 119, 120, 143, 155–65; and "sport
    of attraction," 25, 157–59; and

CPSIA information can be obtained
at www.ICGtesting.com
Printed in the USA
LVOW03s0838091117
555628LV00001B/3/P